D0088297

Studying Christian Spirituality

Studying Christian Spirituality is the ideal introduction for students wishing to discover how spirituality can be understood beyond the conventional boundaries that religions have established.

In nine chapters, the book includes discussion of a wide variety of issues and questions including:

- Definitions of Spirituality
- Context
- God
- Anthropology
- History
- Text
- Human-Spiritual Development
- Spiritual Practice
- Criticism

David B. Perrin explains clearly the traditional relationships between Christian spirituality and theology and history. He also proposes greater connections with the human sciences, such as philosophy, psychology, phenomenology, and sociology, and reshapes the classical approaches to Christian spirituality, its texts, practices, and experience.

Studying Christian Spirituality will enable students to develop a deeper understanding of Christian spirituality's research methods, and its relevance to the world today.

David B. Perrin is President of St. Jerome's University, Waterloo, Ontario and is a former President (2005–6) of the Society for the Study of Christian Spirituality.

Studying Christian Spirituality

David B. Perrin

Routledge
Taylor & Francis Group

NEW YORK AND LONDON

First published 2007
by Routledge
270 Madison Ave., New York, NY 10016

Simultaneously published in the UK
by Routledge
2 Park Square, Milton Park, Abingdon, Oxon OX14 4RN

*Routledge is an imprint of the Taylor & Francis Group,
an informa business*

© 2007 David B. Perrin

The right of David B. Perrin to be identified as the Author of this
Work has been asserted by him in accordance with the
Copyright, Designs and Patents Act 1988

Typeset in Sabon by
Florence Production Ltd, Stoodleigh, Devon
Printed and bound in Great Britain by
Antony Rowe Ltd, Chippenham, Wiltshire

All rights reserved. No part of this book may be reprinted or
reproduced or utilised in any form or by any electronic, mechanical, or
other means, now known or hereafter invented, including
photocopying and recording, or in any information storage or retrieval
system, without permission in writing from the publishers.

British Library Cataloguing in Publication Data
A catalogue record for this book is available from the British Library

Library of Congress Cataloging in Publication Data
A catalog record for this book has been requested

ISBN10 0–415–39473–2 (hbk)
ISBN10 0–415–39474–0 (pbk)
ISBN10 0–415–94477–1 (ebk)

ISBN13 978–0–415–39473–4 (hbk)
ISBN13 978–0–415–39474–1 (pbk)
ISBN13 978–0–415–94477–6 (ebk)

ontents

Acknowledgments

A number of persons have been generous with their time and talent in the preparation of this book for publication. I would first like to acknowledge and thank my colleagues who read drafts of chapters as this book was being written. Their critical and insightful feedback helped me attend to a number of key issues in the study of Christian spirituality that, otherwise, I may well have overlooked: Philip Sheldrake (Durham College) read Chapter 2 on Context; Elizabeth Dreyer (Fairfield University) read Chapters 3 and 4 on God and Christian anthropology; Kevin Gillespie (Loyola College in Maryland) did a second reading of Chapter 4 as well as a reading of Chapter 7 on Human-spiritual development; Kevin Coyle (Saint Paul University) read Chapter 5 on History; and James Pambrun and Andrea Spatafora (both from Saint Paul University) read Chapter 6 on Text. A huge debt of gratitude is due to Anne Louise Mahoney who did a first English edit of the book in its entirety. I would like to thank the staff at Routledge, in particular Lesley Riddle and Gemma Dunn, who have faithfully and most helpfully guided me along during the entire production of the book. It has been a pleasure working with you.

My primary research assistant Diane MacDonald, a graduate student at Saint Paul University, undertook numerous preliminary research tasks in the preparation stages of Chapters 1 through 7. Other responsibilities took her elsewhere before the manuscript was completed. Three other graduate students at Saint Paul University helped do some of the preliminary research for Chapters 8 and 9 on Spiritual Practice and Critical Edges: Michael Rock, Bonita Slunder, and Amanda Rappak. My sister, Nancy Laflamme, constructed the diagram on the "Hermeneutical Interpretation of Texts" in Chapter 6.

ACKNOWLEDGMENTS

Over the last fifteen years I have had the opportunity to teach a number of times the introductory course Christian Spirituality at my former place of employment, Saint Paul University. I am grateful for the many questions and requests for clarification from the students in those courses, which, in the end, helped shape the present volume. I would also like to acknowledge Saint Paul University, which not only provided some funding for the preparation of this book but also generously granted a full-year sabbatical during which time this book was largely written.

# Preface

There is much talk today about perspective and context, both of which shape the biases and prejudices brought to any human activity. This is to suggest that there is no neutral perspective from which human beings carry on their various activities. All human activity including the writing of this book reflects, in some ways, past experiences and current preoccupations of the author. Although I've attempted to be objective in the choice and presentation of the material contained in this book, it would be unbelievable to suggest that these choices weren't influenced by my world view and some fundamental commitments I've made within that world view. One's world view, for better or for worse, is integrally shaped, for example, by past formative experiences, by ethnicity and social location, as well as educational opportunities. Thus, perhaps a few words about me, the author, might help clarify the particular perspective and context within which this book was written. It would be impossible to link what I say below about myself to all the details contained in this book. Thus, I will allow my brief biographical sketch to stand on its own, and you, the reader, can make those links as you see fit in the reading of the book.

I was born into a family of seven children in a rural farm area in central Canada. Although we never seriously farmed, since my father had a full-time career in the Canadian military, we always kept a few farm animals and large gardens. My first university-level studies led me to complete a degree in chemistry. After a two-year teaching sojourn at a high school in Haiti, in a very isolated and small village, my intellectual focus turned to philosophy and theology. This led me eventually to a three-year stay in Rome, Italy, to do graduate studies in Christian Spirituality. These extended periods of time in cultures other than my own have opened my mind up to the diversity of cultures and traditions that make up the global community.

I'm a North American white male, ordained as a priest within the Roman Catholic tradition, and within that tradition, I'm a member of a religious group, the Missionary Oblates of Mary Immaculate. This makes me celibate and a member of a rather large international male congregation. I served three years as a pastor in a congregation prior to returning to school to do doctoral work in my mid-thirties. I strive to be ecumenical in my spiritual practice as well as cultivate openness to spiritual traditions other than Christianity. I have a deep desire to understand contemporary Western culture and how spirituality is emerging within that culture in a broad range of expressions.

*I*ntroduction

Goals of this book

IN GENERAL, THE AIM OF THIS BOOK is to introduce the reader to the exciting and newly emerging discipline of Christian spirituality. In doing so, the aim is also to reshape some of the classical approaches to Christian spirituality (which are more focused on theology and the history of Christian spirituality), in order to develop a stronger link between spirituality and disciplines in the human sciences such as philosophy, psychology, history, sociology, phenomenology, hermeneutics, and anthropology. This is of course not intended to dismiss the key contribution that theology and the history of Christian spirituality have made in volumes that are already available to the reader.

More specifically, this book explores a number of frameworks in order to suggest key questions or issues to keep in mind when studying Christian spirituality. For example, the chapter on God helps increase awareness of the function of models of God in relationship to Christian spirituality: different understandings of God shape Christian spiritualities in very practical ways. The chapter on Christian anthropology helps to demonstrate that the self is not a static, once-and-for-all constructed reality; rather, as the *imago Dei* it is a dynamic entity that grounds the potential for participation in the transcendent life of God. How we view the self has an impact on the way we understand Christian spirituality. Each chapter sensitizes us to critical issues that need to be considered in studying Christian spirituality. Each chapter presents a conceptual framework within which questions can be formulated in relationship to the topics referred to in the chapter title.

Throughout the book, the following question is constantly in the background: What does it mean to think critically in Christian spirituality today? In other words, in studying Christian spirituality, what issues need to be kept in mind when undertaking either personal study or the pursuit of a research project? The answer to this question provides an initial response to what constitutes the core methodological principles in the academic study of Christian spirituality, which are presented at the end of this Introduction. Without going into the details of the various Christian traditions, this book aims to be inclusive and ecumenical in its perspective in dealing with all the issues mentioned above.

Christian spirituality and the human sciences

Today, with the rebirth of spirituality for those in society in general, and not only those who belong to institutional religions, there is a need to rediscover the legitimate place of spirituality within human experience per se. Studies in spirituality need the input from the human sciences to accurately describe the appropriation of the sacred in all areas of life. It is the human sciences that give us broad access to the multi-faceted nature of human experience, for example, from a sociological perspective, a psychological perspective, or an anthropological perspective.

Since Christian spirituality and the human sciences study human experience – even though they do so from their own perspectives and questions – they are good partners in this venture. Human sciences is an inclusive phrase that embraces a wide range of disciplines that study the human component of life: sociology, psychology, and anthropology mentioned above, but also, for example, history, law, and political science. Whereas the questions of Christian spirituality are asked from the foundation of faith life lived in Jesus, the human sciences claim to be neutral in their inquiries. They strive to be value-free in formulating conclusions about what they discover about human life. The human sciences are useful for studies in spirituality because the use of knowledge from the human sciences can help the explorer in spirituality to consider items for reflection that may, at first, have seemed unworthy of consideration.

For example, studies in sociology contribute greatly to a critical understanding of how spirituality is being lived in the marketplace of life, outside the institutional churches or faith-based communities. The practices and beliefs of those living spirituality in this broader context have been carefully recorded and analyzed by sociologists, who possess the appropriate skills to do so. The explorer in spirituality may not have these skills.

Not all contributions from the human sciences may be welcomed in the same way, however. Even though the human sciences are valuable research partners there are some cautions which need to be brought to the fore. These cautions do not negate the valuable resources the human sciences bring to research in Christian spirituality. However, when using the human sciences to do research these need to be taken into account in a critical and conscious way.

First, the human sciences tend toward a reduction of some kind or another. Based on the theory that their findings are applicable regardless of the cultural context, the place, or the particular time period, the human sciences strive to claim some authoritative universal knowledge of the human condition. The tendency to this kind of reduction is less so now than in the later half of the twentieth century. A good number of researchers in the human sciences have recognized the inability to formulate universal theories of, for example, human behavior, group interaction, and how human beings respond to the spiritual dimension of life. However, there still remains a tendency, for some theorists at least, to reduce all human life to some basic common denominators.

Second, while the human sciences do make a contribution to our understanding about life, for the Christian their contribution must be considered in the larger, and unpredictable, framework of human reality. For Christians this would include the knowledge about living and life gathered from belief in Jesus Christ. No matter how solid the theory, people cannot be reduced to the form of evidence that is collected about them, whether that be in the spiritual, psychological, or historical sphere. The mysterious nature of Christian life and the surprising presence of God in the life of the Christian opens up new possibilities for living that surpass the predictability of the human sciences mentioned in the first point.

Third, and closely tied to the second point, since the human sciences have no measuring stick other than what they determine the norm to be within the *human horizon*, they struggle with the claims of certain groups, such as to how things ought to be measured against moral or religious value systems. For example, psychology, when operating at the limits of its competence, as mentioned above, cannot include a commitment of faith. Psychology can describe the state of affairs of an individual life, but it cannot proscribe values around which that individual life ought to be lived. Psychology would struggle to appreciate the future fulfillment Christians, or persons of other faiths, anticipate in the eyes of God or some Divine other. Its field of inquiry – the questions it asks – would not investigate this realm of human living focused specifically on current and future life with God from an explicit faith perspective.

In other words, the human sciences are concerned with the present and past condition of human reality – but not much with the future as it pertains to eternity in relationship to human life. If the future is considered it is because current realities can be gauged to be leading people (whether individually or as a collective) in a particular direction, whether that be political, ecological, or sociological. Christian spirituality draws attention to the non-contemporary aspect of human reality: that of life with God now *and* in the timeless future. This difference needs to be kept in mind when using the human sciences.

But, as already mentioned, both the human sciences and Christian spirituality may reflect critically on the same phenomenon, or the same experience. Each will bring its own set of questions that will determine in which direction its inquiry will go. The questions, therefore, already limit what kinds of answers will be possible.

For example, the psychologist, when a distressed and fragile client asks, "What should I do?" may advise the client to connect more with supportive friends and exercise more often. The psychologist, who has framed the question in a certain way based on the mutual understanding of the client–therapist relationship, then frames the answer based on these points of reference. The spiritual director, faced with the same question, may counsel connection with friends and more exercise, but may also invite the person to reflect on the meaning of his or her distress in the context of prayer and meditation on a specific scripture passage. Like the psychologist, the spiritual director frames the answer to "What should I do?" within the horizon of the particular relationship that has been established between director and directee but involves another component as well: life lived with faith in God as the foundation of the meaning of his or her reality.

> The purpose of this book is to form bridges between Christian spirituality and the human sciences and the humanities in general – and to create a single field for the study of all aspects of Christian spirituality. Christian spirituality, as an emerging field of study, is well positioned to take advantage of all the expertise accumulated in the past 150 years, that is, since modern methods of research developed in the social sciences and the humanities in the mid-nineteenth century.

No one field of study has all the answers

Significant issues in life, and spirituality is one of them, cannot be studied within any one, or even several, of the artificially constructed boundaries placed on the many academic disciplines. Each discipline, to be sure, contributes to the conversation in a unique way. But when it comes to the human condition, no one discipline can claim to control fully the understanding of human life, let alone how God's presence mysteriously animates life in general.

What is more, all academic disciplines interact with each other. They all have fluid boundaries regarding what is included and what is excluded in their own areas of study. This is true because of the unity of human consciousness. The dissection of academic disciplines is a product of the human mind, not reflective of reality in itself.

For example, there is no such object as history or psychology per se. These are inventions of the human mind that make it possible to examine reality from specific perspectives and within a particular set of questions.

If researchers are honest about it, each academic discipline cannot choose to be influenced, or not, by the other disciplines – it is a given that academic disciplines *are* influenced by the other disciplines. The choice rather is between being unconsciously affected by them, or being critically aware of them. What this book undertakes is a conscious and intentional analysis of the intersection of Christian spirituality with other fields of research. This approach can help to clarify and deepen our understanding of the book's own area of reflection – life with God under the umbrella of Christian spirituality in all its dimensions, for example, the personal, the public, and the social.

Refinement of research strategies

Including the human sciences as a central resource in the study of Christian spirituality helps to refine research strategies and define problems and issues in Christian spirituality. In particular the human sciences can help to situate the specific area of Christian spirituality in the wider spectrum of human discourse. In so doing, they provide research methods that can assist, for example, in doing quantitative surveys and analysis of current approaches in Christian spirituality. In this way, we can establish patterns and trends, or situate isolated examples of Christian experience in the broader range of human experience, in order to avoid drawing premature conclusions.

But a word or two of caution is required here. First, just as Christian spirituality as an area of research is rapidly developing today, so too are the human sciences. Because of the proliferation of information and the growing number of specializations in the human sciences, the most that individuals using the human sciences can hope to gain is an overview of the specific field of study being used. This is not to discourage the use of human sciences, but to ensure that expectations for their use are realistic.

Second, and closely tied to the point above, the hurried student must hesitate and reflect before grabbing onto the latest fad in the human sciences, or even proven ideas, as if any of these will provide the full understanding of what is being studied. If it is kept in mind that any one theory from the human sciences is part of the contributions made from a variety of discourses the student will be less likely to rely on it too heavily. The latest fad is a sure trap for the non-specialist in the field, and students in Christian spirituality must be wary of this.

The student in Christian spirituality does not need to have intensive training in any one human science in order to avoid these pitfalls or to make use of the discipline in question. It is perfectly acceptable to search the area of human sciences looking for a specific idea or piece of information that will shed light on the aspect of human experience being studied. This information can help interpret the phenomenon under study in a more meaningful way, but the investigation will never be complete. Part of the art of study in the area of Christian spirituality is to choose the right idea, hypothesis, model, or piece of information. The student selects what appears to be illuminating or helpful but there is always more to come.

So even though the student does not need to become an expert in the field of study from which contributions are being drawn – such as psychology, sociology, or anthropology – he or she does need to be aware of the basic questions involved in the field of study, what each field deals with, and the limits of its contribution. These can be used as a guide in the selection process. Mindful of one's relative ignorance one proceeds to select carefully what is helpful, keeping in mind one's own question for reflection and points of reference. By keeping any one contribution in perspective, current findings and interpretations remain open for further precision as more is learned from other sources. This positions the student to develop a better, fuller, and more meaningful interpretation of the current object of study.

Christian spirituality is self-implicating

From the outset it needs to be acknowledged that Christian spirituality is a self-implicating endeavor. What does this mean? This means that the explorer – whether student, researcher, or casual reader – in Christian spirituality frequently is part of the reality under scrutiny. Not only is he or she trying to plumb the truth and meaning of Christianity in general, but also, and perhaps more significantly, the individual is often directly or indirectly searching for his or her own identity in it all. This does not mean that an individual needs to be Christian or even a person of faith of any kind to study Christian spirituality. There may be other motives for doing so; for example, someone may be learning about it from the perspective of inter-religious dialogue.

However, quite often people are drawn to Christian spirituality due to their questions about life, God, and the search for meaning in life. For this reason, students of Christian spirituality tend to care personally about the answers to questions being pursued; their reflections and discoveries are not merely academic curiosities. Christian spirituality is a field of study where one subjects to critical inquiry, for example, the beliefs, practices, and history of the field and, often by implication, one's own personal clarity around beliefs, practices, and history. From this personal involvement comes the motivation as well as the questions of inquiry that are the source of a greater understanding of Christian spirituality and its ongoing renewal. But this dynamic is frequently seen to be problematic.

Why is the issue of self-implication problematic? It is problematic because it raises questions about the objective quality of studies in Christian spirituality: that is, the scientific solidity of its findings. As mentioned above, students are often drawn into the study of Christian spirituality because of personal questions that reflect real issues in their lives or communities. They want to understand these issues better, both from the perspective of current research and from the perspective of the existential situation in which the questions arose. Yet the personal investment in the questions initially asked may skew the research methodology as well as the interpretation of the results. One's own personal story may become the exclusive reference for evidence in the research being undertaken. This approach would be limiting: an objective study would need to include more data from other sources, such as historical or theological studies.

Studying Christian spirituality is often marked with this tension between one's existential questions and the studying of these questions from objective angles. Methodology in Christian spirituality needs to overcome this tension, or at least deal with it in a conscious and intentional way. Sandra Schneiders, a leading researcher in the area of Christian spirituality, suggests that "Somehow, the researcher has to gain methodologically valid access to subjective data without denaturing the experience or getting mired in the purely private and idiosyncratic."[1] But an objective and scientific approach to Christian spirituality does not need to dismiss the personal investment and world view the student brings to the research. A method that allows for both of these perspectives to contribute to the research and learning process is the hermeneutical method. The hermeneutical method is discussed in more detail in Chapter 1 and is presented as the preferred method in the study of Christian spirituality. Why is the hermeneutical method the preferred method or approach to studying issues in Christian spirituality?

The hermeneutical method takes into consideration the data brought to reflection by the inquirer, but at the same time respects the rational nature of public discourse. If Christian spirituality is to be credible in the eyes of the wider community, it needs to be accountable for the ways it goes about doing research and explaining its findings objectively. Hermeneutical methodology is one way to do this. What is also helpful in the hermeneutical method is that it challenges the rationalistic reception of reality as the exclusive way of being in the world and generating knowledge about the world. Rationalism tends toward a desire to measure and quantify everything; things that cannot be seen and observed are not considered to be real.

Hermeneutical methodology for research accepts that there are other ways of gaining insight into the world that are not exclusively dependent upon the analysis of human experience from a purely rationalistic frame of reference. The concept of rationalism and its impact on Christian spirituality are explored in Chapter 2, Questions of Context. In particular, see the section "Modernism to postmodernism: the context of 'being in-between'." What is shown in this section is the shift from viewing reality strictly on the basis of what can be seen, touched, and subsequently measured, to an appreciation of including in reality things that are not directly observable. For example, faith in God cannot be measured, but it is a powerful force in the lives of countless people. Faith is very real. There needs to be a way of getting access to this human reality. Chapter 6, Questions of Text, explores this potential. In particular, see the section "Why the hermeneutical method of interpretation is helpful."

Christian spirituality, as a self-implicating discipline, acknowledges the struggles between personal and objective approaches. To deal with these, it strives to foster ways to study and do research that include the perspective of the individual or the community, but also include the objective findings of current data from within the discipline or from other sources, such as history, theology, psychology, or sociology. This book is about how all these viewpoints fit together to contribute to a deeper understanding of Christian spirituality, its research methods, and its relevance to the world today.

Methodology for studies in Christian spirituality

Many topics are presented in this book. Each topic has been focused to build up the student's capacity to be critically aware of a wide range of issues that need to be considered when studying Christian spirituality. All of these issues come together in what is called *methodology in Christian spirituality*: that is, the methods used to pursue particular studies in this academic field.

Method, generally speaking, refers to a series of steps constructed by the inquirer to proceed with a study of some topic in a particular field. Method begins with a topic, a question, or a hypothesis the inquirer wishes to investigate in some detail. In order to do the investigation a plan is needed. Since no one method can be used to study all topics, answer all questions, or investigate all hypotheses, each plan or method will be unique. The inquirer decides upon the particular plan or method after asking questions in Christian spirituality such as the following: How am I going to answer this question or investigate this hypothesis? What data am I going to bring forward for study? What do current authors say about the data? Might the data be illuminated further by examining them using questions from a number of frameworks: for example, theological frameworks, historical frameworks, and sociological frameworks? Are there scriptural data that might be useful for the reflection? Are there other sources in the Christian traditions, either ancient or more recent, that may shed light on this topic?

What comes to light is that method involves a conceptual framework, or several conceptual frameworks, within which reflection on some topic, question, or hypothesis may be studied. The use of several frameworks within which a topic is studied makes it possible to do a *critical* analysis: that is, the study is carried out using multiple frames of reference that do not allow any one framework to be the final arbitrator of the results. The different perspectives are allowed to question each other; in so doing, they complement and correct each other. This allows a deeper probing of the topic at hand. Even within a singular field of study there is usually more than one way of understanding the topic. For example, it is emphasized in this book that, within the Christian traditions, there is a plurality of theologies; each breaks open the theological understanding of Christian life in a different way. These different ways can complement and correct each other.

Let's look at an example. If a student wanted to deepen his or her understanding of how Christian meditation leads to growth in personal maturity and awareness of God's graced presence in his or her own life, the student might do some reading in several fields of study. The student might investigate theological frameworks and their understanding of grace; psychological frameworks that deal with human/spiritual maturation; and investigate physiological frameworks that make explicit connections between physical health and prolonged periods of quiet repose. A series of questions may come from, as well as guide, this reading. Questions such as the following may shape a study on the topic of Christian meditation, personal growth, and the role of God's grace: What is meant by grace? How is God's presence concretely experienced in daily living? What role does grace play in Christian spiritual growth? Is there a connection between physical, psychological, and spiritual well-being?

Core methodological principles

Some of the core critical issues that shape the study of Christian spirituality, and thus have been used as selection criteria to shape the content of this book, are indicated below. These constitute key methodological principles in the academic study of Christian spirituality. All of them are explained, in some detail, in the book. These principles are not independent of each other and as a result many of them enter the reflections many times.

1. A broad understanding of spirituality: Chapter 1 emphasizes that spirituality must be understood beyond the conventional boundaries that religions have established. There are multiple meanings of spirituality, for example, social, cultural, and Christian meanings. Many people are interested in the spiritual dimension of life without any commitment to an organized religion. Spirituality is the object of study in such diverse fields as, for example, education, health care, and the workplace. Studying Christian spirituality may include data from these areas of concern to enhance the understanding of Christian spirituality and vice versa.

2. Relationship between Christian spirituality and theology: Chapter 1 explores the relationship between Christian spirituality and some diverse understandings of theology. Chapter 3 presents key theological questions with respect to models of God. What these chapters imply is that, inevitably, Christian spiritualities find themselves in close relationship to Christian theologies. How spirituality is used depends on assumptions associated with the uses of theology. It is stressed that there are different ways of understanding theology as well as speaking of God; each in turn has a different impact on studies in Christian spirituality. This is why a critical understanding of the way theology is being used, as well as its relationship to Christian spirituality, is important. The preferred relationship between Christian spirituality and theology in Chapter 1 is described as a dialectical relationship: each is able to contribute to the insights of the other. Whatever relationship is established between Christian spirituality and theology, this position refutes the notion that theology is the sole point of reference that determines the truthfulness of all the findings of Christian spirituality.

3. Experience as the object of study: This topic is presented theoretically in Chapter 1 but there are many examples presented in detail throughout the book, especially in Chapters 8 and 9. Spirituality involves the study of experience as experience – to put it another way, it involves the critical study of lived experience or experience on the move. A critical understanding of experience makes it obvious that Christian spirituality is not merely the application of theological categories to lived spirituality in everyday life. Rather, it involves a study of human experience that is beyond the boundaries that theology, at least doctrinal theology, establishes for itself. This opens up the study of Christian spirituality to all areas of life, even those not initially thought to be appropriate for study. Critical to the way human experience is analyzed is the model of the experiencing subject being used. Chapter 4 brings forward a number of ways that the self is understood. A particular model of the self will lead to a particular understanding of human experience. Thus, one's understanding of the self is a critical issue closely tied to the issue of human experience.

4. Importance of context: Chapter 2 emphasizes that the study of Christian spirituality cannot be separated from context. Chapter 5 makes the same case, except this time focused on the questions of the context of history. A critical understanding, for example, of cultural place, geography, history, and even architecture is an invaluable resource when studying a particular topic in Christian spirituality. Context is formative of personal and communitarian identity, which, in turn, profoundly affects the way people live their spirituality. Context – political, sociological, ecclesial, and historical issues – needs to be made as explicit as possible when studying topics in Christian spirituality. Sensitivity to the uniqueness of various times and periods in history prevents the inquirer from establishing hard universal norms suggested to be valid in every time and place.

5. Historical consciousness: Chapter 5 treats this issue. How the past is understood in its relationship not only to the present, but to the future as well, is a critical issue to keep in mind when studying Christian spirituality. As current realities dramatically shift, and at a rate that could only be dreamed of half a century ago, the questions of how the past is treated become even more crucial. A series of questions in Chapter 5 is formulated to assist reflection on the way history is used to inform current issues. These questions include: Is the past treated as a hindrance that stops progress today, or is it seen as a rich resource that anchors critical reflection on current issues? Whose past is brought into the present and why? What is the role of tradition? Historical consciousness brings into focus the belief that people are products of their own times, yet their vision for life may provide valuable wisdom for current and subsequent generations. Sensitivity to historical consciousness reminds us that the current researcher also operates from within his or her own cultural horizon. The details of this horizon need to be made as explicit as possible in undertaking critical studies in Christian spirituality.

6. Multidisciplinary approach: Multidisciplinarity is a central methodological principle for studying Christian spirituality. From the beginning of this book it is stressed that no one field has all the answers when it comes to studying human experience. The very nature of spirituality requires a critical examination of human experience using a number of conceptual frameworks. Furthermore, these frameworks need to be allowed to question each other. When this happens students of Christian spirituality may find themselves confronted with conflicting points of view. As students wrestle with these, the art of studying Christian spirituality comes to the fore. Multidisciplinary methodology requires artful and reasoned judgment to carry forward the truest results of inquiries, all the while acknowledging that these results may be provisional until more data enter the picture. Multidisciplinarity recognizes that judgments are always made from within the perspective of a particular world view, one that may shift as the inquirer deepens his or her understanding of the topics at hand. For example, Chapters 1 and 3 give consideration to some specific theological issues, Chapter 2 to sociological ones, Chapter 4 to questions of Christian anthropology, Chapter 5 to those of history, and Chapter 7 is focused on issues in relationship to psychology.

7. Hermeneutical theory: Hermeneutical methodology, explored in Chapter 1 and Chapter 6, places studying Christian spirituality in the realm of interpretive frameworks. Christian spirituality is not merely interested in the content of its field of study – for example, past events or descriptions of various kinds of prayer – but places the inquirer on the path to gaining insight for living today. This approach requires interpretation. Wisdom from the past or present is sought to be appropriated: that is, made one's own. The self-implicating nature of Christian spirituality is emphasized in this Introduction, as well as in Chapter 6. Hermeneutical theory makes the inquirer aware that studying Christian spirituality is not only informative, but also transformative. Interpretation of the past and the present is accomplished through a great range of sources, and not only written ones: for example, texts as well as sculptures, architecture, clothing, and music. The goal in hermeneutical analysis is not to lay bare raw information, but rather is focused on meaning and wisdom for life today. Transformation or conversion is the very heart of the enterprise of Christian spirituality. It provides the perspective from which all truth is finally discerned.

The above seven issues provide key points of reference for those undertaking academic studies in the field of Christian spirituality. Understanding these points well, and seeing how they are reflected in a variety of ways throughout the book, will provide students with a solid basis upon which to embark on particular projects in their study of Christian spirituality.

———

NOTES

1 Sandra Schneiders (2005) "The Study of Christian Spirituality: Contours and Dynamics of a Discipline," in (2005) *Minding the Spirit: The Study of Christian Spirituality*, Elizabeth A. Dreyer and Mark S. Burrows, eds, Baltimore, MD: Johns Hopkins University Press, 18.

1 Questions of definitions

Introduction

WHAT IS SPIRITUALITY? People throughout the world experience spirituality whether they are Christians or not, and even whether they believe in God or not. Buddhism, Taoism, and Confucianism are all forms of spirituality, but have no reference to a God as such.[1] Many people today claim to be "spiritual but not religious."[2] For them, spirituality can be explained as a human phenomenon rather than an explicit belief in the Christian God or any God. How can this perspective be understood? Not everybody may agree that spirituality is possible outside the context of belief in God, but the approach taken to Christian spirituality in this book encourages an understanding of this perspective. Once spirituality is understood in a general way, questions of spirituality that relate to Christian life become clearer.

Since this entire book is about spirituality in general, and Christian spirituality in particular, it only proposes working definitions: that is, definitions that contain the area of reflection without limiting it. The rest of the book then explores the meaning of these initial definitions in greater depth. Working definitions are useful because there is no universally accepted understanding of spirituality, spiritual life, spiritual growth, or even Christian spirituality. Talking to different people, or reading different authors, will produce many ways of understanding both spirituality and Christian spirituality.

Spirituality

William Stringfellow, in his book *The Politics of Spirituality*, indicates the broad spectrum of what the term *spirituality* might mean today. He suggests that it

> may indicate stoic attitudes, occult phenomena, the practice of so-called mind control, yoga discipline, escapist fantasies, interior journeys, an appreciation of Eastern religions, multifarious pietistic exercises, superstitious imaginations, intensive journals, dynamic muscle tension, assorted dietary regimens, meditation, jogging cults, monastic rigors, mortification of the flesh, wilderness sojourns, political resistance, contemplation, abstinence, hospitality, a vocation of poverty, nonviolence, silence, the efforts of prayer, obedience, generosity, exhibiting stigmata, entering solitude, or, I suppose, among these and many other things, squatting on top of a pillar.[3]

But this definition of spirituality is still too broad for the purposes of this book, even as a working definition. In addition, his use of the word *spirituality* tends to focus on particular behaviors and events, rather than the underlying motivation for them, or the capacity of human beings to engage reality in these ways. Something must lie behind the external actions and events that makes the external expression of spirituality possible. Motivation (why people do things) and capacity (the ability to do things or be receptive to them) are also part of spirituality, as will be shown. These aspects of spirituality are more difficult to describe and understand.

Another question that comes to the fore after examining Stringfellow's list is the question of authentic and non-authentic spiritualities. Might some of Stringfellow's categories be excluded as authentic spiritualities? If so, why? It is very difficult to judge different spiritualities as authentic or non-authentic, as well as decide on criteria that would be helpful to do so. There are real tensions with normativity and what is to be considered acceptable. However, despite inherent tensions, there is good reason to give critical thought to some criteria that might help divide acceptable or authentic spiritualities from those that are not. Take, for example, Jonestown. Jonestown, named for its founder Jim Jones, was the communal settlement made in Guyana by a religious cult previously under suspicion for human rights abuses in California in the 1970s. Jonestown gained international notoriety in 1978 when nearly its whole population of about 900 people died in a mass murder-and-suicide ordered by Jones. From any perspective the events in Jonestown are recognized as an inauthentic expression of spirituality that was pathological in nature.

To begin to respond to the question "What is authentic spirituality?" some suggestions about what authentic spirituality *is not* are in order.

First, authentic spirituality is not simply to be identified with the interior and private life of the individual, as reflected in either exterior practices and rituals or interior meditations and reflections. In other words, authentic spirituality is not to be identified with only one part of the life of the person, cut off from other aspects. "Spiritual life" is not separate from "body life," from the entire sphere of human action and human desire. The psychological, bodily, historical, social, political, aesthetic, intellectual, and other dimensions of the human subject of spiritual experience are integral to the understanding of spirituality. As Ernest Becker points out in *The Denial of Death*, his 1973 Pulitzer Prize-winning study of the human condition, human beings are spirit in the world; spirituality is the effort to understand and realize the potential of this extraordinary and paradoxical situation.[4]

Authentic spirituality, therefore, is not merely the way an individual generates meaning in life to feel good about his or her self and world.

Authentic spiritualities involve the integration of all aspects of life in a unified whole. Authentic life refers to living in an overall spirit of goodwill; it refers to a commitment to look critically at oneself and one's relationships as well as an openness to question objectively and regularly all aspects of living. All this is with a view to deepening self-appreciation as well as self-giving to others. This ongoing, objective, and critical stance may open up new, and greater, possibilities for living which are the foundation of authentic spiritualities. For example, negative patterns such as the abuse of alcohol or the excessive preoccupation with buying new things, though they may generate meaning in one's life and even make an individual feel good, are not authentic spiritualities based on the above criteria.

Second, spirituality is not necessarily associated with belief in a God or some other supernatural being. Spirituality, for some people, may be an important sphere of human living without any involvement in a community of believers for whom belief in a God is at the core of their self-identity. But spirituality does not exclude such a belief, either. In the public realm, spirituality may refer to an expression of human life within a particular belief system that includes recognition of the existence of God *as well as* referring to belief systems that contain no such recognition. From Stringfellow's definition above, non-violence and yoga disciplines, for some people, could be appreciated as spiritualities. These do not necessarily have a belief in God at their core. But then the question could be asked whether these two examples are *authentic spiritualities* that "involve the integration of all aspects of life in a unified whole." Authentic spirituality is not all about one's personal life, even if that life is meaningful.

Now that we know what spirituality is not, let us explore what it is. Four primary characteristics of spirituality are proposed as a working definition for spirituality,[5] in terms of the *human dimension* of life. Since they contain no reference to God, the characteristics of spirituality listed below describe a strictly *humanist* perspective.

Humanist understanding of spirituality

First, spirituality is a fundamental capacity in human beings known as *human spiritual nature*. For example, human spiritual nature is engaged in expressions of creative and imaginative art and music, or in self-conscious reflection. Spirituality in this first sense is also the search for meaning, values, and purpose in life, all of which can be nurtured through such things as interpersonal relationships, volunteering time and energy in soup kitchens, or taking part in certain rituals on a regular basis. Human spiritual nature engages in being thoughtful, being empathetic, and at times making heroic choices that involve intense self-sacrifice.

Second, and intimately related to the first, spirituality recognizes that life is bigger than what is happening in an individual's personal world. The awareness that reality is beyond what can be seen and touched is called the human *capacity for transcendence*. *Self*-transcendence includes the human capacity to nurture meaningful and intimate relationships with other persons or other realities because individual human beings are part of a larger whole. In this sense, spirituality is the discovery of how individuals grow in intimacy, interdependence, and self-giving in relationship with other people and the world at large. For example, in the face of the destruction of forests and pollution of water systems, ecological concerns may be the focus of self-transcendence for some people.

Third, spirituality is a *lived reality that is shaped into a way of life*, for example, attitudes, practices, rituals, and behaviors become constant in an individual's life. Even the athletic way of life could be described as a spirituality within this understanding, for it requires commitment, discipline, and frequent repetition of particular skills. Spirituality is not an incidental or once-and-for-all event. Depending on what meaning, values, or purpose in life people have chosen, they will focus their activities and choices to nurture these. In this sense, spirituality is not a special or separate part of human life, or one that is practiced by only a select few. Generally speaking, any human activity that enhances what individuals commit themselves to in life could be considered part of their spirituality.

Fourth, spirituality also refers to *the study of spirituality*. Human beings not only have a human spiritual nature, a capacity for self-transcendence, and an ability to shape these into a meaningful lifestyle; they also have the curiosity to study how people live out the reality of these aspects. How spirituality operates, how it can be improved, and how it fits into family life, the workplace, public life, health, ethics, and so on, may all be the subject of serious academic study. Universities offer courses on these very topics. Analyzing appropriate spiritual behavior for various stages in life may be of interest to the professional academic as well as the amateur explorer. Thus, spirituality can be studied from at least two perspectives. The first involves studying ways of doing things to do them better – how to achieve stated goals and desired outcomes. This could be described as a practical or formative approach to the study of spirituality aimed at personal growth. The second involves studying spirituality from an objective perspective: a theoretical approach. The goal here is to explain the dynamics of spiritual life in relationship to all facets of human living using methods from other disciplines, such as psychology, anthropology, or sociology.

The above four elements culminate in a more precise definition of spirituality: "Spirituality as lived experience can be defined as conscious involvement in the project of life integration through self-transcendence toward the ultimate value one perceives."[6] This definition of spirituality is helpful to describe spiritualities that do not yet include any belief in God, but it does not necessarily exclude them either. For example, the "ultimate value one perceives" could be God.

> Spirituality refers to a fundamental capacity in human beings. It is expressed within human experience before people identify that experience with a particular religious or spiritual set of beliefs, rituals, or ethics. Spirituality, as an innate human characteristic, involves the capacity for self-transcendence: being meaningfully involved in, and personally committed to, the world beyond an individual's personal boundaries. This meaningful involvement and commitment shapes the way people live and allows them to integrate their lives. Spirituality can be clearly identified and studied in human events and written texts, or other forms of expression, such as art and music, desires and motivations. Spirituality is also an academic discipline. Using interdisciplinary methods, the dynamics of the spiritual dimension of life can be analyzed.

Let us now place this understanding of spirituality in the context of human life in general. Human beings naturally ask the big questions from within two inescapable points of reference: life and death. Between these two poles we probe the world to "make sense of it all," to forge meaning within the at times disparate and unconnected events of life. Spirituality, whether or not it is linked to belief in God, struggles with the mystery of the deep questions around the meaning of human life. Human beings live in a world of values, beliefs, truths, hopes, and desires that call individuals beyond what can be seen and touched. The human spirit remains open to the search for authentic truth within the varied experiences of life, establishes normative values, exercises reasoned judgment, and involves the entire human being on the path to self-determination.[7] Understood in this way, spirituality becomes a daily reality that all people share.

The *spirit* of spirituality

Given the working definition cited above, what is the "spirit" in "spirituality"?[8] From the humanistic understanding of spirituality, we can't yet say that it has anything to do with God, since it is human spirit we are referring to. Nor does it have any reference to the Holy Spirit, or the Divine Spirit within the human spirit; these are specifically *Christian* ways of talking about *Christian* spirituality. To honor what countless people experience as spirituality without any reference to God or Divine Spirit or Holy Spirit, there must be another way to talk about the *spirit* in spirituality.

Spirit here refers to human spirit in the sense of human consciousness,[9] a constitutive (fundamental) dimension of human beings. In a way, then, human spirit involves the unique human capacity to be self-conscious. Not only do humans exist as physical bodies that seek satisfaction in physical comforts and needs (for example, food and shelter), or as psyches that feel emotions and respond and react to various psychological situations (for example, anxiety or joy); human beings also exist as human spirit, with the capacity for self-consciousness (awareness of being aware).

To put it another way, human beings are self-conscious creatures.[10] Human beings can therefore be intentional about who they are, and not simply react blindly to external events that stimulate the biological or psychological dimensions of their being.

Think for a moment. Think about reading these lines. You know you are reading something. You are aware now that you are aware of reading these lines, on this page at this very moment. You are extracting meaning from them, and relating that meaning to previous knowledge. Now imagine you are reading a book of profound personal interest. Because of what you read, you may be planning a changed future course of action, or re-evaluating previous decisions. You are recalling your past. This process of self-conscious reflection requires the work of human spirit. Consciousness and self-consciousness are unique to the human spirit; no other animal has this capacity. Let us now look at some specific characteristics of the "spirit" in spirituality.

Spirit is not completely objectifiable

Because of the varied and sometimes complex maneuvers of human spirit, it is not completely objectifiable. Human beings can never say exactly what they are doing with absolute transparency of motive or intentionality. We may act out of the needs of human spirit, but we can never see it directly. The work of the human spirit is observable only through the mediation of human action, intentionality, and human productions (such as art, architecture, and music). For this reason, any study in spirituality must also look beyond the conscious sphere of the individual human life to include the broadest range of human experience. Spirituality has to do with experiencing *my*-self as a conscious and self-reflective entity, but also includes the struggle with the inability to do so at times.

Spirit can deceive and manipulate

Human intentionality and human spirit can be both conscious and unconscious at the same time. Human spirit may be wounded from past events in life, or immature due to a lack of integration. Since human spirit is never completely transparent in life, as seen above, the human spirit may involve itself in strategies of unhealthy risk and hurtful deception or manipulation in order to achieve a particular goal. Part of the task of human spirit, therefore, is to become ever more conscious of intentionality, motivations, and desires.[11] There is a need to work at this part of human growth and maturation by critical reflection on, for example, behaviors, actions, and attitudes.

Spirit involves the deepest dimensions of life

Spirituality, as self-conscious and self-directed intentionality, involves the deepest and most profound elements of human life. Human spirit explores the aspects of life that lie beyond its immediate sphere of experience. It pushes human beings to acquire new skills, experiment with new ways of being in the world, or risk the commitment of a loving relationship. In these ways, human spirit pushes the boundaries of the self further and further into new and unexplored territory. Human beings can always move beyond their current state of awareness and level of knowledge to embrace something more. Human spirit entails mystery, since it works with what is not yet known in all these areas of human life.

After reviewing the above reflection what can we say, generally, about spirituality? Spirituality stands at the junction where the deepest concerns of humanity, and the belief in transcendental values, come together in the movement toward ultimate fulfillment in life. The spiritual center is the deepest center of the person: the place of surrender to authenticity and love. It is here that human beings are open to the transcendent, whatever that is for the individual. It is here that human beings experience ultimate reality and their most profound desires are satisfied.

Spirituality embodies the most significant values of human life. Those values are expressed in practices, ways of doing things, beliefs, attitudes, and decisions. To a certain extent, each individual constructs a spirituality that embodies the purpose and meaning of his or her life. Spirituality is, therefore, built around an identifiable center. Individuals defer to this center in the particular and concrete circumstances of life by deliberately considering the various elements of their lives and how these are lived out concretely, for themselves and for others.

Spirituality in everyday life

Spirituality is lived in the marketplace, in the daily encounters where people work, live, and play. There is no one ideal way that spirituality is lived. Various elements of human spirit will come to the fore in each sphere of activity, but some spiritual paths are more helpful than others.

In their healthiest and most helpful forms, the goal of spiritualities is to construct hope and meaning in the midst of daily life. Hope and meaning open up the mystery of the world, which, in turn, fills people with awe and gratitude that they are part of this infinite universe. Authentic relationships are key to opening up the possibility of belonging to the larger world. These may include intimate, loving, interdependent, and trusting relationships with others; a sense of belonging to the natural world; or a reverence and respect for the physical body. Life-giving and authentic spiritualities ought to make people feel at home in a world of difference and multiplicity; they lead to breathtaking possibilities that bring people to care genuinely for others and the world.

Authentic and life-giving spiritualities are therefore self-liberating: they liberate people from what would keep them narrowly focused on private, narcissistic worlds. Care for others requires individuals to step outside of their preoccupations with self. Human spirit is so big that, to do its work, it needs the whole world in which to act. As a result, no authentic or life-giving spirituality can proceed without some form of community – without relationship to others, to the cosmos, to the greater spheres of human living.

At the same time, healthy spiritualities work against destructive elements that may be present in the world, such as rugged and narcissistic individualism, exploitation of nature, degradation of the physical body, and masculine institutional control. We will be talking about all these ideas in more detail later in the book. For now, we can say that these negative situations have tended to fragment human life. Rather than building up individuals and communities, each in its own way has tended to devalue and exploit them.

As we have seen, human spirit's activities are not restricted to the beliefs, practices, and rituals of the organized, institutional churches. Human spirit strives to explore the questions of the meaning and values of human life in all its expressions, not only those that are more clearly identified within the formalized religious dimension of human living. Our working definition of spirituality, before being identified with the beliefs and practices of a particular faith, points to the striving of the human individual to gather his or her life around a cluster of foundational and self-liberating values and practices, wherever these may be found.

Spirituality marketed as a product

As Stringfellow points out, not all spiritualities are life-giving and self-liberating. Some of the current interest in spirituality is superficial and bizarre. Human spirit is not absolutely benevolent. Without careful attention, it can be led astray, resulting in destructive and harmful human actions. Some spiritualities can be a form of illusive life that feeds the narcissistic self and closes the individual off from the broader concerns of society, from the demands of justice, and from the engagement with reality at many levels. These spiritualities have already been identified as non-authentic spiritualities.

At times, from this illusory perspective, spirituality is marketed as a product. Spiritual counsel, books, and paraphernalia are sold as offering quick-fixes to modern problems. A cursory examination of any bookstore will reveal that there is money to be made on the wave of interest in spirituality at the popular and academic levels. Many of these books are published under the guise of responsible scholarship. The authors are advertised as experts who have been educated and trained in their respective fields of study. Spirituality is in many instances a consumer product, and it sells.

"We consume ideas, junk foods, news, the latest unneeded plastic gadget, or other persons. Anything has the potential for being sold, once a need can be artificially created and then identified with a marketable commodity. Friendship, intimacy, love, pride, happiness, and joy are actually the objects we buy and consume."[12]

To a large extent, the wave of popular spirituality belongs to the area of people's personal and private lives. It is difficult to deny that this approach to spirituality has roots within Western consumeristic culture. In this culture, spirituality is seen not as a process of self-liberating transcendence, but as an activity in its own right that people can use to justify their personal, self-serving agenda and narrow ideology.

A person may feel satisfied pursuing his or her individual needs or agenda of the moment without reflecting on the wider dimensions of human life. Does that option give rise to authentic spirituality? According to the working definition above, it does not. Authentic spirituality takes into account the delicate nature and balance of human growth and development, the wider concerns of society, and the multiplicity of ways that spiritualities are enfleshed in people's lives. Authentic spiritualities are positive human expressions of self-liberating transcendence that are directed toward the common good of humanity. Clusters of values, actions, and choices, such as alcoholism, Nazism, or consumerism, that do not satisfy this broad criterion have mistaken the quest of human spirit, and cannot be considered authentic expressions of spirituality.

People need to be critical (in the sense of careful and thoughtful) of current trends in spirituality, whether they are associated with a religious belief system or not. Taking the attitude that when it comes to spirituality, everything goes, is simply not responsible. As we have seen, spirituality can be benevolent or destructive. Some critical understanding is needed so that people can assess what to encourage and what to discourage.[13]

Given the broad meaning of the term *spirituality*, it is helpful to develop a personal sense of what authentic spirituality might mean, even when there is no belief in God associated with it. Spirituality is difficult to define once and for all and therefore it is important to keep one's mind open to the new and the unexpected. Furthermore, a critical appreciation of what passes for authentic spirituality, as opposed to marketing spirituality for financial profit or for some other utilitarian goal, can be very helpful to avoid getting caught in spiritualities that, in the end, may even be harmful.

Let's review the working definition for spirituality suggested above. It has four characteristics of spirituality that relate to the potential or the capacity for spirituality in people as well as its expression:

1. A fundamental human capacity referred to as human spiritual nature.
2. The human capacity for self-transcendence.
3. A lived reality that is shaped into a meaningful way of life.
4. An area of academic study.

These characteristics help determine what constitutes authentic spirituality.

As mentioned above, some people think it is impossible to have a spirituality without some connection to God. However, that does not prevent people who connect spirituality with belief in God in particular to try to understand how others may view reality without belief in God. Being open to understanding and honoring the perspective of the other person, even in the context of disagreement, is a hallmark of Christian spirituality, which we will explore now.

Christian spirituality

In the previous section, the word *spirituality* was identified as a phenomenon in everyone's life, whether people believe in God or not. The word *spirituality*, among other things, refers to the possibility of living out a spiritual orientation in the real circumstances of life. There are, therefore, *spiritualities*, referring to how spirituality as human phenomenon incarnates or embodies itself in various ways. The topic of this section, and ultimately this book, is Christian spirituality. What characterizes spirituality for the Christian? This question can be answered briefly, but merits much further critical reflection as outlined in the rest of the book. Using the general definition of spirituality from Sandra Schneiders above, spirituality becomes Christian when the Christian God is the ultimate concern of one's life; self-transcendence refers to modeling one's life after the life of Jesus; and the "spirit" in spirituality is identified with the Holy Spirit. Let us examine how this understanding of Christian spirituality has developed.

The history of the word *spirituality* in the Christian traditions

Within the Christian traditions, *spirituality* is dependent on the dynamic relationship between the Spirit of God and the human spirit.[14] This relationship is what characterizes spirituality for the Christian. At the center of Christian spirituality is God's animating, graceful presence. It is God's Spirit alive in people's lives that moves them beyond the boundaries of their fragile selves to give their lives in many different ways to others. For the Christian, God is the foundation for all self-transcendence and for all spirituality. The contemporary understanding of the word *spirituality* can be traced back to the origins of Christianity, its scriptures, and to later developments. The word *spirituality*, however, was not used explicitly in either the Old or the New Testament. But we can examine words in the Old and New Testament, as well as later examples, that give meaning to the contemporary understanding of the term *Christian spirituality*.

Spirituality: the ruach *of God in the Old Testament*

In the Old Testament, the Greek word *ruach* generally refers to the Spirit of God. For example, God's *ruach* or "spirit" was present at the time of creation. This is seen in Genesis 1:1: "God's [*ruach*] spirit hovered over the waters." The Spirit of God was present in other forms as well. In Psalm 104:30 God's *ruach* was portrayed as God's "breath": "You give [*ruach*] breath, fresh life begins, you keep renewing the world." Generally speaking, in the Old Testament, God's *ruach* refers to the creative and dynamic work of the Spirit of God in all of creation. God's *ruach* constantly gives, sustains, and renews life. *Ruach* is the spirit, the power, the life and *heart of God* active in the world. In the Old Testament we see God's *ruach* portrayed in many ways, such as "wind," "hand," and "heat."

Spirituality: the pneuma of God in the New Testament

When translating the New Testament into Latin, the biblical scholar Jerome (345–c.419)[15] used the Latin word *spiritualis* (spiritual) to translate the Greek adjective *pneumatikos*. *Pneumatikos* referred to the "spiritual person," someone who strengthened his or her life in the Spirit of Jesus, who is the source of all Christian life. This is what it meant to live a spiritual life. From *pneumatikos* we derive the noun *pneuma*, which is translated as *spiritus* in Latin from which "spirit" is derived in English. The framework for Christian life is, therefore, life in the Spirit of Jesus, which is also the *pneuma*, the Spirit of God or Holy Spirit. What it means to live in the Holy Spirit can be determined by reading how Paul uses this expression in 1 Cor. 2:14–3:3.

In this passage from Corinthians, Paul contrasts a "spiritual" person with an "unspiritual" person. A spiritual person lives a life guided by the Holy Spirit, a life of "love, joy, peace, patience, kindness, goodness, trustfulness, gentleness, and self-control" (Gal. 5:22). Paul refers to an *unspiritual person* as a *natural person*, or a *psychikos anthrôpos* in Greek, because he or she is guided solely by natural impulses. An unspiritual person is animated by evil spirits and lives a life of "self-indulgence . . . feuds and wrangling, jealousy, bad temper and quarrels, disagreements, factions, envy, drunkenness, orgies and similar things" (Gal. 5:19–21). Paul described this lifestyle as a life of *flesh* (in Greek, *sarx*).

In using spirit as the opposite of flesh, Paul was not speaking of any opposition between the spiritual and the physical. Rather, he was referring to two vastly different ways of living: one being in tune with the Holy Spirit, the other not. In Paul's thought, material is not the opposite of spiritual. Paul's New Testament meaning of spirituality referred to the whole life of the Christian lived under the guidance of the Holy Spirit. This meaning largely prevailed until around the twelfth century.

Spirituality after the twelfth century

Jerome's Latin version of the entire Bible was widely circulated and used after the fifth century. Although he used the adjective *spiritualis* (spiritual) to describe the Christian life, this term was not commonly used in ordinary Christian life. One exception is found in a Latin fifth-century letter by an anonymous writer in which we read: "*Age ut in spiritualitate proficias*" (So, act as to advance in spirituality). The context of the letter indicates that this use retains the Pauline sense of acting according to life in the Spirit of God. Only later, around the ninth century, and then again in the twelfth century, did the word *spiritualitas*, derived from the noun *spiritus*, appear in a Christian text outside of its Pauline scriptural meaning. Regrettably, for the most part, this was not a happy development.

Around the twelfth century, universities were beginning to be established in central Europe. Knowledge, which included philosophical and theological knowledge, was gradually being organized for teaching and learning within the newly formed universities. Thus began the age of *scholasticism*: the bringing together into a systematic whole all that was known about Christian life so it could be understood as a single body of knowledge. The word *scholastic* came to be applied to anyone writing or teaching from this perspective. It was during the development of scholasticism that the word *spirituality* began to be used, referring not only to the Spirit that animated Christian life, but also to anything that pertained to the soul rather than the body. This is the unfortunate part of the change in use of the word *spirituality*. Let us explore this shift in more detail.

During the twelfth and thirteenth centuries, some writers began to interpret Paul's use of the word *sarx* (flesh) as referring literally to the physical body, and his word *pneuma* (spirit) as referring to the human soul. To support this claim the writers referred to the use of the word *spiritualitas* in opposition to *corporalitas* (referring to the material body), which was used in that rare ninth-century text mentioned above. This use changed the Pauline sense of *spiritualis*. The body was seen in a negative light and the soul in a positive one.[16] As a result, spirituality was understood as separate from the life of the body – in other words, from the rest of one's life. Increasingly, spirituality referred to one's interior life, pious practices, prayers, and rituals. It gradually lost its holistic reference to living one's entire life under the influence of God's Spirit, as Paul had taught in the New Testament. The body, or the material world, became identified with the place of darkness and sin, while the spirit (soul) became identified with all that was light and holy. Spiritual life and material life were seen as two separate, and antagonistic, elements of Christian human life. The important thing was to save your soul. Because the body had no role to play in the spiritual life, people tried to subdue it. The roots of the disdain for the body and the exaltation of the soul that are found in later spiritual writings, and even in contemporary ones, can be traced back to this time. What seems to have been overlooked in this view of the body is that Jesus took on human flesh as a way of being in a loving and intimate relationship with the world – not as a way of harshly judging it.

So far we have examined two Christian meanings of the word *spirituality*: Paul's, which referred to the entire Christian life lived under the guidance of the Holy Spirit, and the newer meaning, which identified spirituality exclusively with the life of the soul and, as such, opposed spirit and body. A third definition evolved around the twelfth century as well: spirituality came to mean everything that belonged in the realm of the clerics – the ordained members of the Christian community, as opposed to the laity, the non-ordained members. It represented the authority or ecclesiastical jurisdiction of the clerics in opposition to civil authority, and spiritual goods (such as prayers, rituals, penances, and pious practices) rather than material goods (such as money and land). Even though the first two meanings existed alongside it, this third sense of spirituality dominated until the seventeenth century.

As we have seen, the approach to Christian spiritual life after the twelfth century was increasingly characterized by separation and division:[17]

1. spirituality became associated with interiority and feelings, separate from theology, which was understood as a body of knowledge and beliefs associated with Christian life;
2. due to a greater interest in personal spirituality, spirituality became separated from social involvement (such as social justice issues) and public ethics;
3. since spirituality was focused on personal prayer and meditation, it was gradually separated from liturgy, the common prayer of the Christian community;
4. the clerical state, frequently seen as the heavenly, spiritual way, was seen as separate from and superior to the lay state, frequently seen as the way of the world;
5. spirituality, as supernatural life shared with God in heaven, was viewed as something added on to the natural life of human persons living on earth; and
6. many writers on spirituality viewed growth in Christian spirituality in terms of predefined and universal consecutive or separate stages – independent of the mysterious nature of human experience, the uniqueness of each person's spiritual journey, and the unpredictable action of the Holy Spirit.

Spirituality after the seventeenth century

By the end of the seventeenth century, the meaning of the word *spirituality* underwent yet another shift. This shift was built on the development of the largely personalized and other-worldly spirituality that emerged in the twelfth and thirteenth centuries. During the seventeenth century, spirituality became associated almost exclusively with inner dispositions, the interior states of the soul. Eventually, the term became associated with many bizarre spiritual experiences as individuals tried in earnest to live a Christian life of perfection based on a personal – and somewhat isolated – life with God. For example, in France, spirituality became associated with Quietism, the belief that communion with God is attainable only when one does absolutely nothing. Passive sitting, without thinking or feeling, while waiting for God to enter the soul, is the main preoccupation of the quietist.

Because of the negative connotations of extreme and unusual practices such as Quietism, the word *spirituality* all but disappeared in the mainline Christian vocabulary for nearly 200 years. Other terms, such as devotion, piety, and way of perfection were used to express life in the Spirit. And then, in the early 1900s, the French word *spiritualité* (spirituality) began to reappear in Roman Catholic circles in France. From here it was adopted in English through the translation of texts by prominent French writers. *Spirituality* became the favored word once again. It was initially used, as it was before, to describe spiritual life as separate from the rest of life. Eventually, however, as the twentieth century progressed *spirituality* began to be used once again to refer to the fullness of life in the Spirit, that is, life modeled after Jesus, a life that was available to all. Spiritual life was once again not seen as separate from physical life; spirituality involved the whole person (mind, body, and soul). All the separations that had developed following the twelfth century were now being reconsidered.

Paul's portrayal of spirituality as a way of life lived under the guidance of the Holy Spirit was slowly recovered over the course of the twentieth century. By the 1960s, Christian spirituality took on a new and vibrant significance in the lives of many. Within the scriptural, liturgical, and theological developments of the second half of the twentieth century, this spirituality was not identified with any one Christian tradition. Rather, it was acknowledged that there were a variety of legitimate ways to live out the Christian lifestyle. As a result, a range of Christian spiritualities, all fundamentally related to the power of the Holy Spirit and the life of Jesus as told to us in the Christian scriptures, were deemed acceptable. Christian beliefs and practices are valued as the foundation to give specific shape to spirituality as a fundamental human capacity. This approach gives the unique mix of Christian spiritualities that are recognized around the globe today.

We have given a brief historical overview of the development of Christian spirituality. However, the question "How is Christian spirituality viewed today?" still needs to be answered. Even though there are many ways of living life under the guidance of the Holy Spirit, what do they have in common? Let us turn our attention to this question by suggesting some working definitions of Christian spirituality that are current today.

Christian spirituality – some working definitions

The start of this chapter noted that only working definitions would be provided, since no one definition of either spirituality or Christian spirituality is accepted by all Christian traditions. Given the framework suggested in the section on humanist spirituality, as well as the specific understanding of Christian spirituality outlined in the above section, the following working definitions are suggested in order to help answer the question "What is Christian spirituality?"

> Whatever else may be affirmed about a spirituality which has a biblical precedent and style, spiritual maturity or spiritual fulfillment necessarily involves the *whole* person – body, mind and soul, place, relationships – in connection with the whole of creation throughout the era of time. Biblical spirituality encompasses the whole person in the totality of existence in the world, not some fragment or scrap or incident of a person.[18]

> "Spirituality" (at least in a Christian context) is a useful term to describe how, individually and collectively, we personally appropriate the traditional Christian beliefs about God, humanity and the world, and express them in terms of our basic attitudes, life-style and activity.[19]

> [Spirituality] is the experience of conscious involvement in the project of life-integration through self-transcendence toward the ultimate value one perceives. In Christian spirituality these formal categories are specified by Christian content: the horizon of ultimate value is the triune God revealed in Jesus Christ, and the project involves the living of his paschal mystery in the context of the Church community through the gift of the Holy Spirit.[20]

> Christian spirituality is the daily, communal, lived expression of one's ultimate beliefs, characterized by openness to the self-transcending love of God, self, neighbor, and world through Jesus Christ and in the power of the Holy Spirit.[21]

These working definitions can be summed up in the following way: Christian spirituality is the experience of transformation in the Divine–human relationship as modeled by Jesus Christ and inspired by the Holy Spirit. Christian spirituality is appropriated as a lifestyle within all relationships in the broader Christian community as well as in society in general. While Christian spirituality embraces Christian traditions and beliefs, it also exceeds the boundaries of established religions and their theologies. As such, Christian spirituality is always open to new and unexpected expressions of the way the Spirit of God is actively incarnated in human history, whether within the Christian traditions or from outside of them.

> "One of the most interesting characteristics of Christian spirituality as lived experience is its capacity to be outside or even ahead of theological developments and to introduce into the theological and/or religious purview . . . insights and convictions which stretch the received theological categories and paradigms."[22]

Of course, there is much more to be said about Christian spirituality, and it will be said throughout this book. However, these working definitions orient us toward the subject matter that is of primary concern: the methodological questions at stake when individuals undertake personal formation or academic study in the area of Christian spirituality. As noted above, the approach to Christian spirituality being developed in this book views any one Christian spirituality as larger than its theological points of reference. But this begs the question, what is the nature of the relationship between Christian spiritualities and their theologies?

Christian spirituality and theology

> "THEO" – "LOGY" = *theos* (Greek for *God*) + *logos* (Greek for *word*). Theology is, therefore, "talk about God = God's activity, presence, relationship with people and the world."
>
> "The term 'theology' is widely used to refer to the body of Christian beliefs, and the discipline of study which centers upon them. Theology is a discipline of convictions, an attempt to survey and correlate the matrix of Christian beliefs."[23]

"Nothing can substitute for the personal experience of God. Nevertheless, theology can help believers to describe, explain, interpret and account for their faith. They know *that* they believe in the God revealed in Jesus Christ. Theology makes it easier or even possible to say just *what* it is they believe. With this help they can state their faith to themselves and others."[24]

"Theology may at times be free to explore ideas more abstractly – within the context of eternity – but spirituality is always necessarily tied to the particular."[25]

"Theology is done by the religious community for the community's own maintenance and development, and bases its investigations and developments upon intrasystematic commitments bound up for their justification within the life of the community."[26]

It was stressed above that there is no one definition of either spirituality or Christian spirituality; the same is true for theology. How the relationship between Christian spirituality and theology is understood depends on how they are each defined. For example, in some people's minds theology (understood as the body of Christian beliefs) is the *theory* of Christian life, while Christian spirituality is the *practice* (living these beliefs out, for example, through rites and rituals). But if Christian spirituality is subject to theology, as suggested by the above theory–practice relationship, then theology becomes the point of reference for all aspects of Christian spirituality. From this perspective Christian spirituality disappears as an independent field of study with its own critical questions and methods.

This understanding of the relationship between theology and spirituality is problematic if it is accepted that the Holy Spirit is always accomplishing new things in people's lives and in the world. It is not desirable to reduce Christian spirituality to what is known already in theology, since many areas of research that have greatly increased the understanding of Christian spirituality do not take theological norms as their point of departure. For example, women's studies and environmental studies, which are now taught at many universities, contribute greatly to the understanding of Christian spirituality, and therefore push the boundaries of theological thinking. If theology is an attempt to help understand better the lived experience of Jesus Christ in a systematic way, Christian communities ought to be open to new forms of self-understanding, new language, new symbols and images. All these are born from developments in human thought and experience in their entirety.

Furthermore, there is a body of Christian beliefs only because some people first experienced the life of Jesus and the active presence of God in the world. From those experiences, the Christian community wrote the scriptures and formulated a basic set of beliefs after much careful reflection. So theology is much more than a list of beliefs, it is also a critical analysis of those beliefs and how, for example, they apply to the current world, which is very different from the world of Jesus. Theology involves interpretation, that is, consideration of how it is relevant to current contexts. It also involves discernment about how God is active in a wide range of contexts today. As a result, there are many different theologies: Baptist theologies, Anglican theologies, Lutheran theologies, Orthodox theologies, Roman Catholic theologies, Quaker theologies, and many more. Each Christian tradition may highlight particular aspects of theological insight, resulting in very different spiritualities. There is no one single, privileged body of theological knowledge that reflects Christian spirituality in its entirety. Neither is there one singular Christian spirituality within the various theological traditions mentioned above. For example, there is no single Roman Catholic spirituality, or Baptist spirituality, but within these traditions there are various ways Christian Spirit is expressed and lived. Similarly, there is not one Jewish or one Muslim view of the God–human relationship, but multiple views.

For the above reasons, it may be unfair to use one theological framework to analyze a particular Christian spirituality if the two don't initially have a common point of reference. Just as there are many different Christian spiritualities, even within the various theological traditions, so there are many different theologies. Each speaks normatively from within a specific understanding of a particular tradition. No one theological system can be used to determine once and for all what is normative for Christian belief. What is more, theologies evolve and change.

It is clear that Christian spirituality need not always appeal to theology, at least not exclusively, as the standard for every question being considered. Christian spirituality has carved out its own turf as an area of study because of the following strengths:

1. Its commitment to reinterpreting its storied past, brought to us frequently, and not always accurately, through theological lenses.
2. Its openness to take seriously the various traditions, each with its own contribution, that have emerged from this storied past.
3. Its commitment to a critical analysis of its contexts, histories, and practices as they influence and construct Christian spiritualities.

4. Its readiness to grapple with the often enigmatic and sometimes contradictory perspectives on Christian life reflected in the Christian scriptures.
5. Its acknowledgment of the self-implicating nature of Christian spirituality.
6. Its commitment to an interdisciplinary approach as a significant method in research.

Let us speak more precisely about the relationship between Christian spirituality and theology in methods for the study of Christian spirituality. The theological approaches used to study Christian spirituality will help make the relationship between Christian spirituality and theology clearer.

Methods in the study of Christian spirituality

There are a number of ways to study Christian spirituality. What follows is a brief description of four of these:

1. theological;
2. historical;
3. anthropological; and
4. hermeneutical.

Theological method

As we have just seen above, Christian spirituality and theology are separate, but related, areas of reflection. There are at least two main ways theology can be used in research in Christian spirituality: Doctrinal Approach; and Interdisciplinary Approach.

Doctrinal approach

Theology, as a Christian academic discipline, aims *to systematize* what is known about humanity's relationship with God and God's relationship to all aspects of the world. Theology is also an attempt *to reflect critically* on how the Christian God is in relationship to the world (for example, persons, society, and the natural world) and on how all these parts are in relationship to each other. In a general way, theology's task is to analyze critically what can be objectively believed about God and God's presence in the world. Starting from the revelations about God as reflected in the life, death, and resurrection of Jesus, the Christian scriptures, and the developed traditions (each from within their own parameters), theology describes a coherent system of belief and practices for Christian life.

Those who identify theology essentially as theological *doctrines*, that is, a stable body of beliefs also known as *doctrinal theology*, see theology as the theory of Christian life, and spirituality as the application of these doctrines to the practice of Christian life. The first step in this use of theology as a research method is to determine which categories or doctrines of theology, that is, the known or positive data, are to be used for the study. From there, one would examine how a particular experience fits or doesn't fit this theology.

Because doctrinal theology can be used to dismiss easily certain experiences or findings using a doctrinal theological framework for study in Christian spirituality, this method needs to be used with some care. Divine Spirit is not always predictable within what is known already. Furthermore, it was affirmed above that God is actively present in all areas of human life, not only those that are described as being spiritual or religious in nature. As a research method in Christian spirituality, doctrinal theology can help clarify and evaluate what is experienced, but not necessarily act as the final arbitrator of the value of all experience, or of how God's Spirit is alive in certain experiences. Careful discernment, and not the mere application of abstract categories, is needed to determine the subtle ways God is present in human lives.

For example, "liberation" is a fundamental Christian theological category. God wants human beings to be free. But how is liberation as a *lived* Christian category understood? Is it personal liberation? Political liberation? When Moses liberates his people by crossing the Red Sea with them, and when Jesus heals the blind and the sick, God's liberating presence in the world is demonstrated. But these two scriptural stories of liberation offer differing perspectives. One, at least on the surface, is political; the other is physical. While the theological term *liberation* can help describe the truth that God desires to set people free, it does not speak directly to the lives of individuals and communities today. How does God want people to be free today? And freedom from what or whom? How is it possible to discern the ways God's Spirit is active today? Doctrinal theology, by examining the history of Christian life, has affirmed that God desires human freedom but it cannot speak directly to current realities without some form of interpretation of this constant truth. How God's desire is unfolding in current realities is a question of Christian spirituality, that is, as it explores how people are experiencing transformative, liberating grace today.

Thus, Christian spirituality makes a global attempt to understand experience from *within* its boundaries of reflection (theological ones, for instance) as well as *outside* of them. Christian spirituality, as a separate field of study from doctrinal theology, does not seek to deduce from what is known already about God what Christian living must be, or to describe its theological flavor. Rather, Christian spirituality aims to understand spirituality as it transforms the human subject in Christ and the Holy Spirit in the concrete and often messy situations of life. Christian spirituality aims to understand the phenomena, as well as their effects, through which God's self-revealing love takes hold in the myriad circumstances of human life. To put it another way, Christian spirituality is about the nature of a network of relationships: how they are concretely lived, bring about human growth, and transform people in the Spirit of God.

Viewed from this perspective, doctrinal theology needs to become a research partner or one point of reference – but not the only one – for critical reflection on Christian spirituality. Christian theological categories such as grace, conversion, and repentance can be used to assist in the critical reflection on human experience, but a wider range of perspectives is needed to complete the analysis. For example, from the perspective of psychology, the concept of pre-adolescent consciousness in relationship to adult consciousness may offer insight into the appropriate modes of prayer for each phase of life. How would a seven-year-old pray to God (taking into consideration the psychological, physical, social, and other preoccupations of this time of life) compared with an adult who is married, has family and job responsibilities, or has lived through other key transformative experiences (such as losing a partner to cancer)? From the perspective of doctrinal theology one might ask what theory or model of grace best explains the prayer of the pre-adolescent versus the prayer of the adult. While spirituality inquires about, for example, psychological (age-appropriate language, symbols, and images) and cultural influences, doctrinal theology inquires about how one explains the mystery of God's presence in people's lives from the perspective of known theological concepts.

Interdisciplinary approach

Those who use an interdisciplinary approach as the main framework for reflecting on questions of Christian spirituality see theology as a critical reflection on faith. From this perspective theology, as a research *partner* among possible other research partners, is appreciated as one source for critical reflection on lived human experience, but it does not see itself as the final arbitrator for all the data allowed into the reflection nor for the conclusions drawn from the critical analysis of it. As such theology helps to make explicit that which, to date, has remained implicit in Christian experience or has been excluded in the past.

In this approach, theology is seen not as the firm commitment to a set of beliefs, but rather a commitment to remain open to the growth of knowledge concerning humanity's relationship with God and God's presence in the world. Theology, from this perspective, ultimately involves becoming a *theological person*, that is, one who actively pursues the quest to discover God's surprising and transformative presence in all the dimensions of life.[27]

As Philip Sheldrake, a leading researcher in Christian spirituality, emphasizes, "the contemporary discipline of spirituality depends on some kind of distinction from doctrine, but this is not the same as a distinction from *theology*."[28] The advantage to this approach to theology is that it allows the researcher in Christian spirituality to include, for example, social, cultural, scientific, psychological, political, and historical realities in the reflection that have not yet been included in studies in traditional doctrinal theology per se. Topics as diverse as ecology, music, and architecture will find their place alongside theological contributions in this approach to theology and Christian spirituality.

Theology, in this approach, is used as a critical tool to help understand all these dimensions of human life but if God's abiding presence is not easily recognized in them due to the lack of theological precisions to date, the insights from these experiences are not immediately eliminated from the reflection. In this approach to theology, in the words of Philip Endean, "Theology holds us open to a mystery about which we exclaim and ask questions."[29] From this perspective Christian spirituality and theology are in a dialectical relationship: each is able to contribute to the other. Christian spirituality, ever attentive to the dynamics of human experience in context, may act as an ongoing source of renewal to theology and its doctrinal traditions by contributing new insights to existent theological frameworks. Further to this, Christian spirituality can act as a synthesizing field of study for theology. Philip Sheldrake puts it this way:

> [Christian] spirituality is a synthetic discipline as far as theology is concerned. It holds the varied elements together and prevents the theological enterprise from dispersing into a collection of semi-autonomous disciplines, biblical, historical, systematic, or practical. ... [it] is the holistic heart of the broad field of theology that gives it its shape and meaning.[30]

From this perspective theology, using its current categories and understandings of Christian life, can help clarify and illuminate the findings from

Christian spirituality, that is, the ongoing experience of Christian living in all its dimensions. And Christian spirituality can assist in the renewal and expansion of the understanding of current theological concepts.

Along with theology, the Christian scriptures relate the earliest Christian experiences, provide the initial symbol system upon which Christianity is built, and relate the foundational story of Jesus, into which Christians weave their lives. For this reason the Christian scriptures are the privileged text when it comes to discerning authentic Christian spiritualities as they are lived today. There are also many histories of how Christians have embodied Jesus's story down through the ages. Both the scriptures and the histories of Christian life are integral to studies in both Christian spirituality and theology. Through these disciplines, along with those of the human sciences, today's expressions of Christian spirituality can be evaluated in the context of the key events recorded in scripture, as well as the unfolding history of Christianity.

Historical method

This approach to Christian spirituality primarily uses the stories of how Christian life has been lived down through the ages. These stories are recorded in histories, biographies, letters, sermons, and the like. This method studies Christian spirituality based on the traces left behind that witness to the way people have lived God's presence in the world. The historical method works to establish, for example, the accuracy of documents, the completeness of historical texts, and the factors that may have influenced a particular spiritual figure. From these resources Christian spirituality can be described as it was lived in various eras and places.

For example, the histories of all the Roman Catholic religious orders that were launched at the beginning of the nineteenth century in France, following the French Revolution (1789–1799), could be studied as a research project. During this era many men and women gathered groups of followers to respond to very specific needs in the Christian communities, such as ministering to those in prison, the sick, or the poor. The expansion of these religious orders could be studied in the context of the expansion of the colonial powers (such as England, Spain, and France) into the Americas, Africa, India, and beyond. Many nuns and priests traveled to the New World on trade ships to found new missions. Christian spirituality could be studied in these new settings in relationship to its confrontation with the spirituality of the indigenous peoples of each continent. The expansion of the religious orders was also influenced by the decision of the French government to expel many of them (since the Roman Catholic Church in France was generally viewed as part of the aristocracy, which the Revolution sought to dismantle). Members of these orders had to find new countries in which to live.

Reflecting on all these events may assist in uncovering some insights about how God's Spirit was active during these times. Examining the past may provide some clarity around living Christian spirituality today. It is helpful to know what has happened in the past, and why it happened, so that the activity of God's Spirit may become more apparent in the world today. However, it is important to note that the historical method does not simply involve finding out what happened in the past. There are more complex issues to be considered in using this method for research in Christian spirituality. These are discussed in greater detail in Chapter 5, Questions of History.

Anthropological method

This method sees spirituality as an intrinsic part of the human person. The anthropological approach stresses that spirituality does not start from Christian theological categories, or even from history, but rather from the capacity for spirituality in every individual. This capacity of the individual person was described in the humanist understanding of spirituality above. In this sense, research in spirituality does not first attempt to describe specific Christian experiences within the life of persons, but more basically attempts to describe spirituality generally within the experience of being human.

This approach opens up the questions of spirituality, including Christian spirituality, to cross-cultural and inter-religious contexts. It does not exclude any experiences because they do not appear to be Christian. The anthropological method recognizes Christian spirituality as one expression of spirituality. It considers points of reference such as the history of the tradition, biblical reflection, and theology, but does not use these points as the final arbitrator of the truthfulness or authenticity of a particular experience.

The anthropological method opens up the possibility of the discovery of new ways that God's Spirit is alive in the world outside the known categories of Christian faith life and conventional religious communities. It actively engages other disciplines, such as sociology, psychology, and inter-religious dialogue, to investigate spiritual phenomena. The anthropological method accepts that insights may be gained for Christian spirituality from other religious traditions. Discussion of Christian anthropology and the issues at stake in pursuing questions of spirituality from a Christian anthropological framework are pursued in more detail in Chapter 4, Questions of Anthropology.

Hermeneutical method

The word *hermeneutics* comes from Greek mythology. Hermes, the son of the gods Zeus and Maia, was responsible for bearing messages between the gods and humans. Hermeneutical theory refers to techniques used to tease out the messages and meanings that are not immediately obvious in all sorts of human activity. Hermeneutics, or interpretation, can be applied to texts, human actions, events, or artistic productions – all aspects of human life. Human activity does not speak for itself; it needs to be *interpreted*. If how God is present in human life today is to be discovered, or if there is a desire to uncover fresh insights into how God was present in the past, there needs to be an openness to interpreting life from all angles. An example of how hermeneutical theory operates will be applied to the reading and interpretation of texts in Chapter 6, Questions of Text. In this section the importance of hermeneutics for the enterprise of Christian spirituality overall is emphasized.

Hermeneutics involves not only a multidisciplinary approach, but also an interdisciplinary one. While theology, philosophy, psychology, sociology, anthropology, and so on may all be used to study the phenomenon of human life (a multidisciplinary approach), these disciplines are also brought into dialogue with each other (an interdisciplinary approach). Human experience, as experience, is the common subject of all these disciplines – it is not a unique object of the study of spirituality or Christian spirituality. But each discipline asks its own questions – including the discipline of spirituality. A full account of human experience can be gained only when input from all the relevant disciplines is combined.[31] Coordinating and interpreting the information allows the researcher to accurately name the nature of the experience in question – in Christian spirituality examples include prayer, conversion, growth in the Holy Spirit, and the ways God is present in the world generally.

Through the interdisciplinary approach that hermeneutics offers, it is recognized that human consciousness is singular, and that the human capacity for knowledge is all one. The human mind is not separated into compartments labeled "psychology section" or "spirituality section" or "history section." *Human beings* dissect reality into these various spheres of knowing and being in the world, but reality does not exist that way. The hermeneutical approach recognizes this and opens up the possibility of interpreting the various data and organizing them into a coherent whole while always allowing for further interpretation and meaning to be explored.

When reality is viewed as essentially a singular phenomenon that is expressed in various ways, an openness to the Spirit of God active in all dimensions of human life is nurtured. Some people tend to limit God's presence to those activities that are already seen as theological or religious or spiritual in nature, by appealing to the categories and the experiences already labeled as such. But God cannot be contained within the categories of human knowledge or within a precise set of activities that human beings have determined to be the holy places of Divine activity. God is not present only in churches or only in those activities deemed to be holy. Simply put God cannot be contained within the patterns of God's activity in the world determined by the different faith communities. This is where hermeneutics enters as a method for the study of Christian spirituality.

Hermeneutics gets around the prejudice of where, when, and how God is present in the world by being open to investigating all phenomena within their own parameters of meaning. It thus allows the researcher to attend to issues of the world, in all their complexity, without pre-judging them. For example, somebody may inquire as to how God is present in the secular workplace.[32] The first response may be, "God cannot be present in that big, faceless company!" But if the individual were to take the time to explore a profile of the company – including business practices, employee attitudes, and sponsored activities outside work time – he or she may discover a new way of naming God's presence in the secular world. The disciplines of theology, psychology, sociology, business ethics, and recreation theory may all assist in naming this reality and revealing how God is present in a meaningful way in this sphere of human life.

Management and work are significant activities for most of the world's population.[33] These two activities consume a good portion of the time of a lot of people and are integral to the world's development. When these are viewed through the lens of Christian spirituality, the researcher may be awakened to new ways of recognizing God's loving presence in the world. God establishes relationships with human beings in the most unexpected places and unpredictable times – including human work.

One of the primary aims of studies in Christian spirituality is to reveal and understand God's transformative presence in the world today. To find solutions to today's problems Christian communities cannot revert uncritically to the way things were done in the past, for example, by seeing what was done in the first and second centuries C.E. Clearly, the world was a different reality at that time. For example, the widespread Christian practice of doing penance for one's sins was expressed differently in the earliest years of Christianity than it is today. If today's Christians simply imported past solutions to attend to current issues of penance, they would find themselves sitting in public squares wearing sparse clothing and begging for food for extended periods of time. While penance is still very much a part of many Christian traditions today, the approach has changed. The insight of the need for penance, while valid, needs to be interpreted to be meaningful for today's world. The overall approach of hermeneutics allows this investigation to be open to new ways of living Christian life. Spirituality, including Christian spirituality, as a research area of study "is a comprehensive interpretive scheme, a complex social, cultural, symbolic and linguistic reality,"[34] and hermeneutics allows the researcher to attend to the dynamic tensions inherent in the interplay of these characteristics.

The hermeneutical method involves three essential steps.[35]

1. A *description* of the phenomena under investigation is provided. For example, the musical scores of the German mystic Hildegard of Bingen (1098–1179) would be described. What style of music was it? Was the music similar to other music that existed at the time? At what age did she write it? What was the political and historical setting at the time? How did other people respond to it as reflected in other texts?

2. The information is subject to *critical analysis* that will help explain the phenomenon with respect to other areas of knowledge. This will involve, inevitably, some theological analysis but may include other disciplines such as history, sociology, psychology, or literary studies. For example, from the perspective of theology, does it evoke a particular image of God? Is the historical setting of Hildegard reflected in the music? Are the images used common to the culture at the time or was Hildegard innovative? Did Hildegard write commentaries on her music, giving us insight into the meaning she gave it?

3. The phenomenon is *interpreted* for Christian life today. The task is not only to understand the phenomenon in itself and critically analyze it, but also to understand it in the context of the lived reality today. The Christian community's increased *self-understanding* (with all of the relationships in the world that this phrase implies) is ultimately the end product of interpreting the meaning of the music of Hildegard of Bingen. Thus, what happened in the twelfth century becomes meaningful for those living in the twenty-first century. The question is asked: What meaning is found in the text in relationship to the issues of today's world?

Hermeneutical methodology is the process whereby *knowledge develops* as the inquirer engages in an ongoing process of *mutuality in understanding* – the object being studied is better understood but there is also an increase in the self-understanding of the life of the Christian community. Through this process the Christian community becomes more alert to what is happening today – in the world, in society, in our relationship with God – than to what happened in the past.

Although any of the methods mentioned above may be used to study Christian spirituality, the hermeneutical method best characterizes research into human experience and therefore is the preferred overall method when not addressing specific historical or theological issues.

Let us now briefly summarize this section on approaches or methods to the study of Christian spirituality. Christian spirituality is obviously rooted in Christian tradition, but it does not always remain within the boundaries Christian tradition has constructed for itself to date. Christian spirituality, therefore, is in a position to explore current developments in Christian faith life that may not easily be accepted within current theological norms. As a field of research, it allows a critique of human experience outside a dogmatic framework of theology, and thus has the potential to reshape a strictly theological agenda. Historical and anthropological approaches to Christian spirituality are useful, but limited, since they contain the inquiry to a particular set of questions. Hermeneutical methodology allows Christian spirituality to be interrogated from within the current context of Christian faith life in all of its dimensions, all the while including the insights from past understandings. Hermeneutical methodology, therefore, contains the other three approaches, that is, the theological, historical, and anthropological. Hermeneutical methodology is examined further in relationship to Christian spirituality in Chapter 6, Questions of Text.

Spirituality and religion

It has become fashionable today to distinguish between spirituality and religion. In everyday conversations expressions like "I'm spiritual, but not religious" are heard, or "I believe in God, but I don't need to go to church – I feel God's presence in nature more than in church." For many people today, the spiritual and the religious appear to mean different things. Even if it is agreed that they are different, the obvious questions surface, "How are they different?" and "How are they related?" The relationship between spirituality and religion is as difficult to determine as is the relationship between spirituality and theology sketched above. Let's look briefly at each of these terms and their relationship: religion and spirituality.

Generally speaking, religions tend to be identified with authoritative spiritual traditions and structures that include, for example, clear beliefs, practices, symbols, and texts. All of these aspects are identified with the framework that contains the boundaries of the particular religious tradition. For example, Christianity, Judaism, and Islam are clearly defined religions, and each has its own set of institutional structures, beliefs, and practices. Each has authoritative texts: the scriptures, composed of the Old and New Testaments, for Christians; the Hebrew scriptures for Jews; the Koran for Muslims; and the Vedas for Hindus. These texts go beyond the life of the individual and point to larger faith communities, within which each person is embedded. These faith communities are clearly identified by their common understanding of core beliefs, their acceptance of particular organizational and authoritarian structures, their development of a particular way of viewing the world, and the boundaries that define who belongs within the fold.

For example, if someone were to blatantly deny that Jesus is the Son of God, or to declare that the resurrection of Jesus is a fabrication, that person would need to seriously reconsider his or her claim of membership in the Christian religion. These two beliefs are the very foundation of Christianity: rejecting them implies a rejection of Christianity itself.

Religions tend to develop normative ways of living and being in the world that determine clear directions in life. For example, although they may be interpreted in a range of ways, the Ten Commandments (from the story of Moses on Mount Sinai in Exodus 34) and the Beatitudes (the blessings and teachings of Jesus in Matthew 5) act as a universal code of conduct for Christians. These two scripture passages – in relationship to many others – are frequently used to guide Christian living.

While religions tend to give clear directions in life, many contemporary spiritualities do not. Spirituality is considered a fluid thing, something that relates directly to the concrete circumstances of everyday life in all its complexities. The commitment to diversity and the unexpected is key to spirituality, because spirituality is embodied in the activities of everyday life that have these same characteristics. In the flux and flow of life the living God is encountered. David Tacey describes this point in *The Spirituality Revolution: The Emergence of Contemporary Spirituality* (2004). He states:

> It is enough for spirituality to realize that there is mystery and presence in the ordinary world. The world itself is revelatory of God's presence, so the intense rituals, liturgies and chants become less important in developing and maintaining a compelling sense of the sacred. Reality does not have to be broken by ritual to reveal the sacred, and time does not have to be suspended to admit the eternal. . . . God reveals itself to us not only in scripture, creation, and tradition (the three official sources of revelation), but also in the minor revelations of everyday life.[36]

Spirituality, in practice, does not tend to look for indicators of official religiosity. Rather, it seeks an expression of the intuitive/embodied/felt presence of God in one's life. In this way Christian spiritualities, and their expression in lived experience, are, to a large degree, bound together through *praxis* (practice), and not exclusively through beliefs dictated by religious systems. At the basis of the interplay between individual Christian practice and beliefs shaped by religious systems is Christian community.

Outside a community that supports *and* challenges its members spirituality can become empty. Without some form of community there is the risk of an unhealthy preoccupation with one's own private world. Privatized spiritualities based exclusively on an appeal to personal experience may feed a self-serving style of life that, rather than nourishing a connection to others, may gradually erode the very relationships initially desired. For this reason, a connection (however fluid) between individuals and a community of practitioners is not only recommended, but necessary. Religion and spirituality are not in competition with each other. They reflect different dimensions of the fundamental human quest for self-transcendence, belonging, and meaning in life. While the core values of spiritualities and their religious frameworks are not always the same, they do overlap, and it is very hard to separate them in any definitive way.

Christianity and Christian spirituality

When it comes to Christian spirituality, the core beliefs, practices, and texts of Christianity give some guidance and direction. It is beyond the scope of this reflection to determine what these core beliefs, practices, and texts are, since there are many traditions within Christianity.[37] What is underlined here is the close relationship between Christianity and Christian spirituality – even while acknowledging the vast array of ways Christian spirituality can be lived and practiced. Some individuals may do this tied very closely to the institutional structures (the religion per se) of Christianity, while others are less connected to the various institutions that give expression to the core religious framework.

What is important is the recognition that Christian spirituality is, above all, something lived by flesh and blood people amidst the real circumstances of life. Christian spirituality is not merely the belief in abstract principles, or the faithful following of institutional dictates, it is the personal experience of life lived with God in all its dimensions. Central to Christian spirituality is the modeling of one's own life after the life, death, and resurrection of Jesus under the power and guidance of the Holy Spirit. To put it another way, Christian spirituality is situated within the experience of faith. Christian lives are informed, shaped, and nurtured by what the community as a whole has discerned to be the authentic touchstones (core beliefs such as the resurrection of Jesus). With these touchstones firmly in place, there is room for a wide variety of ways of living these truths in everyday life. In the end, therefore, although Christian spirituality is closely identified with Christianity (the religion as reflected in its institutional authority, structures, and norms), the two are not necessarily identified as one and the same in all their particular expressions.

Christian spirituality and experience

"We had the experience but missed the meaning."[38]

"It may be that in every formulation of belief, there is something which is of permanent value and something which is merely accidental arising from the circumstances under which belief is formulated."[39]

As mentioned earlier, the key way to describe the object of study of Christian spirituality is "experience *as* experience." But what does this phrase mean? Wouldn't it be clearer to say that Christian spirituality studies "experience" in itself? No – there is no such thing as experience per se, any more than there is a such thing as history or religion. All these words, and many like them, are *constructs*. Human beings give them meaning (content) with reference to particular contexts (such as the social, political, and ecclesial) and particular operations of the mind (such as the emotional, imaginative, and thinking). From these sources, and others, content (or shape) is given to human experience so we can study it *as experience*. What we are talking about here is the nature of experience in itself. Let's examine this idea further.

The nature of experience

The word *experience* is used to cover a wide range of cognitive (thinking) and emotional (feeling) operations of human life, without being too precise. At the same time, there is something immediate about experience that leads people to rely on it for claims to certainty and truth. Let's say somebody has worked for five years in an office that distributes food and clothing to the poor. He or she may say, "My experience has taught me what it is like to be without food and clothing." Here the individual appeals to his or her experience – working in an office – to make authoritative claims about knowing what it is like to do without food and clothes. Is this individual to be believed? In everyday conversation, the individual would not likely be challenged to justify such a claim. But, when thought about, perhaps the individual should be challenged – especially if the person, for example, is using this statement to justify being hired, at a higher salary, by another company that does similar work.

It is not uncommon for people to appeal to experience to justify beliefs, actions, and decisions. The appeal to *my experience* is often assumed to be self-authenticating and needs no further verification. When someone appeals to their experience, others tend to accept the information provided on this account. But experience is always ambiguous and subjective. Because it is one person's perception, it needs further critical reflection to endow it with truthfulness and authenticity.

To give someone's experience authenticity and meaning, there is a need to ask a series of questions, like: "*What* did you experience?" "What did it *mean* for you?" "What, specifically, did you *learn* from this experience?" "What *insights* do you have about *yourself* as a result of this experience?" In this way, the person can relate meaningful information or give content to the experience. As Gerald O'Collins, a leading Roman Catholic theologian says, "There is no such thing as purely 'objective,' neutral and non-interpreted experience."[40]

Let's look at another example. If someone says, "I worked in Latin America for 10 years. I've had the experience of living in a society that is riddled daily by conflict. To solve our problem here, we need to follow this (x, y, and z) line of action." These statements may be true, but whether the person's experience necessarily gives him or her the authority to speak on these issues and propose a plan must be decided based on further critical inquiry of the knowledge actually gained from the experience in Latin America.

The following activities, and ones like them, give the necessary content to experience to make it credible and meaningful:

- thoughtful analysis;
- probing questions;
- interpretation;
- conscious reflection on personal biases, emotions, and feelings; and
- dialogue with others combined with openness to critical feedback.

These activities can help people become aware of what was experienced, as well as its meaning. Sometimes the meaning of what happened to people is difficult to identify or articulate. To become mindful or consciously aware of one's experience requires work. Without critical inquiry, experience remains empty. Much of what people experience in life never enters their conscious awareness because they don't actively engage in thoughtful reflection to give events in their lives authentic content.

Furthermore, experience can change, making it even more important for people to critically analyze and reflect on life events. What does it mean to say experience can change? Since experience is essentially a construction based on thoughtful analysis, there may be new insights concerning past events after some time has elapsed. Profound moments and experiences continue to be productive even after they have occurred. For example, there may be new insights into the role an important person played in one's life long after the relationship has ceased. Critical reflection shifts the experience from the past to the present, and forces an individual to rethink how that experience is named and what it means for today. Or perhaps events in the present call individuals to interpret past events differently.

For example, let's say, as a child, an individual hated the way his mother always overcooked the peas, turning them to mush. The overcooked peas became a symbol of how poor a cook his mother was. Later, as an adult, the man pondered the meaning of past events in his life. He became consciously aware that his mother had seven children to raise, in addition to cooking, cleaning, doing laundry, and attending to the needs of her husband. With all these demands on her time he realized she could not be watching the peas so they would be cooked just right. The individual became aware that cooking was just one of the many tasks which the mother lovingly undertook. The mushy peas, then, became a symbol of loving concern rather than careless cooking. As we can see, this experience of childhood changed once it was conceptualized in the overall picture of adulthood. This is an example of how people need to constantly reflect on the experiences of the past, both personally and collectively, to tease out of them the meaning they have today.

Experience as experience

Experience *as* experience acknowledges that experience is not self-transparent; it doesn't speak for itself. Since the content of lived experience is the object of inquiry in spirituality, including Christian spirituality, we need to find a way to get at this lived experience to give it shape. To have had the experience, people need to be able to describe the events in language, critically reflect on them, interpret them (the hermeneutical task of Christian spirituality spoken of above), and probe them for new meaning. In so doing people may need to let go of habitual ways of interpreting events and be open to new ways that the Spirit of God is active in the world.

Being open means that sometimes events and experiences need to be allowed to show themselves (using the critical reflection on experience discussed above), rather than imposing prematurely, or too solidly, the usual ways of seeing and understanding them. This approach is in contrast to dogmatism. The dogmatic approach leads to seeing or experiencing something only in the desired way – the way *one would expect* something to be seen or experienced. Being open to other possibilities allows people to probe their experience – the object of the study of Christian spirituality – within the points of reference established for Christians. But being open to other possibilities also allows the active involvement of God in the world to shine forth in new ways. This approach involves the active participation of human intuition and imagination. People need to trust their hunches – not in a blind way, but by testing them in conversations with others and by thoughtful reflection. Points of reference for interpretation of experience may include the theological, historical, scriptural, and ecclesial – but they may also include a number of other realities, such as gender, age, social context, education, past significant events, and future hopes.

Reflection or meditation on experience as experience leads to an increase in self-knowledge: people come to know themselves better, and perhaps let go of cherished ideas or comfortable self-conceptions. The result may be changes in personal beliefs, which in turn lead to spiritual development. For this reason, experience as experience takes precedence over the categories of theology or religious doctrines.

Experience as experience is, therefore, self-implicating or self-involving, as was said above for Christian spirituality. It involves the thoughtful and imaginative participation of the person in what has been meaningful in life. This process opens the way for being in relationship with oneself, the world, and God in new ways. It leads to wisdom, depth of character, and an appreciation of the relative nature of one's life in the world before God and others.

Conclusion

In this chapter we have examined a number of key terms related to the study of Christian spirituality. There has been no attempt to tie any of these terms to absolute definitions. Rather, the goal is to explore in a general way what each of them means – sometimes from a variety of perspectives. Definitions always include the perspective or bias of the individual or institution formulating them. This is not necessarily a bad thing. Bias gives meaning to the definition, making it useful for self-understanding, and for exploring these realities in settings other than one's own.

If people hold too firmly to definitions that are essentially constructs (words like *religion, spirituality, experience*, and *human spirit*), they risk missing the insights from other people – insights that have grown from a different experience of the world and of God's presence in it. Although experiences are radically different from what one may expect, they may be equally valid. As we will see throughout this book, a range of cultural, social, ecclesial, and political contexts greatly influences the way people engage reality, which in turn determines how they define and use words. An open mind is needed to explore the full range of potential in the way of life called Christian spirituality.

RECOMMENDED READING

Collins, Kenneth J., ed. (2000) "Christian Traditions," in *Exploring Christian Spirituality: An Ecumenical Reader*, Grand Rapids, MI: Baker Books, 61–226. (A section is dedicated to each of the following spiritual traditions: Carmelite, Orthodox, Lutheran, Reformed, Anglican, Methodist, and Evangelical.)

Cunningham, Lawrence S. and Keith J. Egan, eds (1996) "Christian Spirituality," in *Christian Spirituality: Themes from the Tradition*, New York: Paulist Press, 5–28. (Provides an excellent introduction to the meanings of the term *Christian spirituality* from the perspectives of various Christian traditions.)

Dreyer, Elizabeth (1995) "Christian Spirituality," In *The HarperCollins Encyclopedia of Catholicism*, ed. R. McBrien, San Francisco: HarperCollins, 1,216–1,220.

Dunne, Tad (1993) "Experience," in *The New Dictionary of Catholic Spirituality*, ed. Michael Downey, Collegeville, MN: Liturgical Press, 365–377.

Hinsen, E. Glenn, ed. (1993) *Spirituality in Ecumenical Perspective*, Louisville, KY: Westminster/John Knox Press. (From an ecumenical perspective it explores topics such as the nature of spirituality and spirituality in the dialogue of religions.)

Lane, Belden (1988) *Landscapes of the Sacred: Geography and Narrative in American Spirituality*, New York: Paulist Press.

McGinn, Bernard (2005) "The Letter and the Spirit: Spirituality as an Academic Discipline," in *Minding the Spirit: The Study of Christian Spirituality*, eds Elizabeth A. Dreyer and Mark S. Burrows, Baltimore, MD: Johns Hopkins University Press, 25–41.

McGrath, Alister E. (1999) "Theological Foundations for Spirituality: Basic Issues," in *Christian Spirituality: An Introduction*, Oxford, UK: Blackwell, 25–34.

O'Collins, Gerald (1982) "Human Experience," in *Fundamental Theology*, TipTree, Essex: Anchor Press, 32–52.

Principe, Walter (1983) "Toward Defining Spirituality," *Studies in Religion/ Sciences Réligieuses* 12, 127–141.

—— (1993) "Christian Spirituality," *The New Dictionary of Catholic Spirituality*, ed. Michael Downey [A Michael Glazier Book], Collegeville, MN: Liturgical Press, 931–938.

Thompson, William G. (1992) "Spirituality, Spiritual Development, and Holiness," in *Review for Religious*, September–October, 646–648.

Tyson, John R. (1999) *Invitation to Christian Spirituality: An Ecumenical Anthology*, New York: Oxford University Press. (An excellent collection of texts by author and theme. Well indexed for easy location of texts in a particular area of interest.)

Foundation references for studies in spirituality and Christian spirituality

Bibliographia Internationalis Spiritualitatis, Rome: Edizioni del Teresianum (1966–). (An annual collation of bibliography in the area of spirituality, over twenty-two volumes to date.)

Brown, Laurence, Bernard C. Farr, R. Joseph Hoffmann, eds (1997) *Modern Spiritualities: An Inquiry*, Oxford, UK: Prometheus Books.

Classics of Western Spirituality, New York: Paulist Press (1978–). (Over 130 volumes to date. A very important collection of original writings of significant spiritual authors in the West from the Catholic, Protestant, Eastern Orthodox, Jewish, Islamic, and American Indian traditions.)

Cousins, Ewert H. *et al.*, eds (1985–) *World Spirituality: An Encyclopedic History of the Religious Quest*, New York: Crossroad. (Over twenty-five volumes to date. Volumes 16, 17, and 18 deal specifically with the history of Christian spirituality.)

Dictionnaire de spiritualité ascétique et mystique: doctrine et histoire (1937–1995), 17 volumes, Paris: Beauchesne. (See especially the entry under *Spiritualité*, vol. 14 (1990), Columns 1,142–1,173.)

Dreyer, Elizabeth A. and Mark S. Burrows, eds (2005) *Minding the Spirit: The Study of Christian Spirituality*, Baltimore, MD: Johns Hopkins University Press.

Ferrer, Jorge N. (2002) *Revisioning Transpersonal Theory: A Participatory Vision of Human Spirituality*, New York: S.U.N.Y. Press. (Based on the principles of transpersonal psychology, this book examines a thoroughly humanistic spirituality: i.e. in a very general way, self-transcendence is viewed as experiences that extend consciousness beyond the usual boundaries of the body-ego. It is these experiences that are the objects of study in the realm of spirituality.)

Griffith, James L. and Melissa Elliott Griffith (2002) "When Spirituality Turns Destructive," in *Encountering the Sacred in Psychotherapy: How to Talk with People about Their Spiritual Lives*, New York: The Guilford Press, 215–230.

Halverson, Dean (1996) *The Compact Guide to World Religions*, Minneapolis: Bethany Fellowship. (Contains succinct overviews, for example, on Buddhism, Confucianism, Islam, Hinduism, New Age Movement, and Taoism.)

Hanson, Bradley C. (1990) *Modern Christian Spirituality: Methodological and Historical Essays* [AAR Studies in Religion 62], Atlanta, GA: Scholars Press.

Heelas, Paul and Linda Woodhead, *et al.* (2005) *The Spiritual Revolution: Why Religion is Giving Way to Spirituality*, Malden, MA: Blackwell.

Holder, Arthur (2005) *The Blackwell Companion to Christian Spirituality*, Malden, MA: Blackwell.

Ihde, Donald (1971) *Hermeneutic Phenomenology: The Philosophy of Paul Ricoeur*, Foreword by Paul Ricoeur, Evanston: Northwestern University Press.

Kavanaugh, John Francis (1990) *Following Christ in a Consumer Society: The Spirituality of Cultural Resistance*, Maryknoll, NY: Orbis Books.

Leech, Kenneth (1992) *The Eye of the Storm: Living Spirituality in the Real World*, San Francisco: Harper & Row.

Locklin, Reid B. (2005) *Spiritual but Not Religious?: An Oar Stroke Closer to the Farther Shore*, Collegeville, MN: Liturgical Press.

McIntosh, Mark A. (1998) *Mystical Theology: The Integrity of Spirituality and Theology*, Malden, MA: Blackwell.

Magill, Frank N. and Ian P. McGreal, eds (1988) *Christian Spirituality: The Essential Guide to the Most Influential Spiritual Writings of the Christian Tradition*, San Francisco: Harper & Row.

Rahner, Karl (1969) "The Unity of Spirit and Matter in the Christian Understanding of Faith," *Theological Investigations* 6, 153–77.

Schner, George P. (2003) "The Appeal to Experience," in *Essays Catholic and Critical*, eds Philip G. Ziegler and Mark Husbands, Aldershot, Hants, UK: Ashgate, 109–124.

Sheldrake, Philip, ed. (2005) *The New Westminster Dictionary of Christian Spirituality*, Louisville, KY: WJK Press.

Tacey, David (2004) *The Spirituality Revolution: The Emergence of Contemporary Spirituality*, New York: Brunner-Routledge.

Tinsely, Lucy (1953) *The French Expression for Spirituality and Devotion: A Semantic Study* [Studies in Romance Languages and Literatures 47], Washington, D.C.: Catholic University of America Press. (Presents a detailed history of the word *spirituality*.)

Toon, Peter (1990) *Spiritual Companions: An Introduction to the Christian Classics*, Grand Rapids, MI: Baker Book House.

Vitz, Paul C. (1977) *Psychology as Religion: The Cult of Self-Worship*, Grand Rapids, MI: William B. Eerdmans Publishing Company.

Waaijman, Kees (1993) "Toward a Phenomenological Definition of Spirituality," *Studies in Spirituality* 3, 5–57.

—— (1995) "A Hermeneutic of Spirituality: A Preliminary Study," *Studies in Spirituality* 5, 5–39.

—— (2002) *Spirituality: Forms, Foundations, Methods* [Studies in Spirituality Supplement 8], tr. John Vriend, Dudley, MA: Peeters.

NOTES

1 Buddhism developed from the middle of the sixth century to the early part of the fifth century B.C.E. in India. It focuses on the teachings of the Buddha (Siddhartha Gautama) who lived during this time. Buddhism is a philosophy of life and a psychology as much as it is a spirituality. Taoism, also known as Daoism, has as its focus an impersonal cosmic power that gives life to the world. It has its roots in Chinese folk religion popularized by the philosopher Laozi in the fifth century B.C.E. Confucianism dates back to the sixth century B.C.E. when Confucius (551–479) gathered a group of disciples to study ancient texts in China to glean from them wisdom for practical living. This wisdom developed into a way of life that included ritual practices, beliefs, and ways of social interaction.

2 For some analysis of what this means, see Robert C. Fuller (2001) *Spiritual but Not Religious: Understanding Unchurched America*, Oxford: Oxford University Press; Wade Clark Roof (1999) *Spiritual Marketplace: Baby Boomers and the Remaking of American Religion*, Princeton: Princeton University Press.

3 William Stringfellow (1984) *The Politics of Spirituality*, Philadelphia: The Westminster Press, 19.

4 Ernest Becker (1973) *The Denial of Death*, New York: Free Press.

5 These are adapted and summarized from Daniel Helminiak (1996) *The Human Core of Spirituality: Mind as Psyche and Spirit*, New York: S.U.N.Y. Press, 31–39. The overall appreciation here of being able to consider spirituality as a purely human phenomenon is informed by Helminiak's presentation in *The Human Core of Spirituality*.

6 Sandra Schneiders (2005) "Christian Spirituality: Definition, Methods and Types," in *The New Westminster Dictionary of Christian Spirituality*, Philip Sheldrake, ed., Louisville, KY: WJK Press, 1.

7 These activities are a paraphrase of Bernard Lonergan's (1904–1984) fundamental guide to human living. Lonergan names these four innate *norming* processes "transcendental precepts." Briefly expressed, they are: Be attentive (to data), Be intelligent (with ideas), Be reasonable (with facts), and Be responsible (with values). These precepts are not meant to be understood as rules; rather, they point to the internal operating norms by which anyone transcends himself or herself to live in reality. As such, they are the criteria of authenticity. Lonergan uses the term *authenticity* to refer to the quality in persons who follow these norms. Lonergan was a Canadian Roman Catholic priest, theologian, philosopher, economist, and ethicist. For a thorough discussion of his transcendental precepts, see Bernard Lonergan (1997) *Insight: A Study of Human Understanding*. Volume 3 of the Collected Works of Bernard Lonergan. Toronto: University of Toronto Press.

8 See Helminiak, *The Human Core of Spirituality*, 57–58.

9 Human spirit, as identified with human consciousness, is a fundamental cornerstone of the work of Bernard Lonergan.

10 Helminiak (1996) *The Human Core of Spirituality*, 3–39.

11 This is especially important because human desires are frequently shaped by public media, for example, the television industry. "The commodification of

our desires, our values, and ultimately our selves, is, in its most blatant instance, underwritten by our television industry. . . . Estimates of the average American watching-time run from 26 hours a week to the equivalent of 13 straight continuous years of our average life span. Since up to 27 percent of prime time can be given to advertisement, we could possibly spend, on an average, the equivalent of three solid years of our lives watching solely commercials." John Francis Kavanaugh (1990) *Following Christ in a Consumer Society: The Spirituality of Cultural Resistance*, Maryknoll, NY: Orbis Books, 24–25.

12 Kavanaugh, *Following Christ in a Consumer Society*, 23.
13 It is beyond the scope of this book to deal with the issues of spirituality as a potentially destructive force within different religious traditions: For example, refusing insulin to a diabetic and relying on the accuracy of Mark 11:24 ("I tell you therefore: everything you ask and pray for, believe that you have it already, and it will be yours"). For a brief critique of the interaction of spirituality and religion with respect to these kinds of issues, see James L. Griffith and Melissa Elliott Griffith (2002) "When Spirituality Turns Destructive," in *Encountering the Sacred in Psychotherapy: How to Talk with People about Their Spiritual Lives*, New York: The Guilford Press, 215–230.
14 The history of the term *spirituality* in this section is summarized mainly from the following: Bernard McGinn (1993) "The Letter and the Spirit: Spirituality as an Academic Discipline," in *Minding the Spirit*, Elizabeth A. Dreyer and Mark S. Burrows, eds, Baltimore, MD: Johns Hopkins University Press, 25–41 and Walter Principe (1983) "Toward Defining Spirituality," *Studies in Religion/Sciences Réligieuses* 12, 127–141.
15 Jerome's full name in Latin is Eusebius Hieronymus.
16 This contrast was also fed by a rediscovery of the writings of the mystic Pseudo-Dionysius, a sixth-century writer who supported the Greek opposition between spirit and matter. The thought of Pseudo-Dionysius, believed to be the disciple of Paul mentioned in Acts 17:34, was incorporated into the work of many important writers at this time.
17 These are summarized from Philip Sheldrake *Spirituality and History*, (1992) New York: Crossroad, 41–44.
18 Stringfellow, *The Politics of Spirituality*, 22.
19 Philip Sheldrake (1987) *Images of Heliners: Explorations in Contemporary Spirituality*, London: Darton, Longman and Todd Ltd, 2.
20 Sandra M. Schneiders (2005) "The Study of Christian Spirituality: Contours and Dynamics of a Discipline," in *Minding the Spirit: The Study of Christian Spirituality*, E. Dreyer and M. Burrows, eds, Baltimore, MD: Johns Hopkins University Press, 5–6.
21 Elizabeth Dreyer (1995) *The HarperCollins Encyclopedia of Catholicism*, R. McBrien, ed., San Francisco: HarperCollins, 1,216.
22 Sandra M. Schneider (2005) "A Hermeneutical Approach to the Study of Christian Spirituality," in *Minding the Spirit*, 54.
23 Alister McGrath (1999) *Christian Spirituality: An Introduction*, Oxford: Blackwell, 25.

24 Gerald O'Collins (1982) *Fundamental Theology*, TipTree, Essex: Anchor Press, 10–11.

25 Belden Lane (1988) *Landscapes of the Sacred: Geography and Narrative in American Spirituality*, New York: Paulist Press, 6.

26 George Schner (2003) *Essays Catholic and Critical*, Philip G. Ziegler and Mark Husbands, eds, Aldershot, Hants: Ashgate, 100.

27 The term "theological person" is taken from Philip Sheldrake (2006) "Spirituality and Its Critical Methodology," in *Exploring Christian Spirituality: Essays in Honor of Sandra M. Schneiders, IHM*, B. Lescher and E. Liebert, eds, New York: Paulist Press, 25.

28 Sheldrake "Spirituality and Its Critical Methodology," 25.

29 Philip Endean (2005) "Christian Spirituality and the Theology of the Human Person," in *The Blackwell Companion to Christian Spirituality*, Arthur Holder, ed., Oxford: Blackwell, 223.

30 Sheldrake, "Spirituality and Its Critical Methodology," 24–25.

31 Daniel A. Helminiak (1986) "Four Viewpoints on the Human: A Conceptual Schema for Interdisciplinary Studies: I," *The Heythrop Journal* XXVII, 422.

32 For some ideas on how we might articulate a "spirituality of work," see Elizabeth A. Dreyer (1994) "Towards a Spirituality of Work," in *Earth Crammed with Heaven: A Spirituality of Everyday Life*, New York: Paulist Press, 84–99.

33 See Johan Verstraeten (2002) "Beyond Business Ethics: Leadership, Spirituality, and the Quest for Meaning," *Logos* 5:2, 17–39.

34 This is the expression that George Schner applies to studies in religion in general. See his *Essays Catholic and Critical*, 101.

35 These are summarized from Sandra Schneiders, "A Hermeneutical Approach to the Study of Christian Spirituality," in *Minding the Spirit*, 56–57.

36 David Tacey (2004) *The Spirituality Revolution: The Emergence of Contemporary Spirituality*, New York: Brunner-Routledge, 164.

37 For a succinct summary of core Christian beliefs, see Alister McGrath (2006) "A Brief Outline of Core Christian Beliefs," in *Christianity: An Introduction*, 2nd edition, Malden, MA: Blackwell, 114–170.

38 T.S. Eliot, *Dry Salvages* cited in O'Collins, *Fundamental Theology*, 32.

39 John Macquarrie (1960) *The Scope of Demythologizing: Bultmann and his Critics*, London: SCM Press, 11.

40 Gerald O'Collins (1982) "Human Experience," in *Fundamental Theology*, TipTree, Essex: Anchor Press, 44.

2 Questions of context

"As human beings in modern and postmodern societies, we are relearning that a faith that yields an experience of centeredness and 'at home-ness' is intimately related with the experience of 'place.' And 'place' is not an abstraction."

Sharon Daloz Parks, *Developing a Public Faith*

"The world of life, of spontaneity, the world of dawn and sunset and starlight, the world of soil and sunshine, of meadow and woodland, of hickory and oak and maple and hemlock and pineland forests, of wildlife dwelling around us, of the river and its well-being – all of this some of us are discovering for the first time as the integral community in which we live. Here we experience the reality and the values that evoke in us our deepest moments of reflection, our revelatory experience of the ultimate mystery of things."

Thomas Berry, *Developing a Public Faith*

Introduction

ALL SPIRITUALITY IS PARTICULAR. It takes place in a particular context: in a particular location (including its own geography and climate), a particular historical setting (including its political, economic, and social elements), and a particular culture (including its language, symbols, myths, and values). These are the factors that influence and shape the development of spiritualities alongside the dynamics of faith. What is being referred to here is the spirituality of place. Some people may think a spirituality is best explored through studying the writings of its significant figures, prayer practices, rituals, theologies, and so on, but as we will see in this chapter, geography, climate, culture, politics, and other factors, all play a role in the study and shaping of Christian spiritualities as well.

For example, Francis of Assisi (c.1181–1226), a young Italian man, was influenced greatly by the context within which he lived.[1] His spirituality did not emerge as a result of a withdrawal from or avoidance of the social and political issues facing him; rather, it emerged as a result of his embrace of and response to these issues. This is seen in the clear choices he made in his life – choices that were based on his faith.

The son of a wealthy cloth merchant in Assisi, Francis enjoyed as a youth whatever luxuries life had to offer. However, around 1205 Francis felt himself called by God to attend to society's outcasts, particularly the lepers and poor of Assisi. He felt a great solidarity with them, began to share whatever he had, and spent a great deal of time in their company. Through the suffering of those around him, he was gradually converted to identifying himself ever more closely with the crucified Christ. One day, while kneeling before a crucifix in the dilapidated church of San Damiano, he believed he heard the voice of God instructing him to repair the church. And he set about doing so, literally. He toiled to reconstruct the church, which was in shambles. Only later would he reinterpret what he had heard as an instruction to go and build up the people of God.

But Francis's new lifestyle clashed with his family's expectations. As a cloth merchant, his father exploited the poor by underpaying them – not to mention that the working conditions in the factory were atrocious. The empathetic Francis sided with the workers. His father tried to dissuade him from solidarity with the poor and the socially outcast, even to the point of locking him up in the house. But Francis was not to be deterred.

One day, in the public square of the town, Francis gave all the money he had left in his possession back to his father, removed all his clothes as a sign of renunciation of material goods, and publicly committed his life solely to God. Francis embraced "Lady Poverty" as his intimate companion in solidarity with the poor and the sick. Many men were inspired to join Francis, which eventually led to the foundation of the Order of Friars Minor, now commonly known as the Franciscans. The men who formed this group traveled about the countryside helping those in need, preaching the gospel, and living a life of radical poverty.

This brief story of the life of Francis of Assisi shows how Francis's spirituality had social and political references, as well as spiritual ones. As a member of the emerging middle class of twelfth-century Europe, he experienced his father's preoccupation with wealth and exploitation of the poor. Francis heard a different voice in his life. Based on God's call, Francis took up his cross, renounced all semblance of luxury in his life, and happily made his life with the poor and sick around the countryside of Assisi. Context drew him into the life of Jesus in a very practical way. He identified with the crucified Jesus through his association with the suffering poor and abandoned.

Context, or place, shapes personal identity. Environment influences who people are and how they are in relationship to God, others, self, and the world. Place influences the things needed to be attended to in life for survival, work, or recreation (how food is found, how homes are heated or cooled, or how distances are negotiated to travel for work or play). But beyond these pragmatic circumstances of life that are dictated by place the imaginative dimension of human living and the construction of personal identity are also engaged.

Geographic settings and influence on personal identity

A particular geographic location such as the desert may allow for the development of a symbol system and personal identity that are markedly different from another geographic location such as a forested mountain. In the desert, water is scarce. In the desert, dependence on water for survival will surely be a constant. In the forested mountains, meanwhile, water is most likely plentiful. Taken for granted, water present there may be appreciated more for its aesthetic value, than its life-sustaining qualities. Speaking of Jesus as the "water of life," as the Christian scriptures do, may evoke different images and feelings, as well as engage different life experiences, for the person dwelling in the desert than for the person living on the mountain. How the individual identifies meaningfully with Jesus, therefore, may vary depending on whether he or she lives on the mountain or in the desert.

From the above example we see that the symbols and images people incorporate into spiritualities, whether in prayer, liturgical life, or other forms of practice, are all drawn from the real-life experiences shaped by surroundings. The stories told about life, including those that reflect spiritualities, will have been influenced in a real way by the context within which people have lived. This context includes the spatial dimension described by geography as well as the cultural dimension described by disciplines such as sociology, politics, history, and anthropology. In short, the impact of context, described as the meaningful place within which people live, act, love, and so on, is an essential category of human experience that shapes identity at both the personal and community levels. Places act as depositories of human history, and through the memory of that history they continue to generate meaningful events that construct identity at the communal and personal levels.

For these reasons, place – and not just, for example, biographies, histories, texts, rituals, and prayers – must be considered seriously in the study of Christian spiritualities. The recognition, or lack of it, of God's place in *place* is central to the study of Christian spirituality.

The expulsion of God from ordinary place

The recognition, or lack of it, of God's presence in the place people live has a tremendous impact on people's relationship with God and thus on the way Christian spirituality is lived. Where God is located affects the experience of God. Is God located only in churches or in communal meeting places? Or is God's presence also experienced in nature, in the home, in the workplace, and in the marketplace of the everyday activities of life? Looking back over the history of Christian spirituality there is no one way to answer these questions. In fact, the answer depends on the historical moment and the cultural setting examined. For example, in Christian Celtic spirituality, God, or perhaps, more accurately, the Divine presence, was recognized intensely in the workings of nature and was easily discerned in the landscapes of Ireland, Scotland, and England.[2] For the Celts there was a sacredness to everyday place. The opposite is true in many cultures and settings today.

Christian spirituality, regrettably, has suffered, and continues to suffer, from the historical expulsion of God from the physical world and from the everyday places of human encounter. Following the rapid increase of a rational approach to the world and to knowledge in the seventeenth century, scholars and the population at large began to look at the world as a mechanistic body.[3] Science was beginning to unlock the mysteries of the universe. This led to the tendency to describe the world in terms of cause and effect, as if we were describing the working parts of a giant machine.[4] The mysterious nature of the universe tended to get lost, and the mysterious presence of God in that universe was similarly relegated to the sidelines. Knowledge of the world provided by physics, chemistry, and the other developing natural sciences became the norm. With the scientific method, all truth claims had to withstand the scrutiny of empirical testing, that is, described through what can be observed and measured. God cannot be thus examined, dissected, and reported upon, and therefore was dismissed, to a large extent, as irrelevant to the concerns of society. This attitude reached its peak with the great German philosopher Friedrich Nietzsche (1844–1900), who boldly proclaimed "God is dead." Nietzsche was indicating that the traditional values represented primarily by Christianity were no longer useful. Nietzsche affirmed the utter irrationality of human life and that religion was a futile attempt to make that irrationality coherent.

Those who did not accept the scientific perspective on the world were easily left behind as being too naive to embrace the rational and logical reasoning provided by the natural sciences. Science was demonstrating that nature could be explained and therefore did not contain any element of mystery, or presence of God. Christian communities similarly relegated life with God to the sanctuary of temples and churches. The mysterious God was thus "banished from the world" and took up residence elsewhere, in heaven "up there" somewhere, and could only be easily accessed through the portals provided by the organized religions.

Increasingly, God's personal encounter with humanity was dismissed to the privacy of one's interior feelings, which resulted in privatized spirituality. On the communitarian level ritual activity in the cathedrals and churches increasingly reflected religiosity, that is, a scrupulous concern for the outer forms of ritual worship.[5] The former risked the rise of popular piety, expressed in excessive repetition of prayers and scrupulosity, while the latter risked the rise of empty and heartless repetition of ritual performed only in recognized holy places, assuming this was the only way to encounter the Divine in the world. Exceptions to the tendency to restrict worship of God to institutional churches and temples were movements such as the revivalist tradition, launched in both England and New England in the eighteenth century. These movements recognized that God could not be contained in any one place. For example, the Englishman John Wesley (1703–1791) preached in the open air in Bristol and bought a deserted gun foundry near London so he could preach there. George Whitefield (1714–1770), a friend of Wesley's, did the same along the English Atlantic coast in whatever home, barn, or place of business would welcome him. Whitefield later went to New England several times in order to preach outdoors in the same fashion.

With the generalized expulsion of God from the world, Christian spirituality, for quite some time, felt little need to give its attention to social issues. Social issues might have included the following: the denouncement of the injustices of slavery and apartheid in its many forms; the critique of equality issues between men and women; or increasing the public's sensitivity to ecological issues, such as the destruction of rain forests or pollution of water and air. The quiet and active presence of God in the world, in creation, was all but ignored by mainstream Christian spiritualities for several hundred years. God was safely tucked away in the private interior of one's soul and the repetition of ritual in parish churches or other designated places of worship. However, people are coming to recognize now the harm done by the lack of recognition that the world, as a religiously pluralistic society, *is* God's dwelling place. God can be encountered in church and countryside, in mosque and on mountain top, in temple and among trees.

Christian communities are once again coming to recognize the inbreaking of God's holy presence in human encounter and in the mundane and ordinary experiences and places of people's lives. People are coming to recognize the importance of place, of the natural world, of social context in the development and living out of spiritualities: in particular, Christian spiritualities. Slowly God is moving home in order to be encountered in the unexpected places of forest and desert, palace and ghetto, work and home.

As we will see later in the reflection on current developments in the relationship between science and spirituality, even science has changed its perspective on the question of the mystery that is inherently part of the universe.

Images and symbols come from place

Once God's presence is recognized in the many places in which people live out meaningful relationships, there needs to be an effort to consciously strive to be aware of *how* context has shaped spiritualities. Doing so will help understand them better and gain greater insight into them. This is true in the study of spiritualities developed in past ages, such as the movement to the Egyptian deserts in the fourth century,[6] but it is equally true for spiritualities developing today in large urban centers. When dealing with spiritualities from the past, the challenge is to get behind the images and symbols in order to discern the meaning that can be brought forward for living spirituality today.

When dealing with spiritualities developing today, the task is similar: to be open to the meaningful expression of life in the Spirit that is being expressed in symbols, images, and ways that may be initially foreign. This is no easy task. Since the context of another individual or community may be very different from one's own, it takes hard work to bridge the gaps to understand the meaning of what was going on that resulted in a particular spirituality being expressed in a particular way in the past.

For example, even though some people are familiar with addressing God in the image of "Father," many feminist spiritualities (see Chapter 9) today advocate addressing God in the image of "Mother" as well. This shift in naming God may feel uncomfortable at first, but it is important to work at getting behind the naming – that is, attempt to understand *the experience* that is being named here – to discover deeper insights into how God is present in the world today. (See Chapter 3, Questions of God for further reflections on how God is named.) For someone who grew up in a single-parent family with only a mother, the naming of God as "Mother" may be somewhat easier to understand. That person's context of having only a mother-parent may be reflected in the subsequent spirituality that develops in his or her life, through naming God differently. Or, someone who grew up in a hurricane climate where winds wreaked havoc and destruction on the towns, countryside, and people may find it hard to grasp the life-giving and creative nature of the Spirit that is often referred to as wind (Hebrew: *ruach*) in the scriptures.

Place, understood as the context within which people meaningfully live, shapes personality, molds thoughts, and constructs perspective on the world. All these factors have a major influence on decisions and actions. It may not be possible to name consciously how this is true in every aspect, but growing up in one part of the world will have a different impact on one's spirituality than another part would. Imagine if Jesus of Nazareth had been born in Africa or Asia. The images from the natural world that Jesus used in his teachings and outreach would have been quite different! What would it have meant for Christian stories and symbols if Jesus had woven elephants and tigers into his parables instead of sheep and goats? How would people relate to those images of context?

The mysterious mix of a multiplicity of images and symbols, as well as geography and climate, shape lives in ways that are difficult to comprehend. However, not being able to name completely how context affects the development of a particular spirituality, including one's own, need not stop the effort to do so. The human recognition of the way the Spirit is alive in the world cannot be reduced to a set of principles defined once and for all. The desire to spend time in an isolated cabin high atop a mountain or to pause for long moments of quiet before a radiant sunset cannot be explained away by this theory or that. Ultimately, life is lived with the Spirit's gift that is this place, this time, this geography, this set of historical circumstances – all of which shape the relationship with God, others, self, and nature.

Geography and sacred space: the desert and the city

It has already been mentioned that geography can be a central factor in shaping a particular spirituality. Landscape, whether countryside, mountain, or urban, is an active partner in shaping Christian lives.[7] Landscape is not a passive category that should be taken for granted.[8] Inasmuch as people interact with their geographical setting they are shaped in a particular way. The opposite is also true. People shape their landscapes in a dynamic relationship with them. Think of the massive river dams which have been constructed and whose retained waters cover hundreds, if not tens of thousands, of acres of property (such as the Three Gorges Dam project on the Yangtze River in China), or the constant expansion of urban centers with their newly built homes on what were once fertile agricultural lands. Communities shape their landscapes and they, in turn, shape the communities. The world is viewed differently, literally, because of the way people interact with landscapes and geography. Let us now consider two examples of landscapes that are potent contexts for the construction of Christian spiritualities: the desert and the city.

The desert

The desert has been described above as a unique geographical setting that can lead to certain insights about people, God, and the world. Recall some of the great biblical encounters with God that occurred in the desert in both the Jewish and Christian experience: Moses and the burning bush, the Exodus, the life of Elijah; the ministry of John the Baptist, the forty days of Jesus's fasting and temptations, the many trips of Jesus to the desert, and the solitary prayer of Jesus in Gethsemane prior to his arrest. All these events shaped the creative imagination of the earliest Christian communities, leading them to uphold the desert as a unique place of the Divine–human encounter.

What has become known as the Desert Movement of the fourth century in Egypt testifies to the powerful allure of the desert. During the fourth and fifth centuries, many people sought out the seclusion of the Egyptian desert, along the Nile River or near the Red Sea, to live out the remainder of their lives. They lived in natural caves or carved out dwelling places wherever they could. They lived on the little food and water that was available. Andrew Louth, in *The Wilderness of God* (2003), provides some unique insights into how the desert shaped the lives of these Christians, and continues to shape the lives of Christians today.[9] This is true whether the desert is considered in its geographical manifestation, for example, the Sahara Desert, or as a symbol for secluded, isolated places, such as monasteries or retreat centers. The desert, in whatever manifestation, has proven to be a powerful place of encounter with God where great insight has been gained about God and God's world.

Why would this be the case? For one thing the desert is not heavily populated. The desert pilgrim finds him- or herself alone most of the time. The senses are sharpened and awareness is heightened in this apparent void. The stillness of the desert provides times of long uninterrupted silence, allowing the individual to contemplate the mystery of life, the presence of God in that life, and the ways God is mysteriously present in the world. The great expanse of sand and light, the clear blue skies that go on forever, all provoke a sense of God's transcendence, grandeur, and depth. The radiant sun heating the day symbolizes the life-giving force of God. The cool, shadowy light of the moon, revealing as much as it conceals, leaves one vulnerable, not quite knowing what the darkness is hiding. With little food or water easily available, the desert pilgrim experiences the fragility of life, and his or her dependence on gift and grace for all needs. Water takes on a new meaning as the essence of life and the giver of refreshing energy.

The desert pilgrim, in his or her solitude, comes to know the interdependence all must share as members of a single human community. The stranger passing by is adopted as friend, though few words are spoken. Gender, age, and ethnicity are scarcely noticed. Instead, one's common humanity comes to the fore in a true meeting of persons; both know they are dependent on one another for survival in whatever exchanges of material support, esteem, and love they briefly share.

The illusion of human self-sufficiency is unmasked in the desert for what it is: an attempt to not get caught up in the complexity of interpersonal relationships, all the while forgetting that it is through these very relationships that God's word ultimately enters people's lives. In the end, it is discovered that attempts at human self-sufficiency end in despair and loneliness. In short, the desert has the potential to open humanity's eyes to the mysterious nature of the universe and God's presence in the universe. The desert has the potential to invite people to become members of a single community who share a common humanity in God.

The city

The above statement is no less true for the city even though city landscapes, perhaps best called *cityscapes*, are constructed in ways that are radically different from those of the desert. In the desert individuals find themselves largely powerless before the forces of nature, whether benevolent or hostile. Cities, on the other hand, are more directly tied to the imaginative human creations, for example, of architecture, the careful planning (or lack of planning) of transportation systems, parks, marketplaces, and residential and business areas. A critical reflection on the impact of cities on the development of Christian spiritualities is of utmost importance, since so many people today live in cities.

If people are shaped by the environment they have constructed we need to be doubly aware of how cities, and *built environment* in general, have a

By 1990, about 50 per cent of the world's population lived in cities. By the year 2025, it is expected 60 to 75 per cent of people will do so.[10]

role to play in the development of personal and community spiritual well-being. Built environment, defined as the outcome of community planning, design, and implementation, is being recognized increasingly as having an impact on spiritual well-being. Life stories have geography, too, and the bulk of humanity's life stories are now being honed in the context of urban centers. The symbols and images of cityscapes inform and shape these life stories as never before in the history of humanity and in the history of Christian spiritualities.

For example, how something as simple as sidewalks are planned can have a significant impact on the potential for human interaction and a sense of community. Knowing that it is possible to go for a stroll on the sidewalk, safe from traffic, may provide people with more opportunities to develop friendships with neighbors. The availability of nature parks and recreation areas near to residential communities can give a sense of daily renewal and provide one's spirit with a welcome lift: leisurely strolls past natural vegetation and ponds are uplifting. For those who are distant from these natural recreation areas, often the poor who do not have personal vehicles, decisions by city governments to provide efficient and affordable transportation systems are just as important as creating the park or recreation area in the first place. City space, and its accessibility, directly affects human interaction and influences how individuals have access to each other. This is also true for public places of business and commerce. In the small villages of Europe, town squares, with their markets for fresh food, cafés for unhurried conversations, and places of worship, all clustered together, continue to provide a deeply meaningful place for human encounter.

But many modern cities, particularly residential suburbia, lack places like these where significant human interaction is easily possible. Rather, the spaces have been constructed for the mass processing of business of one kind or another. In this context there is the risk of developing the perception that people are mere objects or commodities like the products quickly purchased and easily discarded. This can lead to a sense of isolation and a lack of personal meaning that can ultimately result in a spiritual void or a feeling of aloneness in the world.

> If people find themselves in too many public places for business that lack human imprint (understood as a sense that it is one's humanity that is valued above all), and if the only identity these public places betray is cost-effectiveness, corporate/consumer identity, and the potential for a quick sale, people will soon find their spirits reflecting the same lack of human identity and humanity.

Architecture

There is a kind of language implicit in architecture that goes beyond the usefulness of the structure: architecture indicates how communities situate themselves in this world. Buildings communicate back to those who built them their values, beliefs, and self-images. Even though this is true of all buildings, to some degree, and of human architecture in general, churches serve as a good example of the truthfulness of this idea. Think of the large medieval churches whose spires reached far into the sky with crosses perched precariously on top.[11] This vertical stretch reflected the tendency of the people of the Middle Ages to emphasize the transcendence of God, the distance between God and the earth, as well as the vast distance between the power of God and that of mere human beings. Elevated spires struck feelings of awe in those who looked upon them from lowly dwelling places close to the earth. Humble buildings may also leave their imprint on human psyches, leaving the occupant feeling diminished or even out-of-place.

Authentic place

We spoke above of place as a category that did not merely reflect spatial qualities, such as the physical place in which magazines are kept. Place is a powerful concept that includes the potential for meaningful and purposeful life, *in that place*, beyond its spatial qualities. Authentic place opens up the potential for authentic human encounter. At times people may find themselves in places quite devoid of any potential for meaningful human interaction and literally feel out-of-place. Some refer to this as *non-place*[12]: places such as the passive place of hours spent in front of the television, in an airport waiting room, or in a car driving home on the freeway. It is important, therefore, that cities and urban centers are constructed in a way that diminishes out-of-place experiences and enhances the potential for meaningful connections to others, as well as to the world of nature.

In authentic place, with its reminders of the identity of any particular community which includes where it has come from, and where it is going, encounter with God through the mediation of place can be greatly enriched.

The contribution of sociology to context

As already emphasized, context plays a major role in the flourishing, or stagnation, of spiritualities. Sociology helps describe a different kind of context, social space and place, so that there is an increase in awareness of social factors and their role in the development of spiritualities.

> Sociology is the study of the development of society, social interaction, and the interrelatedness of social phenomena. Its goal is to construct plausible theories of human behavior in society, principally within its communal expression.

Sociology's methodological tools allow it to take into objective consideration social location, which includes such factors as race and ethnicity, gender, age, and financial income. Under its sub-field of sociology of religion, sociology is well positioned to provide valuable insights into how spiritualities take root, develop, and affect communities and groups in diverse settings. Sociology can also help better understand the development of Christian spiritualities in previous eras, giving greater insight into communal developments that led to specific spiritualities in the past.

Geography and physical space affect developments in spiritualities; social and cultural place and space are equally important. The place and space that sociology describes and analyzes is cultural place or social location, the space of human interaction in all its diversity both at the communal and interpersonal levels. Spiritualities do not find their homes merely in churches, synagogues, mosques, or other communal places of worship. Rather, spiritualities are found in the happy mix of daily social, economic, and political meeting places that, in themselves, structure unique environments for the growth of spiritualities.

This is perhaps truer for spiritualities than it is for formally organized religions that tend to find their locus of activity in well-defined spaces and places, such as churches and synagogues or even soup kitchens or other faith-based community initiatives. Because the boundaries for spiritualities are so fluid and not easily defined (compared with those in parochial structures, for example) the challenge is to gain access to these market-place spaces so we can have insight into what is going on. Sociology can readily assist in this quest due to its interest in social interaction in all its manifestations and in all its places. Few boundaries contain sociological inquiry. For the researcher in spirituality, this freedom is most helpful. Sociology can also be helpful in that it is open to all expressions of communal interaction, and may be able to identify spiritual or religious phenomena excluded from inquiry done from a purely spiritual perspective with already recognized spiritual or faith-based groups.

Sociologists, in their quest to discover what is going on, are increasingly turning their research toward the phenomenon of religion operative in society, as well as the increased interest in spirituality in all areas of human interaction. This was not always the case.

The rejection of spirituality by sociologists

At one point, in the earlier part of the twentieth century, sociologists had all but rejected religion and spirituality as areas worthy of critical study. As the processes of rational thought gripped the attention of Western societies, and sociology developed as a field of research after the Enlightenment in the seventeenth century, it was accepted that the influence of religion in society would all but disappear. It was believed by some social theorists that religions would be replaced by philosophy, and that philosophy, in turn, would be replaced by science, including the social sciences. The reasonableness of spirituality was heavily questioned, and thus its place in a reasonable society was cast in doubt. Sociologists, as products of the Enlightenment, saw reason and rational thought as the important drivers that stood behind social interaction. For them, only social phenomena driven by reason could be worthy of serious study. Spirituality and religion, to a large degree, had been assessed as belonging to the non-rational sphere of human life and thus irrelevant to the larger picture of human interaction.

This attitude on the part of classical social theorists has been challenged by a significant number of events.[13] Events such as the 1978 mass suicide of about 900 followers, mostly Americans, of the cult leader Jim Jones in Jonestown, Guyana, and the enormous public outpouring of grief and solidarity with those affected by the attacks on the World Trade Center in 2001, reveal that reason is only one of the forces standing behind human interaction and choices. The decision to participate in a mass suicide can hardly be attributed to the outcome of a calm and collected reasoning process. And the spontaneous responses of caring by so many in the face of tragic events such as the terrorist attacks reveal that society is not merely driven by reason; the heart, displayed in our feelings, also plays a major role in social events and movements. Sociologists are coming to recognize this realm of the human beyond the strictly rational.

The sacred dimension of life is once again coming to the fore, but frequently not within the scope of the organized groups already clearly identified with a particular spirituality. This is where sociologists can assist in getting at and describing new developments in spirituality.

Sociology of religion and spirituality

Sociology, or rather its sub-field identified as sociology of religion and spirituality, is taking spirituality, and its role in shaping the world of social interaction in all of its settings, ever more seriously. Reason and rational thought are being recognized for their *limited capacity* to explain the way human beings respond to events and how they interact. In the postmodern world (discussed in detail below), reason and rationality are not the sole preoccupation. Humans have a deep-seated need to relate in a meaningful way to other human beings. There is something sacred about human interaction, for it is the locus for generating the most profound and meaningful moments, what it means to be human.

It doesn't take world-shaking events like those mentioned above to see how this is true. Think of celebrations, anniversaries, births, deaths, and graduations. These events are not merely passing moments; they endow life with its depth of meaning. Their firm and concrete expressions of meaningful belonging provide stability and a sense of hope amidst the transience of life. They endow human life with a sense of purpose beyond the mere functional realities of everyday life. Even so-called secular events, such as investitures of all kinds or military marches, or what could be described as utilitarian action (for example, the sudden and unreflected action to save someone who is in extreme danger, putting one's own life at risk), can be the settings for profound personal and communal expression of the spiritual dimension of human living. Thus, spirituality shapes social behavior in significant ways.

The opposite is also true. Social behavior can be the basis for profound spiritual awakenings: awakenings that need to be explored with adequate concepts, language, and investigatory practices familiar to spirituality. Dag Hammarskjöld (1905–1961), the Swedish United Nations Secretary General (1953–1961), is an example of someone who underwent profound spiritual experiences and conversion while in active social service. Many today would go so far as to identify Hammarskjöld as a Christian mystic. His life as Secretary General in the United Nations is a witness to the way involvement in the social realm, outside of the boundaries of any group affiliated with a particular spirituality, can be a place of intense Divine encounter. His personal testimony to this encounter is recorded in his journal, simply titled *Markings*, first published in England in 1964 and still read widely today.

Sociology and spirituality as two separate domains of research find much common ground in their concern to break open the meaningfulness of the everyday realities of life. Spirituality is concerned with many of the same questions as sociology, such as those surrounding everyday practices and traditions. Spirituality is similar to other social phenomena in that it can be studied, for example, across different ethnic boundaries, historical time periods, cultural settings, family situations, class divisions, and gender differences. Sociology of spiritual experiences treats spirituality as an empirically observable social fact; thus, sociology can shine light from outside and provide analysis in the area of social interaction that may not be accessible to the theorist or practitioner in the field of spirituality.

Specific benefits of sociological studies in Christian spirituality

Sociology, from within its domain, can provide a sociological understanding of the plurality of ways in which spirituality is relevant in our society today. For example, sociologists can ask these questions, and ones like them:

What is the social benefit emerging from persons and groups engaging in specific spiritual practices [e.g. spiritual pilgrimages or economic development activity in poorer countries]?

How do social benefits differ with respect to ethnic background and social class of those participating in spiritual practices such as tithing (giving a percentage of your income to charity or your church) or weekly communal worship?

Why do young people tend to join esoteric (non mainstream) spiritual movements?

Sociology can help analyze the relationship between world views based on a particular spirituality and cultural conflict, or to understand why some ethnic groups are more involved in spiritualities than others (i.e. how culture affects the development and shaping of spiritualities).

Sociologists can help interpret the differences in the dynamics of how faith-based communities organize themselves. Do Latinos and Latinas, whites, African Americans, and Native Canadians all organize themselves in the same way in relationship to their spiritualities? If not, what are the differences and how do these affect their place in their various social settings? In short, sociology assists in the analysis of the interplay between socio-cultural, political, and spiritual dynamics.

> Sociologists are not concerned about whether God exists; nor are they concerned with the defense of the principles of particular practices, beliefs, or spiritualities.

Through their descriptive analysis of the ways and effects of how human persons interact, whether individually or in groups, sociologists can help us understand how spiritual beliefs relate to the way people see the world and situate their place in that world. Sociology can help spirituality break out of any bubbles within which it has enclosed itself by helping to identify how spiritualities relate to the greater whole, identify their place in that whole, and provide relevant insights on how that greater whole is reciprocally in relationship to them. Sociology can have, therefore, a grounding effect on spiritualities.

For this reason, sociology can provide descriptions and insights about shared meaningful experiences that take place outside the confines of any explicitly spirituality-based community. Sociological studies may help identify alternative shapes and forms of emergent spiritualities, including Christian spiritualities, and how people are responding meaningfully to their situations. How people experience belonging together, with a common purpose and vision, may not at first be named as a spirituality, but could be named as such upon appropriate sociological analysis that may clear the path to see behaviors and relationships in this way. The discovery of new Christian spiritualities, emerging in the marketplace through the watchful lens of sociological analysis, could benefit research in both areas.

The study of Wade Clark Roof entitled *Spiritual Marketplace: Baby Boomers and the Rethinking of American Religion* (1999) is an excellent example of how the sociologist interested in questions of spirituality can contribute to and extend research in spirituality. Roof's understanding of markets and consumer behavior is applied to the study of spirituality to help better understand how baby boomers (that large segment of the population born in the later 1940s up until the later 1950s and who all are expected to retire by roughly 2020) embody spiritualities that reshape traditional religious boundaries and relationships to traditional religious institutions. These consequences inevitably play out in the marketplace of civil and religious activities.

Point of departure for studies in sociology and spirituality

The point of departure for the sociologist interested in spirituality, as well as the researcher in spirituality, is not a tightly constructed set of principles, but rather a series of flexible concepts from which inquiries can be made in order to better understand what is developing in the world, regardless of the context and how it has been previously labeled. Sociology is not just about gathering statistics and subsequent number-crunching associated with quantitative analysis. Sociology, as well as studies in spirituality, are about concepts and their applicability in current lived situations. Both are concerned about trends in society, each from their own agenda of inquiry, that frequently overlap in their concern for the construction of meaningful lives.

> Sociology, with spirituality, also shares the perspectival problem: that is, the quest for neutrality in any study so that the results of research are not harmfully biased from the outset. However, there is no need to leave personal normative concerns behind in order to do respectable sociology or to do studies in spirituality. Perspective, which includes, for example, historical context and personal bias, gives depth and meaning to the questions that are brought to bear on any situation and, as a result, helps gain further insight into the area of inquiry.

It is only when perspective becomes so normative as to block openness to unforeseen outcomes that it becomes problematic. Perspective must be accompanied by openness, even to the point where the validity of truth claims that led to the inquiry in the first place may also be questioned.

Events and situations have multiple causes and multiple explanations that may not be apparent at the beginning of a study in spirituality. Furthermore, research from within the field of spirituality may not provide all the data or tools necessary to do a thorough and critical analysis of the topic in order for the multiple causes and multiple explanations to come to light. For example, spirituality may not have the tools at hand to do an adequate analysis of how social class, gender, and race affect communal self-identity and the concomitant potential for the generation of meaningful communal spiritual practices. Studies in sociology can assist the researcher in spirituality to uncover how these multiple factors affect spiritual practice and self-identity. Likewise, spirituality, from its perspective, can provide a corpus of insights and understandings about the human condition that cannot readily be found within the literature identified as sociological.

Studies in spirituality often overlap with those in sociology, as well as with other social sciences, such as psychology. At times, the researcher in spirituality may need to be informed of how this overlap may be brought to bear on the relevant questions at hand. This is not to suggest that researchers in spirituality must develop finely tuned skills in sociology. However, they do need to be aware of the potent resource that is available to them in sociological inquiry and actively seek out the literature that has investigated the relevant questions at hand or contact sociologists who might assist. Sociologists are trained in the formulation of questionnaires aimed at cutting through predetermined outcomes in order to gain objective responses; they are practiced in helpful interview processes that aim to do the same; and they are schooled in the area of statistical analysis, which makes findings more relevant and insightful for further use. In short, sociologists are trained in the area of information gathering in the social domain. Researchers in spirituality may not have had training in these quantitative and qualitative assessment techniques, and thus stand to gain greatly from studies in sociology for their own research.

Spiritual but not religious

For example, many people today would identify themselves as "spiritual but not religious."[14] Academics teaching courses in spirituality see this attitude reflected in discussions with their students; members of self-help groups may identify their therapeutic exercises as reflecting their spirituality but are not religious in nature; and individuals involved in New Age spirituality (see Chapter 9), including such practices as tai chi, crystals, meditation, or yoga, would not identify these practices as religious per se. How are we, as students and researchers in the area of spirituality, able to skillfully identify how the reality "spiritual but not religious" is reflected in the population at large?

To a great extent explorers in the area of spirituality, including Christian spirituality, are involved with select profiles of the population: for example, those who have decided to take courses in Christian spirituality at the university level. Those involved in university-level education are already a select group of the population – they have the money and time to do this work. This is already not typical of the population at large. Furthermore, the classroom group will most likely not reflect the diversity of ethnicity, gender, economic status, age, denominational affiliation, and so on, of the larger population. So, to attempt to come to an accurate determination of the "spiritual but not religious" segment of the population in general from classroom surveys is problematic, to say the least.

The question is further complicated by the way the question is asked: that is, what definitions the researcher, and those being asked, will assign to the words "religious" and "spiritual." What do people have in mind when they say they are one or the other, or reflect a mix of the two? What do they mean when one is diminishing in influence while the other is gaining in influence? How does the impact of being either "religious" or "spiritual" show in one's life: that is, what makes it credible to be able to say that one or the other is what motivates action, shapes attitudes, and creates a sense of belonging? Is it personal practice or institutional affiliation that prompts respondents to place themselves in one category or the other? Or has it been a significant spiritual experience that tips the scales one way or the other?

Thus, the question of "spiritual but not religious" does not stand alone; it must be asked amidst a number of other questions that, in turn, need to be carefully considered, evaluated, and analyzed together to form plausible conclusions. Most explorers in Christian spirituality might not be equipped to shape a research project that will consider all the sociological variables implied by the phrase "spiritual but not religious," or consider how to select a group of respondents that truly is representative of a population in general and is not just, for example, college-level, middle-class, and Caucasian in the twenty- to thirty-year age level. Nor might a researcher in the area of sociology of religion be equipped to put together satisfactorily such a research project. However, both researchers may combine talents to cover all these concerns.

Modernism to postmodernism: the context of being "in-between"

It is common today to hear that we live in a postmodern world. Books are published on topics such as postmodern architecture, art, culture, and politics, along with many other areas of interest. This may seem a strange way of describing our world, since the word "modern" is also used to describe the very latest gadget or the newest way of doing something. People say "we live in modern times" in ordinary daily speech. Obviously "modern" has more than one meaning.

In academic discussions (among other settings), "modern" or "modernity" is used to refer to a period of time that stretches roughly from the mid-1700s up until about 1950. Even though the shift to the postmodern world was slowly taking shape in various ways at the turn of the twentieth century, only later did it become clear that a shift had, in fact, taken place. The postmodern period thus refers to the period from roughly 1950 up until our own times. Each of these two periods has had its own ways of viewing the world and recognizing how people gained knowledge about the world. Both views have had, and continue to have, a significant impact on, for example, politics, education, law-making, workplace norms, and spirituality.[15] The shift from modernism to postmodernism thus refers to a cultural shift reflected in a change in the way people view the world and situate their place in it.

The modern period

René Descartes (1596–1650), a French philosopher and mathematician, is frequently cited as the individual who launched the modern period. Based on his famous dictum *cogito ergo sum* (I think, therefore I am), Descartes removed religious faith as the organizing principle of all knowledge and replaced it with human reason and rational thought. Descartes and his followers attributed to human thinking the basis for all true and authentic knowledge.

Up until the time of Descartes, we could call it the pre-modern period: personal identity, knowledge (including knowledge labeled scientific during that time), and meaning in life were primarily constructed around a religious perspective of the world. The pre-modern view upheld the importance of human interdependence, and promoted a rather holistic view of the human self. The pre-modern subject also enjoyed an interdependent relationship with nature. The movement to reason and rational thought as the organizing principle of human knowledge and activity in the modern period was to change all of this.

In the modern period no longer would the religious perspective be the foundation of the way people look at the world: rather, the human mind would be held accountable to make sense of the world independent of God. Without referring to Descartes specifically, we saw the impact of his philosophy on society in a previous section, which dealt with the expulsion of God from ordinary place. Because of this so-called enlightened perspective on the world (independence from the shackles of the religious perspective), the initial thrust of modernism came to be called the Enlightenment. It was also known as the Age of Reason. In short, Descartes' *cogito* led society to believe in the potential for the formulation of clear and concise ideas from within the power of the human mind alone – independent of religious beliefs.

Granted, Descartes' philosophy on life was not the only factor that contributed to this movement. Industrialization and significant discoveries in the scientific realm around the same time all helped to shape the modern perspective on the world. New frontiers were being explored in the Americas, and the idea grew strong in the psyches of the population of the Western world that anything was possible with enough hard work, dedication, and commitment. The French Revolution was fed in part by the intellectual ferment of the Enlightenment, but also by political and ecclesial unrest on many levels. Founded on the ideals of liberty, equality, and fraternity for all, the French population exercised its vision of the autonomous self free from the oppressive control of both state and Church by the establishment of the First Republic. A similar event had just occurred with the American Revolution (1775–1783). In North America, the lone cowboy heading off into the sunset, totally self-sufficient, caricatures this individualistic self in these new societies. The image of the frontier homesteader in the harsh, windswept landscape of the North American prairies also captures the ethos of the period.

The modern period became characterized by a rugged individualism and a self-autonomy whereby the principles ordering people's lives were accepted to be found within themselves, not within the state or the Church.

Rational thought and logic assumed a greater role in life and in the discovery of knowledge during the modern period. All authentic knowledge was based on the methods of the new scientific discoveries and organized into clearly identifiable systems of order. The logic of science believed that knowledge could be organized into meta-narratives, that is, one big story, whereby everything could be explained in relationship to everything else in any particular area of human knowledge.

The churches had their own rendition of this principle: uniform belief among all church members was meant to assure conformity and coherence in issues of faith and moral practice. There was an objective nature to the world, understood simply as the ways things are, within the scientific as well as the ecclesial world views: reality, whether that be of the Divine or human domains, was just waiting to be discovered and documented once and for all. What did not fit the belief system in the churches, or could not be proven with objective certainty in the sciences, was easily discarded as irrelevant. Thus the churches fell prey to rationalism with their rationalistic theologies as much as did many groups in society in general.

Along with the countless great and wonderful scientific discoveries, advances in medicine and health care, and construction of labor-saving machines, an exaggerated hope in science and technology grew by the end of the nineteenth century. It was generally believed that all advances in knowledge were progressive and for the betterment of humanity. It was also believed that science and technology would ultimately be able to satisfy all human needs.

Control of nature was the key: the fruits of the land were there for the taking, to be used and exploited for the satisfaction of human consumption, with little thought of the consequences for the land. In terms of economics it was believed that the common good was best served by the individual pursuit of wealth: capitalism, now firmly planted in many countries around the world, was best poised to manage the new wealth of humanity. In the political realm, it was believed that the political judgment of each citizen would automatically lead to right political decisions for all. In this scenario, as discussed above, God was banished from ordinary places. Spirituality and the religious view in general were privatized and removed from public discourse in the community.

The developments in science, economics, and politics were increasingly split apart from religion and spirituality; spirituality could not speak the language of the others and little attempt was made to do so.[16] Science, economics, politics, and other disciplines furnished the language of public discourse, while religion and spirituality furnished the language of private devotions and personal piety. Spirituality, during the modern period, was thus essentially excluded from public place, and knowledge gained from the other disciplines was kept from entering into the beliefs held by religious groups.

The modern period – mid-1700s until about 1950 – is characterized by the following:

- rational thought was frequently in tension with feelings and personal experience as authentic sources of knowledge
- autonomy and independence of individuals emphasized
- neat and tidy systems of knowledge decided what was acceptable
- developments in science and history viewed as always progressive
- exaggerated hope in science and technology
- emphasis on private devotion
- God was expelled from ordinary place
- God viewed as a Supreme Being who rules the world
- God intervened on our behalf but from a distance

But a crack in this publicly held view of the world and of God occurred with a series of dramatic events beginning in the early part of the twentieth century: the First World War (1914–1918); the stock market crash of 1929; the Great Depression (1929–1939); and the Second World War (1939–1945) with its extermination camps, for example, Auschwitz-Birkenau and Lublin-Majdanek, and the use of the atomic bomb – Hiroshima, Japan, August 6, 1945 and Nagasaki, August 9, 1945 – against a civilian population. These events, and others like them, increasingly called into question the world view that had dominated Western civilization for the previous 300 years. These events also cast doubt on the human conceptions of order and the belief that all scientific discoveries were for the betterment of humanity.

Science was no longer exclusively seen as the friend of humanity. After all, the A-bomb and extermination camps that killed countless innocent people were designed and constructed by persons using the advances of science. War after war dislodged tightly held views concerning humanity's capacity to overcome evil in the world through its own efforts. In all of this turmoil God's presence and role in the world was also questioned. How could God let such horror and tragedy happen? Was God really in charge of human history? Even the understanding of God was under attack. A benevolent God that intervened in human history when needed no longer seemed plausible. The autonomous self that relied on reason and logic to solve the problems of the world was no longer credible, either. That same reasonable self was the root cause of much destruction and unrest in the world.

The postmodern period

Thus, by the middle of the twentieth century, new sensitivities began to come to the fore. They include the following:

1. A greater emphasis on the human being as a relational and inter-dependent being became increasingly reflected in literature, art, the workplace, and politics.
2. The emergence of the need for authentic community, in opposition to the individualism that characterized the modern period, became increasingly important.
3. A greater awareness of the limits of science and technology also evolved. Reason *and* feelings are seen as important.
4. The mystery of life – including how human life is integrally connected to the mystery of nature and the natural environment – rose steadily in the consciousness of many individuals and groups during this time.
5. Even science, within its own ranks, questioned the validity of its belief that all knowledge that was worthy of being called knowledge required validation by a strictly scientific method.
6. Meta-narratives – whether upholding views from within society or from the churches, which tended to suppress or ignore anything (or anyone) that did not fit into their dogmatic organizing system – were recognized for what they were: barriers to exploring the new, the imaginative, and the creative edges developing in the world in so many areas of life.
7. One's place in the world, whether that is in the family, the workplace, or society, was once well defined by the social arrangements of modernity. Now this state was increasingly called into question. As a result the place of women, persons of color, minorities of all kinds (including gay men and lesbian women) were undergoing radical re-evaluation in tune with new social, political, economic, and ecclesial perspectives.
8. Within the churches, logic, reflected in carefully constructed theological systems that had been the norm for centuries, was giving way to everyday experience as a potent source for truth in the Christian life.

However, it would be false to suggest that we have passed completely from a modernist to a postmodernist perspective on the world. We can see both the characteristics of modernity and the newly developing sensitivities of postmodernity active in the social, political, economic, and ecclesial systems of the world. Clearly, societies are in a period of transition. Indeed, change and flux are salient characteristics of postmodernism. But this period of change and flux is difficult for many: the familiar, which is being lost, has not yet been replaced by the new. Furthermore, it cannot be suggested that there is a need to sweep aside completely the developments of modernity in order to embrace without critique the postmodern perspective. Both have advantages and disadvantages, as a more thorough reflection beyond the presentation here would reveal.[17] For example, the values of equality and freedom for all, the rise of democracy, the value of the individual, and the improvement of medicine and health care are helpful advances to bring forward from the modernist period.

At times the modernist and postmodernist perspectives compete with one other, depending on which aspect of modernity is still active in the post-modern context. Here is an example: the modernist tendency is to attempt to construct a singular world view on the basis of a stable body of knowledge that is coherent and logical within its own frame of reference. Both Church and state have appealed to this modernist practice in the past in order to construct unalterable laws and norms for their various constituents; at times, they both continue to do so today. However, the postmodernist perspective is at home with a multiplicity of world views that are constructed from varying and different sources of knowledge.

These world views may even compete with each other, but each would be valued for its unique contribution to the construction of meaningful life in different human contexts. Thus, the postmodernist perspective requires a genuine commitment to reconciling differences, rather than a dependence on absolute authority that carries only one perspective of the whole. Some people find this lack of clear direction very difficult. They favor the modernist perspective, which strove to establish inerrant authority. But even though it is true that both the modernist and postmodernist perspectives have an impact on the churches and society today, it is also true that it would be impossible to reconstruct the widespread position that the churches held in society prior to the developments during the modernist period.

The dismantling of clear religious belief – the rise of spirituality

Centuries of secularization during the modern period – the intentional and progressive movement in society away from belief systems that saw God as the guarantor of the meaning of all life – have dismantled to a large degree the appeal of traditional religious systems that were shaped into various church communities. Those who either no longer believed in a God of any kind or who had found the view of the sacred within those systems untenable have for centuries looked beyond the religious norms in order to address questions of meaning in life.[18] Even though many people continued to participate in formal church communities, from the 1700s on, traditional religious systems increasingly were no longer recognized, as they once had been, as harbors of meaningful encounter and places of reposeful refuge amidst the chaos and turbulence of life. This gradual decay in the authority of the churches over several centuries resulted in a great exodus of believers from the 1950s on. At this time, it became more acceptable publicly not to belong to any organized religious group.

The churches had lost their hold on the religious imaginations and allegiance of large segments of the populations in Europe and the Americas, and church attendance declined markedly as a result. People felt free to organize their lives around the new world views that had gradually taken widespread hold in society and that did not contain formal relationships to any church. Those people who continued to attend church services often felt free to tie into the religious system from the perspective of personal choices, needs, and values. This signaled a shift from an obligation to participate according to the norms set down by the churches, to the freedom of personal choice about what to believe and practice.

Truthfulness in the religious traditions that reflected personal experience and insight increasingly became the basis of religious belief and practice, rather than reference to doctrinal norms, inherited habits, or social pressures.

But the exodus from the organized religions mentioned above did not mean that people stopped experiencing something sacred about the world, about themselves, and about others. It did not mean that people stopped searching for hope and meaning in life. Secularization may have produced an unchurched culture but not an irreligious one. People continue to experience something beyond themselves that they describe as the spiritual or transcendent dimension of life. As seen above, sociologists understand that the spiritual is not disappearing from people's lives. But with the disillusionment in science brought about by the tragic events of the first half of the twentieth century and beyond, as well as the deconstruction of the religious perspective in the world launched by modernity, people were not inclined to look to either science or religion for their answers about life.

Reason and logic, whether expressed in civil law or doctrinal norms, were emptied of their capacity to answer the deepest longings of the human heart. In some way, the organized religions were also found emptied of this capacity: human experience, in itself, has taken on new importance as a source of truth for the believer in a postmodern world. The shift to the belief in a world view constructed by human experience, and not one constructed by abstract or intellectual reasoning, is at the foundation of the plethora of spiritualities that are developing in our society today. The shift to people looking at their own lives as sources of profound meaning has pushed them to search for new ways to answer the most important questions of life: for example, the questions of love, belonging, suffering, and death. These are the questions surrounding the spiritual dimension of every person's life. These are the questions that cannot be easily satisfied with stock answers pulled from a ready-made list.

People continue to search for meaning in life that takes them beyond the answers that rational thought, accumulation of material goods, position of power and influence, or sometimes even the organized religions can provide. This search has led many to open up to the mysterious and sacred dimension of life in new ways – ways that have led to a proliferation of new spiritualities.

> People have come to discover that it is not in heady logic or religious rules that we find answers to our deepest questions about life; rather, we find them in the meaningful encounter with the sacred dimension of life, which surfaces in various ways.

This ferment of spiritualities is typical of postmodernism. To a certain degree, postmodernism has restored to the world a certain enchantment and mystery – experienced in the encounter of other persons, in the beauty of creation, or in the imaginative productions of art and literature – that modernity, with its scientific perspective, strove to remove. The place of the experience of the sacred dimension of life for many people today is in the mystery and marketplace of everyday experiences.

A hunger to locate ourselves meaningfully in the world in relationship to this sacred dimension has given birth to new forms of spirituality that can express and nurture this meaningfulness. But people are not necessarily naming this sacred experience in relationship to the Christian God, or to any organized religion. If there is some relationship to any of the major spiritual traditions such as Buddhism, Islam, Hinduism, Judaism, Confucianism, Taoism, or Christianity, it may simply be to borrow this or that practice or ritual that fits the individual's sense of spiritual expression.

Some people have described this as a marketplace approach to spirituality. Whatever else could be said about it, the marketplace approach has opened up the space for new, innovative forms of spiritual practices and for new spiritualities. Some of these will be briefly explored in the last chapter of this book. But the question immediately surfaces: How do we decide which practices are helpful and which ones are not? It is not the purpose here to study critically in-depth criteria that could aid in this assessment. However, a few preliminary remarks on this subject may be useful.

The marketplace approach to spirituality

The vital desire that the Christian believer and the non-believer share in the postmodern period is the desire for a meaningful life expressed in encounters of hope and love with others. There is a hunger in the world today for authentic meaning in one's life, whether one attributes the Christian God as the foundation of this meaning or not. Genuine spiritualities, whether Christian or not, need to strive to name the centers of meaning that nourish our being at all levels. They need to bring together our head and our heart, so we experience our body-selves as a complete entity. Furthermore, postmodern spiritualities do not regard the inequality of men and women as an acceptable way to structure beliefs and practices. In the postmodern vision men and women are equally invited to share their experiences of the sacred in the world. The world in turn will shape belief and practice that reflect the unique contribution of both men and women. Postmodern spiritualities, in general, do not assume that roles of dominance and submission are co-natural in the world, for example, between men and women or nature and humanity.

Constructive postmodern spiritualities are those that take seriously the present world situation and work hard to respond to human needs within the reality of that situation. Spiritualities that strive to reverse the debilitating grasp of modernity's individualism, its subordination of humanity to mechanization, and its exaltation of economic interests to the deprivation of social, aesthetic, and ecological concerns, cannot help but have a positive contribution to make in today's world. The growth of spiritualities that have as their aim key life-giving characteristics – including the formation of community, as opposed to the exaltation of the self-subsistent self; the emphasis on our interdependent relationship with nature, as opposed to the exploitation and control of nature; and the realization that there is a vital need for a multiplicity of voices in order to tell the human story, as opposed to singular controlling meta-narratives – will all contribute toward the betterment of our societies and our world. Indeed, with the current growth of multiculturalism accompanied by religious pluralism in societies all over the world, as well as the revival of some ancient spiritualities, it is increasingly difficult for one cultural or religious expression to dominate any aspect of any society or religious tradition.

Each group or tradition brings its own mix, for example, of customs, practices, rituals, language, and symbols. These are expected to be received as a part of a dialogue whereby each participant has something of value to contribute. Postmodern spiritualities are at home with this diversity and, in fact, welcome it. Constructive peace is the happy outcome of this desire to live in relationship with others despite differences. Indeed, the relational is constitutive of the postmodern trends in spirituality that have given rise to so many expressions of it: the relationship not only with other communities but also the relationship to the natural environment, to one's family, and to one's own culture. All these play a significant role in any spirituality that is going to be helpful in exploring the deeper meanings of life for individuals who exist only in communion with others.

Spiritualities that attempt to rediscover the sacred in the world, that bring back hope and meaning into the living of daily life, and once again recognize the mystery of the universe in all its splendor are worthy of our attention. Thus, currents in spiritualities, including marketplace spiritualities, alongside Christian spiritualities that reflect all of the above need to be nurtured and recognized for the life-giving force that they are in the world.

Christianity claims to be both historical and contemporary – thus the need for contemporary Christian spiritualities that reflect the concerns of today's secularized world. In the end, we can view secularization as a gift – it has opened up Christian spirituality to a rich diversity of religious expressions and made possible new ways of experiencing and expressing the sacred in the world.

What cannot be forgotten is that whatever expression Christian spiritualities embody today, they must be in continuity with the historical origins of the Christian spiritualities passed down through the ages. In this continuity the Spirit is active in forming the community of Christ wherever authentic community emerges – whether within or outside of Christian spiritualities per se.

Karl Rahner (1904–1984), a German Roman Catholic theologian, recognized the gift of secularization as he looked back ten years after Vatican Council II (1962–1965) of the Roman Catholic Church.[19] Rahner pondered on what the Council ultimately had to offer the world. He bluntly recognized that Vatican II was largely a meeting that represented Western, Caucasian (white), developed countries. Most bishops at the Council from African, Asian, or Latin American countries had ethnic origins in Europe or North America. But the Council expressed a burning desire to be part of the new realities in the world, with all the diversity that had taken hold in the last centuries. Rahner was making a case to be part of the emerging postmodern sensitivities that had grown strong in the minds and hearts of people around the world. He knew that Christianity had to break out of its controlling Eurocentric mold if it was truly to be a world religion and a credible witness for Christianity in a cosmopolitan environment.

Secularization, generally understood as a withdrawal from society's self-identification with the local institutions of religion, had opened up new opportunities for Christianity to truly embrace a universality reminiscent of its earliest expressions, and Rahner wanted Christianity to seize this moment of promise.[20] He called for Christianity, without denying its own origins, to take root in radically different cultures, and to be expressed from within those cultures in new ways. This realization was a call for the development of a radical plurality of Christian spiritualities in dialogue with non-Christian spiritualities that already expressed the hopes and dreams of various peoples around the world. This call was not to negate the perspective and gift that Christian spirituality would bring to a common table, but rather to see its gift alongside the gifts of the others.

For Christian spirituality, the unique perspective brought to the table is that of Jesus Christ. For the Christian, spirituality that incarnates self-giving and forgiving love following the witness of Jesus's life, death, and resurrection must be seen to be at the core of what Christian spirituality is all about. However, Christians need to be aware that, at times, spiritualities that are not specifically Christian in nature may greatly assist in achieving this goal as they bear witness to that same reality, albeit in a different way. Postmodern Christian spiritualities are therefore at home in diversity, whether that is in relationship with the Christian traditions or with other faiths such as Buddhism, Hinduism, Islam, or Judaism.

Conclusion

In this chapter, we have recognized the importance that context plays in developing Christian spirituality and spirituality in general. Alongside people's explicit faith commitment are many other references that actively engage people and shape the way they form relationships with others, the world, and God. These references include the economic, political, sociological, geographical, and cultural dimensions of people's lives. The images, symbols, and values that express and nourish spirituality come from within the actual circumstances of life. It is here that people meet the living God – whether in the desert, the city, or somewhere in-between.

In this chapter we have also described the context within which large segments of the world currently live: that is, the state of transition from a modern to a postmodern world. With the development of the scientific method and its accompanying expulsion of God from the ordinary places of human activity in the seventeenth century (the modern period), a wide rift developed between spirituality and the emerging scientific disciplines, including the social or human sciences. This rift left spirituality as something for private consumption. Spirituality was not viewed as a part of everyday life.

Place – that is, the everyday lieu of human encounter – in the modern period was not viewed as having potential for the human–Divine encounter. This attitude contributed to a neglect of issues such as social justice, equality of persons, and care of the environment. With the dawn of the postmodern period, it was once again recognized that the Divine can be, and is, encountered in all the realms of human activity, and is not confined to the specific activities of the organized religions. This recognition has fueled the growth of many expressions of spirituality in society in general today.

Sociology was described as a particularly valuable tool to help locate and describe these emerging spiritualities. Since they are not necessarily found in the normal places such as church, mosque, or temple, there is a need for the analytical tools of disciplines such as sociology to help analyze how people are encountering the spiritual today. Truth claims of statements like "spiritual but not religious" can be helpfully described using sociological analysis.

We come to understand, therefore, that context, whether described by the formal structures of well-recognized faith communities or by the wider dimensions and activities of society, is a powerful cauldron in which our spiritual lives are shaped in profound and surprising ways.

RECOMMENDED READING

Burton-Christie, Douglas (1994) "Mapping the Sacred Landscape: Spirituality and Contemporary Literature of Nature," *Horizons* 21, 22–47.

Daloz Parks, Sharon (2003) "To Venture and to Abide: The Tidal Rhythm of Our Becoming," in *Developing a Public Faith: New Directions in Practical Theology*, R. R. Osmer and F. Schweitzer, eds, St. Louis, MI: Chalice Press, 63.

Downey, Michael (1994) "In the Ache of Absence: Spirituality at the Juncture of Modernity and Postmodernity, *Liturgical Ministry* 3 (Summer), 92–99. (Very helpful for those not too familiar with the concepts of modernity and postmodernity, and how the shift from one to the other affects questions of our understanding of holiness, asceticism, prayer, and God.)

Jacobson, Erico O. (2003) "From the Garden to Jerusalem" and "Learning to See Our Cities: A Theological Approach," in *Sidewalks in the Kingdom: New Urbanism and the Christian Faith*, Grand Rapids, MI: Brazos Press, 34–45; 63–73. (The first section gives a brief account of the history of cities in the Bible, while the second reflects on cities as potential places for spiritual and personal growth.)

Lane, Belden C. (1998) "Connecting Spirituality and the Environment," in *The Solace of Fierce Landscapes: Exploring Desert and Mountain Spirituality*, Oxford: Oxford University Press, 9–21.

Louth, Andrew (2003) "The Desert in the Bible," in *The Wilderness of God*, London: Darton, Longman and Todd.

Paden, William E. (1992) "As Society, So Religion," in *Interpreting the Sacred: Ways of Viewing Religion*, Boston, MA: Beacon Press, 28–47.

Resseguie, James (2004) "Topography: The Landscape of Spiritual Growth," in *Spiritual Landscape: Images of the Spiritual Life in the Gospel of Luke*, Peabody, MA: Hendrickson Publishers, 9–27. (In this chapter, river, desert, lake, and mountain are reflected upon as potent places for spiritual growth.)

Roof, Wade C. (2003) "Religion and Spirituality: Toward an Integrated Analysis," in *Handbook of the Sociology of Religion*, Cambridge: Cambridge University Press, 137–148.

Seasoltz, Kevin R. (2005) "Culture: The Context for Theology, Liturgy, and Sacred Architecture and Art," in *A Sense of the Sacred: Theological Foundations of Christian Architecture and Art*, New York: Continuum, 1–34. (Presents a summary of different cultural periods and contexts: for example, Native American Culture, Hispanic American Culture, and Postmodern Culture.)

Sheldrake, Philip (2001) "Place in Christian Tradition," in *Spaces for the Sacred: Place, Memory and Identity*, Baltimore, MD: Johns Hopkins University Press, 33–63.

Tillich, Paul (1987) "Behold, I Am Doing a New Thing," in *The Essential Tillich: An Anthology of the Writings of Paul Tillich*, edited with a Preface by F. Forrester Church, New York: Macmillan, 271–281.

References to research topics from this chapter

Anson, Peter F. (1973) *The Call of the Desert: The Solitary Life in the Christian Church*, London: SPCK. (Recounts the stories of the kinds of Christian communities that developed in the desert spaces and were intimately shaped by them.)

Baum, Gregory (2006) *Religion and Alienation: A Theological Reading of Sociology*, Ottawa: Novalis Press.

Bibby, Reginald W. (1987) *Fragmented Gods: The Poverty and Potential of Religion in Canada*, Toronto, ON: Irwin Publishing.

—— (2004) *Restless Churches: How Canada's Churches Can Contribute to the Emerging Religious Renaissance*, Ottawa, ON: Novalis Press.

Borgmann, Albert (1992) *Crossing the Postmodern Divide*, Chicago: University of Chicago Press. (Reflection on postmodernism in relationship to cities and citylife.)

Cohn, Robert L. (1981) *The Shape of Sacred Space: Four Biblical Studies* [AAR Studies in Religion 23], Chico, CA: Scholars Press.

Dillon, Michele, ed. (2003) *Handbook of the Sociology of Religion*, Cambridge: Cambridge University Press. (See the Bibliography for many helpful examples of sociological studies of religion and spirituality that could be useful for research in Christian spirituality.)

Dupré, Louis (1998) "Spiritual Life in a Secular Age," in *Religious Mystery and Rational Reflection: Excursions in the Phenomenology and Philosophy of Religion*, Grand Rapids, MI: William B. Eerdmans Publishing Co., 131–143.

Fuller, Robert C. (2001) *Spiritual, But Not Religious: Understanding Unchurched America*, Oxford: Oxford University Press.

Gannon, Thomas and George Traub (1969) *The Desert & the City: An Interpretation of the History of Christian Spirituality*, Chicago: Loyola University Press.

Geffré, Claude and Jean-Pierre Jossua, eds (1992) *Concilium 6*, London: SCM Press. (Thematic issue titled "The Debate on Modernity." Provides a helpful critique on modernity from philosophical, sociological, theological, and ecclesial perspectives.)

Griffin, David R., ed. (1988) *Spirituality and Society: Postmodern Visions*, New York: S.U.N.Y. (Deals with topics such as the following: postmodern vision of spirituality and social policy; postpatriarchal postmodernity; agriculture in a postmodern world; and science and technology in a postmodern world.)

Guardini, Romano (1979) *Sacred Signs*, Wilmington, DE: Michael Glazier.

Handy, Charles (1998) *The Hungry Spirit, Beyond Capitalism: A Quest for Purpose in the Modern World*, New York: Broadway Books.

Harvey, David (1989) *The Condition of Postmodernity: An Enquiry into the Origins of Cultural Change*, Baltimore, MD: Johns Hopkins University Press.

Haworth, Lawrence (1963) *The Good City*, Bloomington, IN: Indiana University Press. (Reflection on the way cities can enhance human life and community.)

Inge, John (2003) *A Christian Theology of Place*, Aldershot: Ashgate. (Thorough presentation of history of place in Western thought, scriptures, sacraments, pilgrimages, and holy places.)

Jackson, Kenneth T. (1985) *Crabgrass Frontier: The Suburbanization of the United States*, New York: Oxford University Press. (Historical reflection on the development of city sprawl.)

Jacobs, Jane (1961) *The Death and Life of Great American Cities*, New York: Vintage Books.

Kemmis, Daniel (1995) *The Good City and the Good Life: Renewing the Sense of Community*, Boston: Houghton Mifflin.

Kunstler, James Howard (1993) *The Geography of Nowhere: The Rise and Decline of America's Man-Made Landscape*, New York: Simon & Schuster.

—— (1998) *Home from Nowhere: Remaking Our Everyday World for the 21st Century*, New York: Simon & Schuster.

Lane, Belden C. (1988) *Landscapes of the Sacred: Geography and Narrative in American Spirituality*, New York: Paulist Press. (See the extensive bibliography in the notes covering all aspects of space and place, such as architectural design, liturgical space planning, and cultural geography.)

—— (1998) *The Solace of Fierce Landscapes: Exploring Desert and Mountain Spirituality*, Oxford: Oxford University Press.

Lilburne, Geoffrey R. (1989) *A Sense of Place: A Christian Theology of the Land*, Nashville, TN: Abingdon Press.

Lyotard, Jean-François (1993) *The Postmodern Condition*, trs. G. Bennington and B. Massumi, Minneapolis: University of Minnesota Press.

McGinn, Bernard (1994) "Ocean and Desert as Symbols of Mystical Absorption in the Christian Tradition," *The Journal of Religion* 74:2, 155–181.

Roof, Wade Clark (1999) *Spiritual Marketplace: Baby Boomers and the Remaking of American Religion*, Princeton, NJ: Princeton University Press.

Schama, Simon (1995) *Landscape and Memory*, New York: Alfred A. Knopf. (A study of the relationship between humans and nature through an examination of the myths of environment. An extensive examination of American identity and American landscape.)

Sheldrake, Philip (1995) *Living Between Worlds: Place and Journey in Celtic Spirituality*, London: Darton, Longman and Todd.

—— (2001) *Spaces for the Sacred: Place, Memory, and Identity*, Baltimore, MD: Johns Hopkins University Press.

—— (2002) "Cities and Human Community: Spirituality and Urban Living," *Theoforum* 33:3, 291–309.

Soja, Edward W. (2003) *Postmodern Geographies: The Reassertion of Space in Critical Social Theory*, London: Verso. (A reflection on how the uses and concepts of space affect social thought and theory. Soja's analysis reinserts the human element back into postmodern spaces that have become devoid of the same.)

Tillich, Paul (1988) *The Spiritual Situation in Our Technical Society*, edited and introduced by J. Mark Thomas, Macon, GA: Mercer.

Whyte, William (1968) *The Last Landscape*, Garden City, NY: Doubleday. (Reflects an excellent understanding of how cities function and the importance of the meaning of a city's history in city planning and revitalization.)

Wuthnow, Robert (1988) *The Restructuring of American Religion: Society and Faith Since World War II*, Princeton, NJ: Princeton University Press.

—— (1998) *After Heaven: Spirituality in America Since the 1950s*, Princeton, NJ: Princeton University Press.

Wuthnow, Robert and John Evans, eds (2001) *The Quiet Hand of God: The Public Role of Mainline Protestants*, Berkeley: University of California Press.

Wuthnow, Robert and Glen Mellinger (1978) "The Religiosity of College Students: Stability and Change over Years at University," *Journal for the Scientific Study of Religion* 17, 159–164.

Wyschograd, Edith (1990) *Saints and Postmodernism: Revisioning Moral Philosophy*, Chicago: University of Chicago Press.

NOTES

1   These events from the life of Francis of Assisi are summarized from Bernard McGinn (1998) *The Flowering of Mysticism: Men and Women in the New Mysticism, 1200–1350*, New York: Crossroad Publishing Company, 42–46.

2   For an intriguing description of Celtic spirituality that studies the questions of place in detail, see the following: Philip Sheldrake (1995) *Living Between Worlds: Place and Journey in Celtic Spirituality*, London: Darton, Longman and Todd.

3   The scientific method attempted to gather clear and precise knowledge about everything, including the workings of nature. Those objects that did not lend themselves to scientific investigation and thus accurate descriptive accounts, such as God, or God's presence in the world, were dismissed as irrelevant to the serious business of life.

4   This movement came to be known as the Enlightenment – that is, humanity became more preoccupied with the human mind and reason as the sole source of knowledge. With this "discovery" came the confidence to make decisions and chart courses of action based solely on the power of rational thought, known as inductive reasoning. See the section in this chapter on Modernism and Postmodernism for further details on the Enlightenment.

5   For a historical presentation of the development of this "dismissal" and the subsequent "retrieval" of God present in the world and in ordinary human experience see Nicholas Lash (1990) *Easter in Ordinary: Reflections on Human Experience and the Knowledge of God*, Notre Dame, IN: University of Notre Dame Press. This text depends largely on the categories of theology and philosophy for its analysis.

6   One of the first persons to set out into the desert and develop a spirituality generated from that context was an Egyptian peasant called Antony. He eventually became known as Antony the Great (c.295–373). Collections of the sayings of some of those who lived in the desert during the fourth and

fifth centuries are readily available. One of the most widely known is: (1975) *The Sayings of the Desert Fathers*, tr. Benedicta Ward, Oxford: Alden Press.

7   James L. Resseguie, (2003) in *Spiritual Landscape: Images of the Spiritual Life in the Gospel of Luke,* uses the physical, social, and economic landscapes found in Luke's Gospel in order to bring new insights to the journey of spiritual growth. The construction of *authentic place* through a consideration of the themes of journey, family life, meals, and clothing, among others, helps us appreciate how *place* expresses and shapes our spiritual values and commitments.

8   The Shakers and Puritans, along with Aboriginal people in North America, are examples of groups that carefully discerned the presence of God in the midst of everyday life in the landscape that surrounded them. For further details on how the Shakers and Puritans discerned God's presence in landscape and geography see Belden Lane (1988) "The Puritan Reading of the New England Landscape" and "The Correspondance of Spiritual and Material Worlds in Shaker Spirituality," in *Landscapes of the Sacred: Geography and Narrative in American Spirituality*, New York: Paulist Press, 103–124; 132–151.

9   Andrew Louth provides an excellent description of how the desert is portrayed in the Bible and how the desert context shapes such things as prayer, self-awareness, and awareness of God in the world. See (2003) *The Wilderness of God*, London: Darton, Longman and Todd, for a description of desert spirituality in general, as well as a description of desert-like situations (monasteries and various secluded dwelling places) that contributed to the development of specific spiritualities. See also Thomas Gannon and George Traub (1969) "Ideals of the Desert," in *The Desert & the City*, Chicago: Loyola University Press, 17–50.

10   Figures from Crispin Tickell in his "Introduction" to Richard Rogers (1997) *Cities for a Small Planet*, London: Faber & Faber, vii. Tickell also indicates that the demand for fresh water is currently doubling every twenty years – a fact that is alarming in itself and further indicates the need to take the development of cities and their requisite resources seriously.

11   For an extensive analysis of how church architecture shapes spiritualities, see Richard Kieckhefer (2004) *Theology in Stone: Church Architecture from Byzantium to Berkeley*, Oxford: Oxford University Press.

12   See Marc Augé (1997) "From Places to Non-Places," in *Non-Places: Intro-duction to an Anthropology of Supermodernity*, tr. by John Howe, London: Verso, 75–115.

13   Notwithstanding the shift that occurred in the movement from modernism to postmodernism with the events between 1900 and 1950 discussed later in this chapter, other more recent events such as those mentioned in this section increased even further the interest of sociologists in religions and spiritualities.

14   The sociologist Wade Clark Roof has done just such an analysis in (1999) *Spiritual Marketplace: Baby Boomers and the Remaking of American Religion*, Princeton: Princeton University Press. A summary of the findings is reported in Wade Clark Roof (2003) "Religion and Spirituality: Toward an Integrated Analysis," in *Handbook of the Sociology of Religion*, Cambridge: Cambridge University Press, 146–148. For example, Roof reports that roughly

59 per cent of the United States population identifies itself as being both "religious" and "spiritual."

15 Our brief, and necessarily simplified, reflection on the transition from modernism to postmodernism concerns spirituality in general, and Christian spirituality in particular. See recommended reading at the end of this chapter for further analysis of this very complex phenomenon in other areas such as those mentioned above.

16 Ross Thompson entertains what is at stake in joining back together science and religion in a postmodern spirituality. See his (1992) "Scientific and Religious Understanding: Towards a Post-modern Spirituality," *The Way*, 32:4, 258–267.

17 For a helpful critique (positives and negatives) of both modernism and postmodernism see Geffré and Jossua (1992) and Griffin (1988) in the bibliography at the end of this chapter.

18 This thesis, adopted in this section, is developed at length in Adam Possamai (2005) *Religion and Popular Culture: A Hyper-Real Testament*, Brussels: P.I.E.-Peter Lang.

19 Rahner ponders these ideas in Paul Imhof and Hubert Biallowons, eds (1986) *Karl Rahner in Dialogue: Conversations and Interviews 1965–1982*, New York, Crossroad, 342–345.

20 Paul Tillich (1886–1965), a Prussian philosopher and theologian, anticipated this same perspective when he wrote the following in 1948: "Our period has decided for a *secular* world. That was a great and much-needed decision. It threw a church from her throne, a church which had become a power of suppression and superstition. It gave consecration and holiness to our daily life and work." But Tillich also names the negative impact of this decision: the impact that postmodern spiritualities are striving to counterbalance. He continues in the same 1948 text: "Yet it [secularization] excluded those deep things for which religion stands: the feeling for the inexhaustible mystery of life, the grip of an ultimate meaning of existence, and the invincible power of an unconditional devotion. These things cannot be excluded. If we try to expel them in their divine images, they reemerge in daemonic images. Now, in the old age of our secular world, we have seen the most horrible manifestation of these daemonic images; we have looked more deeply into the mystery of evil than most generations before us." Paul Tillich (1987) *The Essential Tillich: An Anthology of the Writings of Paul Tillich*, ed. with a preface by F. Forrester Church, New York: Macmillan.

3

Questions of God

"The way you use the word 'God' does not show whom you mean – but, rather, what you mean."

Ludwig Wittgenstein, *Culture and Value*

"A merely infinite God is a pure abstraction, and a merely immanent force within the dynamic unfolding of reality is not God either."

George Schner, *Essays Catholic and Critical*

Introduction

IMAGES HAVE A HUGE IMPACT ON US. In a recent trip to China, I noted that advertising, theater, the arts, and public discourse are directed toward furthering the ideology of the state: that is, state control in all areas of life. The same public manifestation of ideology, albeit focused on consumerism and not state control directly, is evident in the Western world: on billboards and signs, and in advertising in general. Images are powerful tools that work to shape, or even control, our thoughts and actions in particular ways.

Images of God have a similar effect. How people view God influences their ideas about theology, Christian spirituality and faith life in general. After all, there is no one image or model of God that is "*the* model of God" in Christian spirituality or in theology. We all accentuate certain aspects of our understanding of God or of the Divine to the exclusion of others at different times in our lives. A person's understanding of God at ten years old is usually somewhat different when in his or her fifties. Furthermore, a person's understanding of God is shaped by deep unconscious, affective, and relational sources. Although this chapter does not delve into these more psychological understandings of how our models of God are actually shaped, it is important to recognize that our own histories do, in fact, affect and effect the way we view God and the nature of the Divine.

The main point here is the following: focusing on only one model of God at any point in life risks turning into idolatry what is clearly not intended as such. This is a serious issue, and thus warrants critical reflection on the models of God used in faith communities. In this chapter, we will use the terms *image* and *model* of God to refer to the same thing. The words people use to describe God, or characteristics of God as they are perceived, are really models or images of God, since God is beyond all human words. Images and models are made by humans: they are not God. Models of God are constructed to the best of human ability, but they can never exhaust humanity's understanding of God.

If we believe what the mystics (those who report having a personal, intense, and sustained experience of God – see Chapter 7) say about God, we understand that there is no one way to image God fully and describe who God is in Godself. The mystics realized that humans can know very little about God, and yet people tend to solidify God into clear ideas that subsequently dictate well-defined spiritualities that are thought to be valid for all time and all peoples. God cannot be known completely, since God is beyond all human understanding. All talk about God is indirect. In the end, the mystics describe God as "nothingness" or "without being." But they also talk about God with great positive affirmations, such as "pure light," "absolute joy," "rock," or "friend."

The mystics note the love of God embodied in Jesus. They refer to the "creator" and "redeemer." Thus, Christian spirituality refers to God in two complementary ways. One refers to the limits of language about God and is called the *apophatic* way; the other refers to the capacity to name and describe God (albeit incompletely) and is called the *kataphatic* way. These two traditions will be taken up more explicitly later in this chapter. What concerns us now is the effort to describe God with words, which we call models of God.

> The apophatic way of naming God refers to the God of no names who is beyond human understanding; the kataphatic way of naming God uses descriptive words to portray God as experienced in Jesus and through the Holy Spirit.

Names for God suggest models of God that generate insights into the God–human–world relationship. These models of God have a real impact on Christian spirituality, on both the communitarian and personal levels; they influence policy and practice and they inevitably help or hinder the Christian journey. This question or issue is a practical one, since we all have names for God, or describe God in particular ways as we have come to experience God – or, more likely, have been taught – in our lives. But not all ways are equal, and not all ways are helpful. The exaggerated dominance of one model of God may restrict the potential for the development of the relationship with God in a number of ways. The tendency to take models of God as literally true fails to acknowledge that all human naming of God falls far short of the reality. Rather, models of God need to be seen as the Christian communities' best guess at naming God based on ways of being in relationship to God. A critical examination of predominant models of God is therefore important in developing a clearer understanding of Christian spirituality.

Models of God

If we have settled on some favorite way of imaging God, we have likely overlooked a wide range of images and language that could enrich our understanding of God and our own lives. It is not just a question of what is said about God, but about how what is said affects the God–world–human relationship. Many Christians settle on naming God as "Father," "Son," and "Spirit." They take as their basic point of departure the naming of God as Trinity, which is the foundational image of God in Christian spirituality. This is not a bad thing. However, to stop there limits greatly the quality of relationship possible with God. For example, what about God as "Mother," "Shepherd," "Divine Healer," or "Light"? Each of the Trinitarian names can be broken open or expanded to enrich the understanding of relationships with God. Let us look briefly at how this might be possible.

There is no Christian spirituality without the Spirit – the Holy Spirit. God's Spirit, also referred to, among other names, as the Fire of Love, Sanctifier, and Breath of God, is what dwells within the human soul. The Holy Spirit moves people, for example, to love, to act justly, and to undertake heroic actions. Jesus is also spoken of as God's Son, as Redeemer, Savior, and Lamb. God is referred to as Father, Rock, Creator, or Ground. Thus, Christian spirituality involves a triune God, who is both one and three: *the* Trinity, in Christian theologies. But many different words are used to describe this Trinity and the individual persons of the Trinity. Biblical witness, as well as the witness of the developing tradition over the years, has offered a great number of ways of referring to God, or, in the language we are using here, models of God. In more contemporary usage, as well as in earlier Christian writings, we may find reference to God as Lover, Friend, Nursing Mother, or Homemaker. The words Christians use influence their relationship with God and the role God plays in their lives. For example, spiritualities will have different accents for those who see God primarily as Father/Creator, Mother/Nurturer, Jesus, or Spirit. Which person of the Trinity most easily related to will influence any one expression of Christian spirituality in profound and practical ways.

Practical importance of models of God

Our focus is not so much on the doctrinal nuances or dogmatic pronounce-ments about God, important as these are. Rather, we call attention to the impact that the practical, everyday thinking about God plays in constructing and shaping Christian spirituality from day to day. What an individual thinks about God – that is, the dominant models that most quickly come to mind concerning God – influences daily living. One's primary models of God have an enormous influence on such questions as how one views oneself, appreciation (or lack of it) for one's body, how he or she responds to questions of inclusivity and belonging, what style of prayer and worship is adopted, and the role the scriptures play in one's life. All these issues have an explicit or implicit model of God that stands behind them and informs them. For example, if I image God predominantly as Judge who gives punishment when I have failed in some way, then I will feel judged and shameful in my prayer when I reflect on my sinfulness. However, if I image God as Reconciler who grants forgiveness, then I will feel hopeful that I can be reconciled with God in my prayer and find the strength to carry on in a new way. An individual may not even be aware of what model of God is driving a particular action, belief, or feeling. But it will be present if he or she takes the time to think about it.

The God question is important since not only do people shape their actions according to their God models, but they also shape their understanding of themselves. What people believe about God shapes and determines who they understand themselves to be before each other and before God. The way they think about God influences how they think about the human. The opposite is also true. How they imagine the human also shapes their images of God.

Genesis 1:26–27 reminds us that God created human beings in God's own image. Humans also tend to create God in their own image: that is, people build their images of God in accordance with human qualities judged to be the best or the highest. For example, God is named to be Good, Intelligent, or Generous, with the understanding that God is the perfection of all these human qualities. There is a reciprocal relationship between who people understand themselves to be and who they understand God to be in their lives. God is not merely some being out in the middle of nowhere waiting to be discovered and described in a scientific way once and for all. We have clues that assist us in describing God, our relationship to God, and ultimately who we are before God, but the ineffable (unknowable) nature of God does not allow human beings to know definitively the absolute answer to all these questions. Human beings therefore live with models, images, that are instructive but not absolute in coming to know God in human life. It is natural that the models of God created reflect the human understanding of people and the nature of the most profound and intimate human relationships.

If this issue is taken seriously, we come to understand how better to live Christian spirituality freely in modern-day society. Rather than getting caught up in a particular way to view God, there is an openness to the ongoing development of the understanding of God according to the various resources currently available. It is easier to accept that various cultures or historical situations emphasize one aspect of God, sometimes to the exclusion of others. Or, at differing stages in life, individuals or communities may name God differently, according to current needs. For example, when an individual needs reconciliation and forgiveness, he or she may image God as "Forgiver" or "Giver of Peace." In times of celebration and exultation the name for God may be "Joy" or "Happiness." People are challenged to use images of God that speak to their times: images that are relevant to the people of their culture. A teenager may view an image of the Sacred Heart of Jesus and ask, "How can I relate to something like that – a long-haired, weepy-eyed Jesus pointing to a fleshy heart protruding from his chest?" Historically the image of the "Sacred Heart" had a profound meaning in Christian spirituality for many people and it continues to do so today. But we ought not expect this image to speak to people of all ages, personal interests, historical and cultural contexts, and denominational affiliations.

Openness to many models

Openness to a multiplicity of models may lead to a clash among models. But this is acceptable, since no one model of God is adequate. In fact, these models are based on human paradigms that are themselves limited. Furthermore, each model eludes control and precise definition. Jesus well understood this tension in the great variety of names he used for God. Each new naming of God by Jesus challenged his disciples' ways of thinking about God, and continues to challenge us in the twenty-first century. But models that once generated important insights for early Christian communities may no longer do so as the communities change over time, which may attest to the success of those models in helping the community grow.

For example, to talk of God as "King" and "Lord" may have been very important for first-century Christians in the context of oppressive Roman rule.[1] Kings protected their people with armies, provided for them in various ways, and remitted justice. Surely this image of a strong male protector would have been a consoling image of God for the early, persecuted Christian communities. But the image of King also points to other qualities: kings are removed from the common folk; they reside in inaccessible castles amidst wealth and luxury; and they are in absolute control. These latter attributes of God as King do not work well in North American or European cultures of the twenty-first century. Thus, the search for relevant and meaningful names for God needs to expand continually.

It was mentioned above that a multiplicity of models of God will inevitably lead to a clash. For example, the model of King clashes with the Suffering Servant model of God embodied in Jesus. But it was precisely this clash that gave such power to the Suffering Servant way of naming God – a new naming of God that stood in stark contrast to the previous names. However, it is the all-powerful nature of the King model that has been frequently emphasized in the Christian traditions. At times Christians have emphasized the King model to the near exclusion of the Suffering Servant one. Perhaps people feel protected and secure with such a King God; the Suffering Servant model might make people feel exposed and vulnerable. To embrace the Suffering Servant model fully means that the King would have to leave his throne, perhaps permanently.

Whatever the case the clash of these two models leads us to examine critically which images of God have truth value for people today. The truth value of each model of God is measured by its usefulness to speak to significant issues in people's lives. It is not the King God model in itself that is harmful, or even the focus on maleness, it is the limitation of the God–world–human relationship imposed by the King God model that is destructive. The King God model, often taken in its literal sense, is so powerful that there is little room left to image God in alternate ways. A wide range of God images act as a corrective to prevent this narrow viewpoint. Models need to clash with each other to break each other apart and make way for new and creative namings of God.

Models of God reveal a philosophy of life

Images and models of God also incorporate within them a philosophy of life, or a world view. Since the relationship with God is a pivotal and defining relationship in people's lives, a particular model of God reflects the way of being in the world and a particular view of the world. Do I view God primarily as "Judge" and "Prosecutor"? If so, chances are I tend to be judgmental and blaming, since this is how I imitate God. If I view God as the possessor of immense power, then God becomes an authoritarian figure in my life to whom I plead to get things done the way I want. If I view God as distant and not really engaged in the grittiness of everyday life, I will likely view my daily activities as disconnected from my faith life; my faith life will focus on "the other world" where God resides. In this image of God, the material world becomes irrelevant and spiritual activities are removed from everyday life.

Everyone has either explicit or implicit images of God that underlie the way they live their life. No one image is completely accurate, nor is any list complete. People need to trust in their personal experience of God; from that experience words come forth to name that reality. These words are the images of God. These words may need to change from time to time, accurate as they may be when first discovered. God is beyond human capacity to comprehensively image in any one period of time, in any one culture, in any one community of believers, or in any one life. But it is crucial to be aware of the images of God out of which we work, live, pray, hope, and love. In short, images of God profoundly shape Christian spiritualities. In his work on the relationship between language, thought, and action, the French philosopher Paul Ricoeur (1913–2005) convincingly argues that how we name something *becomes what it is for us*. For this reason we cannot take for granted God images. Being open to critiquing God images both positively and negatively is at the foundation of Christian spiritualities. This exercise, practiced throughout life, will go a long way toward helping embody ever more fully the God that eludes all human understanding and *all* human words.

Whether we realize it or not, models or images of God are found not only in faith-based understandings of who God is; they also surround us in popular culture. They abound in art, films, news documentaries, novels, marketing, the business world, advertising, and in just about any other imaginable encounter with popular culture. At times, these models or images may be used in playful ways, harking back to traditional values. For example, the use of images of God sitting in judgment on a throne, angels with wings, clerics in collars, and nuns in full habit have frequently been used in humorous settings to draw attention and thus sell products.

But these images can exploit popular understandings of God in order to co-opt people into a consumer culture. These models of God ultimately reflect a particular way of looking at the world and the way people interact with each other. But far from being neutral, the models are tied to hoped-for outcomes, whether that be the sale of a product or advancing an agenda in a particular religious, political, or social milieu. The media often abuse images of God since it *uses* those images (and *people* along with them) that best suit its own aims – rather than use them to foster relationships with God and with each other. The media use models of God to tie people into various spiritual feelings in order to sell a product or persuade people of an opinion. Models of God used in all areas of life are ultimately practical, since they are tied to larger issues of life and love, whether they explicitly acknowledge this to be the case or not. We need to be aware of whether models of God assist us, or not, to develop a positive attitude to God, between people, and the world. Further examples can help us understand how this is true.

Models of God as a careless despot emerged out of events in the Second World War concentration camps. Who wants to be involved with a God who betrays and plays with human history and lets terrible things happen? Models of God that present God as "up there" somewhere reveal an understanding of God as a distant and other-worldly being not connected to this world. Since God doesn't care, you need to control your own life and live independently from God. Models of God in flowing robes and long white beard sitting on a throne as a judge, or God as an old man holding a ledger to tally people's rights and wrongs, lead to fear that God will punish if people don't behave in a certain way. Nobody wants much to do with a condemning tyrant. In popular society, Jesus is still sometimes viewed as a static lifeless man who didn't laugh or enjoy life, who didn't mix with women or embrace his sexuality, who didn't challenge the structures of power and inequality of his day. These images of God do not empower people today to be responsible stewards of the life given by God. On the contrary, they excuse people from making any real commitment to current social and political issues, since God doesn't seem to bother, either.

Which models of God?

If we say that not all models of God are helpful to spiritualities in the same way, how are we to test the truth claims of the various models? How can we determine which models are more helpful than others? Which models of God should be emphasized and which ones should be downplayed for a particular time and context in history? In particular, which ones are most appropriate *for current times*?

In her insightful book *Models of God*, Sallie McFague asks the following question: "What sort of divine love is suggested by each model?"[2] If the predominant characteristic of Divine love suggested by the model leans toward a condemning, judgmental, retributive kind of love, then there is good reason to ask if that model of God is suited for our times (or for any time at all). If Christians are to model their lives with one another based on their relationship with God, then they would not get very far in building Christian community following this model of Divine love. If the predominant characteristics of Divine love suggested by the model lean toward understanding, acceptance, radical inclusivity, and reconciling forgiveness – all values that Jesus lived in his God–human–world relationships – then this second kind of model ought to be favored. We need to ask whether each model of God is consistent with the life of the Jesus of the scriptures as interpreted in the context of today's postmodern world. Even though today's world is markedly different from the world of Jesus, the followers of Jesus can bring forward his fundamental way of being in relationship to the world, others, and God.

What is helpful from McFague is that she attempts to get a picture of the relationship between God and the world from a *Christian* perspective that is reflected in each model. Buddhists will have a different understanding of the relationship, as will Muslims, Jews, and so on. Difference, however, does not imply that one view is better than another. Each faith tradition contains its own unique richness that embodies the Divine–human–world relationship.

Sallie McFague divides the ways of modeling God into three categories: 1) natural non-personalist (Rock, Water, Breath); 2) personalist (Friend, Lover, Mother); 3) philosophical (Being-itself; ground of Being; Substance). She argues for a greater emphasis on developing personalist models of God, since it is exactly in this arena that people experience God's saving activity.

The expression and embodiment of Christian love in everyday life is at the core of the test for the authenticity and usefulness of any one model of the Christian God. McFague readily admits that models of God useful in one era may not be the most useful in another. Christians need to discern carefully what is appropriate for any one time. Thus, again, critical thoughtfulness is necessary in order to choose models of God that are apt for a particular time and that profoundly reflect Divine love in the concrete circumstances of life.

It is helpful to know what a particular model of God reflects in terms of the values and vision that Jesus brought forth in his own life. Models of God are not built out of nothing; they are not pure abstraction formed from the exercise of logic. It is the life of Jesus that provides the framework for a test of the truth for the various ways of reflecting on God. Thus the following question becomes crucial: How do the ways Jesus lived his life before God, others, and the world apply to the lived reality of Christian spiritualities today? We need to recognize that the models of God that have become predominant in Christian spiritualities in the past are constructed in response to this question. These models are carefully crafted pictures of

God based on a particular interpretation or emphasis from scripture or Christian traditions that reflect particular needs in particular historical times. It is unfortunate that some models of God have been neglected, while others have enjoyed almost exclusive dominance. Thus, the primary question is not the question of which models are true and which ones are false, but rather which ones best reflect and support the truthfulness of the developing Christian spiritualities in current times. Again, this leads to the question of which models of God best reflect the Divine–human–world relationship as lived by Jesus.

Some people may be challenged to shift their model of God from one of dominance and power (a more traditional patriarchal model) to that of a nurturing and co-responsible God (for example, more attuned to postmodern sensitivities that take seriously caring for the earth and promoting radical equality of all people). Brian Wren, a minister in the United Reformed Church in the United Kingdom, has worked extensively on the shift needed from understanding the power of God as dominating to an understanding of the power of God as enabling. In his engaging book *What Language Shall I Borrow?* Wren struggles with the question of God-talk on a very practical level.

The model of a God integrally involved with this world rather than distant and separate from it (a God who ultimately *rules* the world, *controls* it, and single-handedly *saves* it) can lead people to be actively co-responsible for this world with God. The idea of co-responsibility involves the shared task of bringing forth all that is best for this world. In this model people can no longer blame a distant landlord for the world's problems; rather, people understand that their role is integral to the work of justice, peace, shared resources, ecological issues, and, in general, the care of the planet in all of its dimensions.

The individual who understands that all models of God are essentially symbolic, and not literal (as religious fundamentalism would claim), is much more able to deal with the shifting models of God that reflect the religious sensitivities of our own times.

Evolving models of God and cosmology

Numerous cultures in various periods of time throughout history have envisioned reality in different ways. This is to say that each culture operates out of its own vision of the universe, which is referred to as its *cosmology*. Cosmologies reflect the relationships among various elements in the cosmos: matter, nature, earth, planets, sun, stars, heaven (the afterworld), and hell (the underworld; hades).³ Cosmologies are at the foundation of a particular culture's world view. They shape and inform questions about self-understanding, dwelling place of the gods and goddesses, and practical living in all areas of life. For example, temples in many ancient cosmologies were considered to be the meeting place of the three cosmic regions: heaven, earth, and hell, each stacked one atop the other. Passage from one cosmic level to the other was possible through the earthly temple – the cosmic center of the world. Thus, temples were considered to be endowed with a kind of cosmic energy, or holiness, due to this special function allowing passage from one level to the other. To be in the temple was to be at the center of the universe – a powerful place, indeed!

Christian spiritualities have also operated within particular cosmologies. To a large extent, these cosmologies were informed by early philosophers rather than the scriptural witness. But, as we will see, as science became more and more developed, the earlier cosmologies were abandoned for one that reflected more accurately the actual nature of the cosmos.

Shifts in Christian cosmology – the place of the Planet Earth

Until the discovery by the Polish astronomer Nicolaus Copernicus (1473–1543) that the planets rotated around the sun, it was a generally accepted principle that the planets rotated around a *stationary earth* and that human beings lived at the center of the universe. The celestial stars, it was believed, lay beyond the planets and did not move. This cosmology implied a certain hierarchy of the place of humans in relationship to the rest of the created world; humans were at the center of the world not only with respect to location, but also with respect to importance. The natural world took second place to the primary importance of people who lived *in* this world but separate from it. However, even given this hierarchical relationship, Christian culture enjoyed a certain organic relationship with the cosmos, and with nature. There was a certain interdependence between the natural world and humanity. In addition, there was a humility in the face of a nature that disrupted humanity through violent storms, long periods of drought, or pestilent scourges. Such events fostered a model of God that saw God as punishing people for wrongdoing.

Thus, Christianity's earliest cosmology provided the backdrop for spiritual answers to the questions of life and God's place in the world. So dear to Christianity was the earlier cosmology that the Italian physicist and astronomer Galileo Galilei (1564–1642), in partnership with the German astronomer Johannes Kepler (1571–1630), was viciously condemned for upholding Copernicus's discovery (that the sun, not the earth, is at the center of our universe) in the sixteenth century. The point here is that how people see the universe in relationship to the human and to God influences people's self-understanding and the qualities and characteristics of God out of which they shape their Christian spiritualities. Furthermore, how people view matter in relationship to spirit, how concepts such as heaven and hell are understood, and the relationship between nature and humankind is appreciated, all stand in the background and subsequently shape how people practice Christian spiritualities.

The late medieval Church that condemned Galileo in 1633 realized that cosmologies shape belief systems. The Church, in condemning Galileo, was not about to risk a "false" model of the universe that would undermine all the current understandings about the place of human beings in the world, their consequent spiritualities, and God's relationship to that world (an almost magical presence), which had been so carefully constructed and upheld since the second century. However, not all of Galileo's contributions were helpful. Galileo's quest to interpret the world from a strictly quantitative perspective (the description of the world in terms of numeric measurements) led thinkers to dismiss the organic view of the world that held intact the interdependence of nature and humanity, among other things.

Subsequently, when Copernicus's discovery was confirmed by mathematician and physicist Isaac Newton (1643–1727) in 1687, a new cosmology held sway. Newton's proof that the sun is indeed orbited by the earth and the other planets, and that the stars are not stationary, set in motion an understanding of the natural sciences that has dominated the Western world ever since. Newton envisioned the universe as a large machine, each piece moving rhythmically in relationship to the other. But Newton's mechanical model of the universe distanced nature from human life. Human life was not seen to be an integral part of Newton's "machine." The organic, interdependent relationship of earlier times was lost. Nature existed to serve humanity, with no thought to the consequences that such an attitude might have. From such a utilitarian relationship, it was an easy step to human exploitation of the earth.

The first Industrial Revolution in Britain in the eighteenth century proceeded to launch its rape and pillage of the earth, and pollute air, sea, and land. Industrialization also required the consumption of vast quantities of water. Similar industrial revolutions followed in other countries – in France, Germany, and the United States in the middle of the nineteenth century; in Russia and Canada at the beginning of the twentieth century; and in Latin America, the Middle East, Asia, and Africa in the latter half of the twentieth century.

With all this industrial activity taking place on earth, God, understood as having little or nothing to do with care of the earth in the first place, was definitively banished to the distant halls of heaven. God was seen as somewhere "up there," far away from planet earth. Unfortunately, Christian spiritualities, to a large extent, did not concern themselves with reflection on the abuses recklessly launched in the various industrial revolutions. The earth was viewed as a machine at the service of humanity, as understood in the cosmology of Newtonian physics.

As a consequence, life with God was viewed as an interior movement within the privacy of one's own life, but with little consequence or concern for the outer world. Since God did not live in the outer world but in the privacy of the personal soul, the abuse of nature was seen as having little consequence for Christian spirituality. This attitude plays itself out in a disrespect for nature and a tendency to see the natural world as inanimate. Instead of seeing persons and the natural world in an organic relationship of interdependence, it is easy to slip into hierarchical relationships that ultimately risk valuing one to the near exclusion of the other.

However, there were exceptions to the tendency to exclude God from the workings of the world. For example, the English poet William Blake (1757–1827) reflected a kinder relationship to the earth and to humanity in his so-called Prophetic Books. This series of lengthy poems reflected social concerns and condemned eighteenth-century political and social tyranny. In his poetry, Blake stressed the triumph of the human spirit over reason, thus developing a profound Christian spirituality in reaction to industrialization.[4]

Thus, we see how the model of God out of which Christianity shaped its spiritualities in the past few hundred years was informed by a particular cosmology as well as a particular model of the human. It was in the human soul that the encounter with God took place. God was not seen as reflected in nature, or as a part of nature, or encountered in nature. Nor was God encountered in the human body. Humans who interacted with God via the interiority of the movements of the soul such as prayer, remorse, reconciliation, and feelings of piety, rather than through nature or the body were free to exploit nature (and the human body) with little fear of interference from Christian circles.

If we accept that various models of God reflect the historical, cultural, and political times within which they are developed and used, we need to acknowledge that spiritualities are profoundly affected by the same historical, cultural, and political influences. In a postmodern world groups and people no longer operate out of the same cosmology, narratives, and world view that have guided Western thought for the past 300 years or so (the period of modernity). This is not entirely a bad thing. A world view based on a radical split between nature and the Divine, and between soul and body, has caused people to denigrate the earth as well as their bodies. The postmodern world is increasingly sensitive to the intrinsic relationship between nature and the Divine, and is taking ever more seriously a holistic appreciation of the human body. In developing Christian spiritualities, people need to be constantly aware of shifts in models of God and their concomitant cosmologies in order to create relevant spiritualities for current times.

God in a postmodern world

Given various developments in cosmologies, what would a God of the postmodern world look like? Where would this God reside – that is, what dwelling place would be assigned to God in a postmodern cosmology? If the God of modernity reflects a dominant, male, all-controlling King God who lives "up there" somewhere, would a God of postmodernity reflect other sensibilities and be in relationship to the world and the cosmos in a different way? Built into the idea of God as King is the understanding of a Sovereign *Lord* who has absolute control over *his* realm. This model of God fits nicely into the Newtonian cosmology that envisioned a mechanical model of nature that was mostly predictable and that functioned according to well-defined rules. The King model of God thus was consistent with this past knowledge of the universe and the cosmology built as a result of that knowledge. However, if the dynamics of change, randomness, and chance are introduced into cosmology, as well as the human capacity to change the course of history, intervene in nature, and alter other fundamental aspects of human life (for example, through stem-cell research), it would be difficult to find a residing place for the King God who, ultimately, is in control of everything. To lose control would be to lose *his* Kingdom as a reigning *Lord*.

If we acknowledge that all the above-stated possibilities are within the realm of human agency, the King God *has* lost control, as we understand human control. Contemporary science now acknowledges the dynamics of randomness and chance operative in the universe. Advances in science have brought the world far along in the intervention and control of human life. These shifts have altered existent cosmologies and thus invite a challenge to re-evaluate current models of God and God's home in the universe. If the King God no longer has a kingdom under his absolute control, where does God preside? Where does God live?

These questions are a challenge to examine critically what has been taken for granted concerning the primary models of God operative in the Christian and secular culture in the West for many centuries. Subsequent critical reflection must therefore invite a shift in attitudes toward the way God is active in life, interacts with people, and calls forth Christians in various ways to be intimately involved with all facets of human life. Responsible stewardship of the earth is but one example of the way a shift in cosmology and God's place in the world has led to a shift in the Christian's self-understanding before God, others, and the world in general. In short, it has led to various changes in Christian spirituality that continue to be developed in many ways.

Only now are people rediscovering a more organic model of the universe that recognizes the interdependence of humans with the earth. Recent developments in science have re-evaluated the Newtonian model of the universe in favor of a more holistic appreciation of the one world that humans and nature share. This insight has championed a parallel rediscovery that God is alive in and through nature; it accepts as foundational the idea that Christian spiritualities are lived out in the dynamic interconnectedness of God–human–world. This shift has led to major revisions in the way Christian spiritualities are shaped in light of a cosmology that recognizes God as an integral part of the world of nature, and as a part of the earth. This recognition was not foreign to the cosmology of both the Jewish and Christian faiths, but it has been lost over the years, when the emphasis came to be on the radical separation of spirit and matter.

This latter division was more in tune with the ancient Greek cosmology that radically separated earth and heaven, or, more generally speaking, matter and spirit, to the point of disdaining matter and exulting spirit. Since Christianity took shape within the Greco-Roman world, Greek philosophy and its world view also shaped Christianity. The scriptural witness to the holistic unity of spirit and matter, heaven and earth, God and human, was almost entirely lost. Happily, the essential intimate relationship of these realities is being recovered in Christian spiritualities today.

For example, God's immanence in the world is the subject of much reflection in many contemporary Christian spiritualities. In Christian history, many prophets have attempted to remind us of this truth. Perhaps best known is the Italian friar and preacher Francis of Assisi. Francis communed with nature and recognized the intense presence of God reflected there. To this day, his followers uphold the sacredness of the earth as a reflection of the Divine presence. Pierre Teilhard de Chardin (1881–1955), a French geologist, philosopher, and theologian, held that evolution will culminate in the convergence of the material and spiritual dimensions of the world. The spirituality of both Francis of Assisi and Teilhard de Chardin rejects the opposition of the sacred and the profane, positing rather that all of life is imbued with the sacred. God is alive in all of creation, in humanity, and in social and political life.

The paradox thus surfaces: the supreme transcendence of God (understood as God radically different from the cosmos and human nature) shows itself through the overflowing presence of God in nature and the practicality of human love. In the practical restoration of justice, mercy, and love in the cosmos and people, God concretely appears. Transcendence in Christian spirituality is not to be ascribed to the physical location of God "living somewhere else" but rather to the eruption of something quite different (Divine Love) in the concrete situations of the here and now through human action. The transcendence of God is seen in human activity. People work to bring about a just world, to mitigate the debilitating situations and divisions that prevent people from fully embracing authentic Christian life.

Mahatma Gandhi (1869–1948), the great pacifist from India, recognized this truth in a negative way. He was known to have indicated that Christians truly believe only *half* the message of Christianity. That is, Gandhi thought that Christians easily believed that Jesus was truly God, but they had a harder time accepting that Jesus was also truly human. Gandhi is calling Christians to a spirituality that recognizes the reality of the Divine-human active in the world. Martin Luther King, Jr. (1929–1968), African-American activist who promoted civil rights, also recognized this fact in his struggle against the oppression of persons of color and their exclusion from mainstream social and political life in the United States. His social conviction boiled up from great reserves of moral force; his action was based on the spirituality of belief in the Incarnation. Martin Luther King, Jr. advocated the termination of segregation between whites and persons of color in order to create more authentic forms of inclusive community based on the equality of all. Like Jesus, both Gandhi and King were killed for their beliefs.

The apophatic and kataphatic ways

As we saw earlier, a central issue in Christian spirituality is the task of speaking adequately about God. All God-talk, all images or models of God that interpret the signs of God's presence in the world, cannot fully name or grasp the reality of the Divine-In-The-World. Even though people can speak truthfully of God, God is *never* to be equated with what can be said about God. Thus there is a certain "is" and "is-not" about God language. Even the greatest attribute we use to name God – God is Love – is not up to the task of getting at the reality of God. We say "God is Love," but this is based on the human experience of love, of God and others. We are thus led to the two distinct ways of talking about God that exist within the various Christian spiritualities: the apophatic way (affirming that we cannot know God) and the kataphatic way (affirming that we can speak of God). Let us now consider each of these ideas.

Apophatic spirituality

From the earliest days of Christianity, Christian spirituality has realized the impossibility of knowing God in Godself. Here are some examples of writers who emphasized the unknowability of God.

John Chrysostom (347–407) advanced this position in his treatise *On the Incomprehensibility of God*. A Spanish writer, John of the Cross (1542–1591), speaks of God as *nada* (nothing) in *The Ascent of Mount Carmel*. For John of the Cross, the created order is disproportionate with God; there is a radical difference between God and what God has created, and this gap prevents people from naming God. God is, therefore, *nothing* identifiable with human language or imagery. Dionysius the Pseudo-Areopagite affirmed the same position in the sixth century in his work *The Mystical Theology*. The anonymous English fourteenth-century writer of *The Cloud of Unknowing*, who was inspired largely by Dionysius, is one of the most influential apophatic writers in the history of Christian spirituality. The author of *The Cloud* emphasized that God lies beyond the cloud of darkness and can be known only through the movements of love. Below is an example of aphophatic writing taken from Dionysius. In this text from *The Mystical Theology*, Ch. IV, Dionysius is describing God as the "universal Cause" who is unknowable, but not impersonal or without understanding, in terms of any way human beings have of describing this Cause.[5]

> The universal Cause transcending all things is neither impersonal nor lifeless, nor irrational nor without understanding: in short, that It is not a material body, and therefore does not possess outward shape or intelligible form, or quality, or quantity, or solid weight; nor has It any local existence which can be perceived by sight or touch; nor has It the power of perceiving or being perceived; nor does It suffer any vexation or disorder through the disturbance of earthly passions, or any feebleness through the tyranny of material chances, or any want of light; nor any change, or decay, or division, or deprivation, or ebb and flow, or anything else which the senses can perceive. None of these things can be either identified with it or attributed unto It.

This emphasis on the realization that God is beyond human understanding, the apophatic approach to our understanding of the God–human–

world relationship, is also known as the *via negativa* (negative way). The apophatic approach stresses the limitation of what can be known directly or even indirectly about God. It recognizes that God is beyond all human knowing and all human language, even though there are attempts to name the experience of God in people's lives. Writers working from the perspective of the apophatic tradition have emphasized the absolute transcendence of God – that is, God transcends, or is beyond, the human capacity for knowing God.

Kataphatic spirituality

The kataphatic approach (also at times spelled with a "c" – cataphatic) focuses on the experience of God and the capacity to name that experience in the God–human–world relationship. Positive affirmations about God in word, symbol, image, and nature constitute the kataphatic approach in Christian spirituality. This is also known as the *via positiva* (positive way). The kataphatic approach to God-talk acknowledges the ability to positively name who God is for people. Although Dionysius's thought reflects the apophatic approach, his thought is also a remarkable example of the kataphatic approach. In *On the Divine Names*, Dionysius explores various names for God, such as Beautiful, Good, Life, Wisdom, and Eternal. Dionysius is concerned with describing how the unknowable God is made known in the beauty of creation through these various qualities. This is demonstrated in the following text from *On the Divine Names*.[6]

> We give the name of "Beautiful" to that which shares in the quality of beauty, and we give the name of "Beauty" to that common quality by which all beautiful things are beautiful. But the Super-Essential Beautiful is called "Beauty" because of that quality which It imparts to all things severally according to their nature, and because It is the Cause of the harmony and splendour in all things, flashing forth upon them all, like light, the beautifying communications of Its originating ray; and because It summons all things to *fare* unto Itself (from whence It hath the name of "Fairness"), and because It draws all things together in a state of mutual inter-penetration. And it is called "Beautiful" because It is All-Beautiful and more than Beautiful, and is eternally, unvaryingly, unchangeably Beautiful.

Julian of Norwich (1342–c.1423) is another writer who demonstrates the kataphatic way. She was an Englishwoman who experienced a series of visions revealing the goodness, generosity, and love of God. Julian's visionary experiences from around 1373 are recorded in her book *Revelations of Divine Love*. This book contains the naming of God as "Father" and "Mother." It describes God as the "true spouse" and the human soul as God's "beloved wife," and calls Jesus "Mother, brother, and savior." The kataphatic way, then, is an active attempt to plunge the depths of the experience of God using human language that is familiar. People's feelings, imaginative wanderings, and creative expressions in art and music can all contribute toward the kataphatic tradition in Christian spirituality.

Conclusion

These reflections have underlined the truth that images of God are not created out of nowhere: images surface from within human experience of the Divine. Models are also drawn from the traditions. Different elements are nurtured and emphasized in different times, contexts, and places. Models of God surface in response to specific needs – a particular aspect of God is emphasized because of the circumstances of the life now being lived. As these images come forth the Christian communities critically reflect on them, keeping in mind the Christian witness of those who have gone before, the scriptural witness, and the needs of the current times to hear the liberating word of God in a particular way.

The problem with traditional models of God is that they are often held to be absolute givens. As a result, it is exceedingly difficult to dislodge them from the predominant places they have assumed in liturgical prayer, hymns, sacred art, and, perhaps most significant, in the psychic formation of individuals and communities. Regrettably, this dynamic can block being open to new ways of imaging God, or recovering ways that have been lost or largely neglected in earlier traditions, that can nurture the relationship with God in creative and exciting new ways. The task is to interpret in fresh ways past traditions and carry forward from them what is needed as correctives for different times. For example, in discussions of the concept of salvation somebody might ask the following question: "What do we need to be saved from today?" Asking this question will cause us to reflect on the "saving power of God" and uncover images of God that are best suited to express this kind of salvation. Christian spiritualities are based on credible understandings of God in relationship to the real concerns and issues (positive and negative) of the world today. Fresh models of God will provoke fresh ways of acting and being in the world.

Thus, openness to new ways of modeling God to grow in relationship to this God, who is beyond all *image*-inings, is vital for renewal on both

Thought, belief, and action are all closely linked. This affirmation calls for an end to absolute models of God that, ultimately, stifle Christian spiritualities as organic, dynamic, and living responses to God's Spirit alive in the world. God's Creative Spirit continually calls the Christian communities to newness in the ways they live out their relationship with God, others, and the world in ever-changing times.

the personal and communitarian levels. The search for new models of God may even include a look beyond the Hebrew scriptures and the New Testament to find convincing models for different times and places. What doesn't change is the same fundamental issue: that is, the dynamic nature of the Divine–human relationship. Helpful models of God are those that point the Christian communities in the right direction in order for God's Self-revelation to take hold in their lives. This approach is fundamental to Christian spirituality: the nurturing of the breakthrough of God in reality, in people's lives. Such an approach calls for deep pockets of trust that God's Spirit is alive and active in the world.

It is important that the witness to God's presence in the world is acknowledged in earlier times, as well as in current realities. Sometimes the experience of God has been shaped into specific spiritualities. For example, the people of Latin America in the 1960s and 1970s began to become acutely aware of being oppressed by political and social structures that keep them poor and in servitude. In this context, and through their prayer and liturgical life, they began to experience the liberating Spirit of God. It is God who ultimately brings freedom from oppression. Latin American writers such as Gustavo Gutierrez began articulating this insight and shaped it into a spirituality of liberation relevant to the people of Latin America. Gutierrez's seminal work, *We Drink from Our Own Wells: The Spiritual Journey of a People*, published in 1984, recounts the story of the felt experience of God's liberating presence in the lives of the people of Latin America. As a result, one of the meaningful names for God in the Latin American context is Liberator.

Spiritualities interpret the saving love of God active in the world. In turn, these spiritualities name God. Relevance to the lived situation of people is what gives a model, image, or name of God authority in any one period of time, culture, or historical setting. New spiritualities arise because something doesn't fit anymore in our way of imagining God's relationship to the world and in the interpretation of the earliest accounts of Jesus in the New Testament and in subsequent expressions of Christian self-understanding.

Christian communities today are looking for inclusive, non-hierarchical ways of modeling God. Models that emphasize the distance of God from the world, or the domination of God, need to be left behind in order to foster models that suggest nurturing, supporting, and reciprocal relationships between God, humanity, and the cosmos.

Personal God images reflect God's activity in the world in a network of intimate relationships that Christians strive to live every day. Relationships between mother and child (Nursing Mother) or committed partners (Intimate Lover) speak powerfully about God's potent presence in the world. These models of God are directly linked to the experiential dimension of human life; we come to know God from within the experience of God in everyday life.

Christian spiritualities are thus not concerned directly with all the traditional dogmatic questions of systematic theology that may flow from a particular model. Rather, its models of God focus on the expression of the experience of God and the relationship God has struck with the world in all its dimensions. This is to say that in Christian spirituality, we are not preoccupied with an ordered system of models of God that do not risk clashing with each other. As mentioned above, the clash of models serves well to break open and balance the contributions to the expression of the God–human–world relationship that each model characterizes. In contrast to many Christian theologies that rationalize opposing perspectives or models into complementary ones, Christian spiritualities are called to allow the models to speak for themselves and at times clash with each other as they highlight some aspect of the God–human–world relationship. Inadequate images of God result in inadequate spiritualities – ones that do not, and cannot, respond to the challenges of life today.

At a practical as well as theoretical level, authentic Christian spiritualities stem from adequate and truthful images of God. Models of God that directly or indirectly undermine the truth of the Incarnation subtly undermine the capacity to be truly sensitive to the immanent God. Jesus modeled social involvement, not a privatized spirituality. He advocated action toward peace, reconciliation, freedom, and all expressions of justice. Furthermore, how the role of the Spirit is understood in the Trinity is crucial to Christian spiritualities. The Spirit provokes growth, change, conversion, truthfulness. In short, the Spirit moves people beyond complacency; it keeps the human spirit soft and malleable. A variety of models of God need to speak to these expressions of God's presence in the world. Various Christian spiritualities will highlight at times the work of one person of the Trinity and, to a lesser degree, the contribution of the others. And yet there is a need to continue to acknowledge God's commitment to the world through the Triune God. No one image is rich enough to capture the work of all three; no image is complete. Christians are called to bring to light a diversity of models open to interpreting the rich ways that God is alive in the world.

RECOMMENDED READING

Grenz, Stanley J. (1996) "The Postmodern Ethos," in *A Primer on Postmodernism*, Grand Rapids, MI: William B. Eerdmans Publishing Co., 11–38. (Provides an indication of the postmodern view reflected in such varying areas as architecture, pop culture, television, filmmaking, theater, and art.)

Howells, Edward (2005) "Apophatic Spirituality," in *The New Westminster Dictionary of Christian Spirituality*, Philip Sheldrake, ed., Louisville, KY: WJK Press, 117–119.

Leech, Kenneth (1981) "Believing in the Incarnation and Its Consequences," in *The Social God*, London: Sheldon Press, 25–38.

McFague, Sallie (1987) "A New Sensibility," in *Models of God: Theology for an Ecological, Nuclear Age*, Philadelphia: Fortress Press, 3–28. (Provides a good reflection on the power of language and why a new way of talking about God is needed during our time.)

Mollenkott, Virginia R. (1993) *The Divine Feminine: The Biblical Imagery of God as Female*, New York: Crossroad Publishing Company.

Mueller, Mary Louise (1977) "The Many Faces of God in the Hebrew Scriptures," *Spiritual Life* 23:4, 195–204.

Ruffing, Janet (2005) "Kataphatic Spirituality," in *The New Dictionary of Christian Spirituality*, 393–394.

Sheldrake, Philip (1987) "Prayer and Images of God," in *Images of Holiness: Explorations in Contemporary Spirituality*, London: Darton, Longman and Todd, 62–75.

References to research topics from this chapter

Cattin, Yves (1992) "The Metaphor of God," *Concilium* (1992/4), 57–73.

Grenz, Stanley J. (2001) *The Social God and the Relational Self: A Trinitarian Theology of the Imago Dei*, Louisville, KY: WJK Press.

Johnson, Elizabeth A. (1993) *She Who Is: The Mystery of God in Feminist Theological Discourse*, New York: Crossroad Publishing Company.

Lane, Belden (1988) *Landscapes of the Sacred: Geography and Narrative in American Spirituality*, New York: Paulist Press.

Lerner, Gerda (1986) *The Creation of Patriarchy*, Oxford: Oxford University Press.

Levinas, Emmanuel (1969) *Totality and Infinity: An Essay on Exteriority*, Pittsburgh: Duquesne Univeristy Press.

McFague, Sallie (1982) *Metaphorical Theology: Models of God in Religious Language*, Philadelphia: Fortress Press.

—— (1987) *Models of God: Theology for an Ecological, Nuclear Age*, Philadelphia: Fortress Press.

Marion, Jean-Luc (1991) *God Without Being*, Chicago: University of Chicago Press.

Mitchell, Donald W. (1991) *Spirituality and Emptiness: The Dynamics of Spiritual Life in Buddhism and Christianity*, Mahwah, NJ: Paulist Press.

Ricoeur, Paul (1977) "Study 7 / Metaphor and Reference" and "Study 8 / Metaphor and Philosophical Discourse," in *The Rule of Metaphor: Multidisciplinary Studies of the Creation of Meaning in Language*, Toronto: University of Toronto Press, 216–313.

Schner, George (2003) *Essays Catholic and Critical*, Philip Ziegler and Mark Husbands, eds, Aldershot, Hants: Ashgate, 76.

Sells, Michael (1994) *Mystical Languages of Unsaying*, Chicago: University of Chicago Press.

Slater, Peter (1981) "The Transcending Process and the Relocation of the Sacred," in *Transcendence and the Sacred* [Boston University Studies in Philosophy and Religion, volume 2], eds Alan M. Olson and Leroy S. Rouner, Notre Dame, IN: University of Notre Dame Press, 40–57.

Wittgenstein, Ludwig (1980) *Culture and Value*, G.H. von Wright, ed., and Peter Winch, tr., Chicago: University of Chicago Press, 2nd edition.

Wren, Brian (1990) *What Language Shall I Borrow? God-Talk in Worship: A Male Response to Feminist Theology*, New York: Crossroad Publishing Company.

NOTES

1   For further details see Brian Wren (1990) *What Language Shall I Borrow? God-Talk in Worship: A Male Response to Feminist Theology*, New York: Crossroad Publishing Company, 137–124, from where this example is taken.

2   Sallie McFague (1987) *Models of God: Theology for an Ecological Nuclear Age*, Philadelphia: Fortress Press, 92.

3   For example, an exposition of various elements of the cosmology of Aboriginal peoples in North America and how it affects their spirituality can be found in, Belden Lane (1988) "Seeking a Sacred Center: Places and Themes," in *Landscapes of the Sacred*, New York: Paulist Press, 45–65.

4   William Wordsworth (1770–1850), also an English poet, was another bright light of hope. As a youth he developed a keen love of nature – his poetry reflects the direct experience of the senses as they encountered the events of everyday life. The passion and zest for life was Wordsworth's inspiration. Wordsworth, along with Samuel Coleridge, published *Lyrical Ballads* in 1798. Samuel Coleridge, another English poet, is well known for his poem "The Rime of the Ancient Mariner," which was included in *Lyrical Ballads*. Blake, Wordsworth, and Coleridge rejected the popular controlled structure of English verse to create free-flowing poetry.

5   From Clarence Edwin Rolt (1920) *Dionysius the Areopagite: On the Divine Names and the Mystical Theology*, London: SPCK, 199.

6   From Rolt, *Dionysius the Areopagite*, 95.

4 Questions of Christian anthropology

"A significant aspect of the quest for meaning is the search within ourselves for answers. To find them, we must trust that the divine speaks to us through our intuition. And to do this we must recognize our own divinity, get to know our souls and learn how to nourish them."

Lucinda Vardey, *God in All Things*

"We did not have to ask to be created. God himself moved by the ardor of his love created us in his image and likeness in such dignity that the tongue cannot express, nor can the eye see, nor the heart imagine how great is the dignity of a person."

Catherine of Siena, *Le Lettere di S. Caterina da Siena*

Introduction

> Anthropology seeks to describe the essential characteristics of human beings and how those characteristics shape culture, beliefs, and practices. Anthropology thus responds to questions like "What is the nature of human being?"; "What constitutes human life?"; "Who are we as human beings in relationship to the world around us?"; and "How do human beings shape their world and the world of others in relationship to their beliefs?"

CHRISTIAN ANTHROPOLOGY has struggled with the above questions since the origins of Christianity, but modern anthropology as a secular academic discipline is a fairly recent development. Modern anthropological theory dates back only to the late 1800s. Britain's Edward Tylor (1832–1917) is considered the pioneering author in modern anthropological investigation. His research focused on religion in primitive cultures.

However, our interest here is not a general survey of anthropological theory, nor even a general survey of Christian anthropology in its various forms. Rather, our interest is focused on the insights that Christian thought contributes toward developing a Christian understanding of human nature: "What does it mean to be human from a *Christian* perspective?" Reflection on this question will provide the essential framework for a specifically Christian anthropology. Christian anthropology has an important contribution to make in today's rapidly changing world that is continually challenged to think in new ways about what constitutes basic human identity and life.

Given new insights provided by disciplines such as psychology, sociology, and even the natural sciences, the question of what constitutes the specific characteristics of human beings has taken on new significance. Let's look at a few examples of how advances in these fields of study are causing people today to examine critically the notion of what it means to be human.

Due to recent advances in medical science and engineering, the human person, with his or her natural physical attributes, is no longer a permanent given. Individuals can be molded, reshaped, and significantly altered through medical procedures. Cosmetic (plastic) surgery is a burgeoning industry in North America and Europe. But the human person has not only become plastic, it has become bionic. The increased use of mechanical devices, such as pacemakers, titanium hips, and artificial hearts contributes to a new perspective on how humanity is viewed. As the exchange of body parts (for example, livers, hearts, kidneys, and even faces) becomes more and more possible, and more controversial issues associated with stem-cell research arise (for example, growing human body parts on animals for human transplants), the notion of what it means to be a human being changes. This raises a number of significant questions. For example, "At what point might society eventually draw the line and no longer recognize some persons as *human beings*?"; "What constitutes the essential characteristics of being human?" and "How do these characteristics influence how individuals, groups, and societies shape the world?"

Reproductive technology also brings new perspectives on what constitutes the natural state of human life. The human body can be chosen man or woman through processes that separate male and female sperm. Furthermore, the increase in sperm banks all over the world allows people wanting to conceive the choice of physical body characteristics, intelligence, and other qualities exhibited by donors. Research in psychology on gender and transgender choices is also changing views on human life. Some individuals no longer recognize themselves as male or female according to their physical, biological makeup, but describe their gender according to deep-seated psychological orientations. This perspective is explored in Chapter 9 under the section "Gender." Some would challenge the presumption that there are only two genders – male or female – claiming that a continuum of genders lies between these two poles.[1]

Christian spirituality needs to pay close attention to all these issues. After all, Christian spirituality is generally described as a spirituality of the Incarnation because Jesus took on human flesh. How people view that flesh (understood as the whole human person, and not just the physical body), therefore, will influence how they view Christian spirituality and life today. There needs to be a critical reflection on how new perspectives on human beings are integrated into the Christian understanding of the human body, human nature, and Christian living in general. What we are speaking of here is a specifically Christian anthropology. What insights, from a Christian perspective, may be brought to respond to the question of the nature of human beings and human relationships? Christian anthropology is a challenge given the twenty-first-century developments mentioned above.

One of the most common ways Christians have defined what it means to be human relates to the creation story. As Genesis 1:26–27 suggests, human beings are created in the image of God. From this idea have come various reflections on Christian anthropology – on how Christians, with their particular beliefs and perspectives on the world, answer the questions of what it means to be human before the Divine. Christian anthropology, and anthropology in general, relate to Christian spirituality. The view of what it means to be human profoundly affects the way people are in relationship not only to God but, just as importantly, with each other and the world. How and why this is true is the subject of reflection in this chapter.

The *imago Dei*

Christian anthropology centers on the core belief that human beings and human life reflect the image of God. In Chapter 3 we saw that there are many ways to imagine God, to image God. So what does it mean for human beings to be created in the image of God, to be the *imago Dei* (as often expressed in Latin)?

The term *imago Dei* finds its origins in Old Testament anthropology and is further developed in the New Testament. Genesis 1:27 states it succinctly: "God created human beings in God's own image; in the image of God God created them; male and female God created them." The idea of *imago Dei* is also reflected in the New Testament: for example, 1 Cor. 11:7 and James 3:9. But *how* humanity reflects the image of God has been widely debated; no one way of understanding this concept has been accepted throughout the history of Christian spirituality or across the various Christian traditions. Nevertheless, how any one group of persons answers this question is of utmost importance for Christian spirituality, since how people understand themselves to be reflections of God's image will inform and shape their Christian identities and practices. Given the diversity of the ways *imago Dei* has been understood and lived out over the centuries, we ought not to be surprised at the diverse Christian spiritualities that have sprung up as a result.

Even though there is no solid agreement about how the *imago Dei* is understood, there are at least two distinct ways of looking at its meaning. Different writers emphasize one or the other, or perhaps borrow from both.

First, *imago Dei* could refer to certain characteristics that human persons possess that resemble the characteristics assigned to God. Rational thought and free will are frequently cited as two significant characteristics that reflect the *imago Dei* in personhood. This way of viewing the *imago Dei* was favored from the thirteenth century until the time of the German reformer and former Augustinian monk Martin Luther (1483–1546).

Luther favored a second approach to interpreting the *imago Dei* that refers to the relationship that human beings share uniquely with God. This approach focuses on the image of God reflected in the characteristics of this relationship. From this perspective the *imago Dei* is less about specific characteristics that humans possess and more about what people do, how they live out their lives together with God and with each other. The French theologian and reformer John Calvin (1509–1564) picked up Luther's idea and focused on the *imago Dei* as the mirroring of God's life that shines forth in righteous living. For Calvin, the *imago Dei* entails the actual living out of Divine life in the here and now, which constitutes the foundation of the Divine–human relationship.

Neither the first nor the second way of interpreting the *imago Dei* is the only interpretation, however. Søren Kierkegaard (1813–1855), a Danish religious philosopher, taught that the *imago Dei* was reflected in works of love accomplished within relationships between people, with God, and the cosmos. Kierkegaard believed that since God is love, the image of God can be reflected only in acts of love.

There is also the issue of the ambiguity with which the Christian traditions have interpreted the meaning of *imago Dei* with respect to the perceived differences between men and women. It is true that from the beginning, as we saw in Genesis 1:27, God created *both* men and women as *imago Dei*. However, due to gender dualism (for example, men perceived as being superior to women) that was widespread in the culture during the time of the birth of Christianity, men and women were not seen as true equals in Christianity either.

Furthermore, men were identified with the widely accepted superior qualities of mind, reason, and spirit, while women were identified with the inferior qualities of bodiliness, affectivity (feelings), and materiality. Because of the existent inequality attributed to men and women, it was only a short step to identify men with these qualities more closely resembling those belonging to God, while women were given secondary status. Some early Christian writers went so far as to identify women as the source of evil tendencies in human life in general. Thus, in Christianity, human nature has been seen as being embodied in two different and unequal ways.

The sub-discipline called *feminist anthropology* has worked hard in the last few decades to reverse the debilitating influence of dualisms in their many forms in Christianity. But, in practice, dualistic thinking is still very much alive. For example, some Christian churches (and secular workplaces, too) refuse to grant women the most senior positions of leadership or to ordain women for ministry in Christian communities. When these situations occur, it is implied that, in fact, men and women do not reflect equally *imago Dei*. However, this is simply not the case. Both men and women, equally, do reflect the *imago Dei* as we will develop our understanding of it in this chapter. Feminist anthropology is reflected in many writings on *feminism* and *feminist spirituality*. You can read more about both of these topics in Chapter 9 in the section on "Feminism."

Given the diversity of ways of understanding *imago Dei*, it is generally helpful to take a critical stance on how *imago Dei* is being presented (explicitly or not) in various Christian spiritualities. When reading about a particular Christian spirituality the following question may be asked: "Does this particular Christian spirituality reflect true equality of men and women on all levels?"

Given the range of meanings attributed to *imago Dei* across the centuries, it is helpful not to view the concept from too narrow a perspective. At a minimum, however, in Christian anthropology whatever attributes are brought forth as belonging to the *imago Dei* are held by both men and women as equals in God's creation.

In the following pages, we will examine various aspects of what it means to reflect the *imago Dei*. Ultimately, what characterizes the *imago Dei* in these pages are the ways in which the Christian community follows the teachings and practices of Jesus – not as singular individuals, but as a faith-filled community. The attempt to focus life on Jesus, together in community, is the inspiration for Christian spirituality and for how God's image is reflected equally in all human beings.

The nature of the self

The word *self* comes up frequently in everyday language. People talk about "self-respect," "myself," "self-determination," "self-help," "yourself," "him/herself," and so on. All of these expressions refer to the subject of investigation of anthropology: the human person. Thus, when we refer to "self" or "person" or "human being" in this book we are referring to the same thing. What is the nature of the self that people so often mention in everyday language and that we have been alluding to in this chapter? Let's take a more critical look at this term.

Philosophers, theologians, psychologists, and sociologists, among others, have struggled over the years with questions about the nature of the self. In a general way, the self is what makes "me" a distinct entity, different from "you." It is the cluster of identifiable characteristics, composed of all parts of an individual's being as a composite unity, that constitutes the individual as a personal "I." This perceived identity – or, perhaps better, this perceived self-awareness – is a fundamental human experience. When asked "Who are you?" the natural response is to begin a sentence with an identifiable "I" and attach to that "I" identifiable characteristics that reveal, at least in part, an individual person with personal beliefs, attitudes, and opinions, along with a personal history.

Identification of the self refers to a unique capacity of human beings, as different from other animals, to relate the past, present, and hoped-for future into a stable and predictable awareness of "who I am." The self therefore refers to the acknowledgment that human beings are unique, each with particular characteristics, but who also reflect a common humanity different from the animal world.

In Christian anthropology and Christian spirituality, questions of the self are brought forward not as an autonomous independent being, but as a self in relationship to others, the world, and God. A number of fundamental issues provide the foundation for reflection on these relationships and give an initial response to the question of the nature of the self. These will be described briefly to offer some understanding of human nature in general, and will act as a foundation for the Christian anthropology developed in the sections that follow.

Characteristics of the self

First, the self is understood as the whole human being. It is not exclusively the non-material expression of humanity, since it also includes the physical body. The self is understood to be a dynamic complex that evolves in its particular cultural, historical, political, and social contexts while engaging all levels of one's person: for example, feelings, desires, body, spirit, rational thought, and intuition. Even though people may talk about any one of these to the exclusion of the others, they all exist within a continuum that is the whole human being.

Second, the self is not a given, not a mere artifact to be discovered after earnest searching and exploration somewhere "within." This position causes us to reflect with some critical questioning on everyday expressions such as "I want to be my true self," or "I want to discover the inner me," or "I just want to be who I am called to be." The "true self," the "inner me," and "who I am called to be" all need to be reflected upon critically if we hold to the basic position that the self is essentially a construction in time and space. This does not mean that these everyday expressions do not have truth value, but people need to think carefully about what is meant when these expressions are used.

Thus the quest of discovering "my true self" is a fiction, inasmuch as we understand the "true self" to be some already composed and fully constituted self. The self is not hidden away in the deepest parts of the human body merely awaiting removal of the layers of debris that are piled upon it and that hide it from view. Rather, the self is continually being constructed and is susceptible to change. New experiences shape the self in new ways. The "true self" is more easily accepted as a metaphor of the self that is most compatible with the values held to be true by someone: either those already realized, or those being nurtured that are not yet fully integrated.[2]

Third, the reflection on the self takes as its point of departure that there is a self that can be known: that there is a stable and identifiable "I" that possesses learned beliefs, attitudes, and opinions that situate the individual in a personal existence. The ability to deal responsibly with the varied and often complex issues of life requires a fair degree of personal stability. In order to engage in critical reflection with others, an individual needs to be fairly certain of the solidity of his or her own values and how these values have critically shaped his or her opinions.

Fourth, beyond what can be known of the self as revealed through actions, attitudes, or decisions, other aspects of the self escape us: we can never be fully and completely present to ourselves. The *self shows itself* in different ways, such as what we do and the values out of which we live. However, what we have available to us concerning the self are really only *representations* of the self. We do not have direct access to the self and therefore cannot pin down once and for all a complete description of ourselves (or anybody else). Rather than seeing this point as a negative aspect of the self, we ought to see it as one of the self's greatest strengths: the self eludes absolute description; it remains flexible and malleable in the changing moments of life. The nature of the self is unstable; it remains open to the newness of life and allows change to occur.

And yet the self does have an identifiable center, as stated above. This center is understood as a locus of traits by which I and others know it is me. Yet this awareness of who I am, the self as agent within the context of one's own life, cannot be so solidly construed that it becomes once and for all completely identifiable and absolutely predictable. There is a certain mystery that permeates the identity of each and every human person. This mysterious nature of the self is referred to as the *transcendent* nature of the self, which we will examine in more detail in a following section.

Fifth, we are thus faced with the paradox of the self: it is both stable (we can identify an "I") and unstable (the "I" is open to change) within the changing realities of my life. An answer to the question "Who am I?" is linked to the evolving possibilities in my life. The answer to the question "Who am I?" is neither a mere résumé cobbled together from the past, nor an inventory of the present, but also includes the potentiality of the "I" in the future. Who I am now is linked to my future, inasmuch as my imagination connects me to potential new paths in my life based on current hopes, dreams, and desires.

Sixth, the notion of the self is culturally defined. In India, for example, the idea of the self is largely defined by a transpersonal awareness – that is, the self is defined by the matrix of relationships within which a person lives. This matrix of relationships includes other persons, nature, and the cosmos. This definition is in contrast, let's say, to the North American notion of the self, which tends to focus more on the self as a separate, private, and individual entity. Since there is a tendency to focus on the characteristics of the self as defined within the parameters of the self per se, the notion of the self as culturally defined deserves special attention and will be explored in more detail below.

In conclusion, so far, when we speak of the nature of the self we are referring to all these characteristics:

1. the self as the whole human being;
2. the true self as a work in progress;
3. the self as an identifiable and stable entity but who is open to growth and change;
4. the recognition that there is no direct access to the self;
5. the paradox of the self as both stable and unstable;
6. the self as culturally defined.

These characteristics of the nature of the self, although not uniquely Christian, are at the foundation of the Christian anthropology being developed in this chapter: human beings created in the image of God.

Of particular interest is the way the self is defined within its cultural matrix. Let's take a brief historical look at how the question of relationships has profoundly defined the nature of the self in the past. This will help us understand that the nature of the self is defined by its inherent characteristics, but it is also defined by its cultural relationships and the way society views human beings. With the dramatic cultural changes taking place today, as we saw in the opening pages of this chapter, sensitivity to cultural shifts as contributors toward our understanding of Christian anthropology, and thus Christian spirituality, are as important as the inherent characteristics of the self mentioned above.

The self as defined by culture: the pre-modern, modern, and postmodern self

Pre-modern self

During the pre-modern period – that is, until the seventeenth century – being a person in the West was largely defined by factors outside the individual. From the earliest Greek times until roughly the seventeenth century, an individual's place in the world was determined by his or her social role, financial status, and family situation. These spheres of influence, which people were born into, defined – to a great extent – who they were as individuals and their sense of personhood. Their personal identity, then, was defined first and foremost by the external communal dimension of life. Human agency (where one is able to act and have an influence) was predefined and permissible only according to the status one held in this world. People were not seen to be free and independent within their own intentions, hopes, dreams, and choices.

Modern self

In the seventeenth century, as the modern period began, a shift occurred in this notion of the person. This shift, to a large extent, was introduced by the French philosopher and mathematician René Descartes. Descartes is credited with the launch of the idea of the *modern self*. The modern self, understood as the private and independent self, began to receive greater recognition in Descartes' notion of what defined the human person. With freedom to exercise free will beyond the narrow lot of the life assigned to people through their social status, they were able to move beyond what was previously recognized as their fate.

With Descartes' recognition of the autonomy of the individual, with individual rights, freedoms, aspirations, and free agency, society moved away from its understanding of the self embedded in its communal moorings. The individual is hence seen with his or her *own* interiority, independent of the various external spheres of influence. Put briefly, Descartes' philosophy of the human person reflected the possibility of the self's presence to itself. His famous dictum "I think, therefore I am" captures the core of this new way of looking at the self.[3] During the modern period, thinking or rational thought was seen as the major characteristic of what it meant to be human, to the point that a person was popularly defined as a "rational animal" – a definition which dates back to the Greek philosopher Aristotle (384–322 B.C.E.).

Postmodern self

In the postmodern world, as we saw in Chapter 2, more and more people are working to look at the self in a more holistic way. That is, there is a greater awareness that persons are not "rational animals" exclusively, but are defined by their capacity for imagination, creativity, and feelings as well as for their capacity to think critically, analyze, and come to logical conclusions. Thus we see that the nature of the self may not have changed in itself over the centuries, but particular aspects of the nature of the self have been emphasized more or less in different time periods and cultural settings. What people perceive to be the reality, whether it be absolutely true or not, influences the way they think and act. Therefore, close attention to the cultural impact on our understanding of the self is in order. This is true for our current understanding of the self as well as the way people look at the past. What is at stake here?

Issues at stake: the changing notion of the self

The marked changes from the understanding of the pre-modern self to the modern self to the postmodern self cause us to question any tendency to apply the postmodern understanding of the self, with all its psychological, philosophical, and moral precision, to those who lived in earlier times. The problem is this: when people from the past are studied, their stories need to be appreciated from within their own self-understanding and their own cultural definition of selfhood. This was their reality; to interpret their experience from within a modern or postmodern view of the self would not do them justice. Researchers or readers in Christian spirituality need to keep this point in mind when undertaking, for example, biographical studies of spiritual authors who lived in times radically different from their own. Before attributing to people who lived in the past qualities such as free will, social belonging, and the role of the imagination, as understood from current perspectives, there needs to be a careful consideration of the definition of the self, of personhood, that shaped them during their own times.

One point appears to be clear regardless of what time period is being considered or who is being investigated when writing biography, personal or otherwise: the self is hard to pin down and cannot be adequately described. Whatever emphasis is put on the nature of the self, the self is a multi-faceted reality. Different aspects of the self come to the fore during various moments of an individual's life. Careful attention needs to be paid to this fact in writing about one's own life, as well as reading or writing about the lives of others.

But the recognition that the self first is a convoluted mix of body, spirit, feelings, desires, and so on, and, second, the emphasis on each aspect varies according to cultural and historical settings, does not prevent us from attempting to know as much about the self as possible. This is true both at the objective level of theory of the self as well as knowledge about the self at an individual and personal level. The development of self-knowledge has been recognized by many men and women as a fundamental prerequisite for spiritual and human growth. It is to this aspect of human and Christian anthropology that we now turn.

The nature of self-knowledge

From the inscription above the gates of the ancient Greek temple at Delphi, we receive the command: "Know thyself." This maxim, often iterated by the philosopher Socrates in the fifth century B.C.E., has been reflected in popular wisdom down through the ages. In Christian spirituality the same exhortation to be self-aware, to know who one is, and to be in touch with one's feelings, hopes, strengths, and weaknesses is underlined as important. Equally, Christians are advised to bring to consciousness their values, their personal histories, and their moments of grace as well as moments of despair. This exhortation to self-knowledge implies that to be aware of one's life history, the values that inform it, how one's life has affected other people, and so on, is a good thing. Why is this so?

Self-knowledge is linked to responsibility toward one's own life, others, and creation as a whole. Self-deception or self-ignorance makes people vulnerable to erroneous decision-making and misjudgment, since decisions are made out of a false sense of self. Therefore, a critical and honest reflection on one's life history, previous decision-making, and current attitudes and values contributes to greater self-consciousness. An increase in self-consciousness opens up the possibility for a longed-for intimacy with self, others, and God, since the only self an individual can bring before another to genuinely love is the self that is known – warts, wrinkles, and all! Intimacy and love are major goals of self-knowledge. Self-knowledge is also linked to the care of others. People who are self-deceived because of self-ignorance bear a greater risk of failing to respond appropriately to the needs of others. Not yet being aware of their own genuine needs, those who lack self-knowledge find it difficult to know the needs of others and then struggle to meet those needs in a healthy way.

The self and self-knowledge are linked inasmuch as the self is constructed through critical self-inquiry and self-evaluation during the range of experiences in life. The self is linked to self-knowledge in a dynamic interaction of discovery and insight that results in the reshaping of who an individual is currently and who he or she desires to be over an entire lifetime. With conscious awareness of how lives have been shaped in the past and are taking shape now, people can more truthfully and helpfully shape the future of their own lives as well as assist others in this task.

Teresa of Avila (1515–1582), a Spanish mystic and nun, often spoke to the other nuns in her charge about the need for self-knowledge. She taught that there was a close link between self-knowledge, personal humility, growth in generosity toward others, and general progress in the ways of the Lord. One of her books, *The Interior Castle*, describes growth and development in the spiritual life. She admonishes the reader to begin the spiritual journey with a critical look at one's self-knowledge: to begin with a certain humility and honesty about self-knowledge. Teresa possessed little formal training or theological education, but she was a practical woman who, from her own experience, learned how important self-knowledge was in the spiritual journey. Indeed, she viewed it as the starting point for spiritual growth:

> It is a shame and unfortunate that through our own fault we don't understand ourselves or know who we are. Wouldn't it show great ignorance, my daughters, if someone when asked who he was didn't know, and didn't know his father or mother or from what country he came? Well now, if this would be so extremely stupid, we are incomparably more so when we do not strive to know who we are, but limit ourselves to considering only roughly these bodies.[4]

But self-knowledge as indicated by the maxim above the temple gate at Delphi, and in the writings of Teresa of Avila, is a difficult ideal to attain. This is precisely because of the elusive nature of the self, which we have already discussed. Because the self cannot be fully identified and conceptualized, it is not possible to attain full self-transparency. However, this is not really the goal to begin with. The goal is to *strive* to overcome the tendency to be strangers to ourselves in order to assist us in our living. Self-knowledge helps people take a certain responsibility for their lives and the lives of others by consciously guiding personal actions and decision-making now and for the future. Self-knowledge allows people to be more objective as they are confronted with differing and potentially conflicting situations. Furthermore, greater self-knowledge more easily opens people up to the potential of transformation and conversion in life. If we know ourselves better, we will more easily be able to identify potential areas of growth and discover how to go about achieving that growth.

Careful attention to personal experiences through critical self-reflection, or careful listening to feedback from others, are important practices that nurture self-knowledge. As we will see in Chapter 8 on Spiritual Practice, there are many ways to enhance self-knowledge. Examples include journal keeping (the construction of the narrative or story of one's life) and spiritual direction (meeting regularly with another person to reflect on faith life). These practices can contribute significantly to self-knowledge, with all of its attached history, values, and consequences.

Self-knowledge does not merely involve introspection – the isolated self looking inward for insight – for it is inextricably linked to how others know one another in the crucial instances of life. Self-knowledge involves *response* to such fundamental human movements as love, guilt, shame, respect, and forgiveness, all of which are experienced in the context of the self in relationship to others. Family and friends can be a valuable source of self-knowledge, since they are the ones who experience individual persons in these moments and are poised to give honest feedback during these fundamental human situations. Individuals need to have the openness, courage, and humility to ask for this feedback.

Self-knowledge needs to be continually tested against the actions of one's life and the framework within which it is essentially situated in life. Since there are a number of ways of approaching the self, individuals need to keep testing the congruence of various modalities of the self in their different existential manifestations. The accuracy of self-knowledge needs to be constantly open to revision in the context of the community of persons with whom individuals habitually live. The self grows out of, and is shaped by, a multiplicity of relationships with other selves. In other words, the personal self finds its home in a community of persons, and cannot be understood in isolation from other persons. In Christian spirituality, desires, motivations, feelings, attitudes, and other such characteristics of the self are understood only in relationship to the world outside of the self – for example, in relationship to other persons, nature, and God.

We may not always get it right. Self-knowledge is not served up on a tray elegantly laid out for proper viewing. Furthermore, there is no point in life when we are no longer susceptible to illusions or misunderstandings about the self, or are beyond self-deception. For this reason, we need others to assist us regularly in the journey to achieve self-transparency and truthful living. Every point of arrival in our journey of self-knowledge is likewise a point of departure. There is always more depth to who I am. This is the Christian journey mapped out against the call to conversion and *metanoia* issued by Jesus during his earthly life. This insight reveals the fragility and, at the same time, the hopefulness of the Christian pilgrim as Christians recognize that all things are made new in him through adherence to his call of love, reconciliation, and peace.

Profiles of the self

Up to this point we have discussed specific characteristics of the self and self-knowledge. We have made some suggestions concerning the nature of being human. These characteristics are the foundations of a specifically Christian anthropology. In this section we will extend the use of these characteristics by developing three profiles of the self that rely on them, thus extending our understanding of a holistic Christian anthropology.

These profiles are understood as specific dimensions of the self that take on particular importance in everyday living: 1) The Transcendent Self; 2) The Narrative Self; and 3) The Body-Self. Together, these three profiles help us understand how the *imago Dei* is lived out in the ordinary experiences of daily life and assist us in constructing a specifically Christian anthropology.

The transcendent self

Are we destined to shape ourselves within the confines of human knowledge and everyday living as expressed in psychological categories, scientific terms, societal norms, or even the current values of the communities to which we belong? Can we describe the potentiality of the self by referring to aspects which surpass the self completely? The simple answer to these questions is "yes." Although we accept that people exist in space and time, we also maintain that part of human nature is the capacity for transcendence. Transcendence here is understood as the capacity to appeal to that which surpasses the human condition altogether in order to shape who people are, what they are called to, and what they are to believe. Thus understood, transcendence does not refer exclusively to the sacred or to God, but is a much bigger concept that refers to human potentiality.

The capacity for transcendence is a fundamental quality of the self and a unique characteristic of human beings – it grounds knowledge and freedom. The recognition of the transcendent quality of the self is a refusal to reduce human transcendence to the causal laws of science, the rational function of the human mind, or even the creative capacity of the imagination. The self cannot be reduced to a series of objective functions or to objective knowledge about the self. The self is inherently grounded beyond itself, which means that the self is not self-establishing. There is something inherently mysterious in the human that grounds the capacity for transcendental values such as justice, reconciliation, love, and peace. These values cannot be reduced to human pragmatism: they are the product of a call from elsewhere, however we define or describe their point of origin.

For Christians, this call from elsewhere originates in God – the transcendent self both reflects the *imago Dei* and strives to embody it ever more closely. Created in the image of God, human beings both reflect the image of God and participate in God's Divine nature. This is the source of the transcendent self as described here. Christians speak of the core of this *imago Dei* as being the soul, the place of the indwelling of God in the human person. It is this indwelling of God in the human person that grounds the transcendental nature of the human self. It makes possible the actualization of transcendental values, such as self-giving love, even to the point of death. Of particular importance in this regard is the life of Christian mystics.

Christian mystics witness profoundly to the transcendental nature of the self. The mystics have continually shown that transcendence belongs to the nature of the truly human self. Regrettably, there has been a recent trend to de-emphasize this aspect of the human. The self is frequently reduced (whether consciously or not) to its immediate and lowest common experiences. This is seen in the frequent description of people in Western cultures as the "now" generation – people expect everything in the immediate moment and only believe in what can be immediately seen. Failure to recognize the transcendental nature of the self (and of life in general) is to reduce the self to less than what it is. Implicit in this reduction is the diminishment of human freedom, creativity, imagination, hope, and capacity for love. The issue of the transcendent self is a significant one today because the autonomous, independent, and privatized self emphasized in the seventeenth century is still very evident in cultures today.

Grace and sin

Central to Christian anthropology is the reality that God is actively present in human life through the power of the Holy Spirit – the Spirit of God and Jesus Christ. Christians refer to this activity as God's grace active in their lives. It wells up from the core of human being, enlivening and inspiring people to become ever more identified with the *imago Dei*. Grace is not an abstraction, a theological idea. People need look no further than their own lives to see how this is true.

People experience God's grace in moments of sorrow, when they feel loved even though they have no reason for feeling that way, or in moments of joy when they celebrate some success in life. Other ways that God's grace manifests itself in life is in moments of insight and clarity of thought; in the desire to assist a troubled stranger; or in the making of unpopular choices that show the concrete living of Christian values, such as witnessing to the equality of all persons. Grace is any gift from God.

The Christian experience of God's grace, in other words, is the experience of God's self-communication through gifts of faith, charity, and hope. These gifts are freely given, even amidst experiences of failure – failing others, or failing oneself. Grace is not earned, nor does it come as a reward – it is graciously, freely, and lovingly bestowed by God, even when people have failed in some way.

Thus, in Christian anthropology we also acknowledge this aspect of humanity – the inability at times to rise to the challenges of life that result in real failures. These failures are known as sinfulness, which results from the ambiguity experienced as human beings: the desire, on one hand, to live a perfect life of love and charity, yet, on the other hand, the incapacity to always do so.[5] Sin, which is essentially due to this human ambiguity, is seen in the betrayal of relationships. Sin is revealed in the breaking down of the bonding of persons – it is a breakdown of loving and caring relationships with oneself, others, God, and the natural world. Sin is a description of the ways people have not achieved the goal of living fully the *imago Dei* in the here and now.

The good news is that God's grace, the Spirit of God and Jesus Christ, dwells within to strengthen and guide, especially when people lose their way in the often ambiguous and messy situations of life. God's mysterious presence is active in many ways in people's lives – so many ways that they cannot begin to be counted or named.

The narrative self: the self as a tale told

Most people like to tell stories. People gather after a week at work or school and tell others "what happened." During a wedding anniversary reception, individuals recount highlights from the couple's life over the years. Beyond these casual events of storytelling are more focused attempts to tell one's story. Autobiography is one of these. After a lifetime of experience and reflection on that experience, someone describes the events surrounding achievements and losses, joys and disappointments, successes and failures in an autobiography. Seemingly disconnected events are knitted together into a sustained narrative of happenings that tell the story of a life, even though it is still incomplete. Other ways people tell their stories is in a spiritual direction relationship, or through the notes kept in one's personal journal or diary.

Such storytelling may have profound consequences for people's lives. Telling one's story is not merely to provide information to someone unfamiliar with our life, or to explain how something happened and why. The narration of stories plays a significant role in personal identity formation. Thus we can speak about the narrative self: my self as constructed, shaped, and developed through narrative (storytelling) activity.

At play during the various moments of telling one's story is a selective process that determines which events in life are most meaningful and important. On the surface, the process is simple: from the many experiences an individual has had over the years, his or her memories drift toward certain events that are more important, for whatever reason. These selected events act as points of reference against which the whole of one's life may be interpreted. By selecting some particular events, whether from last week or ten years ago, and piecing them together into a *coherent whole*, people weave together their life story into a *meaningful whole*. The result is the development of one's personal identity through the story told and interpreted in relationship to one's past. The pulling together of the various events into a whole also gives meaning for the present, as well as directs the individual into a meaningful future. Thus we speak of a narrative self, an identification of the self that is constructed on the story of the past as it relates to the present and projects people into the future.

The construction of this narrative self also allows people to try on different identities. First, what may seem important today from the past may not seem so in the future. Or what wasn't important previously suddenly becomes key due to the new meaning people give the event or due to subsequent events that color previous events in a new way. Second, given the impossibility of the total transparency of the self to the self, it is not entirely sure that the way people have told their story is in fact the way their story unfolded. People employ their imaginations to envision themselves in different ways. Short of a level of self-deception that involves lying, the phenomenon of shaping one's story according to perceptions that may not be fully correct can provide the opportunity to try on different identities of the self.

We always have the possibility of telling our story in the mode of *as if it were in fact the case*. The way we see ourselves, in fiction or in fact, gives us a way of being-in-the-world in new and innovative ways. Again, this dynamic does not function if the intention is to deceive and manipulate. But we must at least consider that how we see ourselves is frequently how we would like to be! Slowly, over time, through self-identification of how we would like to be, and subsequent transformation, we can grow into that person.

The fluid nature of the self allows this dynamic to take hold of people in various ways. For example, somebody, let's call her Anne, may admire a particular historical figure, or someone currently involved in her life. For some reason Anne may already identify with that person. Maybe that person's values are close to Anne's values and that person's accomplishments already help shape her own goals. As a result Anne may try to emulate the other person through particular spiritual practices or good works in her community or faith group. Anne might even consider joining a group with which the person she admires is strongly identified. All of this leads Anne to integrate that person's story into her story, as well as to integrate her story into that person's story. Imitation of the other is not merely taking on external action. Rather, imitation is tied to the values and motivations that underlie that imitation. The narrative self can shift significantly as people find even more ways to construct meaning in their lives through their connections at the level of the narrative self.

The Spirit in the Christian narrative

In Christian spirituality the Spirit is constantly at work weaving life stories, and the life stories of faith communities, into the story of Jesus. The birth, life, death, and resurrection of Jesus form the backdrop for the narrative self of every Christian. From the story of Jesus are highlighted particular events that bring his life into a meaningful whole. These same events are available to Christians to inform, compose, and shape their own lives. Jesus fed the hungry and visited the sick and invites people to do the same. Jesus worked to eliminate oppression and unjust structures and again invites people to do the same. The invitation, therefore, is to shape and tell one's individual Christian story using the story of Jesus's own life. In this way the story of Jesus *really becomes* one's personal story. Christians find their self-identity in Jesus in relating in a meaningful way to how he lived his life. Paul of Tarsus is a dramatic example of this dynamic at work. Paul, as a Jew who had previously persecuted the Christians, came to know his life through the eyes of Jesus. Jesus's story became Paul's story, even to the point of persecution and physical death.

In Christian spirituality, even death does not end one's story in Jesus. As Jesus was raised from the dead, Christians too participate in that defining event of Jesus's life. In the Spirit of Jesus, the Christian life lived now has, as its ultimate end, the embrace of the fullness of God's reign, which Jesus realized in his resurrection. Participating now in what is the hoped-for future is the heart of Christian spirituality and constitutes the foundation of Christian faith. This faith in the fullness of God's reign transforms the self, since it constantly restructures the Christian's self-identity into who he or she hopes to be in the fullness of time: a person, for example, of peace, reconciliation, self-giving love, and justice. More and more, the Christian's character is called to reflect the character of Jesus. More and more, the Christian's life story is taken up into the life story of Jesus, which includes the dynamics of his life: joy, peace, forgiveness, reconciliation, justice, and so on. In all of these aspects is anticipated the event of his resurrection – and the Christian's, too.

Jesus's narrative story: the agape of God

At the basis of the narrative self is the profound dynamic of love: loving and being loved. In Greek this dynamic love is referred to as the *agape* (a-ga-PAY) of God. The primary character of God is God's self-giving love, which gives birth and shape to Christian communities. The narrative self is always an interpretation of one's self-understanding in relation to God's infinite horizon of love that calls people to be in relationship to others in a similar kind of way. Love poured out for others points to the communitarian dimension of the narrative self. The narrative self is always tied into the events and traditions of the communities and groups to which somebody belongs. Since the primary goal of Christian communities is to seek out the other in love, in reconciliation, and in peace, any individual story is always a shared story in the context of the life of others who participate in these same goals. Love can only operate in the context of community – relationship with others.

As a Jew, Jesus formed a community with a narrative identity based on the past events of the Jewish people. The story of the Jewish community, and God's Spirit that shaped that community, became the backdrop for the story of the followers of Jesus. But we also know that Jesus transformed the meaning of significant events in the Jewish community through his own life story. In a similar way, the earliest Christian communities give contemporary Christian communities a certain self-identity through their foundational events. For example, the way the early Christian communities developed prayer practices, different from the Jewish traditions of prayer, still influences contemporary Christian communities. You can read more about this in Chapter 8 in the section titled "Prayer." However, contemporary Christian communities are also called to assist in the transformation of Christian life in light of the reign of God anticipated to embrace all parts of life in the end times. The narrative self within a community of persons, therefore, ultimately participates in the narrative of the triune God as creator, redeemer, sustainer, and transformer of all life. The *imago Dei* of the narrative self exemplifies the life of the triune God in the story of today's world while keeping a watchful eye on the fullness of the embrace of God that comes from the future.

The narrative self has a social dimension that reflects the *imago Dei*. The *imago Dei* is ultimately a communitarian *imago*. The *imago Dei* is not a personal inward reality that is characterized by the privatized self with his or her personal potencies. Rather, the *imago Dei* is reflected in the communitarian dimension of living together as faithful followers of Jesus with all the consequences that flow from identifying our story with his. The autonomous self, with his or her personal and private story unrelated to the community, is a false reflection of Christian anthropology. The fallacy of the isolated self comes to light when we understand that the Christian narrative self is integrally involved in the life story of others who also make the claim to be the disciples of Jesus. Personal identity is thus not solely realized, and perhaps not even primarily realized, from an inward turn, but rather is derived from being-in-relationship with others. The narrative self constructed through the insertion of one's story in the story of the Christian community is fundamental in Christian anthropology.

Within Christian spirituality there exists a multiplicity of ways to embody Christian life. One way of living Christian spirituality may be appropriate at one point in life, but may not suit another. One's affiliation to different communities or groups may also add to the richness of one's self-understanding. Involvement in social justice groups, faith groups, environmental concern groups, and so on, can contribute a better under-standing of one's narrative self – the story of a self that is defined by its relationships to the wider narrative community.

The body-self

The body-self refers to the physical body that is identified with a "me." People say, "this is my body." People describe their body in terms of height, weight, state of health, and so on. This tends to lead exclusively toward a description of the body in terms of its materiality, its physical nature. However, at various points in history different appreciations of the body have been held. During the time of Jesus, two central or major lines of thinking influenced how people thought about the human body: the Roman

BODY

Body,
that place where I discover
Spirit of life.
Torso,
of affective pleasures
that are shared.

Not mine,
not yours,
but emerging inbetween.
I know you not
but for this
time of flesh.

You know you not
but for this
receiving.

How else are we
to be becoming
before Eternity?

No other way to incarnate God,
but to risk all the mistakes
as God did.

My God,
to live life,
and howl in the wind!

Climb trees
stretching upon a limb
jump into time.

Falling I embrace
all of your body,
encountering Life itself.

David B. Perrin (1991)

and the Greek perspectives. Although the immediate influence during the time of Jesus was evident in the Roman perspective on the body, it is helpful to acknowledge the significant influence of the Greek perspective. Thus, we speak of the Greco-Roman world in which Christianity was born, and whose thinking about the body greatly influenced Christian anthropology and spirituality in many areas. Let us briefly examine some of them.

The Greeks glorified the body. We could say that Greek culture was body-centered. This is seen, for example, in the importance given to the Olympic Games, performed in the nude in order to exalt the body, which were held every four years between 776 B.C.E. to 394 C.E. To a large extent physical training, endurance, competition, and bodily pleasures were more highly prized than mental activity and its associated pleasures. However, another Greek school of thought regarded the body as the tomb of the soul, which indicated a certain disdain of the body. Socrates (466–399 B.C.E.) was an influential Greek philosopher who regarded the soul as a prisoner within the body. Thus the inferior quality of the body in relationship to the soul was emphasized. Plato (427–348 B.C.E.), a student of Socrates and a very influential philosopher in his own right, held that the body prevents people from being truly free, since the soul was held captive in the body. The separation of the body and soul (the soul held as superior and the body held as inferior) is known as a form of dualism. In this model, material reality was seen as inferior to spiritual reality. This dualistic perspective was reflected in other areas of life. For example, women (identified with the affective passions and with earthly material reality) were seen as inferior to men (who were identified with the intellect and with the rational powers of the mind).

One group of people who embraced these values in a particular way in the Greek world around 300 B.C.E. were called *Stoics*. The Stoics developed a philosophy of life today referred to as *stoicism*. As the Roman Empire expanded, with the eventual conquering of the Greeks, stoicism became the most influential philosophy in Roman life. Stoicism upheld the dualistic nature of the body and developed an approach to life that was largely intended to keep the body (the lower, corruptible part) in check in order to save the soul (the higher, immortal part). Stoicism exerted a strong influence over Christianity during its earliest years and, as a result, a dualistic approach can be discerned in many early Christian thinkers and even in some places in the Christian scriptures.

The conflict between soul and body was evident during the earliest years of Christianity. Some early Christian writers upheld the dignity of the whole person, while others emphasized a dualistic framework of the body and held in disdain its irrational impulses, feelings, and uncontrollable behaviors. The tension between these two models is evident throughout the history of Christianity. For example, on one hand the writings of the Flemish woman Hadewijch of Antwerp, a thirteenth-century Beguine, describe a way of knowing and loving God that passionately involves the physical body. Her writings, in the form of letters, poems, and recorded visions, demonstrate in a positive way the erotic and highly sensual nature of the love that humans share mutually with God. On the other hand there is *The Cloud of Unknowing*, written in the fourteenth century by an unknown author, that tends to cast the physical body in a negative perspective. This book has been highly influential in the past and continues to attract readers today. However, its suspicion of the body reflects a spirituality that is largely detached from the concerns of everyday reality. Rather, its focus is on interior prayer, private contemplation, and personal holiness.

The continued ambivalence toward human sexuality is rooted in a negative appreciation of the body as inherently sinful. The persistence of the idea of the inherent sinfulness of the flesh continues to leave its mark in our Christian thinking, living, and practice with respect to various issues regarding human sexuality and spirituality. For example, some people continue to see the physical body as something to be conquered, subdued, and put in place – in favor of the rational and cool control of the intellect. This is true especially with respect to issues of sexuality – to be out of control, that is, to let the body freely enjoy the physical pleasures of marital love, without guilt or shame, is still repulsive for some people. A positive approach to human sexuality – understood as the desire for intimacy and communion and not mere genital activity – is foundational to a mature Christian spirituality that recognizes the role of passion (*eros*) as the raw material of relationships and communion with others. A negative approach to the body and sexuality is contrary to a religion that focuses on the Incarnation as its founding event.

The fact that Jesus took on human flesh and joined together into the same self both humanity and divinity opposes a dualistic approach to the body. The body and soul, understood as embodying the material and non-material aspects of the self, are an integrated whole – a psychospiritual unity. We are flesh animated by spirit. The self, as body *and* soul, fully participates in the life of the Holy Spirit and is a reflection of the *imago Dei*. At times one may speak of the body, mind, or spirit for the purposes of clarification or exploration, but it is important to bear in mind that, according to Christian anthropology, people are a singular unity.

Thus, a healthy Christian anthropology places a positive value on the flesh and sexuality. People will never take serious joy in their bodies if they are burdened with constantly trying to escape from them in order to live in some form of spiritual bliss outside the body. It is essential to emphasize the part of the Christian tradition that gives a positive evaluation to the body and sees it as the very place from which God's grace originates. For example, early Orthodox spirituality (the spirituality of Eastern churches that evolved out of the ancient Greek-speaking churches; e.g. the Greek Orthodox Church and the Russian Orthodox Church) stressed a very positive evaluation of the body, linking the similarity between physical human love and Divine love. A healthy Christian anthropology rejects the idea that spirituality is disconnected from the human body or human sexuality, or that the desires of the flesh are inherently sinful. A balanced Christian spirituality of the body recognizes the fleshy character of grace and the movement of the Spirit in life through the human body. This position is not to deny the choice that some make to live celibate lives. Celibacy can be a powerful witness to Christian love and embodied sexuality. However, the choice for a celibate lifestyle ought not to be lived as a choice that puts at odds the body and the spirit. Celibates and non-celibates are equally challenged to live holistic and integrated lives that recognize the grace of embodied life.

Healthy Christian spiritualities thus avoid dualisms that oppose body and spirit. The Spirit of God is involved in all parts of people's lives. Practical everyday life is not separate from one's spiritual life. One's sexuality is not split off from one's mind, feelings, and rational processes. The body is as involved in Christian spirituality in a positive way as is any other aspect of the self. However, since the long-standing traditions within Christian spirituality are permeated with both dualistic and holistic (psychospiritual) approaches to the body, it is important to examine critically teachings on the body, keeping in mind a holistic approach. Let's take as an example the Christian scriptures. Both positive and negative aspects of the body-self can be found in the writings of Matthew. Matthew 25:35–6 emphasizes the positive care we ought to extend to the body, while Matthew 18:8–9 seems to denigrate the body.

THE AMBIGUOUS APPROACH TO THE HUMAN BODY IN THE NEW TESTAMENT

Positive appreciation of the body as shown in Matthew 25:35–6: "For I was hungry and you gave me food; I was thirsty and you gave me drink; I was a stranger and you made me welcome; naked and you clothed me, sick and you visited me, in prison and you came to see me."

> *Negative* appreciation of the body as shown in Matthew 18:8–9: "If your hand or your foot should cause you to sin, cut it off and throw it away: it is better for you to enter into life crippled or lame, than to have two hands or two feet and be thrown into eternal fire. And if your eye should cause you to sin, tear it out and throw it away: it is better for you to enter into life with one eye, than to have two eyes and be thrown into the hell of fire."[6]

Thus, reference to scriptural texts concerning one or the other approach to the body cannot be left to stand alone. Usually they must be complemented by other scriptural texts or by reference to further developments in the Christian traditions and their practices. Holistic philosophical and psychological accounts of the self or actual descriptive accounts from men and women of what has been helpful in developing integrated approaches to the body can also be very useful. All these sources can be used as correctives in reflection on different Christian spiritualities and their approach to the body as a reflection of the *imago Dei.*

> A critical understanding of the body in Christian spirituality is important, because there is no singular approach to the body that is consistent or readily accepted throughout the Christian traditions. The body can be viewed in a positive or negative way; for example, as a sacred or secular entity; or as material or spiritual. Attitudes to the body even play themselves out after death. Following physical death, the body remains the most dominant symbol of the self. People go to visit the burial sites of their loved ones. The closeness to the physical place of interment of our loved ones brings us close to them in spirit.

Any paradigm of the body will immensely influence how the body is treated and, subsequently, how life is lived in the everyday. In essence, therefore, views on the body play themselves out in significant ways in Christian spirituality. Issues of asceticism, contemplation, prayer and worship, mysticism, spiritual practice, and the like will all be influenced by an understanding of the body as a reflection of the *imago Dei.*

In conclusion it needs to be acknowledged that different spiritual traditions will suggest different notions of the self, that is, will suggest different models of the self, or emphasize some characteristics over others. Thus, it is important to be conscious of the predominant model of the self that is being used in Christian spirituality at any one time.

Conclusion

Reflections on the questions of Christian anthropology developed in this chapter ground the possibility of human agency – that is, the self-determination of the human person as well as the human person acting under the impulse of the grace of God. This perspective challenges the view that the self is the result of the passive reception of the randomness of life. The self does not spontaneously happen, but is the result of the movements of human freedom, beliefs, and values.

Fundamental religious beliefs and values, such as the equality of all persons in Jesus and the sacred nature of all life, are what drive the Christian self and what ground the self. These beliefs and values involve all aspects of human-being: minds, souls, bodies, and feelings, as well as hopes, joys, pleasures, and fears. Thus, the expression "become who you are" needs to be carefully considered. It has been emphasized that the self is "constantly under construction," given all of these aspects of the self examined above that shape it in a seamless continuum.

Self-knowledge is needed to establish the truthfulness of one's own journey as well as to take responsibility for others. Freely Christians are called to take responsibility for each other in Christian spirituality. Self-giving is constitutive of the self in Christian spirituality. In other words, the transcendental self is constituted in the free human movements of love, forgiveness, and reconciliation – in the context of a community of persons. Through interaction with the other, who cannot be contained or measured in one's own terms, people are constituted as individual selves, but always persons alive to ever greater potentiality in the lives of others.

We have acknowledged that the self is always open to the future of new possibilities. As free agents in the Spirit of God, people are not held as passive victims of their past. The past can always change its meaning for people as they become increasingly aware of their life stories and of how God has been alive in their lives. The integration, or sense of wholeness in one's life, is never achieved once and for all. New possibilities challenge people to deepen their self-understanding. For the Christian, this self-understanding always takes place before God, others, and the world. Therefore, it requires an acceptance of self-transcendence as a fundamental characteristic of human life.

Self-transcendence involves moving beyond the narrow confines of one's own life. Often it means leaving behind the false sense of oneself revealed in the debilitating effects, for example, of one's biases, oversights, and misjudgments. Generally speaking, self-transcendence refers to the capacity to leave behind one's small and limiting world to be authentically interested in the world of others. As people become less and less preoccupied with themselves they are free to become ever more involved in the lives of others. In Christian spirituality we could describe this movement of self-transcendence as being *self-forgetful*. Self-forgetfulness, that is, letting go of one's personal preoccupations and concerns, allows one to embrace issues elsewhere that need attention, such as causes for justice, environmental issues, praying with and for others, and assisting those in need of greater resources.

In Christian spirituality, the self is not autonomously self-constituting or self-creating but molded, shaped, and re-formed within the context of multiple relationships. All these relationships are enlivened by the Spirit of God, who shapes the Christian ever more perfectly into the *imago Dei*. In Christian spirituality this is what it means to be human.

RECOMMENDED READING

Ahlgren, Gillian T. W. (2002) "Julian of Norwich's Theology of Eros," in *Spiritus* 5:1, 37–53.

Destro, Adriana and Mauro Pesce (1998) "Self, Identity, and Body in Paul and John," in *Self, Soul and Body in Religious Experience*, eds A. I. Baumgarten, J. Assmann, G. G. Stroumsa, Leiden: E. J. Brill, 184–197.

Paulsell, Stephanie (2002) *Honoring the Body: Meditations on a Christian Practice*, San Francisco: Jossey-Bass Wiley Imprint.

Ryan, Thomas, ed. (2004) *Reclaiming the Body in Christian Spirituality*, New York: Paulist Press.

Synnott, Anthony (1997) "Body: Tomb, temple, machine and self," in *The Body Social: Symbolism, Self, and Society*, London: Routledge, 7–37. (A precise history on shifts that have taken place in the way we view the body since the time of the Greeks.)

Timmerman, Joan H. (1994) "The Sexuality of Jesus and the Human Vocation," in *Sexuality and the Sacred: Sources for Theological Reflection*, eds James B. Nelson and Sandra P. Longfellow, Louisville, KY: WJK Press, 91–104.

Williams, Rowan (1996) "The Body's Grace," in *Our Selves, Our Souls & Bodies: Sexuality and the Household of God*, ed. Charles Hefling, Cambridge, MA: Cowley Publications, 58–68.

References to research topics from this chapter

Bourgeois, Warren (2003) *Persons: What Philosophers Say About You*, 2nd edition, Waterloo, ON: Wilfrid Laurier University Press.

Dupré, Louis K. (1976) *Transcendent Selfhood: The Loss and Rediscovery of the Inner Life*, New York: Seabury Press.

Grenz, Stanley J. (2001) *The Social God and the Relational Self: A Trinitarian Theology of the Imago Dei*, Louisville, KY: WJK Press.

Jopling, David A. (2000) *Self-knowledge and the Self*, New York: Routledge.

Helminiak, Daniel A. (1987) "Four Viewpoints on the Human: A Conceptual Schema for Interdisciplinary Studies: II," *The Heythrop Journal* XXVIII:1, 1–15.

McGuire, Meredith B. (2003) "Why Bodies Matter: A Sociological Reflection on Spirituality and Materiality," *Spiritus* 3, 1–18.

Mischel, Theodore, ed. (1977) *The Self: Psychological and Philosophical Issues*, Oxford: Basil Blackwell.

Misciatelli, Piero, ed. (1940) *Le Lettere di S. Caterina da Siena*, Florence, Vol. 1, Letter # 21, 65. Translation by Carola Parks (1981) in *Western Spirituality*, Matthew Fox, ed., Santa Fe, NM: Bear & Company, 249.

Modell, Arnold H. (1993) *The Private Self*, Cambridge, MA: Harvard University Press.

Neisser, Ulric and David A. Jopling, eds (1997) *The Conceptual Self in Context: Culture, Experience, Self-understanding*, Cambridge: Cambridge University Press.

Reiss, Timothy J. (2003) *Mirages of the Selfe: Patterns of Personhood in Ancient and Early Modern Europe*, Stanford, CA: Stanford University Press.

Synnott, Anthony (1997) *The Body Social: Symbolism, Self, and Society*, London: Routledge.

Taylor, Charles (1989) *Sources of the Self: The Making of the Modern Identity*, Cambridge, MA: Harvard University Press.

Vardey, Lucinda, ed. (1995) *God In All Things: An Anthology of Contemporary Spiritual Writing*, Toronto: Alfred A. Knopf, 20.

NOTES

1   For a thorough analysis of gender and issues related to it see Sherry B. Ortner (1996) *Making Gender: The Politics and Erotics of Culture*, Boston, MA: Beacon Press.

2   See George Lakoff (1997) "The Internal Structure of the Self," in *The Conceptual Self in Context*, Ulric Neisser and David A. Jopling, eds, Cambridge: Cambridge University Press, 98.

3   This is the conclusion of his seminal book *Meditations of First Philosophy*, first published in 1641.

4   Book I, Chapter 1, Paragraph 2, *The Interior Castle* cited from *The Collected Works of St. Teresa of Avila*, Volume Two, Kieran Kavanaugh and Otilio Rodriguez, tr., Washington, D.C.: Institute of Carmelite Studies, 1980, 284.

5   A philosophical and theological analysis of the sources of this ambiguity is presented in David B. Perrin (1997) "Asceticism: The Enigma of Corporal Joy in Paul Ricoeur and John of the Cross," *Pastoral Sciences*, 16, 135–162.

6   *The Jerusalem Bible*, Standard Edition (1966) New York: Doubleday & Company.

5

Questions of history

"The past has revealed to me the construction of the future."

Teilhard de Chardin, in Yves Congar,
"Church History as a Brand of Theology"

"The older distinction between fiction and history, in which fiction is conceived
as the representation of the imaginable and history as the representation of
the actual, must give place to the recognition that we can only know the actual
by contrasting it with or likening it to the imaginable."

Hayden White, *The Writing of History*

Introduction

History as an academic discipline

THE STUDY OF HISTORY on the amateur level was popular from the
sixteenth to the mid-nineteenth centuries.[1] Apparent truth, as told by
historians, was sometimes regarded as more interesting than the imaginative
novels of the day. Whoever had the interest, as well as access to records
and documents, wrote non-critical narratives based on the events of the past
– partly for education, but partly also for broad-based interest. History as
an academic discipline was still very much in its infancy then. The formal
development and recognition of history as an academic discipline would
take place between the mid-nineteenth and the mid-twentieth centuries
during which time history departments were created in the universities.

These departments trained professional historians, and methods were
established for correct historical inquiry. But it was believed that all that
was needed to establish the absolute truth from the past was to stick to the
facts as depicted in archival documents. History was deemed to be self-
explanatory. Furthermore, it was considered to be value-free, as if the
bias or mindset of the researcher did not influence any aspect of historical
inquiry. All this was to change in the mid-nineteenth century, when
critical methods for historical inquiry began to take shape. These methods
were largely based on parallel developments in the social sciences, such
as anthropology, sociology, and psychology. Later in this chapter, in the
section on the nature of historical inquiry, we will examine some of the
critical insights that came to the fore around the 1930s and radically
influenced the way history was studied and written. For example, the
presumptions mentioned above (that "facts" need be gathered only from
the documents, that history is self-explanatory, and that history is value-
free) were shown not to be true.

History and Christian spirituality

The study of the past is not often in the forefront when it comes to practical questions of living the Christian life. For example, a 250-page book describing in detail the nature of visionary literature around the twelfth century may seem to have little to do with Christian spirituality today. Why even bother with such a topic? But we are all writers of history; we are all involved in the events of today that will become the history of tomorrow – even if only in small ways. Whether we are aware of it or not, I suspect we all hope that someone in the future might express some interest in our past – that is, in the lives that we are living today.

However, it is important to keep in mind that people today live in the heritage of the long-dead. Current social systems, political systems, ways of thinking, languages, cultural perspectives, as well as spiritualities, are all connected to the lives of the ancestors, both recent and not so recent. The past has an enormous influence on current populations. Current populations live the consequences of the decisions made by those who went before them. In this way the past continues to live in us – it has a legitimate claim on our lives and it engages and critiques our experience today.

It is important, therefore, to study the past with an attentive eye to its successes and failures, to its sadness and joy, to its accumulated wisdom about life so we can better understand the world and ourselves in it. Furthermore, the study of history gives perspective to life. The issues people are dealing with today, as important as they are, may pale in significance when viewed alongside events from the past. Knowing where people have come from can make the world, and people's lives, less mysterious and more meaningful today.[2] When history is appreciated in this way, it becomes apparent that studying it is a practical thing to do.

Similarly, when Christians study the history of Christian spirituality, they usually do not study it out of idle curiosity – that is, as history for its own sake. Rather, it is often studied to enrich and better understand Christian spirituality today, that is, the historical context within which current spiritual practices and traditions are rooted. People come to know themselves, their practices, and their beliefs better when they take seriously the lessons learned from the past. Even though the issues from the past were wrestled with in very different contexts than current times, many issues remain fundamentally the same. Issues, for example, that concern human relationships, personal growth and meaning in life, justice and support for the disadvantaged, and care of the earth are all perennial in the history of Christianity. In studying how people in the past struggled with these issues, much wisdom can be gained for living today and tomorrow.

For example, if experiences of prayer are studied from the second and third centuries, the following questions might surface: How did their communal practices of prayer evolve? What elements from the experience of prayer of the early Christian communities are reflected in prayer life today? Why were some aspects continued while others were left behind? Which elements from the early Christian experience of prayer might contemporary faith communities want to retrieve to enrich their prayer lives today (for example, the early Christian experience of praying *to* the Spirit as well as praying *with* the Spirit)?[3]

To gain a thorough appreciation of Christian prayer as practiced during the second and third centuries, a researcher may have to study the larger social, political, and cultural contexts of the early Christians. The Roman thinking view on the human–god relationship would have influenced the early Christian practice of prayer. The Romans taught that the gods were distant, not part of the everyday life of the citizen. Christians believed that God was close and in intimate relationship with them. Studying the history of prayer will show how these two opposing perspectives played themselves out in the experience of the early Christians living in a culture that was predominantly Roman. Let's bring this example into our current context.

Some people today, as we saw in Chapter 3, still experience God as remote and disconnected from everyday life. Could contemporary students of Christian spirituality learn something from the early Christian experience of prayer to bridge the gap between these two views of God in their contemporary pluralistic society? How did the early Christians speak of God, that is, what symbols and images did they use to describe this closeness of God to non-Christians? A study of the history of Christian prayer may help answer these questions.

Studying the history of Christian spirituality has little, if anything, to do with studying a dead past. The past is still very much alive today. But we cannot look to the past without a critical appreciation of the issues at stake. This chapter examines the key issues faced when the history of Christian spirituality is studied.

What is history?

"In literary terms history is concerned with the drama of life, with what results through the characters, their decision, their actions, and not only because of them but also because of their defects, their oversights, their failures to act."[4]

As an area of study, what distinguishes history from, let's say, physics, chemistry, and biology is the difference in the object each studies. The natural sciences study universal systems of knowledge. History as an academic discipline involves the particular events of life that are scrutinized not by universal laws, but by local values, circumstances, and the dynamics of interpretation. In short, its points of reference are almost entirely contextual: history is shaped by what is happening in the event being studied and by those around it.

But studying history is not merely an attempt to satisfy one's curiosity about what happened, who did what to whom, and who said what. History includes a significant number of sub-fields, each of which can be a valuable resource in the study of Christian spirituality.[5] For example, demographic history is the study of the critical role of population size, growth, and age in determining many aspects of life. The history of social roles and change is the study of individuals in relationship to society in general. This latter example also involves "the identification of social status groups and social classes, and the analyses of social institutions, structures, values, and patterns of individual and group social mobility."[6]

Along with these is the history of mass culture, which includes the study of popular beliefs, social rituals and festivals, the de-Christianization of society, and the popular culture of the working classes. Urban history includes whatever happens in cities. Largely quantitative, it concerns itself with urban geography and ecology, urban religion and social values, urban sociology, politics, and administration. The history of the family embraces

> kinship ties, family and household structures, marriage arrangements and conventions and their economic and social causes, changing sex roles and their differentiation over time, changing attitudes toward and practice of sexual relations and changes in the affective ties binding husband and wife, and parents and children.[7]

We will not be studying any of these separate areas of history – our interest is more in the questions of history itself. But it is important to keep in mind these various areas of history and their potential contribution to studies in Christian spirituality.

Even though numerous divisions exist in historical study, we can simplify matters by using the word *history* for two basic categories. First, it refers to what actually happened in the past: that is, the *events*. Second, it refers to the *processes* undertaken to construct the historical past. Let us look now at each of these categories separately in relationship to Christian spirituality.

The events of history

From this perspective, the student of the history of Christian spirituality would study as accurately as possible the history of Christian spirituality from the first century up until the present. He or she would include the history of events such as the move that many men and women made in the fourth century to the desert in Egypt to live a life of solitary holiness, the fourteenth-century English mystics who had extraordinary insights into God's gracious presence in their lives, and the stories of specific men and women who made notable contributions to Christian spirituality through founding religious orders or launching charitable works for those in need. By going back through the evidence and establishing with some certainty "what happened," one could attempt to develop a singular history of Christian spirituality, relating a sequence of events in chronological order from the beginning of Christian life up to the present.

But history is not characterized by an even flow of events seamlessly leading their way into the present and future. Rather, it is better characterized by "breaks, ruptures, crises, and the irruption of changes in thinking – in short, discontinuity."[8] For this reason, the development of a linear and singular concept of the history of Christian spirituality is not possible. Countless events are always happening simultaneously. Some aspects of the story may end as others are beginning. History is more aptly characterized by a network of relationships, akin to a spider web that, beaten in the wind, has developed holes and, literally, loose ends. While a strand of the story may be picked up later, this does not necessarily mean there is a direct causal relationship with what happened earlier.

Furthermore, there are always events surrounding the main event of current interest that guides any history along. These additional events may or may not have had an influence on the main story but each has its own history and its own points of reference. We are led, therefore, to speak of histories – of history in the plural. In other words, the history of Christian spirituality is not one but many, because it is linked to specific contexts, each with its own ecclesial, political, social, and cultural framework.

The history of Christian spirituality is structured alongside the dynamics of the history of society in general, but there is not a "sacred history" and a "secular history" – all is bound together within God's Spirit active in the world. Each history of Christian spirituality that addresses a specific series of events (e.g. the expansion of monasteries in Europe in the thirteenth century) or traces a theme over an extended period of time (e.g. Christian prayer in different time periods) needs to be free to tell its own story on its own terms, but must also take into consideration the wider societal context.

Furthermore, the attempt to write an accurate and complete general survey of the history of Christian spirituality, even when taking into account the wider societal context, is simply not possible and not desirable.[9] Cross-cultural variances and different theological points of reference, cosmologies, anthropologies, and models of God must also be considered.

For example, there is a tendency to tell the history of Christian spirituality from an exclusively Western European perspective (largely shaped by the norms of Western Greco-Latin theology, as we saw in Chapter 2). The viewpoints of the Middle East, India, Latin America, Asia, and Africa are all but ignored.[10] And where Europe has exported its Christianity – for example, to Latin America – the history of Christian spirituality in that part of the world is almost inevitably told from the perspective of the conqueror. Western European Christian spirituality is held up as the norm by which all indigenous expressions of spirituality are judged. This method of constructing the history of Christian spirituality is blatantly unfair and unjustly biased. For this reason, specialized studies by individuals who have some in-depth knowledge of the specific social, cultural, political, and theological context stand a better chance of constructing a more accurate history of the Christian heritage. These histories have a dynamic relationship with other expressions of spirituality, as well as with a range of forms of Christian spirituality with which they are in contact.

Clearly, analysis and interpretation are needed to tease out how events are related and what they mean. Furthermore, judgments need to be made to decide what is to be included in any one historical question. This leads us to the second way of using the word "history." This second way refers to the *processes* involved in accurately depicting the historical past. Some of these have already been described above. Let's look at others now.

The processes of history

The word history refers to the representation of the past as reflected in the work of historians – how historians go about telling the story of the past. To construct the story, they carefully analyze the evidence. They also do a number of corollary tasks such as establishing and naming periods of time that reflect primary values and shifts in perspectives. They give these periods names that interpret what was happening then. In so doing, they must not only make judgments on what happened, but also assess dominant forces and describe the dynamics of change that shaped a historical period. The Reformation is a case in point.

The Reformation, largely identified with the reformer Martin Luther (1483–1546), was a movement in the sixteenth century in response to certain excesses of the Roman Catholic Church. For example, the Roman Catholic Church had begun to accept money that people paid to have their punishment for their sins canceled after they were granted forgiveness in the sacrament of reconciliation. This was known as the selling of indulgences. The money raised in this way was being used, to a large extent, to fund the building of St. Peter's Basilica in Rome. Luther, meanwhile, believed that God's Spirit was a free gift. It was not a result of human achievement, and it could not be purchased. He embraced a spirituality of the Gospel that freed individuals from such things as the oppressive penances put on people in the sacrament of confession (which frequently led to scrupulosity), the buying of indulgences, the piety attached to relics (artifacts associated with saints), and celibacy as the ideal path to holiness.

Some historians mark the beginning of the Reformation with Luther's publication of his dissent from Roman Catholic teachings in 1517. This date views the Reformation largely from the perspective of the ecclesial institution and politics. But the average faith-filled person was not affected by this singular event until much later, perhaps as late as the beginning of the seventeenth century, after it had time to trickle down into the lives of ordinary churchgoers. From this latter perspective, the Reformation is viewed as an event in which ordinary people participated and made their own judgments of the issues mentioned above. Thus, depending on the point of departure, the beginning of the Reformation is signaled as an institutional event (the break between the Church's teachings and Luther's theological norms earlier in the sixteenth century) or as an event of the common masses of people (a new perspective that profoundly affected the Christian spirituality of masses of people in Europe earlier in the seventeenth century). Cutting history into periods, we can see, is arbitrary in many ways but also reveals judgments tied to the biases of the writer.

The above example shows that historians help structure the historical past so we can understand it better. This allows people to have a better grasp of the present. What historians are trying to do in the construction of history is to develop a sense of *historical consciousness*. Historical consciousness means people attempt to situate events in the context of the past as well as their meaning for their present lives. Where people have come from, along with the processes, shifts, and transitions that have shaped current realities, is at the core of what we call historical consciousness.

But the past cannot be viewed solely from the perspective of our current knowledge, beliefs, and values. If we do so, we are subject to the error of *presentism*. Presentism refers to the tendency not to allow the past to be viewed from within the parameters of its own setting. It risks dismissing as irrelevant important aspects and events of the past because they do not fit into the categories of today. To avoid presentism, the student of history must view events from the past from within their own points of reference before mining them for insights to apply to life today. The same goes for words. If students of history apply uncritically their contemporary understanding of words to the past, they may make mistakes in describing the past.

For example, between the eighth and the twelfth centuries *conversion* and *winning souls* usually referred to someone who was entering a monastery.[11] If a person had a conversion, he or she embraced monastic life and thus his or her soul was won. At that time, the lifelong commitment to being a monk or nun was seen as the perfect way to live Christian spirituality and reach Christian perfection. The word *religious* (used here as a noun) was reserved for those who embraced the monastic lifestyle or joined formally religious orders. Laity were not considered to be religious; to a large degree, we still make this distinction today.

However, after the thirteenth century, reference to conversion and winning souls took on broader meanings as mendicant preachers (people who were not necessarily clerics) roamed from village to village, preaching the Gospel to those who lived outside the monastery walls. In Europe during the twelfth and thirteenth centuries people began to recognize that Christian spirituality could be lived outside the formal structures of the institution (epitomized by the monasteries). Popular religion began taking its place alongside the formal institution on the other side of the monastic wall. Due to this increase in lay spirituality, conversion and winning souls began to refer to bringing all people to penance and thus winning their souls through preaching.

Clearly, language in Christian spirituality was used in different ways at different times. We need to be sensitive to this fact and not presume that words we use today mean exactly what they have meant previously. Let's look at another example, the word *feminism*, in relationship to events taking place in the twelfth and thirteenth centuries.

The contemporary understanding of feminism is sometimes uncritically mapped onto the lay women's movement, known as the Beguine movement, in the thirteenth century in the Rhine Valley in Europe. During this time being a nun was almost the only option available for women who wanted to dedicate their lives in a special way to the Church. The Beguines were single lay women who chose to live together, hold assets in common, share a common life of prayer, and provide service to others – outside the framework of the established orders often controlled by men. These informal arrangements gave religious meaning to women's ordinary lives.[12] But although some people today may describe the thirteenth-century experience as "feminism," the word means something very different there. If this is not acknowledged, we risk letting current feminist concerns overtake the authentic concerns of these thirteenth-century women. They were responding to their own issues. For example, as lay women their common prayer reflected the marked increase in popular piety, and their poverty offered a counter-example to the accumulation of wealth in the developing urban centers. The Beguine movement had its own points of reference that will help people understand it. The Beguine movement can still be used to gain insight into feminism today, but we must understand that the context was different for the Beguines. A student studying feminism from the perspective of the experience of the Beguines needs to artfully (and accurately) interpret the Beguine reality before bringing forward insights into contemporary times.

Besides avoiding presentism, there is a need to be cautious about importing absolutes from the past into the present without critical analysis. When persons of privilege and power look uncritically to the past to justify current beliefs and practices, it is very easy to end up with a form of social control. This can happen both in society and within the churches. Present circumstances must always be considered. Just because something was done a certain way in the past does not necessarily mean it should be done that way today. The argument of precedence – that is, it was first done that way – is hardly defensible when we think about the great many changes that have occurred in society and churches over time. The nostalgic return to the past in order to defend current practice, and even some beliefs, tends to conveniently ignore the developments of history and the changes that have taken place between then and now. Each generation must retell its own history, interpreting the past in light of the truth of life today. Great truths from the past will be brought forward, but with a critical understanding of how they fit into current realities: "The past remains constant, but history changes."[13] The past does not change in itself, but the current population's relationship to it does as new information, perspective, and meaning emerge from within current contexts.

Let us now return to the main point here: What is history? We need to bear in mind that what really happened, and what historians suggest happened, may be two distinct things. The representation of the past is fraught with choices, value judgments, and interpretations. In this chapter, the focus is on history: we are concerned with the process of constructing history and raising issues that affect the choices, value judgments, and interpretations historians are called to make. Our goal here is not to tell the story of a particular event or person from the past, but to inquire into the nature of historical inquiry itself.

The study of the history of Christian spirituality is important, since Christian history, and history in general, is tied to the Christian's self-identity, belonging, and purpose in life. Christian spirituality is built on a real history that consists of the lives of flesh-and-blood people. Jesus actually lived and died. He ate and drank with other people, performed public acts, taught in the synagogues, and traveled extensively through the area of Galilee. How Christians tell the story of all these events is important, for it laid the foundation for future Christian belief and practices. The same is true of the community of followers of Jesus. They based their actions and beliefs on what they observed and what was recorded to be the actions and beliefs of Jesus and his followers. Christian communities – today and in the past – have lived under the guidance of these historical accounts ever since.

The nature of historical inquiry

The sources of historical knowledge

The sources for the history of Christian spirituality may take the form of histories written with a view to keeping alive the memory of certain important events for future generations. The biographies and autobiographies of men and women who have made a significant contribution provide another source of information. The Christian patrimony also includes a huge inheritance of art, such as paintings, sculptures, frescoes, mosaics, and relief carvings, as well as music, poetry, icons, stained-glass windows, and religious paraphernalia of all kinds (for example, objects used in prayer and worship or items of popular piety). All these traces of the past may be used to piece together the history of Christian spirituality.

The architectural design of churches and places of worship is another source of the history of Christian spirituality.[14] For example, Margaret Miles, in her important book *Image as Insight*,[15] describes how architecture and imagery used in fourth-century church buildings display prominent aspects of Christian spirituality that are markedly different from those recorded in books by the intellectual elite (bishops, priests, and emperors) of the time. To get a feel for Christian spirituality of the fourth century, Miles emphasizes the need to start with "the images available daily to the whole community instead of with texts written by a few."[16] Church architecture and the images used to adorn the interiors of churches were particularly significant. The leading features of the newly built Christian churches (known as Constantinian churches, since Constantine was the emperor of Rome at the time) were "hugeness, a simple plan and exterior, and a gorgeous interior."[17] Due to the large windows and light interior walls, the buildings were well illuminated. Art of every kind engaged the spirit and senses of all who walked through the doors.[18] The architecture and lavish imagery personified a spirituality of openness and accessibility to all who wished to come and join in Christian communal prayer life. Thus we see the contrast between the literal and the visual testimony to the past: the textual evidence focuses on theological definitions and dogmatic precisions, while the architectural and visual evidence reflects the universal invitation to all persons to participate in the newly founded Christian faith.[19] The discovery of a universal way – that is, accessibility of salvation for all (of any faith) – that characterized early Christian spirituality of the fourth century is strongly supported by the visual and architectural evidence and not the written, textual evidence. If only the textual evidence was studied, there would be a risk of missing out on important aspects of early Christian spirituality.

More is to be gained by a study of the non-visual evidence: the art adorning the walls of the Christian places of worship came from many strata of society, and not only the upper levels. The result was that the entire Christian community, and not just the learned elite, shaped Christian spirituality of the day. We can thus question the commonly held belief that the images adorning the walls of churches and meeting places for prayer up to the fourth century were merely intended to educate the illiterate poor into the ways of the faith. Rather, these images were intended to "arouse strong emotions" and inspire awe in all who viewed them, as Gregory of Nyssa (c.335–395), a bishop and influential writer, confirmed.[20] The churches were built to accommodate artistic works of all kinds, and with a wide range of themes. "Excitement with a *via universalis*, a way of salvation for all people, could not have been more strongly and directly reflected and communicated than it was in the architecture, the images, and the statues of Constantinian churches."[21]

Let us briefly look at another example that shows how non-textual sources play a significant role in the construction of the history of Christian spirituality and its expressions.[22] During the third and early fourth centuries, images of Jesus focused on his human qualities. He was frequently portrayed in various biblical narratives, such as the Good Shepherd with the sheep or the Teacher with crowds of people. Whatever the setting, the images usually included other people clothed just like Jesus. The bearded-young-man Jesus was portrayed in the acts of "healing, teaching, or working miracles." However, toward the end of the fourth century and into the fifth paintings of Christ "enthroned in glory," "presenting the new law to the apostles," "triumphantly entering Jerusalem" and the like began to appear. These latter images emphasized Christ's divinity rather than his humanity. This change in imagery reveals that a new kind of spirituality was being nurtured. Instead of a spirituality reflecting Jesus's closeness to the people or giving universal access to Jesus as portrayed in the earlier images, a spirituality of "glory, majesty, and power" that shows Jesus as removed from the life of the common citizen was emerging. In the latter images there is the sense that Christianity was becoming triumphant. The "imperial Christ" takes precedence over the "human Jesus" as we move into the fifth century.[23] This shift in imagery is not a mere curiosity for the art historian.[24] Rather, it is essential evidence for the authentic study of shifts and trends in the history of Christian spirituality.

The limits of historical knowledge and method

How securely based is the knowledge of the past? The past cannot be known directly, as if it were passing before us on a movie screen. What we do have access to are the remnants of the past that give witness to what happened. This is true even if meticulously detailed written accounts of events are available. We could read these accounts and imagine we were there, but in the end the account of what happened still lies between us and what actually transpired. History, then, is mediated by what is left behind so that the historian can piece together and interpret, as best he or she can, the events of the past. Can this evidence be trusted as factual? Yes – but only to a certain degree, as we see in this section.

The historian cannot, as in a scientific inquiry in a laboratory, repeat the experiment of the past to confirm the data upon which he or she may base the conclusions. The historian can only string together facts that have been more or less determined to be true, into narratives that reveal what happened. Certain factors prevent the historian from constructing the story of the past in such a way that it is beyond reproach and further clarification. The historian can trust the evidence of the past, but only so far, as the following points emphasize.

Historical knowledge is always incomplete

All sources of historical knowledge are incomplete from at least two perspectives.

First, not everything left behind has been found; some of it may never be recovered. Much of what has been produced at some point in the past has been either lost or destroyed by later generations. Wars and fires have taken their toll, as has the disappearance or destruction of countless manuscripts and pieces of art through loss, human negligence, theft, or the inability to recognize the importance of some materials for future generations as cultural, political, or spiritual interests shifted. More evidence may yet be discovered, however, causing current interpretations to be shown to be erroneous. Accounts of some historical events may need to be revised according to current understandings and information. For example, it was a long-held view that since the beginning of Christianity, the parish church was the normal meeting place for common prayer and worship. However, more recent research has determined that "until the year 1000, it remained common for people simply to assemble from time to time around a cross."[25] It was only later, perhaps around the eleventh or twelfth century, that parish organizations began to put more elaborate structures into common prayer and liturgical practices, thus making churches the focal point (even geographically) of village life.

Second, not everything was recorded. History, in the first sense of the word we mentioned at the beginning of this chapter, also includes information for which there is no direct record of any kind. This has left gaps, at times quite large, in the records of what happened. To fill in the gaps, the historian must make intelligent guesses, infer what happened, or present several hypotheses, all of which may be within the range of probable truth. Sometimes the historian infers what happened in the past by examining what happened in later events (i.e. for such-and-such to have happened, this other event must have happened first). Clearly, imagination is a vital tool for the historian. It helps construct hypotheses that can then be tested against known information. In the end, the historian cannot assume that he or she has a full account of the past, no matter how complete or accurate it may appear to be.

Furthermore, at any one time there may exist several competing interpretations of the past. All of them may contribute toward the understanding of the past, but none of them completely. For example, the popular perception today is that demons (generally understood as personifications of the devil) were a source of intense fear for early Christians. In early Christianity, prayers were thought to be a protection against the devious presence of demons. Some of these prayers were expressed in pre-baptismal exorcisms. But were these exorcisms, and rituals like them, really intended (and believed) to banish the presence of demons from the life of the newly baptized Christian? When this question is critically examined in early Christian texts, we see that they were not greatly concerned with "neutralizing the power of the devil, who is not considered capable of inflicting real harm, nor with getting rid of demons, who are portrayed as targets for the monks' mockery, rather than as sources for their fear."[26] A closer look at the attitude toward the devil and demons in early Christianity, as presented in the study "Early Monks, Prayer, and the Devil," by the historian J. Kevin Coyle, reveals that rather than present occasion for serious harm, demons were instead ridiculed.[27] The early Christians were not as preoccupied with the devil as some have suggested.

Given these two large gaps in historical knowledge (not everything left behind has been found and not everything was recorded), it is problematic to construct histories based on absolute enduring truths.[28] Given the possibility that new information may be discovered that could in turn lead to fresh insights and understandings, it is unrealistic to put too much emphasis on the concept of enduring truths that could provide an unchanging framework around which the histories of Christian spirituality are constructed.

The belief that historical events can be presented in a complete, accurate, and absolute fashion is called *historicism*. For Christian spirituality, historicism can cause other problems: it tends to reject events that do not fit into strict historical verifiability, such as the miracles of Jesus or his resurrection. Furthermore, historicism can lead to the belief that only one version of history, based on so-called facts, is correct, shutting out all other alternatives. Such convictions have been the cause of wars. In one example, the Christian Crusades from the eleventh to thirteenth centuries were fought on the premise that only Christians had a right to the holy city of Jerusalem;[29] the Muslims were to be expelled at all costs. When we recognize that all representations of past events are partial and incomplete, we tend to foster a greater openness to dialogue and give serious attention to other points of view.

The selection of the facts of history

Data from the past are gleaned from the objects of historical inquiry (for example, books, letters, manuscripts of all kinds, art, and population censuses). But these data are not yet history or historical accounts as the historian would understand them today. Once the data have been established with sufficient certainty, history is the weaving together of the data into a coherent and meaningful story. This is the role of the historian. The data are used by the historian to establish the facts in order to explain what happened from the perspective of the person writing the history. Data, in themselves, do not lead to understanding the past, as we have used this term in the previous chapter. Data do not speak for themselves. Data provide a kind of text to assist the historian in interpreting what happened, but this is always open to revision as more data come to light. The historian may be challenged to revise the factual account of what happened, why it happened, and what relationship this account of the past has to life today.

For this reason, the facts excluded in any historical account can sometimes be as significant as those that are included. Furthermore, what one age finds important from the past may be different from what previous ages found important.[30] Historical accounts are therefore a *selection of the facts* put together for the purpose of a plausible reconstruction, explanation, and interpretation of the past from the perspective of the current historian. However, and regretfully, sometimes historians tend to reconstruct the story of the past to legitimize or explain current positions and make them the norm.

When collecting the facts, the historian has already betrayed himself or herself in understanding what is important. From this perspective the facts constructed from the data are tainted. Therefore, when historical facts are selected as relevant to telling the story, it is crucial to identify the criteria used to select them in the first place. Why were some facts included in the historical account while others were left out? The historian may plead the limitation of space, or the irrelevance of some of the data. However, use of space and relevance are both determined by the importance given to the facts selected. There is no value-free account of history. Sources, even highly reliable ones, can be interpreted in various ways according to the presumptions and biases of the historian. It is not enough to know that something was said or written: equally important is who reported it as said or written.

History is usually written by the winners, for they were able to go on to tell the story – *their* story – of victory over the vanquished. The victors are in a position to tell the story of why their victory was the better outcome. Subsequent generations must depend on the victors for knowledge of the vanquished. It is reasonable to expect that the victor will likely diminish the contribution and perspective of the vanquished and attempt to eliminate their voices.[31] An extreme example of this dynamic is the elimination of all textual references to Arianism – the denial of the full divinity of Jesus Christ, which was held by Arius (256–336) and his followers in the third and fourth centuries. After the position of Arius was condemned in the fourth century, there was a massive destruction of all writings that reflected his position. We would know very little about Arianism today if it were not for his opponents who quoted Arius in their own documents. The point here is not whether Arianism is correct or not, but, rather, how the victorious have, at times, sought to eliminate completely the voice of the vanquished.

When we look back through the history of Christian spirituality and the history of nations, can we honestly say that the victor was always right?

Too often, and too easily, the losing side or underside of history is dismissed as irrelevant, especially when it comes to questions of belief. Sometimes the past that best follows the lines of uniformity rather than welcoming healthy pluralism is uncritically favored. This is regrettable; even irresolvable conflict that presents alternative or complementary perspectives may shed new light on what happened in the past. Historical coherence to make the so-called facts fit comes at a high price if the historian overlooks what really happened and what the valuable contributions from the different perspectives were. To compensate for the tendency always to favor the victor and the uniform position, a certain skepticism must accompany sound historical inquiry. Attention to those on the periphery, those who do not fit easily into the mold, may be exactly where the Holy Spirit is working "to make all things new."

For example, largely excluded from Christian spiritual history is the voice of the Dutch Christian humanist Desiderius Erasmus (c.1466–1536). Humanism is a philosophical approach to life that emphasizes the dignity and worth of each and every individual. It also argues that human beings are rational beings who possess within themselves the capacity for truth and goodness. Thus, for the humanist, the world is not viewed from the perspective of Christian belief, but from within its own parameters, and is still judged to be good. Erasmus, although a devout Roman Catholic, believed that the humanist approach to life had some merit. He reflected this belief in his own writings (e.g. *Institutio principis Christiani* [1516] and *Colloquia familiaria* [1518]). But because the humanist perspective did not reflect the dominant religious voice at the time, his writings have largely been ignored ever since.[32] Given the strength of humanism in today's world view, perhaps historians, theologians, and researchers in Christian spirituality would do well to go back and see how Erasmus integrated the humanist perspective within his own Christian writings to speak of *Christian humanism*.

If the history of Christian spirituality has been largely written by well-educated male, celibate clerics, then we must at least ask the question, as we did with the writing of texts in general, of how less-educated people – women, married and lay people – figure in histories of Christian spirituality. Who was left in and who was left out in any historical inquiry? This is a key question. Knowing who was left out of the story may be more meaningful for Christian spirituality today than knowing who was included.

What we are affirming here is that Christian spirituality is lived within the formal structures of faith communities, but it is lived outside those structures as well. Both sides have contributed enormously to the history of Christian spirituality, but persons of power and privilege (that is, those within the structures) have been the ones in a position to write about it. For example, until very recently, the history of the poor and the disenfranchised has been left out.

Historians need to scrutinize possible intentions of the writers of history, as well as their own personal assumptions and interests, before beginning historical inquiries. Self-awareness and self-knowledge are vital. Bias in historical inquiry is assumed and is not necessarily harmful. What is harmful is the unstated or unconscious bias of the historian, which may overlook the contribution of entire groups of people, or interpret the data and facts in ways that do not accurately reflect the events of the past. Both of these may be the result of another agenda at play.

This is especially problematic if a particular ideology figures significantly in the reasons for the historian's writings. Theological or political ideologies can shape the story of the past beyond recognition. For example, is it more accurate to refer to the *discovery* of America or to refer to the *conquest* of America in the fifteenth century by the Europeans? After all, there were inhabitants in North America long before the various European groups arrived. What we see is that historical inquiry and the establishment of facts is based on both subjective elements (for example, personal interest, potential for personal gain, and biases) and objective elements (for example, critical methods of inquiry and analysis).

If people look to the past primarily to find reasons to support their current understandings and ways of doing things they risk remaining blind to the rich lessons from the past that can continually teach new things. If it remains blind to the lessons of the past as well as to the newness of the present, history can be used to limit the awareness of the activity of the Holy Spirit in today's world instead of enlightening people to its movements.

Another issue to consider is the use of secondary literature to substantiate a current belief. Usually, with good reason, the tendency is to accept uncritically published scholarship from the past. Once one researcher establishes a plausible explanation of what happened, his or her research may be quoted in subsequent publications. After a period of time, a significant number of scholars can be found to be quoting each other, substantiating the same point at hand. But all of this support for a scholar's position really rests on the accuracy of the *one* original study, not further critical scholarship. Something is accepted to be true since so many individuals of reputation believe it to be true. When the historian goes back to original documents, he or she may discover something quite different from what later scholars were led to believe.

For this reason, it is important that a full history of the topic be made before beginning a new scholarly study – for example, at the level of a university doctoral program – on a theme in the history of Christian spirituality. This will allow a critical examination of the sources that may open up the topic at hand. The latest work on a particular topic does not necessarily guarantee accuracy or completeness. Sometimes people are happy with the facts as they stand and are quite willing to use them without critical analysis. The status quo may support positions of authority, privilege, and power, making tampering with the past undesirable. But, the honest historian cannot overlook the possibility that the past is yet to be mined for a fuller and more complete picture.

Historical remnant is part of a greater whole

The removal of an event from concurrent events happening around it may be necessary to limit the research or to bring into focus a particular example to make a point. But even though each historical event is an object of interest in its own right, it is still connected to other events that influence and shape it. By discovering these events, which may include the larger cultural, political, or religious contexts, the historian completes his or her under-standing of the primary investigation in some way. This affirmation leads to the conclusion that all historical knowledge is socially, culturally, and politically conditioned.

For example, the expulsion in 1492 of the Muslims from Spain, where they had enjoyed religious freedom for 700 years, cannot be understood as a strictly religious event meant to ensure the triumph of Christianity. It was also a political event. It was King Ferdinand of Castille and Queen Isabella of Aragon who united their territories in Spain and required religious conformity by all, which led to the expulsion of the Muslims. But religious conformity was not merely to enrich the lives of the Christian faithful, but also to ensure the political stability the king and queen needed to extend their political power and interests even further. The decision to expel the Muslims had an enormous influence on the history of Christian spirituality, but it was primarily a political decision. Up until this time, Christians and Muslims had lived in relative harmony. Now they were enemies.

The historian's task is to connect the dots to describe and interpret past events accurately. This task can be done only when the larger context is included. Often, an investigation beyond the initial area of inquiry will be required; the historian's job is never complete. Since history is a cumulative discipline, there is always more evidence to add to the reflection as it becomes available. This new evidence may be drawn from new critical research within the area of Christian spirituality, or from other fields of inquiry, such as the sociological or political. What we see, then, is that historical understanding refers not only to an understanding of the events in themselves (their value, meaning, and purpose), but also to their interconnections and interdependence in the wider societal context.[33]

In this section we have outlined the nature of historical inquiry. We can summarize some of the main ideas under the following points:

- sources for historical inquiry are many: texts as well as art, music, stained-glass windows, architecture, and the like;
- the writer of history always has biases that need to be taken into account by both the author of the history and its subsequent readers;
- the contributions to historical accounts need to come from all strata of society – not just the affluent and those in positions of power;
- historians do not have direct access to the past; rather, they rely on traces of the past to construct histories;
- since history is a construction of the past, as new evidence becomes available history can change;
- there will always be large gaps in history; the construction of history relies on the need to interpret evidence from the past as well as to infer or intuit what may have happened due to what is known in previous and subsequent history.

History of Christian spirituality and theology

Sources for the histories of Christian spirituality cannot be placed completely under the umbrella of theology, since doing so would cause them to lose their historical contexts, which give a practical understanding of events, relationships, and Christian phenomena in general. Theology tends to abstract principles from the particular experience of men and women during a specific era and make these principles normative for all time, all contexts, and all people. They thus become the great organizing principles for all spiritual experience in the history of Christian spirituality. This is a problem.

Historical events, for example, whether depicted in the frescoes painted on the walls of the catacombs of Rome in the second century, in the musical scores of Hildegard of Bingen from the twelfth century, or in the portrayal of life as a journey by John Bunyan's (1628–1688) *The Pilgrim's Progress* in the seventeenth century, need to be dealt with on their own terms. This allows them to speak their truth from within the context in which they were born.

This means that as historians examine sources for the history of Christian spirituality, they do not necessarily need to first submit them to the strict and sometimes limiting categories of theology. These categories reflect what is known already about God's Spirit in the world, or what has been clarified about God's salvific presence in the past. God may be present in another way in the future, or may have been present in a different way in the past than presumed thus far.

Although historians cannot study historical data without an interpretive framework in mind, the historian of Christian spirituality does well to examine the evidence from a number of perspectives. If historians begin examining sources strictly from a unified theological framework, they may view them from within predetermined categories that have their own problematic historical, dogmatic, polemic, and political origins.[34]

> The history of Christian spirituality cannot be guided by the known categories and concepts of theology only. Using these exclusively as the historian's guide might cause the historian to miss out on what went unnoticed or was not included due to its being outside the accepted theological categories at the time. Being open to the as yet unexplored phenomenon of Christian spirituality may result in being surprised by new readings of the historical past that are not contained within known theological categories.

For example, if we assume that holiness is defined only by the norms of theology within a particular historical period, we may lose sight of the fact that holy men and women are reflections of the norms for holiness that operate in various societies and historical periods. Holy men and women are produced by, and belong to, their own cultures and communities.[35] An individual who is recognized as a universal example of holiness is just that: an example. The contemplative woman who spent the bulk of her life in silence behind monastery walls in the twelfth century exhibits a different kind of holiness from the single mother today who, valiantly and selflessly, struggles day in and day out to provide food and shelter for her two children.

All expressions of Christian holiness can never be exhausted since, as new needs within history call forth fresh gifts from individuals, the appreciation and understanding of holiness will shift accordingly. If historians cling to a narrow theological understanding of holiness as they delve into the lives of men and women from the past and present they may miss out on innovative expressions of the way the Gospel has been incarnated in a range of times and places. Christian holiness is not a theological category of human experience independent of time, place, and culture. Rather, it is an expression of the many imaginative and creative ways God's Spirit has enlivened men and women to respond to the needs of the times.

In the history of Christian spirituality, historians and researchers in general can incorporate various ways of examining the objects of Christian spirituality, alongside the strictly historical and theological. There is also the need to discern the interior dimension of historical investigation: the intentions, feelings, and mentality of those involved. Interpretive methods in the history of Christian spirituality can include analysis from various disciplines to help gain a meaningful perspective on this dimension of investigation.

Also, because it is not desirable to align the histories of Christian spiritualities with any one theology, neither can they be aligned with any one denominational community (Church). Theologies and models of Christian communities (Churches) are closely linked. Including one inevitably includes the other, which further restricts the potential for picking up missed strands of the rich histories of Christian spiritualities. Even though the historian may be tied to one faith tradition or another, he or she needs to be open to moving beyond the boundaries set by either its theology or its self-understanding as a faith community. This openness allows the as yet unknown aspects of Christian spirituality from the past to emerge either within his or her own tradition, or from within the traditions of others.

Christian spirituality and its *particular* history

The object of study in the history of Christian spirituality is more than a history of events and the persons who influenced or played a part in them. It is more than a study of the traces of the past reflected in paintings, music, or architecture. The history of Christian spirituality also includes a history of the *phenomena* of Christian spirituality interpreted through the invisible signs of God's self-giving grace alive in the hearts of men and women down through the ages. These phenomena surpass the strictly historical, the events that can be verified according to science. Miracles, physical healings, changes of attitudes, the acceptance of Christian values, the resurrection of Jesus, and other events can all be admitted into the collection of what happened in the history of Christian spirituality, even though they may have left no physical traces.

Stories from the past not only reveal what happened, but they also tell how people interpreted or perceived Christian Spirit active in their lives. They strove to live purposeful and meaningful lives based on how they discerned God's active Spirit in the world – the phenomena of Christian spirituality referred to above. Let us look at the life of Augustine of Hippo to examine this point further.

Augustine of Hippo (354–430) lived in the northern part of Africa. In the early years of his life, he felt empty and lost. As a young person he had participated in different religious movements, but none of them responded to his deepest longings for life. After encountering Ambrose, the Bishop of Milan, he was reintroduced to Christianity and tried to adopt it as his way of life. However, Augustine also enjoyed the pleasures of a concubine – pleasures he believed were contrary to his Christian commitment. They had a child together. Caught between his desire for a satisfying sexual life and intimacy with God (two things Augustine could not reconcile), Augustine suffered a lot. But he desired God greatly and believed that God was also seeking him. One day, while sitting on a bench in a fenced-in garden, his bible beside him, he heard a voice that said "take up and read." (The voice was from one of the children playing on the other side of the fence.) Believing this to be the "voice of God," he picked up his bible, which was open at random, and read from Romans 13:13–14. This passage exhorts the reader to "put on the Lord Jesus Christ, and make no provision for the flesh, to gratify its desires." The words struck Augustine like a thunderbolt. On the spot he resolved to embrace Christianity with all his heart. He sent away his concubine and was baptized into the Christian faith. He later became a priest and Bishop of Hippo. His writings became very influential and have touched the lives of countless Christians over the centuries.

This series of events from the life of Augustine of Hippo leads us to ask questions like "What happened in the garden?" or "Did the event happen at all?" From a strictly historical perspective, we can question what Augustine heard and whether he reported it accurately ten years later (the garden event occurred in 386 and he only wrote about it in 396). Was it the "voice of God" speaking through one of the children? Were they playing a game that involved instructions to "take up and read"? These questions are hard to answer. What is known by Augustine's testimony in his autobiography is that he *perceived and believed* this to be the voice of God for him. So powerful was this perception and belief that it changed the rest of his life. We can speak, therefore, of the *conversion* of Augustine – not as a historical event that somebody saw, but one that happened, in much the same way the historian can infer or construct other events of history.

This aspect of the nature of the history of Christian spirituality – phenomena that do not easily withstand strict historical verification – needs to be taken seriously. Given the evidence of Augustine's own witness to what he believed happened, as recounted in his autobiography, along with the subsequent actions he took as a result of his embrace of Christianity, this story *is what happened.* And it is recounted as part of the history of Christian spirituality as such. What distinguishes this story from other historical accounts (for example, in the political realm) is the affirmation of the grace and Spirit of God alive in areas of human life, which cannot be proven using the type of proof used to verify other historical events. God's Spirit in the world works in human lives in surprising, and often unseen, ways that only become evident in later events.

The nature of Christian spirituality, in terms of its history of events and peoples, and even in terms of its art and architecture, shares much in common with historical research as a scientific discipline. However, this phenomenal perspective also needs to be considered seriously. If the phenomenal aspect which accepts as legitimate the categories of grace, inspiration, conversion, belief, martyrdom, piety, and the like, is not acknowledged there is the risk of excluding that which does not easily lend itself to strict historical verification. Miracles, healings, and other extraordinary events such as spirit possession and exorcisms are an integral part of the history of Christian spirituality. When this is acknowledged, we gain some access to, and understanding of, the interior dimension of the history of Christian spirituality, which can then be studied with its own suitable methodology. There is a branch of philosophy that develops research methods to deal precisely with these kinds of issues. It is called *phenomenology.* It is beyond the scope of this book to go into the details of this research method, however, a few reflections on it might provide the spark for the interested reader to pursue this topic elsewhere.[36]

Phenomenology is dedicated to developing ways to show or bring to appearance phenomena as they are, that is, to describe something within its own capacity and points of reference. Phenomenology constructs a method "which might lay open the processes of being in human existence in such a way that being, and not simply one's own ideology, might come into view . . . phenomenology . . . [opens] up the realm of the preconceptual apprehending of phenomena."[37] Given the methodology of phenomenology it could be a very important tool for studies in Christian spirituality, and spirituality in general, with respect to the study of things like conversion, spiritual development, and the effects of grace. All these phenomena cannot be viewed directly but are important parts of the lives of Christian figures written about in history books.

Let's take another example of a phenomenon which is difficult to confirm given the guidelines of strict historical verification: the Christian martyrs. Who are they? Up until the fourth century, the Roman emperors did not recognize Christianity as a legitimate religion. Christians were publicly persecuted – often before large crowds. Many Christians were threatened with death if they did not renounce their faith. A significant number chose death. These men and women, and those down through the ages who gave their lives for their faith, are known as Christian martyrs.

Dramatic descriptions of martyrdom, in paintings or in books, complete with graphic details of physical torture and suffering, may be dismissed by the serious historian as wild exaggerations of what really happened,[38] reduced to the decision of a fanatic few who meaninglessly gave their lives out of personal weakness. However, these images of martyrdom play a significant role in the history of Christian spirituality: they witness to the power of personal commitment to the Christian faith (this is the phenomenon that is being studied – not the actual death of the person). So strong was the martyrs' personal commitment to the legacy of Jesus that, rather than renounce the truth of his self-giving love, they chose to die with him in spirit and in body. This is the lot of the martyr. Martyrdom has little meaning outside this context.

But how can the faith of these men and women be verified in a scientific way? Some people might suggest that it is nearly impossible to do so except to say that the act of self-giving love unto death, in itself, is the truth behind the historical event of Christian martyrdom. Does acknowledging this latter position require the eyes of faith – as it required the faith of the martyr to give up his or her life to witness to the truth of the life, death, and resurrection of Jesus? These are the kinds of questions asked by believers and non-believers alike when it comes to a determination of the meaning of martyrdom, its authenticity as a Christian act, and its truth value as a witness to Christian faith.

Truth in the history of Christian spirituality implies more than admitting such-and-such happened, as chronicled in the history books of Christian life. It also involves *why* it happened – that is, the interior dimension. The example of the martyrs shows that relationship with God is reflected in the selfless acts of men and women who lived profoundly their personal love-relationship with Jesus. The nature of that love-relationship, ultimately one that is characterized by faith and modeled on the life, death, and resurrection of Jesus, is the truth of embodied Christian life. Christians trust that, in the end, God's self-manifestation and self-giving can be translated into the concrete history of human beings.

But frequently, spiritual phenomena are hidden from direct observation, as we saw in the examples of Augustine and the Christian martyrs. Augustine *inferred* that the child's voice was that of God; he *inferred* that what he subsequently read was a message from God *for him*. Augustine's conclusions were based on faith. And so were those of the Christian martyrs – their faith gave them the freedom to embrace martyrdom. Since faith is invisible in itself, many events in the history of Christian spirituality could not count as data for historians who understand history from a purely scientific perspective. But that does not mean that these events must be dismissed as such.

There is a truth proper to Christian spirituality that cannot be verified by purely scientific historical analysis but instead has its foundation in faith. Reality is multi-layered, consisting not only of what is observed as historical events in the natural world, but also the personal dimension of human nature that is not directly observable. Historical method in the study of the history of Christian spirituality needs to include, as much as possible, the multi-layered nature of reality. All areas of human experience, therefore, should be the subject of historical inquiry.

Between the historian who has no commitment to any faith (or perhaps is antagonistic to all faiths) and the historian who is very much faith-filled, there appears to be, at times, an unbreachable gulf. As seen above, the perspective or world view of the historian functions as a criterion of selection when it comes to what is to be counted as the data of history, and what is to be excluded. For the rationalistic historian, it is more difficult to include in historical accounts the data of history not defined by the boundaries of rational thought. Such a historian may find it problematic to take seriously things like miracles. But this is where a paradox arises. Just as the historian who admits the truths of faith must infer what happened to someone like an Augustine, the purely rationalistic historian must infer what happened to lead to, for example, the great stock market crash of 1929. The past is never entirely available to us. We have access only to fragments of evidence.

The history of Christian spirituality is thus challenged to find appropriate methodologies for its investigations of what happened that employ sound historical methods of investigation but that also take seriously the religious commitment to which it is in service. In this way, historians build up credible accounts of the ways history, as history that is credible, witnesses to the real events of God's life in the world. Of particular interest are the extraordinary stories of men and women whose biographies recount numerous strange and miraculous happenings throughout their lives. These accounts are known as hagiography (HAG-EE-O-GRA-FEE).

Even though hagiography has often been dismissed as wildly exaggerated accounts aimed more to witness to personal holiness than to describe historical events, it is worth a closer look.

Christian hagiography

Hagiography is a style of writing that is usually found within biographies and autobiographies.[39] It relates extraordinary events in the lives of holy people, often described as saints, to reveal their exemplary lives or to advance other purposes.[40] The difference between hagiography and ordinary biography or autobiography is that hagiography describes events that did not necessarily happen, in order to idealize a person's life or to make some other point.

For example, the *Life of Antony*, composed by Athanasius of Alexandria (c.293–373) around 357, was written to encourage the monastic life and to demonstrate the nature of true holiness: the capacity to exercise control over demons. Antony (c.250–356) was a hermit who lived in the Egyptian desert and who practiced an extreme form of asceticism. Athanasius recounts Antony's miraculous powers, which he exercised in his numerous encounters with diabolic forces. His victories, according to Athanasius, were a sure sign of Antony's personal holiness. Obviously, Athanasius favored a particular kind of asceticism and monasticism, which he sought to exemplify in the *Life of Antony*. But whether Antony struggled so overtly with demons and devils in the ways suggested by Athanasius is open to interpretation. Athanasius clearly had another agenda: to characterize the path to holiness as the triumph over evil in this world, achieved by the ideals of asceticism and fostered in the monastic life as a whole.

Hagiography is frequently found in religious literature from the Western European Middle Ages, from about the sixth century to the sixteenth. These are often referred to simply as *Vitae* (lives) in Christian spirituality. These *Vitae* reflect different models of holiness, as the understanding of holiness changed through the years. But hagiography is also found elsewhere: for example, in political biography or the recounting of very difficult or near-impossible journeys. The tendency to exaggerate to make specific points seems to be part of human nature. But hagiography is not mere exaggeration; there is something far more significant at play.

For example, in our own lives, we may embellish the facts to make the point of how impossible a task or journey was. We end up the hero; we succeeded against all odds when others may have failed. As we recount our perilous past, we know that the actual goal is not to relay historical fact, but to demonstrate the accomplishment of the impossible. Most of us can probably recall using hagiography at some point. In a similar way, the lives of holy men and women in Christian history have often been recounted using hagiographic content.

Hagiography in Christian spirituality intends to bring to the reader not historical facts, but the stories of men and women who demonstrated Christian heroic virtue according to the norms of the times. Their lives, as described in hagiography, are meant to inspire, move, or engage the reader into action. Thus, hagiography is not meant to be an accurate reporting of the past; it is meant to disclose the truth of the virtue of someone's life, so that others are inspired to live in the same way.

Hagiography is historical only to the extent that there is some link to historical reality – for example, the individual lived in such-and-such a time, setting, and place – but the incidents recounted in the text may be quite fictitious. This is not a problem in hagiography. Thus, reading hagiography to find out the kernel of the truth of what happened is misdirected. Although it may be desirable to try to uncover factual truth within hagiography, it is not enough to separate the extraordinary from the ordinary. The value of the story lies in what is not true, that is, the extraordinary, rather than what could be proven with historical certainty, that is, the ordinary. In hagiography the world and the life of the individual are described in a way that brings forth deeper truths about the world and about life: the possibility of the exceptional, the novel, the holy, the heroic, in the here and now. If it happened once, in that person's life, it can happen in yours or mine.

Hagiography gains plausibility because it uses the tools of historical writing, mixing factual content (however minimal) with embellishment. Thus, hagiography results in a kind of historical account that may have happened. The factual content often reflects the same spiritual, social, political, and economic realities seen in other literary genres, such as poetry or short stories. In this way, hagiography is rendered credible because the context, perhaps described in a similar way as in other published works, is believable. Furthermore, real issues are dealt with in hagiography. Hagiographical accounts reflect real pain and distress in life, real concerns, real joys, real hopes. A lot is going on beyond what is in the text itself. The reader is meant to be taken up into these real issues and respond to them in his or her own life, as did the person in the story. Understanding hagiography does not lie in recounting only the meaning of the story but also in being swept up by its literary and imaginative force.

Thus, when reading the lives of holy and saintly people in the history of Christian spirituality, it is a mistake to scoff at anecdotes that are clearly not representative of the historical past. Rather than dismissing these stories, there is a need to ask about the deeper meaning of the events as they fit into the overall life of the individual as well as the historical, political, cultural, economic, and ecclesial context in which the individual lived. Underneath the extraordinary, what truth about the Christian life is being told in these events? What message is being brought to awareness today? How might people take up that message in their own lives?

Role and place of tradition in the history of Christian spirituality

The history of Christian spirituality is full of traditions. These traditions involve beliefs, attitudes, rituals, prayers, and practices that give witness to the ways relationship with God and with each other has been understood and lived out in the past. At the same time traditions anchor enduring truths for the lives of the present and future members of Christian communities. Thus, as generation after generation recognizes the meaningfulness in certain beliefs, attitudes, prayers, or practices, traditions take shape. Tradition is different from history in that history usually refers to the entirety of the past. Tradition refers to what first has been received and then is intentionally transmitted to future members of communities because it holds special importance in the life of the community.

Traditions, therefore, are not suddenly born. They evolve over time, slowly taking form in the consciousness and practices of faith communities. At a certain point, a group may identify what has become a tradition, but only after looking back and identifying what has been faithfully brought forward by the faith-filled community over time. Christians trust in the presence of the Holy Spirit to guide the community and to renew it through its grace-filled presence. Traditions that are brought forward capture the truth of the Spirit's guidance for future generations.

What Christians receive from the historical past, therefore, is not merely facts or perceptions concerning what happened as history. Rather, they receive beliefs, persuasions, and convictions. Based on these beliefs, persuasions, and convictions, Christians live today in continuity with the past, but always interpreting the received traditions within the current context. Christians thus talk of *living* traditions within the history of Christian spirituality. Traditions situate current generations within what previous generations have found meaningful, and thus become the source of possible truth for contemporary Christians as well. But this does not happen without interpretation – the past is not brought blindly into the present. Tradition is the recognition that there is an exchange between interpreting the past as it has been received and interpreting the present as it is now lived. The result may be changes or shifts in the traditions, for while there is continuity in traditions, there are also innovations. Fidelity to spiritual traditions must give way to creativity that may involve "not only deeper insight, but also new insight, and even correction and purification."[41]

The past offers contemporary people meaningful insights into the living of life that continues to be nourishing today. People living today are heirs to the past, but not in a passive sense – traditions survive only when they are subject to interpretation that continues to bring them to life for current living. Christians trust in the presence and influence of the Holy Spirit in renewing traditions as they are lived, so that Christian spiritualities may be shaped in fresh ways for the world of today and tomorrow.

Conclusion

History has been described in this chapter as a fundamental partner in the study of Christian spirituality. Without history, it would be impossible to know what the Christian community has lived in the past, nor what needs to be brought forward for the future. Without some knowledge of Christian history it is nearly impossible to understand Christian life today. The history of Christian spirituality gives a context within which we can understand the journey of those who have lived in the past, and how this informs the lives of those who live in the present.

But history is not simply an accurate retelling of past events to assist us in understanding the present – an explanation of how Christians arrived at this time and place in their historical development. The work of the historian does involve the discovery and accurate retelling of past events, but it also involves the discovery of "lost beliefs, lost values, lost outlooks on life, and perhaps lost insights and understandings,"[42] which are just as important. The work of the historian is to help understand how people thought, what they believed, how they related to their world, and how they perceived themselves in that world. These are the real treasures that historians offer. By looking at the artifacts of the past, they are able to bring to life the aspirations, hopes, and dreams of persons and peoples from times past.

Christian spirituality, in its search for ever more authentic expressions and appropriations of the life of Jesus, needs to pay close attention to the work of the historian. Only in doing so will it be possible to recover from the past what is useful to transform the present and direct us into the future.

History helps people break out of the tendency to accept the world as it is – as it was received and previously lived. With the study of history we understand that we are historically conditioned creatures who are, to a large extent, directed by our pasts. Christians also come to know that the Holy Spirit has enlivened people in diverse situations for there is no one way to live out the richness of God alive in the world.

RECOMMENDED READING

Becker, Carl L. (1971) "What Are Historical Facts?" in *The Dimension of History: Readings on the Nature of History and the Problems of Historical Interpretation*," ed. T. N. Guinsburg, Chicago: Rand McNally, 29–40.

Delooz, Pierre (1979) "The Social Function of the Canonization of Saints," *Concilium* 129:9, 14–24.

Holt, Bradley (2005) *Thirsty for God: A Brief History of Christian Spirituality*, 2nd edition, Minneapolis: Fortress Press.

Principe, Walter H. (2004) "Broadening the Focus: Context as Corrective Lens in Reading Historical Works," in *Minding the Spirit: The Study of Christian Spirituality*, eds Elizabeth A. Dreyer and Mark S. Burrows, Baltimore, MD: Johns Hopkins University Press, 42–48.

Sheldrake, Philip (1992) "The Nature of History," in *Spirituality and History: Questions of Interpretation and Method*, New York: Crossroad, 9–31.

References to research topics from this chapter

Alberigo, Giuseppe (1970) "New Frontiers in Church History," in *Concilium* 7:6, 68–84.

Bouyer, Louis *et al.* (1963–1969) *A History of Christian Spirituality*, 3 volumes, tr. Mary P. Ryan, London: Burns & Oates.

Breisach, Ernst (1983) "The Christian Historiographical Revolution," in *Historiography: Ancient, Medieval, and Modern*, Chicago: University of Chicago Press, 77–106.

Congar, Yves (1970) "Church History as a Branch of Theology," *Concilium* 7:6, 89.

Cousins, Ewert H. *et al.*, eds (1985–) *World Spirituality: An Encyclopedic History of the Religious Quest*, Vol. 16, 17, 18, New York: Crossroad. (About twenty-five volumes to date.)

Coyle, J. Kevin (1998) "Early Monks, Prayer, and the Devil," in *Prayer and Spirituality in the Early Church*, eds P. Allen, R. Canning, and L. Cross with B. J. Caiger, Everton Park, Queensland: Centre for Early Christian Studies, Australian Catholic University, 229–249.

De Certeau, Michel (1988) *The Writing of History*, tr. Tom Conley, New York: Columbia University Press.

Ferro, Marc (1984) *The Use and Abuse of History: Or How the Past is Taught*, London: Routledge & Kegan Paul.

Kieckhefer, Richard (2004) *Theology in Stone: Church Architecture from Byzantium to Berkeley*, Oxford: Oxford University Press.

Laycock, Steven W. and James G. Hart (1986) *Essays in Phenomenological Theology*, Albany: S.U.N.Y. Press.

Leclerq, Jean (1968) *The Spirituality of the Middle Ages*, tr. the Benedictines of Holme Eden Abbey, Carlisle, London: Burns & Oates.

Lonergan, Bernard J. F. (1996) "History," "History and Historians," in *Method in Theology*, Toronto: University of Toronto Press, 175–196; 197–234.

Pourrat, Pierre (1927–1955) *Christian Spirituality*, 4 volumes, tr. W. H. Mitchell, Jacques and Donald Attwater, London: Burns, Oates and Washbourne.

Seasoltz, Kevin R. (2005) *A Sense of the Sacred: Theological Foundations of Christian Architecture and Art*, New York: Continuum.

Stanford, Michael (1986) *The Nature of Historical Knowledge*, Oxford: Basil Blackwell.

Stone, Lawrence (1977) "History and the Social Sciences in the Twentieth Century," in *The Future of History*, ed. Charles F. Delzell, Nashville, TN: Vanderbilt University Press, 3–15.

Tosh, John (1984) *The Pursuit of History: Aims, Methods and New Directions in the Study of Modern History*, London: Longman.

Van Engen, John (1986) "The Christian Middle Ages as an Historiographical Problem," *The American Historical Review* 91:3, 519–552.

Weiler, Anton (1970) "Church History and the Reorientation of the Scientific Study of History," *Concilium* 7:6, 13–32.

White, Hayden (1978) "The Historical Text as Literary Artifact," in *The Writing of History: Literary Form and Historical Understanding*, Robert H. Canary and Henry Kozicki, eds, Madison: University of Wisconsin Press, 60.

NOTES

1   This brief history is summarized from Lawrence Stone (1977) "History and the Social Sciences in the Twentieth Century," in *The Future of History*, Charles F. Delzell, ed., Nashville, TN: Vanderbilt University Press, 3–15.

2   Meaning in life is a peculiarly human experience and is very difficult to define. History, as Bernard Lonergan indicates, is intimately tied to the generation of meaning in our lives. He states: "In the concrete physical, chemical, vital reality of human living, then, there also is meaning. It is at once inward and outward, inward as expressing, outward as expressed. It manifests need and satisfaction. It responds to values. It intends goals. It orders means to ends. It constitutes social systems and endows them with cultural significance. . . . The many expressions of individual living are linked together by an intelligible web. To reach that intelligible connectedness is not just a matter of assembling all the expressions of a lifetime. Rather, there is a developing whole that is present in the parts, articulating under each new set of circumstances the values it prizes and the goals it pursues, and thereby achieving its own

individuality and distinctiveness." (1996) "History and Historians," in *Method in Theology*, Toronto: University of Toronto Press, 211.

3 For an example of how we can look to the past to enlighten our understanding today with respect to the Spirit and prayer, see Frederick E. Crowe (2004) "The Spirit and I at Prayer," in *Developing the Lonergan Legacy: Historical, Theoretical, and Existential Themes*, Toronto: University of Toronto Press, 294–303. This is a good example of how fresh insights can be teased out of previous understandings about prayer using contemporary analytical tools – in this case, the use of Bernard Lonergan's notion of "interiority."

4 Lonergan, "History and Historians," 179.

5 These examples are taken from Stone, "History and the Social Sciences in the Twentieth Century," 22–23.

6 Stone, "History and the Social Sciences in the Twentieth Century," 22.

7 Stone, "History and the Social Sciences in the Twentieth Century," 23.

8 Paul Ricoeur, "Toward a Hermeneutic of Historical Consciousness," in *Time and Narrative*, Volume 3, trs. Kathleen Blamey and David Rellaner, Chicago: University of Chicago Press, 217.

9 The following authors tend to present the history of Christian spirituality as one – that is, as a seamless continuity from one historical era to the next: Pierre Pourrat, Louis Bouyer, and Jean Leclercq. For example, Pourrat, sometimes referred to as the first historian of Christian spirituality, built his four-volume history on the assumption that whatever forms spirituality manifests itself in, the same spiritual doctrine was at the center of it. The same fundamental spirituality was at work – there was merely a difference in style and presentation. See the bibliography for reference to the works of all three authors. However, the more recent publication of the three volumes that deal with Christian spirituality in Ewert H. Cousins *et al*, eds, *World Spirituality: An Encyclopedic History of the Religious Quest* (1985–) characterizes the uniqueness of various eras and different ways of appreciating the spiritual quest.

10 Philip Sheldrake (1992) *Spirituality and History: Questions of Interpretation and Method*, New York: Crossroad, 94.

11 This example is summarized from John Van Engen (1986) "The Christian Middle Ages as an Historiographical Problem," *The American Historical Review*, 91:3 (June), 546–547.

12 See Caroline Walker Bynum (1988) "Religious Women in the Later Middle Ages," in *Christian Spirituality: High Middle Ages and Reformation*, Jill Raitt, ed., Volume 17 of *World Spirituality: An Encyclopedic History of the Religious Quest*, New York: Crossroad, 121–139.

13 Michael Stanford (1986) *The Nature of Historical Knowledge*, Oxford: Basil Blackwell, back cover.

14 A remarkable study in this regard is Richard Kieckhefer's (2004) *Theology in Stone: Church Architecture from Byzantium to Berkeley*, Oxford: Oxford University Press. Kieckhefer suggests that church architecture can also reflect different models of God. He states: "If one basic purpose of church design is to call attention to the holy present in the context of sacred space and sacred symbols, there are various ways to achieve this goal. It may seem plausible that the different visions of ecclesial aesthetics are correlated with

differing notions of God: that a cathedral of impressive dimensions and design, with intricately articulated space and with a dazzling array of symbolic ornament, will speak of a God known chiefly through works of culture; that a refined and dignified space with white walls and broad uncolored windows suggests a God revealed mainly through the reading and preaching of scripture; that a relatively small and low, comfortably domestic environment invites an awareness of God as present within the gathered assembly; that a yet smaller space, with interior walls of unconcealed brick and with dim and indirect lighting, will serve best as a place for private meditation on an inwardly present God." (133)

15 Margaret Miles (1985) *Image as Insight: Visual Understanding in Western Christianity and Secular Culture*, Boston: Beacon Press.

16 Miles, *Image as Insight*, 41.

17 Richard Krautheimer (1980) *Rome: Profile of a City, 312–1308*, Princeton: Princeton University Press, 18, cited in Miles, *Image as Insight*, 45. R. Kevin Seasoltz holds a similar perspective with respect to the reflection of Christian spirituality in church architecture in the fourth century: "From an architectural point of view, the early Christian basilica manifested a profoundly symbolic interpretation of Christian life in the world. The concepts of center and path were especially important. An emphasis on interiority was common to all early Christian churches. In a sense they were conceived as interior worlds representing the eternal city of God. A simple treatment of the exterior served to emphasize the inward thrust." (2005) *A Sense of the Sacred: Theological Foundations of Christian Architecture and Art*, New York: Continuum, 98.

18 "Examination of the visual evidence of the fourth-century churches shows that Christianity accepted and placed within its own context a wide variety of pagan, Jewish, and imperial images and themes in an effort to build all human beings into the church of Christ." Seasoltz, *A Sense of the Sacred*, 98.

19 "Literary evidence from the fourth century focuses on theological debate, creedal definition, and political repercussions, but visual evidence provides material for reconstructing the larger context within which these struggles took place. If we begin with visual evidence we notice, when we subsequently examine literary evidence, the implicit prominence, even in texts of the theme of a *via universalis* [universal way]." Miles, *Image as Insight*, 42–43.

20 *Patrologia Graeca* 46, col. 572 cited in Miles, *Image as Insight*, 44–45. "The instructional value of an image consists not of the communication of information but of the power of the image to engage and train the will through the perceptions." Miles, *Image as Insight*, 45. Other influential writers, such as Augustine of Hippo, also held this view.

21 Miles, *Image as Insight*, 53.

22 This example is summarized from Seasoltz, *A Sense of the Sacred*, 101.

23 For more examples of this nature see F. Thomas Mathews (1993) *The Clash of the Gods: A Reinterpretation of Early Christian Art*, Princeton: Princeton University Press.

24 For a visual history of the ways Jesus has been illustrated throughout history in Christian art, and thus reflects dominant spiritualities associated with Jesus in various time periods, see Jaroslav Pelikan (1997) *The Illustrated Jesus Through the Centuries*, New Haven: Yale University Press. This illustrated

history is divided into themes that depict various "faces" of Jesus, such as "The Rabbi," "The Monk," "The Teacher," and "The Liberator."

25 Van Engen "The Christian Middle Ages as an Historiographical Problem," 542.

26 J. Kevin Coyle (1998) "Early Monks, Prayer, and the Devil," in *Prayer and Spirituality in the Early Church*, P. Allen, R. Canning, and L. Cross with B.J. Caiger, eds, Everton Park, Queensland: Centre for Early Christian Studies, Australian Catholic University, 248.

27 See J. Kevin Coyle, "Early Monks, Prayer, and the Devil," 230 for references to this alternate position.

28 Philip Sheldrake (1992) *Spirituality and History*, 84.

29 This brief note on the Christian Crusades is not meant to simplify what was, in fact, a very complex series of events that led to this horrific period in the history of Christianity. The origin of the Crusades is also very closely tied to political events in the Middle East, expansionist ambitions of land-hungry knights and noblemen, and the rich commercial opportunities that would result from the occupation of Jerusalem by Christians.

30 John Tosh (1984) *The Pursuit of History: Aims, Methods and New Directions in the Study of Modern History*, New York: Longman, 118.

31 As Giuseppe Albergio comments: "It is not by accident that Western Church history has totally neglected the history of the Eastern Churches since the schism. Only the sixteenth-century reformers, having broken with Rome, began to take an interest in Eastern Christianity. Rome had rejected it, as well as them." (1970) "New Frontiers in Church History," *Concilium* 7:6, 70. The schism being referred to is the break between the Eastern (e.g. Greek and Russian) and Western (European) churches due to deep cultural and political differences that could not be bridged. Although this break developed over a number of centuries, the traditional date for the separation is 1054.

32 See István Bejczy (2001) *Erasmus and the Middle Ages: The Historical Consciousness of a Christian Humanity*, Leiden: Brill.

33 Bernard Lonergan, "History and Historians," 211.

34 See Alberigo "New Frontiers in Church History," 68–84 especially page 75. Alberigo also brings the anthropological issue to the fore in historical studies. He states: "There is a rather delicate problem yet to be resolved, about the kind of anthropology that is needed to underpin the kind of . . . history we have been talking about. Historians . . . will have to examine more closely . . . their conception of what man [*sic*] really is, and, above all, their formulation of working hypotheses and their sorting out of priorities on this basis." (83)

35 Philip Sheldrake (1992) *Spirituality and History*, 85.

36 The use of phenomenology to study Christian spirituality has scarcely begun. Much work could be done here. To see how theological studies are using the resources of phenomenology see Steven Laycock and James Hart, eds (1986) *Essays in Phenomenological Theology*, Albany: S.U.N.Y. Press.

37 Richard E. Palmer (1969) *Hermeneutics: Interpretation Theory in Schleiermacher, Dilthey, Heidegger, and Gadamer*, Evanston: Northwestern University Press, 128.

38 Margaret Miles describes the impact and use of visual representations of martyrdom in the church of the German Hungarian College, Santo Stefano

Rotondo in Italy. Between 1582 and 1583, thirty frescoes of martyrdom scenes were painted in this church, still the largest circular church in the world. The Jesuits, a religious community of men founded in 1540 by Ignatius of Loyola used these images to instruct and inspire their new members, known as novices. As she says: "In these lurid scenes of torture and slaughter, the severed limbs of dismembered saints are numbered, as in anatomical paintings of the time. The paintings are carefully described by rather lengthy inscriptions in Italian and Latin. Jesuit novices were instructed to memorize and mentally affix to each scene a short prose piece or poem of devotion. This program of simultaneous visual and verbal exercise was apparently highly effective in training Jesuit novices for a sacrificial life of contemplation in action." *Image as Insight*, 122.

39 This presentation is summarized largely from Edith Wyschogrod (1990) *Saints and Postmodernism: Revisioning Moral Philosophy*, Chicago: University of Chicago Press, 3–30.

40 See Peter Brown (1981) *The Cult of the Saints: Its Rise and Function in Latin Christianity*, Chicago: University of Chicago Press *and* Pierre Delooz (1983) "Towards a Sociological Study of Canonized Sainthood in the Catholic Church," in Stephen Wilson, ed., *Saints and Their Cults: Studies in Religious Sociology, Folklore, and History*, Cambridge: Cambridge University Press.

41 Sandra Schneiders (1991) *The Revelatory Text: Interpreting the New Testament as Sacred Scripture*, New York: HarperCollins Publishers, 78.

42 Stanford, *The Nature of Historical Knowledge*, 50.

Questions of text

"The ways in which we 'experience' the world are wrapped up with our concerned engagement with 'the world.' This interpenetration is textuality."

Beryl C. Curt, *Textuality and Tectonics*

"A text, in effect, 'fixes' discourse [speaking], preserving its meaning when the event of speaking passes away. So consideration of the 'textuality' of the text is first of all important because it reveals how meaning can be expressed, preserved, and conveyed over temporal and cultural distance."

David Pellauer, "The Significance of the Text in Paul Ricoeur's Hermeneutical Theory"

Introduction

EVERYBODY LOVES A GOOD STORY. Whether it is told on the big theater screen, performed as an opera, or read from the tattered pages of a favorite childhood story book, we all enjoy participating in storytelling and story-receiving in differing ways throughout our lives. My life is no exception. While growing up on a small farm, I spent many evenings huddled in the large, well-used armchair by the fireplace, absorbed in a tale of fiction. I loved to read, and through reading I participated in the most gallant and tragic of human quests; from climbing Mount Everest to sailing across the world to conquer unknown lands, I was there, *really*, taking part in these noble adventures! Stories have that effect on us: they take us to the action, transform us into one of the participants, and draw us into the intrigue that seeks to be resolved.

In Christian spirituality, many texts that have been passed along in the traditions act upon people in the same ways: they take the reader to the heart of the action. They transport the reader into their world so he or she can take part in what the text is all about. This is not to suggest that the Christian texts are fiction, as I described storytelling above. But, fiction or not, texts in general – and the dynamics that play out in the life of the individual and community when reading them – hold many things in common. Texts play a central role in the development of Christian spiritualities, since these texts bring their readers into a world of values and action that reflect the long-standing wisdom of the Christian traditions. Numerous kinds of texts within the Christian traditions could be used as examples. Keep in mind, however, that not all these texts are of the same quality or hold the same level of importance.

Obviously there are the biblical witness of men and women and their stories of life with God, with each other, and within the cosmos at large.

The biblical text is a primary text for the development of Christian spiritualities. In fact, we could describe the scriptural witness to the saving activity of God's love as *the* classical text.[1] It holds special prominence in the life of the Christian communities. However, many kinds of other texts are also of great significance in Christian spiritualities. These include the many biographies and autobiographies of the lives of Christians. Christian prayer books, hymn books, sermons, letters, and poetry also reflect and nourish Christian spirituality today. But what about Christian musical scores, statues, paintings, architecture, and other works of art that have come down through the ages as expressions of Christian spirituality? Could these also be read as texts? Indeed, all these cultural expressions could be read as texts.[2] How we understand that this is the case will be examined below in detail. For now we can acknowledge that the word *text* comes from the Latin word *texo* meaning "to weave" or "to construct." Hence, any woven meaning in some form or other is a text according to the Latin origin of the word.

Let us call to mind the central issue of this chapter: the nature and the use of texts. This is what is known as *textuality*, the reflection on how and why texts, even those from the distant past, can be meaningfully read and interpreted today. This reflection is important for us since Christian communities use texts for many purposes such as prayer, recording past experiences of God in their lives, and articulating the truthfulness of their beliefs.

As we reflect on textuality, the following questions surface: How do texts function in developing Christian spiritualities today? What issues must we pay attention to in selecting and reading texts from the Christian historical past as well as those being developed in the present? Which texts should we pay attention to, and why? Communities today are experiencing a plurality of spiritualities; each one is named by specific boundaries or frameworks, such as feminist spiritualities, political spiritualities, black spiritualities, or liberationist spiritualities. What role does the life experience of the reader bring to the current meaning and appropriation of the text from within these boundaries or frameworks?

All of the above-mentioned questions require serious reflection, since texts play a major role in affirming Christian belief and practice in so many important ways. As explorers of Christian spirituality, we will most likely find ourselves often turning to texts from the past and present – for academic study, personal edification, and spiritual nourishment, or out of casual interest. Christians read and interpret these texts for various reasons: they look to the writings of important historical figures to guide them; selectively adorn places of worship with inspiring art; use poetry to gain insight into the deeper poetic dimension of life; and so on. Because texts in many forms continue to function as an integral part of Christian belief and practice, we must reflect critically on the way they are used and interpreted.

What is a text?

Normally the word *text* is used to refer to *written* language. Texts are produced by taking up pen and paper, or in today's more high-tech world, by typing on a computer keyboard. But, in our understanding of text in Christian spirituality, a much broader definition of the word seems to be needed. Not only have men and women left behind written texts as witnesses to their sublime experience of God, but we also have other expressions of these experiences. For example, could we not consider as texts the primitive drawings left on the walls of the catacombs of Rome in the first century? And what about the musical scores and paintings of the German mystic Hildegard of Bingen, who gave witness to her visions from God through these mediums? Or, could the complex forms of religious paintings and statuary of the baroque period (seventeenth century), which convey drama, movement, and tension between the material and spiritual worlds, not be considered as texts? The short answer to this question is a simple "yes."

> The textual objects for the study and interpretation of Christian spiritualities cannot be reduced to *written* texts. Beyond written texts Christians have left witness in numerous other forms to the way God's Spirit has been active in their lives, for example, music, statuary, and paintings. All these forms could be considered as meaningful traces that witness to God's Spirit in the world, and thus be open to interpretation, each in their own way.

We therefore affirm that texts are more than written records. We do not make this affirmation naively, simply because it suits our strategy to include a range of forms of witness to God's active Spirit in the world. Language theorists agree.[3] Paul Ricoeur, the French philosopher of language, for one, affirms that the concept of text covers a broad spectrum of realities. It includes any work of culture – that is, any inscribed expression of human existence – whether that be in written text, musical score, painting, statuary, symbol, image, architecture, or other artforms. All these media give expression to human life and have the potential to make truth claims about reality.[4] Whether such an expression is found in a book, statue, or piece of music, it sets up a world of relationships beyond its own immediate boundaries and invites the reader, viewer, or listener into the task of interpretation. For example, the expression on the face of a statue (sad, longing, joyful, hopeful, etc.), gestures of the hands (outstretched, arms folded, pointing, wringing, clasped, etc.), even the colors (dark, light, monochromatic, mixed, etc.), all speak to realities other than the concrete existence of the statue in itself. Through these gestures the viewer is drawn into levels of reflection beyond the appearance of the immediate statue. The viewer is led into the task of interpretation through these variables of the statue: What does the statue say?

Let's reflect on the above with a particular statue in mind. Most of us are familiar with the statue of *The Thinker*. Sculpted by the French artist Auguste Rodin (1840–1917) in 1881 *The Thinker* sits unclothed on a rock, torso leaning forward, head held up by a solitary hand, eyes gazing pensively toward the earth. The intense emotion in his face prompts the viewer to conclude that he has something important on his mind. The statue quickly directs the viewer to ask this question: "What is so important that the thinker sits undistracted while the rest of the world drifts by?" If we look a little further into the origins of *The Thinker*, we discover that it is part of a collection of sculptures which depict various scenes from *The Divine Comedy*, written by the Italian poet Dante (1265–1321). *The Thinker*, who sits at the gates of hell as depicted in Dante's work, appears to be reflecting on the meaning of life and his potential banishment to the fires of hell. Our attention may subtly shift at this point: instead of wondering what is so important for the person depicted in the statue, we are invited to reflect on the meaning of our own life and its future prospects. In a way similiar to that of interpreting written texts, we, or the viewer in general, have traveled the route of interpreting the statue.

Our interest here is the truth claim that these media make concerning life with God, and the human expression of it. Meaning can be expressed and preserved over temporal and cultural distance through these artforms. They take up and voice the truthfulness of the way God has been in relationship to God's people. Let us briefly look at a second example from the world of artistic expression: that of Hildegard of Bingen.

In the paintings of Hildegard of Bingen, we can see a struggle to break free from accepted patterns of oppression (feudal master over common laborer; man over woman; cleric over lay person). Her cosmic vision of inclusivity and equality of all people, as expressed in her art, gives witness to this dimension of God's saving plan for the world. Hildegard's expression of the sanctity of all life is another powerful dimension displayed in her artistic work.[5] She recognized that there is a deep relationship between the love of God, the love of the world, and artistic expression. The expression of life's beauty through art brings people into relationship with God, and with one another, in ways that cannot be anticipated. Art that moves people to rejoice and be happy, or to cry and be mournful, directs people's emotions toward the transcendent nature of life just as written texts do. Art produces worlds in which people's imaginations can wander and thus open up new possibilities for their lives. The example of Hildegard of Bingen, which is not unique by any means, challenges us to be open to all kinds of textual witness to the ways God's love is lived and celebrated.

Perhaps a more obvious example is the expression of spirituality found in the icons in the Eastern Christian traditions.[6] Icons are painted images of God or holy people, often on pieces of wood and sometimes adorned with gold paint or even precious stones. They were used for worship and veneration in churches as reminders of God's presence in the world. Henri Nouwen, a Roman Catholic writer on Christian spirituality, has written a short book on how to pray with icons called *Behold the Beauty of the Lord*.[7] It gives rich insights into how we can *read* icons and become more aware of God's saving presence in the world.

All these expressions – statuary, music, and icons – could be considered as legitimate texts, and as ways that the Christian traditions have been appropriated and made available to be passed on to future generations.

In summary, texts, by which we imply all the media described above and not only written texts, fix the meaning of human experience in some objective form that is then open to interpretation and re-interpretation in various settings and time periods. Because of these characteristics of texts, we are able to bridge the gap between historical time and the lived time of the world as we know it. But we cannot construct this bridge without taking into account the interpretation process. Let us examine that process now.

Interpretation of texts

From the very outset of this reflection, the objective nature of the content of texts is affirmed. What does this mean? Simply put, texts can often be identified as being about something that we can describe in concrete terms, even if only very generally. For example, the Spanish mystic Teresa of Avila, in her book *The Interior Castle* (1577), tells about a large castle with many rooms. She guides the reader through the rooms using colorful images and detailed descriptions. But is the text *just* about a castle and its many rooms?

As the reader progresses and begins to put the interpretive clues together, he or she realizes what Teresa is describing: the journey of transformation in and through the contemplative love of God. *The Interior Castle* has become well known for its insightful description of transformation in the contemplative life.

However, even though Teresa describes this journey in detail, there is something unique about the journey for each and every individual. She invites the reader to bring his or her own experience of journeying with God as one of the elements in the interpretation of the text. Including one's personal experience emphasizes the subjective element of the interpretation process. Thus we can say that the text challenges the individual to reflect upon his or her own journey as it relates to the journey narrated in *The Interior Castle*.

Teresa reminds us that the reader brings valuable perspective to the interpretation of the text. This helps shape the current meaning of the text in situations that are not specifically described or anticipated there. How could Teresa possibly have described everybody's journey from her own time, let alone those countless readers in the future? Thus, each individual is invited to read and interpret the text from the perspective of his or her own experience.

A helpful approach to interpreting texts that respects the objective content of the text and gives a place to the subjective experience of the reader in the meaningful interpretation of texts is called a *hermeneutical* method of interpretation.[8] As we saw in Chapter 1 the word hermeneutics comes from Hermes in Greek mythology, the name of the messenger of the gods to human beings. Hermes, the son of the gods Zeus and Maia, was responsible for bearing messages between the gods and the human world. Thus, hermeneutical theory refers to techniques used to tease out the message given in texts. But the hermeneutical method of interpreting texts proposed here does not merely answer the question "What does the text mean?" but rather, "What does the text mean *for us today?*" In order to answer this latter question two things need to be held together in productive tension: the objective content of the text, and the subjective experience that the reader brings to the reading and interpreting of the text. Let us now examine both of these poles in more detail.

The objective content of texts

The first pole, the objective content of the text, is what the text is about: what the text says about life, about spirituality, about something. But acknowledging that the text has something to say does not necessarily admit that there is some absolute meaning in the text in and of itself, let alone meaning that is settled once and for all time periods and circumstances. Texts come from particular historical settings and are always read and interpreted within subsequent historical settings that may shape their meaning in new and different ways.

> Texts in Christian spirituality are not instruction manuals. They are texts that use metaphor, figures of speech, parables, poetry, and other imaginative literary devices to convey meanings and truths about life, about people, and about God, but these truths are not immediately available.

It is because these texts are so highly charged and open to multiple meanings that the interpretive task is needed in the first place. Think, for example, of the fourteenth-century writings of the Englishwoman Julian of Norwich (1342–c.1414). In her *Revelations of Divine Love*, also known as *Showings*, Julian recounts her painful love affair with Christ. Her religious experience would have been shaped by the enormous loss of human life due to the black plague spreading across Europe at that time. From the first pole the reader asks the question "What does the text mean?" There may be an intended meaning in the text as planned by the author, but this is not the final goal of hermeneutical interpretation. The reader could stop at saying that Julian's visions represent an imaginative attempt to give meaningful expression to the absurdity of death that surrounded her in the small English town of Norwich and throughout Europe in general. But how does this acknowledgment help the reader understand the experience of death and pain today? The reader needs to go further than merely acknowledging the origins and truths of the text related to its time of production. The second pole in the interpretive process is needed to bring the text meaningfully forward into current times.

The subjective meaning of texts

The second pole, tied intimately to the first, is the importance of the perspective that the individual brings to the reading and interpretation of the text. The reader, with his or her own life experience, will always read texts from this embodied perspective. Just as we need to acknowledge that texts have a history of interpretations that are brought to bear on current interpretations, we recognize that one's personal past shapes the perspective from which texts are read and interpreted. Christian spirituality, as an academic field of study, acknowledges the importance of the experience of the reader, which gives texts new life. The reader is involved in a life-world – a world of family life, work, prayer, self-giving, faith community, and so on. From this second pole the reader asks this question: "What does the text mean today, given that the current life-world is most likely quite different from the life-world during which the text was written?" Answering this question is the true hermeneutical task. With this question, the text has the potential to be brought forward from the past and taken back up into living speech in the life of Christian communities today.

A dynamic relationship exists between the two above-mentioned poles. The reader is informed by the objective content of texts but is also able to gain new meanings from texts because of the subjective elements he or she brings to the text.

> The cumulative experience of our lives, our history of relationships, and the current existential situation within which we find ourselves – in short, our life-world – are all brought to bear on the current reading of the text. The task before us in interpreting texts is to make the transition from the life-world of the text to our own life-world.

The two poles of objectivity and subjectivity, although each individually recognized, are inextricably linked in the development of the understanding and appropriation of texts. When texts are approached in this way the texts are kept supple and fluid, and room is left for the dynamic nature of life, and the active presence of God through the Holy Spirit, to enter the world through the interpreting of texts. When the objective and the subjective nature of the text are kept in productive tension, then Christian communities more easily remain open to new ways that God speaks to renew them within a changing and developing world. It is this kind of reading and interpretation of texts that gives great hope that classical texts, as well as those lesser-known texts in the Christian traditions, can be brought forward into current times so new meaningful insights may be gained.

Thus far we have acknowledged the two poles that need to be kept in tension in order to interpret texts in a helpful way. The first pole – respecting the text itself and giving it an active voice – has another name: it is the moment of *explanation*. Through techniques of analysis the reader is able to explain the content or life-world of the text. The second pole – respecting the experience and the life-world that the reader brings to the text – is the moment of *understanding*. Here the text is brought into active dialogue with the actual circumstances of a life. Let us now consider these two moments further to see how they are developed and how they interact with each other.

The *explanatory moment* of interpreting texts

To read a text and interpret it according to various methods of study is to explain the text. For example, a person can read a text and determine its *theological* concepts or themes. The result would be a theological interpretation of the text according to known theological categories from the perspective of a particular theological tradition. A reader could approach the same text from a *psychological* perspective, describing the psychological states of characters in the text, their interaction with each other, and how their states of mind may have shifted from the beginning to the end. A psychological reading of the text might describe the meaning of the text as a reflection of the significant events in the life of the author (traumatic childhood experiences, for example). Or, a reader could study the historical and cultural setting, again, of the same text to determine how it reflects significant events during the time it was written. This is known as *historical criticism*. The meanings of particular words or phrases, and how they have evolved through time, could also be part of the study of a text. This is *literary criticism*. Studying a text's genre (e.g. poem, hymn, narrative, parable, sermon, letters, monologue), overall structure (structural analysis), metaphors, figures of speech, and so on, would help the reader get at the objective explanation of the text – that is, what kind of meaning the text intends to bring forward.

All these critical analytical tools can be used to gain insight into the sense of the text. Limiting reading and analysis to one method may not reveal the full depth of the content of the text. Using two or more methodological approaches – such as literary criticism and theological interpretation – will take the project further.

Reading the text from a number of perspectives, e.g. theological, historical, or literary, is very helpful in the initial phase of interpretation. They help describe what the text is about in order to describe the life-world of the text, but do not yet access the meaning of the text as it intersects with the world today.

For example, when someone first reads the poem by the sixteenth-century Spanish mystic John of the Cross entitled the *Spiritual Canticle* (1584), he or she discovers a story about two lovers roaming the countryside, seeking each other.[9] Along their journey they encounter animals and beautiful country vistas. Eventually, they find each other and consummate their love. That is the story that the *Spiritual Canticle* tells, but this is only a surface reading. To get to the deeper meaning, one first needs to do a careful study of the text. This study and analysis is the explanatory moment of interpreting the text. It is akin to the process of exegesis which biblical scholars carry out with respect to biblical texts.

In analyzing the *Spiritual Canticle*, the reader can undertake historical-contextual studies to see how the language of the text reflects the culture of sixteenth-century Spain, during which time the poem was written; literary-textual studies would explore the sources of the rich images and metaphors; thematic-symbolic studies would develop the recurring themes; theological studies would describe and connect the poem to common theological beliefs of John's time. On this latter point (the theological beliefs of John's time), the *Spiritual Canticle* could be interpreted as descriptive of the threefold classical spiritual itinerary, explored in Chapter 7. All this work is necessary. Some scholars contribute to scholarship in Christian spirituality on this level, as an end in itself. And this is an important part of work being done in the academic field of Christian spirituality today. They clarify the meaning of the text as the text presents it, in itself, to the reader.

However, interpreting a text is not an end in itself when it comes to understanding the text in relationship to current realities. The goal is not always to understand *the text* better from one of the perspectives described above. Interpreting a text from within the parameters of its production is quite different from interpreting a text in a contemporary context. In explaining the text the reader may have explained various components of it: explained the historical and political setting that gave production to it, explained it in relationship to the life of the author, and explained its theological points. But he or she has not yet moved to the task of *understanding* the text in the context of *the world of the current reader*. This task is yet to be accomplished. We'll see how we can move beyond the moment of explaining the text to understanding the text below. For the moment, let's examine other ways of getting at the explanatory moment of textual interpretation.

Texts are not only about describing realities that may result in the transmission of knowledge – literary, cultural, political, theological, and so on – but they are also about the task of helping the current reader make sense of his or her own life.

Other ways of describing the explanatory method of interpreting a text are to talk about: 1) author-centered interpretations; 2) text-centered interpretations; and 3) reader-centered interpretations. Each of these may enlighten the reader's explanatory knowledge of the text.

Author-centered interpretations of texts

Some methods of interpretation search for the author's intended meaning in texts, either by objective analysis or by bringing the text into dialogue with some of the author's other writings. Within an author-centered reading, absolute priority is given to the intended meaning of the text as stated (implicitly or explicitly) by the author. In short, an author-centered reading focuses on the development of the text within the life-world of the author and how his or her world affects the interpretation of the text. This leads the reader to focus on a psychological analysis of the text: the text is explored through the mind of the author.

Although this is helpful as one source in the interpretation process, to remain with the author's immediate meaning may limit the work of the text. Such a process keeps the text at the level of explanatory interpretation. If the reader insists on getting at the meaning of the text through an investigation of what the author intended, the reader may get caught at a dead end. There is always more meaning in texts than even what the author may have immediately intended. That is why texts continue to speak in varying cultural and historical moments. In some ways, a text is independent of the author, and of the world in which the text was produced. Acknowledging this truth allows us to bring texts into active dialogue with our own world.

Text-centered interpretations of texts

A text-centered reading takes into consideration that once an author has written a text, he or she in some way loses control over it. The text takes on a certain independence from the time within which it was written, as well as from the intended meaning of the text as stated by the author. Texts float free in history. A text-centered reading, therefore, takes seriously what is actually written and is now before the reader.

Text-centered readings strive to be as objective as possible – they don't ask about the author, the intended audience, or the context. Text-centered interpretations ask how the text is put together, its overall structure, and how it develops from one part to the next. It identifies the literary characteristics of the text. A text-centered reading may track the way characters in the text change roles or are eliminated from the text, and so on.

Reader-centered interpretations of texts

Reader-centered interpretations bring to the text a particular lens or perspective through which the text is read. We've mentioned some of these already: theological or historical interpretations or one through the lens of a feminist critique. Let's explore a bit further what a feminist critique might include.

Applying the principles of a feminist reading to the text may open it up to new readings and new meanings (whether the reader agrees with these readings and meanings or not). A feminist critique might expose the injustices of sexism, the abuses of patriarchal power structures, and oppressive dualisms that are implied, if not explicit, in the text. This exercise may challenge the reader to be more critical (in the sense of becoming acutely aware of what is being read) when interpreting these texts. Texts are written within specific cultural moments and will reflect certain biases (both helpful and less helpful ones). Acknowledging this reality requires that readers approach texts, even classical ones that have proven to be of great value over the years, with a critical eye.

The problem was, and is, readers may have read texts and unknowingly (perhaps like the author did) used them to re-enforce the status quo of the cultural moment – both the positive and the negative aspects – without consciously realizing it. Feminist analysis of some texts has exposed the narrowness of some thinking and thus presents a challenge to reconstruct people's perspectives in a significant number of areas such as those mentioned above. The result has been, overall, a retrieval of women's many and diverse contributions to spiritual life and to society. As presented in Chapter 9 a number of recent books remind us that women were powerful agents in the unfolding story of God's Spirit in the world. These books correct an imbalanced view of God's redemptive presence in the world as dominated by masculine structures and perspectives.

To summarize, then, the explanatory moment of interpreting a text has its own dynamics even though it has links to the moment of understanding the text. When we first read a text we understand it at a certain level, however superficially. The text cannot fail to be about something. This initial encounter can then be modified, authenticated, and deepened by applying various critical analytical techniques.

In general, the notion of explaining a text involves a reading that makes the text more transparent. For example, it may situate the text in the setting of its origins, make explicit theological or spiritual principles that are implicit in the text, or develop it in relationship to other texts that seem to be about the same thing. In the above example of the *Spiritual Canticle*, the reader may notice that it closely resembles the biblical Song of Songs. This moment helps develop one's critical perspective on the text, but is not yet the moment of understanding the text.

The move to understanding the text shifts the reader to the second phase of the interpretation project: that is, to ask the question of how the text is relevant in the here and now. The task of interpretation is ultimately to take the text back up into discourse as event in the life of the reader. The text thus becomes living speech once again.

The *moment of understanding* in interpreting texts

As indicated above, the properly hermeneutical task is to understand the text from the perspective of the life of the current reader, who asks certain questions: How does the text enlarge the world in which he or she now lives? How does it give a better understanding of what it means practically to live in that world? Reflecting on these questions, and others like them, opens hitherto unseen possibilities for living with a new vision for the world as well as one's place in it. The information gathered from the explanatory phase of interpreting the text is carried forward to ask the questions of the text's current meanings. The explanatory phase, which describes the life-world of the text, is essential. It will guide the reader along, but is not given the final say on current meanings.

In order to understand the text there is a need to be mindful of the life-world that the readers bring before the text. Texts are always read by flesh-and-blood people who believe, suffer, hope, forgive, find joy in life, love, and so on. How does the text speak to the current world, the situation now, in which believing, loving, and forgiving take place? What new possibilities for life does the text open up as it shapes anew ideas about God, people and communities, and the world in general?

The life-world of the current reader includes the life-world of the text, that is, the understanding of the text available currently to the reader. The text and the life-world of the reader both have their own sociological, political, ecclesial, and spiritual sensitivities, but the two life-worlds are linked. The encounter is informed and guided by the explanatory phase, whose insights gave a preliminary understanding of what the text is about. However, new questions and new data may expose new meanings as the text is read at a deeper level. But we must not forget that, alongside the current reading, past interpretations are available from the community of readers who have received this text down through the ages. After all, texts are read within interpretive traditions that cannot be ignored. These are all brought to the current project of interpretation – not to clarify meaning in the text at a conceptual level (this has already been done in the explanatory phase), but to gain meaning at the level of human life. Gain in the meaning of a text is not merely a conceptual gain: it plays itself out in the realities of life. The life-world of the text is thus brought into dialogue with the life-world of the reader, which opens us up to new ways of seeing the world and, as Christians, life with God.

The hermeneutical reading and interpretation of texts follows a few simple steps that can be summarized in this way.

First, a text is read with a question in mind, as vague and imprecise as this question may be. This is true even if the text is read for personal edification. The text is chosen keeping in mind that the content of the text may shed some light on personal questions. At this level, the reader has encountered the text in a naive reading and interpretation of it, but the reader has an intuition or a hunch that the text has something to offer. So the reader keeps going.

Second, to deepen the critical awareness of the text, the reader may choose to reread it through a particular critical lens, such as literary criticism, historical criticism, feminist perspective, or theological framework. Through these readings of the text, the reader can critically explain, from the perspectives of each method, or even from the perspective of the author, the inspiration behind the first production of the text. With this, the reader has passed beyond a naive reading and interpretation of the text. But these readings ought not to exert absolute normative control over the text's meaning today. There is no meaning or truth in a text per se, regardless of which framework has been used to get insight into the text. And so the reader continues.

Third, with the above information in mind, the text is allowed to confront current realities in the reader's life. The life that is being lived, with its own world view and its own critical awareness of the social, political, and church milieu, is allowed to encounter the depth of the text. The experience of the reading subject is brought forth: the joys and accomplishments, pains and anguish of a life are brought to bear upon the text, and the text upon this life. To understand the text is to allow oneself to follow the path of thought that the text opens up. At this level, the reader discovers what the text is about, how it may be taken back up into living speech, to be performed again in the hopeful life of the reader.

The above method of interpreting texts shows how the perspective of the reader can be brought to bear on the text in order to gain new meaning from it. To explore this idea, let's remain with the thoughts presented above on a feminist analysis of classical texts. Women who have experienced the wonder of pregnancy and childbirth may now have insight into the creative, birthing nature of God, and thus may spontaneously name God using feminine terms. Having become mothers themselves, they may find it natural to speak of Divine Motherhood. This, in turn, may lead them to read, for example, scripture, in an entirely new way.

Let's take a specific example from the Old Testament. The biblical figure of *Hokmah/Sophia* (spoken of in Prov. 1:20–33; Prov. 8; and Prov. 9) may take on new meaning following the act of childbirth. *Hokmah* in Hebrew, *Sophia* in Greek, was a street preacher in the market.[10] Recognized as a prophet, she identified herself with life itself, and is related to the act of creation (Prov. 3:19). A close analysis will reveal that Sophia's self-description in these texts is remarkably similar to Israel's description of the unnamable God. The birthing mother would find it a short step to identify Sophia with a feminine naming of God, for Sophia helps name the feminine, creative attributes of God. Since God is mostly named in masculine terms, a feminist analysis, combined with the shared experience of birthing, opens up the possibility of new language to describe God and thus new understandings of how God is present and active in the world. These understandings may, in turn, open up reconsideration of the roles men and women are invited to assume in the various Christian churches.

This example shows that the life-world of the reader has a critical role to play in the current meaning of texts. But neither the text, in itself, nor the experience of the reader, in itself, is taken as absolute; a balance of the two needs to be achieved. The text may give fresh insight into one's personal experience, and that experience may open the reader up to explore new meaning in the text. As mentioned above, the meaning of the text can be developed methodically, through the explanations of various studies of the text. This, in turn, affects understanding. And so the cycle continues as new explanatory methods, such as a feminist critique, are incorporated into the text's encounter with the life of the reader. An ongoing and deepening

Hermeneutical Interpretation of Texts
In Christian Spirituality

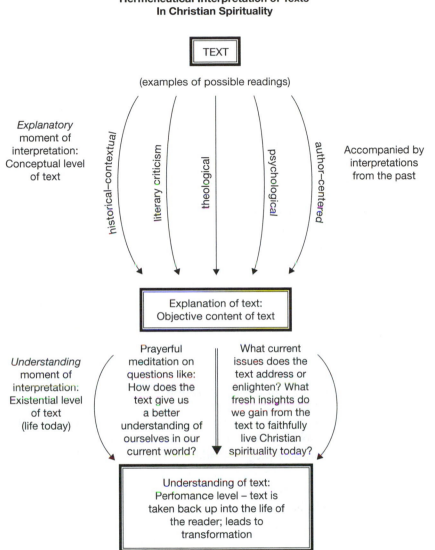

TEXT

(examples of possible readings)

Explanatory
moment of
interpretation:
Conceptual level
of text

historical–contextual

literary criticism

theological

psychological

author-centered

Accompanied by
interpretations
from the past

Explanation of text:
Objective content of text

Understanding
moment of
interpretation:
Existential level
of text
(life today)

Prayerful
meditation on
questions like:
How does the
text give us
a better
understanding of
ourselves in our
current world?

What current
issues does the
text address or
enlighten? What
fresh insights do
we gain from the
text to faithfully
live Christian
spirituality today?

Understanding of text:
Perfomance level – text is
taken back up into the life of
the reader; leads to
transformation

understanding of the text takes place through the movement back and forth between explanation and understanding. New understandings are continually added to the text by augmenting the objective information accumulated about the text. In this way, the text may introduce correctives in the way things are viewed so that current understandings are enriched and expanded.

With this hermeneutical method a dogmatic approach to interpretation (the text means one thing and one thing only, for all times and all places) is avoided. Dogmatic interpretations tend to exclude the life experience of the current reader. We are therefore led toward a reading that takes the life experience of the current interpreter into consideration of the actual meaning of the text. This approach is important since merely trying to tease out the concepts or meaning in the text – that is, explain the text – may not allow for the actual context and religious experience that the reader brings to the current reading and interpretation of the text.

This fundamental problem is often overlooked in the reading and appropriation of texts within the Christian traditions. The result has been the tendency to make texts too hard and too dogmatic, thus weakening their capacity to speak within new historical settings far removed from their time of origin and so provide fresh insights. The two horizons – of the text and of the reader – must meet in the reading and interpretation of texts so the text may be truly understood. Both horizons are taken seriously in a hermeneutical reading of texts.

Summary: explanation and understanding

Even though explanation and understanding form a unique interpretive method, they can also be identified separately by the kinds of knowledge and relationships that they each engender, as the following shows.

Explanation
- produces knowledge that does not need to be gained by personal experience;
- aims at clarifying abstract knowledge according to known categories; logical consistency, based on reason, is fundamental to its method;
- questions are brought to the text as an object to be studied; questions are not necessarily

Understanding
- produces knowledge based on human experience; knowledge is personally acquired;
- aims at clarifying knowledge in relationship to what is known on the personal, intuitive level; logical consistency is not fundamental to its method;
- involves personal life of the reader; individuals find themselves being personally

linked to the personal life of the reader; one-way relationship to text;

- analysis of text appears to be non-evaluative but does contain the bias of human interest: that is, one's own world view;

- knowledge gained by explanation is accessible to all through rational thought;

- knowledge remains at the level of concepts based on empirical investigation; closed within itself.

questioned and interpreted by the text; two-way relationship to text;

- bias (world view) is appreciated as being the place of meaningful encounter between the text and the reader; bias is a positive factor in the text's interpretation;

- knowledge gained by understanding is a personal knowledge; it shows itself through the performance of the text in action/life;

- knowledge is open to transcendent dimension of life and is productive of meaning; open to personal transformation.

The reading and interpreting community

When I refer to "the reader" above and elsewhere in this chapter, I am not referring to a singular reader with his or her own private interpretations. Rather "the reader" refers to the entire reading community that is receiving the text, even though this community does so through individual readings and interpretations that are always partial and open to further interpretation and appropriations.

It is the entire community, with its beliefs, practices, and language, that provides the context for the appropriation of texts, even if the reading is by the solitary reader-interpreter. People grow up within a particular historical community that first shapes their ideas, gives language to express those ideas, and provides a particular perspective informed by, for example, specific faith, cultural, sociological, and political frameworks, that inform the context brought to the reading.

A reading community is thus implied, or implicitly present, in any individual reading of texts. Furthermore, the reading community can bring one text in relationship to another. In Christian spirituality inter-textual readings and interpretations situate texts in the broader tradition and wisdom of the Christian communities.

Through its collective wisdom, the reading community is able to embrace new meanings in the texts that are already important in the life of a particular Christian community, or to embrace texts that hitherto have been largely unnoticed. Sometimes new meanings or new texts are noticed first by gifted individuals who have taken the time to study and ponder the texts, but a singular interpretation does not definitively fix the meaning of the text in the life of the community. The community may receive the new meaning of the text through the life of the individual who has understood his or her life differently, and goes on to witness to that difference within the community. The community then takes notice and thereby is opened up to embracing the new potential of the meaning of old or new texts. A key component in this process is the context or voice that the entire tradition, represented in the reading/interpreting community, brings to the authenticity of any one reading/interpretation of a text. When the reading/interpreting community as a whole accepts an interpretation of a text, this is an important factor in the interpretation being considered valid.

Why the hermeneutical method of interpretation is helpful

If we use a method to interpret a text that will always disproportionately favor our own predetermined perspective on the text (whether the perspective comes from the community or from our personal reading) we are less likely to discover something new about the text and about ourselves. This approach, after all, would defeat the purpose of going through the work of carefully interpreting texts: we read and interpret texts not only to understand the text itself (what it is about), but also in order to find new meaning in it for life today.

Therefore, the hermeneutical method encourages readers to be as open as possible before the text, and to employ a method that will allow the text to speak without absolutely imposing upon it predetermined meanings. This is not to deny, or to suppress, the life experience and perspective brought by the reader to the text. As mentioned above, these are part of the dynamic tension brought to any one reading. But just as it is essential to bring one's own life experience to bear upon the text when it is being read and appropriated, the text must be given an active voice in the reflection. In this way texts are productive. Texts are always brought back to life *in a life*, in the life circumstances of a real flesh-and-blood person. That is why a hermeneutical reading is the favored reading – there is room for both the text and the life experience of the reader to be brought forward.

A hermeneutical reading of texts is a helpful method that:

1. allows texts to speak in different times and places;
2. uses numerous analytical techniques (for example, literary analysis, theological analysis, feminist analysis) to open up the text;
3. acknowledges that interpretation always takes place in particular circumstances (for example, historical, political, and ethical circumstances) that have an impact on the meaning of the text;
4. values the personal life story as one of the factors that the reader brings to the text in order to tease out current meaning;
5. goes beyond a search for facts or objective information (knowledge) that the author wanted to convey to the reader;
6. acknowledges that texts only make sense in the context of a life; they are meaningful only inasmuch as they assist the reader, and the reading community, to encounter the text as a dynamic, transformative event.

In Christian spirituality, the transformative event includes transformation of the life of the individual, the Christian community, and the world in which we all live. Seeking to understand a text is therefore not merely to ask the question "What does the text mean objectively?" (that is, what the main ideas and concepts are in the text), but to ask and respond to the question "What does the text mean for today?" Exploring this second question may call individuals and communities to make choices in order to transform their lives or to take a particular stand on an issue in the faith community or in society. This is true whether scripture, biography, poetry, or any other genre is being read. Understanding a text always corresponds to being in a particular situation in a particular time, with its own parameters of meaning that calls people forth in new ways.

Truth claims in a text

In Christian spirituality truth claims in a text show themselves in action, in the ethical sphere in movements such as human justice, love, self-giving, and reconciliation. Interpretation of a text shows itself in action in the world, rather than in intellectual confirmation of the author's intentions or in conceptual knowledge that fits nicely into a systematic framework. In Christian spirituality, texts do not point people toward the historical past or to systems of absolute knowledge as much as they point people toward the prophetic future and help find new ways of being in an ever changing world. What is being suggested here is that texts, with their figures of speech, poetic metaphors, multiple layers of meaning, plays on words, and so on, never allow themselves to be reduced to one final and absolute meaning. There is always something more to be sifted out from them.

> The goal of reading and interpreting texts is not merely to bring the text from the past into the present, but through understanding the text to give a life today a more hope-filled future.

This approach to textual interpretation marks a shift from previous ways of reading and interpreting texts. Oftentimes in the past, people sought absolute and objective meaning in a text. The task of interpretation may have been to describe the meaning as determined by what the author said about the text; or to determine the meaning of the text by reducing its meaning to that of particular words, symbols, and images as they related to pre-existent bodies of knowledge; or to unearth the cultural use of these during the historical and political period in which the text was written. Ultimately, however, even though the explanatory moment places the text in a life-world, it falls short of getting at the meaning of the text for people today. All this work is necessary to assist in getting at the meaning of the text, but ultimately texts are understood when they become media for self-understanding in the world today.

Texts are performative

It has already been emphasized that to understand the text, and not merely to clarify its conceptual content, is to understand oneself and one's world better in front of the text. This understanding culminates in proposed possibilities for action and conduct. In the end, the reader is challenged to *perform* the text in his or her life. Authentic interpretation results in an authentic performance, for texts are performative in nature. They clue people into ways of acting and being-in-the-world. (The parables of Jesus are especially powerful examples.) Once this phase of reading and interpreting texts is entered, the reader has finally passed into a hermeneutical reading of the text, and not merely an objective interpretation of the text that terminates in truth claims based on dogmatic knowledge contained in the text. As a result of hermeneutical interpretation an enlarged self is given a new way-of-being in the world, instead of dogmatic truths. A hermeneutical reading of a text delves into the meaning of human existence in the here and now, not in some distant (or even near) past that is referred to or described by the text.

Prejudice as key to interpretation

The reader wants to avoid the pitfalls of an exclusively subjectivist reading, but he or she also wants to allow perspective, the context of the reading subject, to enter into the current meaning of the text. A hermeneutical reading of the text considers one's concerned engagement with the world: what is currently of significance, actual preoccupations, and timely existential questions. Ultimately, therefore, the reader always brings prejudice to the reading of a text. The reader brings a historical context, life experience, and actual values to weigh in on current interpretation of the text. In a hermeneutical reading of texts, biases are not to be set aside. Instead, they form a critical contribution to a current reading; they provide the lens with which the reader can make particular readings of the text.

The hermeneutical approach to reading texts brings into dynamic tension what the reader already knows and what he or she does not know about life. These two dimensions of knowledge continually play back and forth with each other. The reader engages the text with what he or she knows already, yet allows the text to open up new perspectives about the world, self, and God. As the reader is opened up he or she can go back to the text to read again, and potentially gain even further new meanings.

For example, someone may read Jesus's call to Matthew: "Follow me" in Matthew 9:9 (a call he or she experiences personally), one way at the age of twenty, but an entirely different way when in the late sixties. Following Jesus with all the energy and vigor of a twenty-year-old may mean something radically different than someone in his or her late sixties who may be facing retirement, health problems, or the loss of a spouse. Mixed in with these personal readings of the text there is always the communitarian level of what it means to follow Jesus, which may include specific actions, choices, and beliefs.

This dynamic of reading and appropriation, appropriation and rereading, is repeated endlessly as the text is received in different historical and cultural settings down through the years. The tradition from within which the text was read previously is preserved, for the current reader cannot discount the wisdom of the original community that found meaning and thus life in the text. However, it needs to be kept in mind that the current reading community finds itself linked to previous readings and interpretations that form part of the context of the current reading and interpretation.

Evolution of meanings of a text

The original meaning of a text may become standard in the tradition from which it evolved. It may even take on a primary role in determining the identity of the community that has appropriated the meaning that is expressed in liturgical rites and rituals, forms of ministry and governance, or specific doctrinal beliefs. This is called the *sedimented meaning* of the text: meaning that is more or less fixed. But, as we have emphasized, *innovative meanings* can be derived from texts as social, historical, political, ecclesial, and other circumstances change. Texts that have withstood long histories of moving back and forth between sedimented and innovative meanings are the ones often called *classic texts*. These texts have stood the test of time and continue to be an ongoing source of new insight and meaning in life; they challenge normative ways of thinking, believing, and acting. Let us examine the nature and use of classic texts in more detail.

Classic Christian texts

As we have just seen, the term *classic text* is used to describe foundational texts that have been used repeatedly over the centuries to gain valuable insights into beliefs and practices in the development of Christian spiritualities.[11] Classic texts come to contemporary Christian communities through their long history of effects: they continually effect or bring about the renewal of the self-understanding of the Christian communities through their capacity to inspire, revitalize, or even shock. As such they anchor the foundational beliefs and practices of Christian communities but are also sources of renewal.

Classic texts display a certain amount of normativity – with respect to the standard perspective some truth is viewed, or with respect to a particular issue or belief with a specific Christian tradition. Readers may recognize, or see mirrored, in classic texts, moments in their experience that are nothing less than the truth of life as they have come to know it. But they also recognize in classic texts their capacity to open people up to new ways of viewing themselves and their world, for such texts can upset dramatically conventional opinions. In brief, classic texts "are those texts that bear an excess and permanence of meaning, yet always resist definitive interpretation."[12]

Given these characteristics of classical Christian texts, we may think of Origen's (c.185–c.254) *Commentary on the Song of Songs*, Augustine of Hippo's *City of God*, Walter Hilton's (1340–1396) *The Ladder of Perfection*, Marguerite Porete's (d. 1310) *The Mirror of Simple Souls*, or Teresa of Avila's *The Interior Castle*. But can there be a clearly identified collection of texts that may be referred to as "classic"?

This is a fundamental question in Christian spirituality. Many of those texts that have been identified as classic texts were written by a very small segment of the population (often culturally privileged, highly educated males who were celibate, from Western Europe, and clerics). Are there texts written by others (such as women, married persons, or persons partnered in other ways, non-clerics, or those belonging to minority and other ethnic groups) that can contribute in a significant way to the development of Christian spiritualities if only their voices are given a chance? The issue of which texts are classic texts and which ones are not thus involves more than merely pinpointing those texts that have been identified as such in the past.

Opening up Christian spiritualities to those voices that have been muted in the past is useful for a multitude of reasons, including historical ones (manuscripts that were lost or incomplete), ideological biases (the reflections or conclusions in the texts didn't fit into beliefs or practices of the time), or church governance structures (writings reflecting women in positions of power were largely ignored). Thus, the concept of classic texts can be questioned in at least two ways, both closely related. The first has to do with the list of texts currently identified as classics – or, perhaps better, those texts that are excluded from receiving this description. The second has to do with the limited and limiting content of currently accepted classical texts. Let us look at both these issues.

Texts identified as classic texts: the problem

The problem here is that the choice of classic texts has revolved around a self-selecting circular process:

1. Texts were written from within a particular world view that reflected the limited knowledge and experience of the people of the times; naturally practice and beliefs are written up in texts from the perspective of the historical, social, theological, spiritual, and political world of the day.

2. Texts found to reflect the dominant values of those in control, and in positions of privilege, whether Church or state, became more easily accessible

and were affirmed as normative by those persons in positions of power and privilege; good reasons were found to ignore texts, or particular interpretations of texts, that did not affirm the dominant perspective of those of position and privilege; there was a controlled reading of texts.

3. Subsequently, in future generations, the texts first chosen as normative because they sustained the status quo were anointed as classic texts; these texts became *the* resources to authenticate or correct current trends, beliefs, or practices with respect to dominant positions of power and privilege; current practice and beliefs are made to conform to the positions reflected in texts that may have been written with radically different world views; new experiences or insights that do not conform are considered unacceptable or even heretical;

4. Classic texts, rather than opening communities up to new perspectives and new meanings, *can be the source of the exact opposite*: an affirmation of the status quo that resists change because they tend to silence competing voices and perspectives; new experiences of life with God in an ever changing world not reflected in classic texts may be ignored.

As a result of the above circular movement, new readings, based on new methods of interpretation, may be excluded because they threaten the status quo. New or developing ways of experiencing God are thereby sacrificed to the ideology of the classic text.

Classic texts can undo the hermeneutical dynamics, presented in this chapter, through a process of self-selection. This process of self-selection would naturally exclude texts that are not in line with normative understandings, whatever these might be in current times. For example, questions about the way Christians view their relationship with God (God as authority figure or God as friend?); the way people grow and mature in spiritual life (a linear development or circular development?); or the way power is shared equally between men and women (may women be admitted to ordained ministry or can only men authentically hold this role?) have received various responses at different points of history.

All perspectives that are identified as normative in texts of any given time period are considered very fine when the texts are being read by those who stand to gain the most (those in positions of privilege) or by those who can use the texts to sustain their current ways of doing things. It is a well-established fact that the power holders in any culture, whether from the political, social, or ecclesial perspectives, favor particular texts that recommend a way of life and beliefs that maintain the status quo for the power holders. Contradictory voices (and thus certain texts themselves) can be excluded today because the original text excluded those voices when it was first written.

Texts identified as classic texts: a possible solution

Although certain texts that continually speak truthfully to current historical situations are favored, there is a need to welcome voices – from the past or from new, emergent texts – that may offer fresh and invigorating ways of living Christian spirituality. When the list of texts favored by any one Christian community becomes so authoritative that other voices are excluded, there is a need to critically examine the rationale for these choices. As times change and communities develop new knowledge in all areas of life, we can expect God's Spirit to blow in unfamiliar ways that might lead to new textual voices from the past or present for nourishment.

The goal is not to establish once and for all a closed list of classic texts, but to bring into critical dialogue a range of voices. In this way communities are invited to continually reflect critically on their place in the world in relationship to God. The term *classic text*, therefore, needs to be used with some flexibility and fluidity. Even texts that have been received down through the ages in a consistent fashion and have taken on the stature of classic texts can be opened up to new readings when brought into dialogue with new knowledge and new texts. This is to suggest that even those texts identified as classic texts which have anchored a tradition and given it coherence need to be continually subjected to the dialectic of explanation and understanding described above.

New interpretations of old (classic) texts

As we discussed above, a hermeneutical interpretation of texts involves the current reading community, as it has done all along, in the actual interpretation of the text. Furthermore, hermeneutical interpretations affirm that there is more in the text than has been previously uncovered, because of the newness that subsequent generations may bring to current interpretations. Thus, when past readings are unmasked for what they are (a partial or limited perspective of the whole), or new critical lenses are brought to a reading of classic texts (for example, deepened understandings in psychology or anthropology), current readers may discover insights that until now have remained hidden in the text.

> Classic texts can reactivate the most critical and creative paradigms, already expressed in beliefs and practices of traditions, while shaping them in new ways for those traditions. Classic texts can develop an enriched sense of self, of authenticity, and of integrity in life. They can lead to transformation and conversion.

But the reader needs to be open to allow this to happen, which means allowing various perspectives to build this enlarged sense of self. The reader cannot exclude conflicting voices without first critically engaging them in serious conversation with each other. Past choices of what to include (or not include) as worthwhile choices for further study or edification in Christian spirituality may have been guided (or misguided, as the case may be) by a number of factors.

Some of these factors were skewed world views (dualist perceptions of the world that saw material realities as inferior to spiritual ones and the body as inferior to the soul); faulty paradigms of male dominance (men's spiritual experience seen as more authoritative than women's); elitist perspectives (the poor and uneducated could not possibly have anything to contribute); and clerical bias (those ordained as clerics or those who have taken vows as religious are holier than the non-cleric or non-religious).

That is why current readers in Christian spirituality need to be open to new and creative ways of reading and interpreting texts. Classic texts, even those that have been interpreted in a standard way for centuries, may surprise current readers with new insights into life with God and with each other. Classic texts may provoke and challenge people to new ways of being in the world, or act as correctives to current perspectives. Classic texts are not read exclusively with the hope of affirming the current identity of communities, but to suggest the identity of these communities in the future. A hermeneutical approach to their reading allows them to function in this way and be sources of transformation.

Above we examined the self-selecting circular choice of classic texts; this same issue applies within the reading and interpretation of texts. A reader may be tempted to interpret a text in a certain way because that is the way it has always been interpreted. Rather than allowing oneself to be radically open to new experiences or fresh insights in a critical reading of the text, he or she may favor the traditional readings. This approach is not helpful when the text appears to be speaking in a new and different way, if only the reader would listen. The current reader needs to trust that one's life experience counts for something in the interpretation of even those texts that have long been standards in the way life is viewed. If something does not fit between a reading of the text and one's life, it may be time for some serious reflection and critical analysis of past and present interpretations of the text. But it may also be time to reflect critically on one's own life: perhaps the text is challenging the reader to change in some way. It is not easy to decide which is the way to go; thoughtful and critical reflection goes a long way in assisting to tease out the truthfulness of classic texts as they are read in the context of today's world.

Classic texts belong to specific communities

What needs to be kept in mind is that people will always read and interpret texts with their own prominent biases. We've already affirmed that this is not, necessarily, a bad thing. The texts determined to be dominant in any one setting are, for example, culturally, socially, or politically specific. This is to say that those texts that reflect current positions will be favored; they will come up in conversations more often since they reflect who readers understand themselves to be and what their values are, and so on. Because this is the case, certain classical texts are more specific to some Christian communities than they are to others.

Differing groups will favor or emphasize one aspect of Christian spirituality while another community may favor another since they recognize themselves more easily in the chosen texts. Thus, it is a very difficult, or at least risky, business to speculate about what might be dominant or marginal texts for another community or individual. Dominant texts may be shaped by a variety of means and for a variety of purposes that are specific to individual faith communities.

Furthermore, communities will favor differing interpretations according to the lens through which they read texts. For one person or community a particular image, let's say of God, organizes their entire belief system. This then shapes spiritual experience and the interpretation of texts. Addressing God as "Eternal King" or "Nursing Mother" defines a relationship of a particular quality or level of intimacy. Interpretations that lie outside of the expected range of these titles may be set aside as being irrelevant (or perhaps even irreverent!). For other persons or communities, a cluster of rituals or a firm commitment to specific beliefs and doctrines may be the lens through which texts are read and interpreted, and subsequently given classical status or not. Christian spiritualities that do not hold Mary, the mother of Jesus, in prominence will most likely give little attention to the long list of Marian feast days celebrated by others.

Classical texts are thus community specific. Each community will develop its own list of texts that they favor – texts that reflect their prominent patterns of spiritual practice and the belief systems that sustain it. Southern Baptists may favor texts that value external conversational prayer with God experienced as close and intimate. Quakers may favor texts that value silence and inner listening to the voice of God. Again, the concept of classic texts needs to be kept fluid. Any given community will see certain texts as classic, but not others. This does not make one collection of classic texts more valuable than the other, for all of them have something important to offer.

Classic texts, by their very nature, are identified as reflecting and breaking open the experience of the reading community in different historical and cultural settings. The many ways of living the mystery of God are authenticated by the great many approaches to reading and interpreting the various texts that have come down through the ages in the Christian traditions. The hermeneutical perspective allows texts from previously marginalized groups within the Christian traditions to bring their voices forward, and to be tested, in conversation with those already recognized as valuable and normative voices.

Conclusion

Texts from the past have proven to be powerful resources for the shaping of spiritualities in many forms. As these same texts are read today, we recall that they were written from a different perspective on the world, with different cosmologies, with different models of God, and different models of the self. Thus, when Christian communities read texts today, the task is not primarily to link themselves to some distant past through the text, but rather to allow the text to speak to their situation today. This is why interpretation, or hermeneutics, as we have described it here, is necessary.

The above presentation has affirmed the value of the text in itself, but also affirms the life experience that the contemporary reader or reading community brings to the interpretation of the text. The Christian communities have gained much insight through the faithful living of the Spirit of Jesus over the past 2,000 years. Furthermore, as a result of great advances in a number of disciplines, world views, conceptions of the self, and favored ways of modeling God have shifted significantly within different Christian communities. All this newness needs to confront the actual and current reading and interpretation of texts. This method is what we have called the hermeneutical method.

What we come to understand with such an approach to texts is that traditions, understood in this context as sedimented interpretations, can be broken open or shaken up. Traditions are linked to culture and normative interpretations of texts. Once the culture shifts, the normative interpretation of texts will often shift as well. This, in turn, will break open the tradition to new expressions (innovations). This does not mean that the previous expressions of the tradition were false, but, with God's graceful Spirit alive in the world, Christians discover anew, or ever more truthfully, how that Spirit is alive and calling forth people in new ways. With time, the innovative interpretations born from new readings may once again fall prey to sedimented interpretations. As individuals, communities, or cultures settle comfortably into what were once new paradigms, and the world around them shifts once more, the process will undoubtedly be repeated again.

In a special way, in Christian spirituality, the Christian scriptures are recognized as the normative text that guides Christian living and belief. But even this text is subject to the dynamics of interpretation and appropriation that we have outlined in this chapter. The Christian scriptures are also open to multiple and deeper meanings than Christian communities may have given them in the past.

RECOMMENDED READING

Miles, Margaret R. (1985) "A Hermeneutics of Visual Images," "Images and Texts," and "Images and the Life of the Body," in *Image as Insight: Visual Understanding in Western Christianity and Secular Culture*, Boston: Beacon Press, 27–39.

Schneiders, Sandra (1991) "The Problem and Project of New Testament Interpretation," in *The Revelatory Text: Interpreting the New Testament as Sacred Scripture*, New York: HarperCollins Publishers, 11–26.

—— (2005) "Spirituality and Scripture," in *The New Westminster Dictionary of Christian Spirituality*, ed. P. Sheldrake, Louisville, KY: WJK Press, 62–67.

Sheldrake, Philip (1992) "Interpreting Spiritual Texts," in *Spirituality and History: Questions of Interpretation and Method*, New York: Crossroad, 163–187.

Tracy, David (1981) "The Classic," in *The Analogical Imagination: Christian Theology and the Culture of Pluralism*, New York: Crossroad, 99–124.

References to research topics from this chapter

Curt, Beryl C. (1994) "Textuality," in *Textuality and Tectonics: Troubling Social and Psychological Science*, Buckingham: Open University Press, 36.

Martin, David (1972) *Art and the Religious Experience: The "Language" of the Sacred*, Foreword by Thomas Altizer, Lewisburg: Bucknell University Press.

Pellaver, David (1979) "The Significance of the Text in Paul Ricoeur's Hermeneutical Theory," in *Studies in the Philosophy of Paul Ricoeur*, Charles E. Reagan, ed., Athens: Ohio University Press, 103.

Ricoeur, Paul (1965a) *Fallible Man*, tr. Charles A. Kelbley, Chicago: Henry Regnery Company.

—— (1965b) *History and Truth*, tr. and introduction by Charles A. Kelbley, Evanston: Northwestern University Press. Includes: "Objectivity and Subjectivity in History," 21–40.

—— (1973) "The Task of Hermeneutics," *Philosophy Today* 17, 112–128.

—— (1974a) *The Conflict of Interpretations: Essays in Hermeneutics*, ed. Don Ihde, trs. Willis Domingo *et al.*, Evanston: Northwestern University Press. Includes: "The Problem of Double Meaning as Hermeneutic Problem and as Semantic Problem," 62–78.

—— (1974b) *Interpretation Theory: Discourse and the Surplus of Meaning*, Fort Worth: Texas Christian Press.

—— (1975) "Biblical Hermeneutics," *Semeia: Experimental Journal for Biblical Criticism* 4, 27–148.

—— (1977a) *The Rule of Metaphor: Multi-disciplinary Studies of the Creation of Meaning in Language*, trs. Robert Czerny with Cathleen McLaughlin and John Costello, Toronto: University of Toronto Press.

—— (1977b) "Toward a Hermeneutic of the Idea of Revelation," *Harvard Theological Review* 70: 1–2 (January–April), 1–37.

—— (1979) "The Hermeneutics of Testimony," *Anglican Theological Review* 51:4 (October), 435–461.

—— (1981) *Hermeneutics and the Human Sciences*, ed., tr., and introduction by John B. Thompson, Cambridge: Cambridge University Press. Includes: "The Hermeneutical Function of Distanciation," 131–144; "Metaphor and the Central Problem of Hermeneutics," 165–181; "Appropriation," 182–193.

—— (1984) *Time and Narrative*, vol. 1, trs. Kathleen McLaughlin and David Pellauer, Chicago: University of Chicago Press.

—— (1985) *Time and Narrative*, vol. 2, trs. Kathleen McLaughlin and David Pellauer, Chicago: University of Chicago Press.

—— (1988) *Time and Narrative*, vol. 3, trs. Kathleen Blamey and David Pellauer, Chicago: University of Chicago Press.

—— (1990) "Hermeneutics and the Critique of Ideology," in *The Hermeneutic Tradition: From Ast to Ricoeur*, eds Gayle L. Ormiston and Alan D. Schrift, Albany: S.U.N.Y. Press, 298–334.

—— (1991a) *A Ricoeur Reader: Reflection and Imagination*, ed. Mario J. Valdés [Theory/Culture 2], Toronto: University of Toronto Press. Includes: "Mimesis and Representation," 137–155; "Narrated Time," 338–354; "Between the Text and Its Readers," 390–424; "Life: A Story in Search of a Narrator," 425–437; "Poetry and Possibility," 448–462; "The Creativity of Language," 463–481.

—— (1991b) *From Text to Action: Essays in Hermeneutics II*, trs. Kathleen Blamey and John B. Thompson, Evanston: Northwestern University Press. Includes: "On Interpretation," 1–20; "Philosophical Hermeneutics and Biblical Hermeneutics," 89–101; "What is a Text? Explanation and Understanding," 105–124; "Explanation and Understanding," 125–143; "The Model of the Text: Meaningful Action Considered as a Text," 144–167.

Wyschogrod, Edith (1990) *Saints and Postmodernism: Revisioning Moral Philosophy*, Chicago: University of Chicago Press, 3–30.

NOTES

1 For a helpful understanding of how this is true, see "Infallibility and Inerrancy" and "Authority and Normativity," in Sandra Schneiders (1991) *The Revelatory Text: Interpreting the New Testament as Sacred Scripture*, New York: HarperCollins Publishers, 53–59.

2 For an example of how art and architecture lend themselves to the interpretive process, see Margaret Visser (2001) *The Geometry of Love: Space, Time, Mystery, and Meaning in an Ordinary Church*, Toronto: HarperPerennial Canada. As Visser states on page 4: "Churches are laid out with a certain trajectory of the soul in mind." Likewise, texts are laid out with a particular trajectory, a place in which we are invited to dwell and to be transformed.

3 On Ricoeur's notion of "text" see: Paul Ricoeur (1991) *From Text to Action: Essays in Hermeneutics II*, tr. Kathleen Blamey and John B. Thompson, Evanston: Northwestern University Press. In particular see: "What is a Text? Explanation and Understanding," pp. 105–124 and "The Model of the Text: Meaningful Action Considered as a Text," pp. 144–167. David Pellauer describes Ricoeur's notion of "text" in the following way: "Taking it to its limit, the entirety of human existence becomes a text to be interpreted." (1979) "The Significance of the Text in Paul Ricoeur's Hermeneutical Theory," p. 109.

4 Edith Wyschogrod goes so far as to apply the concept of "text" to "persons and their relations." See (1990) *Saints and Postmodernism: Revisioning Moral Philosophy*, Chicago: University of Chicago Press, 19–25, 30.

5 An excellent article that connects mystical experience directly with the artist is the following: Evelyn Underhill "The Mystic as Creative Artist," *Understanding Mysticism*, (1980) Richard Woods, ed., Garden City, NY: Doubleday, 400–414.

6 For an example of how an eighth-century Roman icon of Mary may be interpreted in a similar way as a written text, see Visser, *The Geometry of Love*, 30–32. On her assessment of the relationship between the interpretation of images and texts in general, see "Images and Texts," in *The Geometry of Love*, 29–35.

7 Henri J.M. Nouwen (1987) *Behold the Beauty of the Lord: Praying With Icons*, Notre Dame, IN: Ave Maria Press.

8 Hermeneutical theory, as developed in this chapter, takes its inspiration from the work done by the French philosopher of language Paul Ricoeur. Ricoeur,

in fact, was influenced by other philosophers of language, such as Hans-Georg Gadamer and Martin Heidegger, along with a host of others who have been working on methods to critically interpret texts. Ample references are given to Ricoeur's own writings in the research materials. A recommended single introductory volume to Ricoeur's work is: David E. Klemm (1983) *The Hermeneutical Theory of Paul Ricoeur: A Constructive Analysis*, Toronto: Associated University Presses.

9   For a detailed example of how the explanatory moment in interpretation functions, see the following: David B. Perrin (1996) "Foundations for a Hermeneutical Interpretation of the *Cántico espiritual* of Juan de la Cruz," *Science et Esprit*, XLVIII/1, 61–84 and David B. Perrin (1996) "Implications of Hermeneutical Methodology for the Interpretation of the *Cántico espiritual* of Juan de la Cruz," *Science et Esprit*, XLVIII/2, 153–174.

10   This brief description of *Hokmah/Sophia* is taken from Elizabeth Johnson (1993) *She Who Is: The Mystery of the God in Feminist Theological Discourse*, New York: Crossroad, 86–90.

11   In 1978 Paulist Press launched a book series by well-known as well as lesser known authors who have contributed to Christian spirituality down through the ages. There are currently over 130 titles in *Classics of Western Spirituality*. This collection has made a significant contribution to studies in Christian spirituality. See "Review Symposium: The Twenty-fifth Anniversary of the Classics of Western Spirituality Series, in *Spiritus* 5:1, Spring 2005, 88–110.

12   David Tracy (1987) *Plurality and Ambiguity: Hermeneutics, Religion, Hope*, San Francisco: Harper & Row, 12.

7

Questions of human-spiritual development

"Faith and human development designate essential elements of human experience. They are . . . distinct perspectives that belong in dialogue. Through the dual lenses of developmental psychology and faith informed by religion and theology, our human condition becomes more fully visible."

Felicity B. Kelcourse, *Human Development and Faith*

"Spiritual development is the ongoing integration that results in the self-responsible subject from openness to an intrinsic principle of authentic self-transcendence."

Daniel A. Helminiak, *Spiritual Development*

Introduction

MOST PEOPLE TODAY would easily accept the concept of the stages of human development. These stages are readily identifiable in the biological life cycle: we are born, then grow from infancy to early childhood, to adolescence, to adulthood, and then to our senior years. This seems obvious enough. However, stage theories, along with describing biological growth and aging, also imply a sense of progress and development that could be described as a maturation process on more levels than the strictly biological.

We expect the behaviors, attitudes, values, and wisdom of the twelve-year-old to be different from those of the seventy-year-old. People in later life tend to expand their world view and they experience in a concrete way the interconnectedness of all things. Thus, questions of human development need to take into consideration the biological, the psychological, the sociological, and the spiritual. When it comes to describing how these stages take place, their major characteristics, and the transition period from one to the next, a wide spectrum of opinions is available.

Notable psychologists who put forward a range of theories or models of human development include Jean Piaget in *The Child's Conception of the World* (1969); Lawrence Kohlberg in *The Psychology of Moral Development: The Nature and Validity of Moral Stages* (1984); and James Fowler in *The Stages of Faith: The Psychology of Human Development and the Quest for Meaning* (1981).[1]

Spiritual writers who present various descriptions of spiritual life as a journey with different stages include Augustine of Hippo in *City of God*; Walter Hilton (d. 1396) in *The Ladder of Perfection*; John Bunyan in *The Pilgrim's Progress*; Gregory of Nyssa in *Life of Moses*; and Teresa of Avila in *The Interior Castle*. The details of one such description of human-spiritual development, according to the insights of John of the Cross, will be taken up below in the section on the classical spiritual itinerary. Of course, during the time of John of the Cross (sixteenth century), and up until the time of the Enlightenment, spiritual and human development were largely viewed as one and the same thing.

> Until the seventeenth century, the religious world view saw all life through the eyes of faith; human development was no exception. Human development was carefully mapped out in conjunction with the Christian's understanding of the way God's Spirit was active in the world, in the community, and in the life of the individual Christian.

The significant numbers of ways of looking at human development and, at the same time, spiritual development are closely related to the time period in which they were developed and used. Different time periods reflect differing anthropologies, cosmologies, theological or spiritual doctrines, and more or less developed psychological frameworks. For example, the ancient Greek culture recognized that the life cycle was rooted in the larger reality of the cycle of nature and the relationship with the gods. The Greeks recognized the body as being part of nature and thus linking human life and development to nature's cycles of regeneration: birth, death, and rebirth. This theory offered a framework within which the Greeks could understand human development. Christian spirituality, with its religious world view that recognized the Spirit of God active in growth and conversion, offered another model of human growth and maturation linked to the *imago Dei* discussed in Chapter 4. Our modern and postmodern view of the world, informed by contemporary scientific, psychological, and sociological insights, provides us with alternative theories of human development.

What we see, therefore, is that there are many different ways of understanding what it means to grow and mature as a human being. What this chapter seeks to do is bring into dialogue theories of human development (in a general way) with insights from Christian spirituality concerning the same. What we want to underline is that psychology can contribute to our understanding of human maturation but the opposite is also true: Christian spirituality has much to offer psychological theory.

In this chapter we will also examine some descriptions of human-spiritual development as they are presented from writers within the Christian traditions. In particular we will examine the concepts of mysticism, asceticism, and the threefold classical spiritual itinerary.

Fundamental points of reference: models

The Christian God

Today, Christian spirituality is challenged once again to provide its own perspective on human growth and maturation. This is a difficult challenge given the dominant scientific view of the world and a greater understanding, from a psychological perspective, of the human person. But the task is not to dismiss one side of the discussion in order to embrace fully the other. Rather, the task is to allow various models to contribute a fuller understanding of human-spiritual development from differing perspectives. These models (or perspectives) can be tested out against the cumulative experience of men and women over extended periods of time.

As witnessed through the writings of the Christian authors mentioned earlier, their models of spiritual development closely reflect their personal experience – experience that resonated in the personal lives of those who read their works. For that reason alone, they merit close attention and are a resource for critical reflection on spiritual and human development by future generations as well.

Christian witness to spiritual and human development down through the ages does not reflect clinical trials that result in the construction of theories of human growth. Rather, their descriptions reflect what men and women actually experienced, and articulated as best they could, in their journeys of human growth in the context of Christian life. For example, the image of *ascent* was often used to describe the maturation process as a movement toward perfection in God. Given the cosmology operative at the time (God lived "up in heaven"), this image spoke significantly to the general Christian population. Walter Hilton's *Ladder of Perfection* (fourteenth century) and John of the Cross's *Ascent of Mount Carmel* (sixteenth century) use ascent imagery. Teresa of Avila describes spiritual and human development in a vast array of colorful images as the pilgrim makes his or her way through the many rooms of the "castle of the soul" in *The Interior Castle* (sixteenth century).[2]

A great many notable Christian writers had a profound grasp not only of the way God was operative in human life, but also of the way development occurred on a human, psychological, level.

Even though a John of the Cross or a Teresa of Avila did not separate human development from the spiritual, their work contained accurate psychological insights. Current studies on these classical spiritual authors frequently incorporate recent findings in psychology, and the human sciences in general, to describe human development even more helpfully. What must be preserved, however, is the unique Christian perspective brought to these studies.[3] Christian spirituality recognizes that the Christian journey toward God is more about God looking for us than it is about us looking for God! This principle is at the center of any model of psycho-spiritual growth for the Christian.

But there are other points that need to be kept in mind when reflecting on human development. Let's look at some of these now.

Models of growth: other points of reference

More recent views recognize that human development is not strictly linear. This belief does not negate the understanding that life is progressive, but it does challenge us to see that people have never arrived once and for all at any one stage or level.[4] Furthermore, there is a great variation in the way life is lived across the planet. Culture has an impact on human development and the unique way it is described; each culture and time period has its own symbolic system, metaphors, and descriptive language. One way of outlining human development cannot be assumed to be valid for all. Once we recognize this fact, we may also call into question the capacity or the need to name, with absolute certainty, distinct stages of human life and growth that are universally valid.

Models of human development that are more flexible, that take seriously the variables of culture, language, symbols, spirituality, and so on, that are unique to different time periods and different cultures are generally more helpful. Those that use cyclical imagery, or imagery that is not unidirectional, are also useful in accommodating the great number of ways people journey. Sometimes individuals move two steps forward, only to find themselves taking one step back at a later date.

Any description of human development can be viewed as a model, a tentative outline that points in the direction of how human development is understood to be taking place. Models are beneficial in that they help gain insight into human experience and name that experience in ways that others can identify with.

Definitive stage models of human growth are suspect for another reason: they imply a hierarchical passage from one level to the next. This is a significant issue. In Christian spirituality, all people are understood to be equals (but not necessarily identical) before God. The idea of seeing some people as more advanced and others less advanced in terms of spiritual development can thus lead to a perilous result: levels of spiritual development can quickly devolve into reflections of lifestyle and career choices as privileged ways to holiness. Furthermore, Christian holiness does not reside exclusively in the merits of an individual person, but rather in the collective journey of a people being transformed in God together. For example, in a hierarchical approach the cleric could be seen to be more advanced in spiritual maturity than the lay person; the daily churchgoer could be seen as more holy than those who find alternate ways to celebrate their spirituality.

Cultural and sociological settings also affect the way human-spiritual development is evaluated and described. Spiritual traditions – such as from the Buddhist, Hindu, or Muslim faiths – that do not reflect a particular way of describing Christian human-spiritual development will always lose out if the Christian stage models and patterns of development are considered to be definitive. The Dalai Lama and Howard Cutler maintain that "some spiritual paths may be more adequate for different psychological and cultural dispositions but that does not make them inferior or superior to other spiritual traditions."[5] God's call to holiness is universal; it is extended equally to all persons in all places.

Given the tentative nature of the models, as well as the spontaneous and free self-giving of God through God's Spirit, it is at our peril that we identify people as being in a particular stage of human-spiritual development in a definitive and absolute way.

Models of growth do not have the last word on the matter. Human development models must not be generalized beyond the witness provided by the concrete life that is being lived and to which the model is ultimately being applied. Models, when applied to a person's life, may be true in one way, but not true in another. At times hard work is required to carefully discern what a given person is living. Each model has a limited range of applicability; each can potentially contribute to our fuller understanding of human development in the enormous array of contexts within which we live.

Summary: models of human-spiritual development

- Different perspectives or models of human-spiritual development need to be considered in order to correct and complement one another;
- models need to be tested out against the cumulative experience of men and women and not used in the abstract;
- down through the ages Christian spiritual writers have contributed valuable psychological insights on human growth;
- human-spiritual development is not strictly linear in nature;
- culture has an impact on human-spiritual development; therefore, universal models of human-spiritual development must be used with caution;
- linear models of human-spiritual development that recognize definitive and separate stages of growth need to be carefully considered in relationship to concrete human experience and the Christian understanding of the universal call to holiness;
- psychological models or theories are just that, the best attempt to express useful patterns in terms of human-spiritual development, but they are not the final word on the matter.

The intersection of psychology and spirituality

Psychology is the study of human behavior and experience: how human beings sense, think, learn, know, and interact with one another and their environment. Psychology collects and organizes these findings into psychological theories that aid in understanding human behavior.

Psychology can be distinguished in at least three ways. First, it can be viewed as a scholarly field of study. Researchers in the field of psychology are employed, for example, in universities to advance knowledge in this area. The focus here is on empirical studies, that is, the development and evaluation of a range of psychological theories. Second, psychology can be exercised as a professional practice, often referred to as clinical or therapeutic psychology. Some men and women devote their lives to assisting others to live better and more integrated lives. Many different therapeutic models have been developed to help counsel people in times of distress and personal need. Third, psychology in our times has become a popular industry. Self-help books and aids to personal maturity and integration have become readily available in many bookstores. At different times all three of these approaches to psychology enter the reflections below. Let's first examine the first of these three areas, the origins of the empirical approach to psychology.

The beginnings of psychology: the empiricist agenda

Although the issues of psychology have been debated since the time of the Greek philosophers Plato and Aristotle (in the fifth and fourth centuries B.C.E. respectively), psychology, as a distinct area of scientific study, is a relatively new discipline that dates back only to the late nineteenth century. The development of modern methods in psychology is attributed to persons such as Wilhelm Wundt (1832–1920), Sigmund Freud (1856–1939), John B. Watson (1878–1958), and Carl Rogers (1902–1987). The psyche – that human capacity that is concerned with personality development, mental functions, and emotions – was studied by these pioneering psychologists and others in ways that paralleled the methods of inquiry used in the natural sciences, for example, in disciplines such as chemistry or physics.

Early psychologists, caught up in the modern view of the world discussed in Chapter 2, believed that human mental processes, as separate from the physical body, would lend themselves to rational methods of study and observation much like those used to study the physical earth. Many early psychologists believed that religion and spirituality were too irrational, were based on superstition, or arose from misleading primitive world views, and did not lend themselves to this kind of scientific inquiry. After all, there is no strict scientific evidence for belief in the soul or spirit as understood in the Christian traditions.

Some psychologists also believed that religion and spirituality harbored authoritarian structures that needed to be shed if the individual was to find his or her own inner strength for healthy adult living. Freud went so far as to say that religion was only an expression of a person's repressed sexuality and, worse yet, was an expression of collective neurosis. Thus, religion and spirituality were dismissed easily as more of a hindrance than a help to human growth and health during the initial phases of the development of psychology as an independent discipline in the latter part of the nineteenth century. It was during this period that the psychologizing of human experience began. Human experience was essentially detached from religious language and ways of interpreting how people live in the world.

Since Freud and Watson, for example, were highly influential psychologists, and each developed his own widely accepted approaches to psychology (both of which were antagonistic to religion to some degree), it is not surprising that religion and spirituality remain on the periphery of much work done in psychology today. It didn't help that another popular figure at the time, Karl Marx (1818–1883), a German political philosopher and revolutionist, held a similar suspicion toward religion. As Marx's commonly quoted phrase attests, he believed that religion was "the opium of the people" and that it masked authentic engagement in the real spheres of human life – that is, the social and the political.

> From the perspective of the founding figures in psychology, as well as that of much modern political theory based on Karl Marx, the subject of psychology was determined to be that of the *verifiable* and *observable* aspects of human mental life. Little or no attention was given to those aspects of life – specifically the spiritual aspect – that did not easily lend themselves to this form of study.

Much psychological theory and practice continue to be built on the premise that psychologists can accurately observe, through external responses, the healthy or unhealthy aspects of an individual's mental or psychic disposition. This perspective is held to be valid, since the human person is viewed as a biological machine. Human consciousness is attributed primarily to the brain's physiological processes, involving electrical charges, neurons, synapses, and the like. The traditional psychologist is trained to interpret the various ways the psyche presents its current state of affairs through symbolic forms: that is, images, language, and text. The expression of an individual's life through these media is interpreted and mapped out against the normative universal human experience.[6] Much of the work establishing normative universal human experience is accomplished by the empirical psychologist, for example, by doing research with human subjects in a university setting.

In determining the congruent or incongruent expressions of human life in the case of a particular individual with respect to the established norm, it is the clinical psychologist or therapist who picks up the work. A clinical psychologist may recommend certain behavior modifications, attitudinal shifts, exercises, or other forms of remedy to help an individual feel better in relationship to whatever problem is being presented. But a psychologist, dealing with the individual within a strictly empirical framework, is unable to deal with or entertain the questions of the individual focused on authentic or absolute meaning, transcendence, authenticity, or the ultimate good in human life. Typically, these are questions that deal with the spiritual dimension of human life: that is, spirituality.

So, what about those issues in life that intersect with the deeper dimension of meaning in life: issues often provoked by experiences of mental illness, loss, or uncertainty? What if the individual who seeks assistance to deal with these critical moments of life finds such a meaning in his or her religious views on life or in spiritual practices that are a significant part of his or her life? Even the person who is not a self-confessed believer in any religion or who does not adhere to any formal spirituality may have this kind of experience at some point. How might this material be included in a psychological or therapeutic reflection?

For example, many people may have what is called a mid-life crisis, where there is a heightened awareness or awakening of another plane of living that has been neglected until then. This sphere of human life seems to push itself into the consciousness of the individual from beyond his or her normal day-to-day awareness. These movements can be characterized as toward embracing life beyond a person's limited sphere of values and beliefs to take on universal values and points of view. The limitations of his or her ways of doing things, and knowledge accumulated to date, become apparent against the backdrop of something more being experienced in the human quest. During this time, there is a drive beyond the personal world, a move to self-transcendence that dislodges the individual out of a limited and fragmented way of viewing the world, self, others, and the cosmos. As a result, the person may begin to question past actions, current beliefs, and the future meaningful trajectory of his or her life.

These are the questions and issues that characterize the human quest as different from that of other living creatures. At times these questions and issues come to people as if out of nowhere, uninvited, but nonetheless real and powerful. Empirical or quantitative psychology (psychology that works out of the framework of measurements and quantifying research methods), even though it may greatly assist in the reflection on these issues and identify helpful responses, provides an incomplete picture of the human being and therefore incomplete responses to the questions of life. There is a spiritual dimension of the human that is not fully recognized by a strictly secular or empirical view of the human.

Thus, empirical psychology must be able to appeal to a larger framework, other than a strictly empirical one, if it hopes to be able to deal with these deeper questions of life. The concern is not that the self explored by the empirical psychologist was not deemed good, or responsible, or ethical. For many people, however, something happens that radically displaces a good chunk of familiar terrain in their personal world, and this needs to be addressed in a different way. An expanding world, which is both exciting and terrifying, becomes the horizon of meaning of the growing and maturing adult, with all the complexities of family, friends, work, partnership, children, and so on that adult life brings.

Once the psychologist acknowledges these questions as legitimate, he or she will have shifted the focus from pure psychology and moved into the realm of philosophical inquiry. Outside any specific spiritual framework, philosophy entertains answers to the eternal questions: questions of humanity's place in the universe, birth and death, humanity's purpose for existing, and so on. What is the ultimate truth of life? What is the meaning of life or better, the meaning of *my* life, in the total sphere of reality? What can account for humanity's spontaneous movement toward ultimate truth? This movement – what is perhaps better described as a human quest – has been debated and tracked by philosophers and theologians since time immemorial.

All these questions point to a sphere of human life beyond the strictly psychological, or at least the psychological sphere reflected in its empiricist agenda. Indeed, should an individual become preoccupied with questions of transcendence and meaning, the empirical psychological approach is ill suited to respond. For the empirical psychologist, questions and answers about meaning can be responded to from the perspective of energy (motivation) and drives (what people are spontaneously drawn toward). These perspectives cannot adequately deal with the deep pockets of yearning within the human heart. The *meaning of meaning* is therefore also at stake with respect to what psychology and spirituality can offer. Meaning in life in Christian spirituality has to do with where people situate themselves in the world with respect to others, God, and relationships of all kinds. Meaning in empiricist psychology could simply focus on personal goals and personal fulfillment.

> Psychology, if it is to accept and deal with the full range of human inquiry and experience, must legitimize and make space for the deeper questions asked by people down through the ages.

Since psychology struggles to deal with what is ultimately and most basically human, it cannot afford to avoid these larger questions of deep meaning and inquiry into self-transcendence. But is empirical psychology (which essentially believes that we gather knowledge only through the human senses) equipped to deal with questions of profound meaning, of ultimate truth, authenticity, and of transcendence?[7] If an individual believes in God or a Buddha[8] this adds another dimension to the whole that psychology must be able to account for and deal with in a responsible and life-giving way.

Psychology and spirituality: partners or rivals?

Some psychologists have recognized the limitations of dealing with mental health as a strictly secular quest. They began giving serious attention to the spiritual dimension of life and its psychic manifestations. Thus, much work is being done today that deals with the intersection of the concerns of psychology *and* the concerns of spirituality.

Important psychologists such as William James (1842–1910), Carl Jung (1875–1961), and Abraham Maslow (1908–1970) took the spiritual dimension seriously in the development of persons. James's *The Varieties of Religious Experience* (1902), even though it takes an empirical approach, is a sympathetic psychological account of spirituality and mystical experiences. Jung, even though he held an ambivalent attitude toward Christianity, broadened Freud's psychoanalytical approach to include interpreting mental and emotional disturbances as attempts to find personal and spiritual wholeness. Maslow studied extraordinary human experiences as healthy expressions of self-actualization in an attempt to achieve one's greatest human potential.

Following the lead of these and others working to address the spiritual aspect of life, some psychologists developed a sub-field of inquiry within the broad-based area of psychology called *psychology of religion*.[9] Students of spirituality and Christian spirituality will find a great deal that's of interest in the field of psychology of religion. David Fontana narrows the topic and refers to *psychology of spirituality*,[10] but it is the broader term, psychology of religion, that is used most often to describe the interests of psychology in relationship to spirituality and religion in general.

Psychology of religion involves the psychological study of various aspects of religion, such as doctrine, myth, ritual, human transformation, and community.

However, psychology of religion often focuses on the quantifiable aspects of spiritual involvement, with little attention being paid to the personal spiritual journey *as such*.[11] Factors that might be considered for measurement could include: purpose in life, experience of transcendence, and values such as self-giving (altruism).

Despite advances, reflected in the publications that do deal positively with the relationship between psychology and spirituality, mainstream psychology has not yet completely embraced the significant questions of life brought to the fore by the spiritual quest.[12] Attention to the journey of growth and transformation, and not just the measurement of attitudes, values, or practices, needs serious attention if different psychologies are going to make further contributions to reflection on the specifically spiritual dimension of life as understood by Christian spirituality. The fact that psychology, as a whole, still has a way to go to integrate the specific faith dimension of individuals into its critical reflections is ironic.

Although the spiritual life (in its inner dimension as well as its adherence to a faith tradition that believes in God) is not directly observable and thus is difficult to assess scientifically, the same is true of the object of psychology: the human psyche. Furthermore, given the startling ability for Christian spirituality to affect and change people's lives (for better and, at times, for worse) it is surprising that mainline psychology is not more proactive in integrating research in Christian spiritualities (as well as other faith-based psychologies) into its central preoccupations.

This is not to say that psychology of religion has not developed its own set of followers and practitioners to make positive contributions to the field of Christian spirituality. The enormous amount of literature on the subject, both popular and academic, will testify to its importance. For example, the psychological theories of Roy Schafer, Kenneth Gergen, Amedeo Giorgi, Carol Gilligan, and Pamela Cooper-White, are excellent resources to begin to meet the task at hand.[13] Yet reflection on Christian spirituality is not always readily accepted into mainline thinking in psychology. As a matter of fact, some psychologists continue to give a clear negative evaluation of religion and spirituality.[14]

Some psychologists see or use psychology or psychotherapy in itself as a substitute for or a form of spirituality. Inasmuch as psychologies "propose frames of orientation and devotion," "meanings and values," "beliefs or norms," "visions or virtues," or "credos and commitments," they covertly embody spirituality or religion.[15] In short, any proposal from a psychologist involving ideals of living are unwittingly religious and spiritual in nature – it entails belief systems and norms for living.

Briefly stated, empirical psychology, even though it may greatly assist in the reflection on these issues and identify helpful responses, provides an incomplete answer because its picture of the human being is incomplete.[16] There is a spiritual dimension of the human that is not fully recognized by a strictly secular view of the spiritual nature of the human. However, the recognition of the spiritual nature of the human in the domain of concerns of both psychology and spirituality testifies to the importance of these two disciplines engaging in critical reflection.[17]

Understandably, religious views and spiritual attitudes reflect an inner domain that is not directly observable, and therefore not measurable. The psychologist or psychotherapist who is not trained to deal with this dimension of the self – or, more importantly, who is not dealing with this dimension *of his or her own life* – may feel ill equipped to allow material from this level of the client to enter into the therapeutic process. But the point is, whether the psychologist speaks to this dimension directly or not, the framework out of which he or she works will, inevitably, involve an implied belief and value system.[18] Because of this, therapeutic processes operate as covert religions and spiritualities and increase the risk of the creation of a personal (artificial) world based on self-referential reflection. This narcissism could keep the client from facing his or her real problems, which may be spiritual in nature. Therefore, the framework behind any particular psychological theory needs to become explicit in the use of psychological theories in the study of Christian spirituality.

Interest in psychology, in relationship to spirituality (Christian or other spirituality), is growing for a number of reasons.[19]

- Both psychology and spirituality deal with the inner dimension of human reality. We see this in the fact that spirituality is increasingly appreciated as being concerned with the profound meaning in life rather than the beliefs of a particular religious tradition.

- Since spirituality is connected to the concrete and personal lived situation of the individual in relationship to his or her world, many people see spirituality as having a greater claim on our lives over the public observance of ritual that is often associated with religions.

- In addition, there is a growing acceptance in society as a whole that concern about the spiritual dimension of our lives (regardless of how this is expressed or practiced) is not something that is added on to what is fundamental to the human condition in itself. In other words, spirituality is increasingly being recognized as a fundamental dimension of the person. This shift in attitude has led to a greater acceptance of spiritual matters being treated in the psychologist's therapeutic setting.

We can conclude this section by saying that psychology and spirituality are partners in the exploration of human-spiritual development. But we must not lose sight of the fact that it is an ambiguous relationship and thus critical scrutiny is in order prior to buying into any one particular psychological model when exploring questions in Christian spirituality. For example, let's look closer at one branch in psychology that has been sympathetic to the concerns of spirituality in general: transpersonal psychology.

Transpersonal psychology

An example of a specific sub-field in the general discipline of psychology that holds promise in contributing positively to research in spirituality is transpersonal psychology. Transpersonal psychology focuses specifically on spiritual phenomena. The word *transpersonal* refers to "experiences in which the person's sense of identity and self goes beyond (trans) the usual sense of self to encompass wider aspects of humankind, life, psyche, and the cosmos."[20] Transpersonal psychology thus takes seriously extraordinary experiences such as mysticism, out-of-body experiences, near-death experiences, ultimate values, and spiritual healing.[21] It recognizes that the human body operates beyond the limits set by space and time as these are understood from a strictly scientific perspective. It also refuses to accept that any human action can be understood completely as a result of identifiable causes that preceded it (cause and effect).

> Transpersonal psychology views the mechanistic model of the human as limited and incomplete, and insists that spirituality has a central place in the understanding of what it means to be human. It is at home in working with the composite model of the human being: human beings are products of physiological and spiritual characteristics which somehow form the human body as a singular entity.

Transpersonal psychology also recognizes that human behavior is influenced by forces outside of its own personal psychology. Even though transpersonal psychology greatly expands what it is willing to include in its inquiry, it does not lay claim to belief in a personal God that lies behind human growth, conversion, and maturation. There is still a tendency within transpersonal psychology to minimize the contribution that faith (within its own framework of specific beliefs and practices) may make to holistic health.

Thus, the findings of transpersonal psychology, even though they are friendly to the spiritual quest, must always be considered from within the perspective of Christian beliefs and practices in order to benefit from what is helpful and leave behind that which is not. For example, Christian mysticism, the healing nature of the experience of grace, literary traditions, and experiential witness of growth in the Holy Spirit are all valuable resources for critical thinking on human life, happiness, and maturation. In short, the accumulated wisdom of the Christian traditions on the questions of human development has much to offer. When this wisdom finds itself at odds with current psychological theory and praxis, pause for reflection is in order.

At times, transpersonal psychology tends to foster strictly privatized spiritualities: perhaps private meditation is upheld as the singular spiritual practice necessary for a balanced spiritual life. This may give the impression that Christian spirituality, in its communitarian and social expression, is unnecessary, and that privatized spirituality, in one form or another, can adequately replace it. If such a position is taken, the communitarian practices and social involvement of Christian spiritualities may be left behind. One of the hallmarks of Christian spirituality as a whole is the expression of its beliefs and practices by persons-in-community, not privatized selves cut off from the larger community and traditions.

Christian spirituality emphasizes the growth of persons-in-community – not as privatized persons indifferent to the broader needs and social concerns of the world. Christian spirituality that reflects self-giving and is rooted in a keen desire to enhance the life of others as modeled on the life of Jesus can potentially provide a positive influence on such things as moral values, interpersonal relationships, and life philosophies.

Christian spirituality has the potential to shape communitarian life and enhance well-being in the life of the group on all these levels. Spiritual beliefs, experiences, and practices enhance personal *and* social well-being, as has been witnessed by many men and women down through the ages. Chronicled in its many history books are the lives of Christian men and women who have led fulfilling lives and contributed enormously at the community level. This is not to say that Christian spirituality leaves the life of the individual behind. Personal image, esteem, moral values, and so on can also be enhanced through a serious appropriation of Christian spirituality. But self-interest in its various expressions is not *the* primary goal of Christian spirituality as it is lived out in the life of the individual.

While psychology can have a completely mechanistic view of the self, as we saw above, spirituality, and in particular Christian spirituality, views the self as the *imago Dei* (see Chapter 4), the image of God who gives generously of oneself, as reflected in the Christian traditions. A privatized or mechanistic view of the self is unable to account adequately for this aspect of the Divine–human relationship, which is fundamental to Christian spirituality. Thus, within Christian spirituality, any psychology that is indifferent to or cannot allow the fundamental dimension of the Divine–human relationship or the communitarian dimension of Christian spirituality into its reflections needs to be carefully reconsidered.

In the above sections we have stressed the need to consider carefully any psychology which we may wish to bring into dialogue with Christian spirituality. This cautionary reflection does not negate, however, the tremendous contribution psychology, overall, makes to insights in Christian spirituality. Let us look at some of these now.

Psychology's contribution to spiritual-personal well-being

First, psychology can help people reflect on their identity and formulate their life story in a coherent and clear manner, especially during periods of grief, despair, remorse, or intense pain. Thus organized, it can furnish helpful insights into their lives and their personalities that may help to identify positive steps to move through these issues. Psychological counseling may help identify unconscious inner emotional disturbances that lead to outbursts of anger or help bring to the surface self-esteem and self-image issues that can cripple the individual. Dealing with these issues consciously in a caring and understanding environment can contribute significantly to a positive sense of self that, in turn, leads to spiritual wellness. Viewing life from a healthier perspective can contribute to an enhancement of a sense of the meaning of one's life within the Christian story and help situate oneself in a more meaningful place in society and in one's life in general.

Second, psychology can help revise one's perspective on reality as life changes or as an individual naturally grows from childhood through to the senior years. Psychology has made it clear that there is a real progression in the way human beings grow and develop throughout their lives. The need for personal well-being on all levels alters as people mature amidst the changing circumstances of life. The progression of years frequently requires a shift in our maps of reality and in our priorities, which need to be updated continually throughout life to take into account one's personal and social situation. Some individuals have difficulty making the required adjustments in their personal world views so they can adapt to these changing circumstances and stages of life.

The place an individual carves out in his or her life for a newly established career when twenty-something will most likely be very different from the place given to a well-established career when sixty-something and preparing for retirement. If attitudes to one's career and the place it occupies in one's life have not adapted appropriately in this forty-year span, some reality checking may be needed. The same is true of Christian spirituality. Various points in life contain age-appropriate beliefs and practices for expression of Christian spirituality. What may be appropriate behavior for an eighteen-year-old in terms of psycho-sexual maturity may not be appropriate for the forty-five-year-old. Psychology can help sort out healthy and unhealthy expressions of the self that are age-appropriate and that reflect the context in which people live.

Third, psychology can be of great assistance with a task that is dear to both psychology and spirituality: the task of transcending the ego. Here the ego is understood as the center of the human person that willfully directs human action toward one's personal goals; the end result is personal well-being. Essentially the ego is self-centered and as such it believes it must fight for itself in the world. The goal of psychological and spiritual growth is to move beyond the boundaries of one's ego, which is essentially self-serving. The self-serving ego is probably helpful, and perhaps even necessary, in the earlier stages of life, as people establish primary goals around career and family. Such a perspective can be debilitating in later years, however, when adults are invited to foster attitudes that contribute to the greater good of humanity on a much broader level.

Both psychology and spirituality understand that human happiness and fulfillment are based on the shift from ego-centeredness to other-centeredness. Such a shift frequently takes place in a radical way during the middle years of life, but it ought to be fostered throughout one's journey of growth and transformation. With this shift comes the adoption of transpersonal values – that is, values that do not serve simply one's own personal agenda or the agenda of a consumer society to which the ego is constantly prone to submit. Rather, the ego is challenged to continually let go of its self-serving tendencies so it can experience the freedom of being available for the service of others.

Fourth, with the tremendous rise in spiritualities born from various interests, psychology can help discover those that are genuinely useful in the quest for meaningful human life and set aside those that are essentially pathological in nature. Spiritual beliefs and practices that appear to be expressions of illness, and not authentic human self-actualization, can be named as such by psychologists. This is not to disregard the rich variety of valid spiritual expressions and practices both within and outside of Christian spirituality. Rather, spiritualities that are clearly expressions of illness – for example, extreme body mutilations, weird sacrificial practices, and cultic suicidal practices – can be named by psychologists as deviant expressions of self-actualization as opposed to spiritualities that merit further attention and support within the wider community.

Psychology and spirituality as commercial ventures

In a similar way to popular spirituality (see Chapter 1), psychology has become a commercial venture, that is, it has in some instances become a popular industry. The two have become almost inseparable in the minds of many people. For this reason there is a risk of moving away from critical self-introspection toward consumer manipulation. Many self-help books, available in bookstores and supermarkets, are based on psychological insights yet are placed in the spirituality section.[22] Some religious communities and programs for preparation in ministry initiate new members and practitioners with a bevy of workshops based on psychological tools, such as the Myers-Briggs personality type indicator[23] or the Enneagram.[24] Both of these tools have been used to explore such topics as Christian prayer styles and images of God. Both have had a positive impact on Christian spirituality.

But even though exposure to these types of tools may stimulate a deeper desire for critical self-reflection based on new knowledge of the self, in the end it is the individual who must ask the questions "who am I?" and "what is the meaning of my life?" Only when these questions are asked from a personal horizon of meaning do they have the potential for transforming human life. The individual himself or herself must engage personally in the journey of human-spiritual development. Psychological workshops, aids, or self-help books, as valuable as these may be, are not a substitute for the personal work that needs to be done in relationship to living lives of faith.

We are led, then, to understand that spirituality is not psychology and psychology is not spirituality. Psychological life and spiritual life, although intimately connected, are not one and the same. Christian spirituality cannot be reduced to the point where one omits the gratuitous movement of God's grace and presence in life through the power of the Holy Spirit. For the Christian, the surprising presence of God's personal self-giving stirs up moments of transformation, growth, and healing, and soothes in moments of grief, loss, and extreme pain.

From the perspective of Christian spirituality as a whole, then, Christian models of growth and maturation must be allowed to question strictly psychological models of the same. In doing so, the success of the Christian experience is taken seriously and what it has to offer as correctives or enhancements to psychological theories can be explored. Many Christian spiritualities have proven track records on the quest for human happiness and meaning in life at both the personal and social levels.

Of course, there is no magic formula within Christian spirituality that guarantees such an outcome. But it cannot be denied that countless generations have lived purposeful and meaningful lives based on the beliefs and practices of Christian spirituality. Psychological theories could learn much from these experiences. While the categories of psychology continue to be helpful in the study of many questions around spirituality, the categories of spirituality, and specifically Christian spirituality, may lead to new insights in psychological theory.

> Psychology needs spirituality, along with other fields of study such as ethics and theology, to help it reflect on what constitutes living a good life. Christian spirituality can make an invaluable contribution to this goal with its holistic anthropology; its openness to reconciliation, forgiveness, and peace; and its long history of transformative practices such as meditation, prayer, and spiritual direction.

The experience of Christian human-spiritual development: Christian mysticism and asceticism

Ideas on mysticism and asceticism often surface in conversations on Christian spirituality and human and spiritual development. This is because the experience of mysticism and the practice of asceticism are both part of long-standing traditions in Christian spirituality. They relate to how Christians, at least traditionally, have talked about human-spiritual growth.

You may read popular accounts of "saintly mystical raptures" or "harsh ascetic disciplines" describing individuals' experience of transformation while on the road to "spiritual perfection." Christian art that captures subjects in moments of mystical bliss, or sporting physical signs of bodily mortifications under the guise of asceticism, are not uncommon. But these images display only a small part of what mysticism and asceticism have meant in the long history of Christian spiritualities. They could even be said to be caricatures of what the authentic traditions teach on these two important Christian concepts.

The history of Christian spirituality is filled with a great variety of stories of men and women who were true mystics and who brought forth in their writings helpful ascetic practices of one kind or another. The goal here is to understand what mysticism and asceticism have to offer human development in a specifically Christian context and within the broader parameters of Christian spirituality. Given the vast spectrum of writings and research on Christian mysticism and asceticism, the presentation below can only be considered an introductory one. The interested explorer of Christian spirituality will find ample references for exploration listed in the bibliography at the end of this chapter.

Christian mysticism[25]

Within the Christian traditions, mysticism has often been viewed as an advanced state of spiritual life – one that reflects a greater degree of human development, or holiness, or state of Christian perfection as demonstrated in ecstatic or extraordinary experiences. Yet this does not seem to be accurate, given the witness of many men and women who recount the close experience of God in their everyday lives and at the same time struggle with the ordinary ups and downs of life. Children, too, are noted to have experiences that are genuinely mystical – that is, they have an experience of the intimate, loving presence of God that comes spontaneously and freely. Quaker John Wooman (1720–1772) relates just such an experience at the age of seven. While reading the twenty-second chapter of the Book of Revelation, he had a profound sense that "God is here," and he felt united with the whole of life.[26]

> Christian mysticism is part of the potential reality of everyday life. Without negating those expressions of Christian mysticism that may include extraordinary moments such as auditory experiences, levitations, or visions, the foundation of Christian mysticism is the ongoing intimate presence of God active in the everyday life of the Christian.

Christian mysticism is not the privilege of a select few, as has often been emphasized in the Christian traditions. Nor is the incidence of mystical

experience necessarily a sign of advanced stages in human-spiritual development. Furthermore, how one defines mysticism after acknowledging these
basic positions is dependent on many other factors within individual cultures
and time periods. Grace Jantzen, in her study *Power, Gender, and Christian
Mysticism* (1995), goes so far as to say that mysticism is a social construction
and is tied closely to knowledge, power, and politics – not to mention gender.

Given that the experience of mysticism is so widespread, dependent on
context and perspective, and varied in its expression, it is very difficult to
define it in a general way that applies to all traditions. Each tradition or
spirituality will have a preferred way (or number of ways) to express this
widespread reality. Bernard McGinn, a contemporary writer on mysticism,
indicates that mystical experiences are "religiously specific experiences:
Buddhists have Buddhist mystical experiences; Jews Jewish ones; and
Christians have mystical experiences relating to Christ."[27] Whether there is
some common core to all these expressions of mysticism is thus called into
question. The problem of defining mysticism in a way that would apply to
all traditions was signaled in a succinct way in 1922 by Cuthbert Butler,
an English monk. Butler's observation remains true for us today. He states
in *Western Mysticism* (1922):

> There is probably no more misused word in these our days than
> "mysticism." It has come to be applied to many things of many kinds:
> to theosophy and Christian science; to spiritualism and clairvoyance;
> to demonology and witchcraft; to occultism and magic; to weird
> psychical experiences, if only they have some religious colour; to
> revelations and visions; to other-worldliness, or even mere dreaminess
> and impracticality in the affairs of life; to poetry and painting and music
> of which the motif is unobvious and vague.[28]

Given the variety of ways mysticism is understood, the goal here is to grasp
how Christianity has defined for itself its own mystical tradition without
assuming that it is normative for all spiritual traditions. A brief history of
the word *mysticism* will help establish the usage as it has developed in
Christian spirituality.

Origins of the word mysticism

The origin of the word *mysticism* lies in the Greek word *muein*. *Muein*
implies something closed – for example, one's eyes or lips. From the Greek
word *muein* was constructed a group of words including *mystikon*,
mysterion, and *mystes*, which were used in connection with the Greek

mystery religions.[29] *Mystikos* referred to secret or hidden rites known only to the initiated of these religions in the Greek culture that existed around the time of Jesus.

Examining the life of the New Testament community reveals the Christian use of these words. For example, the word *mystical* developed from *mystikon*, which alludes to the secrets of God that concern the salvation of the Christian community – particularly the mysterious nature of God's love for humanity as revealed in Jesus Christ.[30] The mystery of God's love that is spoken of in the New Testament is therefore not something mysterious in the sense that it is hidden, but mysterious in the sense that it remains obscure, even in its revelation in Jesus Christ. God's love is inexhaustible, even in its generous outpouring; it is inaccessible in the sense that it is a gratuitous gift from a personal and loving God. At the core of Christian mysticism lies the awareness that there is only one *mysterium*: God.[31] The remote God is experienced as near in a mysterious way. This nearness opens up that kind of experience that Christianity refers to as mysticism.

Mysticism: the experience of God

Mystical experience is experience of the immanence of the wholly other God, in contrast to the experience of God as distant. At the heart of Christian mysticism, therefore, is the conception of God not as a transcendent Other but as an immanent Self.[32] The essence of the teaching of Christianity on mysticism is rooted in the firsthand experience of God embodied in the world in the person of Jesus Christ. This point of departure diminishes somewhat the significance of the distinction between an immanent and a transcendent God. Christian mysticism emphasizes not so much the experience of an extrinsic Other who, at times, intervenes in the order of the world from elsewhere, but rather a personal God who emerges from within a common world that humanity and God already share.

The goal of Christian mysticism is not primarily an act of union or a particular moment of encounter with the Other. The goal is to live one's entire life *in* the *mysterium* called God.[33] God is primarily the *mysterium* in virtue of God's self-bestowal, not in terms of particular or partial knowledge we may have of God.

Thus, mysticism is best understood not through the intellect, the act of knowing the *mysterium* by the expression of particular knowledge, as through feeling, the dynamic of experiencing and living the *mysterium*.[34] For example, in the following passage, John of the Cross expresses the strong affective side of mysticism that results from the awakening of the Christian to the abiding presence of God in the world:

> For this awakening is a movement of the Word in the substance of the soul, containing such grandeur, dominion, glory, and intimate sweetness that it seems to the soul that all the balsams and fragrant spices and flowers of the world are commingled, stirred, and shaken so as to yield their sweet odor, and all the kingdoms and dominions of the world and all the powers and virtues of heaven are moved; not only this, but it also seems that all the virtues and substances and perfections and graces of every created thing glow and make the same movement all at once. (*Living Flame of Love* 4,4)

This does not mean that knowledge does not have a place in Christian mysticism. Particular knowledge of God's self-bestowal in the world is a secondary consideration, however, which must always point back to the *mysterium* (God), which grounds and verifies it.

Everyday mysticism

This understanding of everyday mysticism is in contradiction to an understanding of mysticism as special revelations or visions, or the involvement in other-worldliness. Nor should mysticism be understood as a state of personal holiness, as mentioned above. This can lead to a form of illusion that feeds the narcissistic self and closes the individual off from the broader concerns of society. To view the mystical state as the state that most perfectly reflects Christian excellence is to risk denying the social character of Christianity and to place mysticism within the confines of one's private devotional life.[35]

Our understanding of mysticism refocuses the life of Christians on the daily reality of their world in creative acts of Christian belief, hope, and love. God's self-communication emerges from within the routine experiences of believing, hoping, and loving. The mystical experience is, therefore, not a higher stage of the Christian life. This is true even though mystical experience (i.e. borne by the grace of God's Spirit alive in one's life) is distinguishable from other experiences of Christian living. The mystic gives witness to the profound yet quiet creative presence of the Incarnate God actively transforming the lives of ordinary people. God eats at the tables of ordinary people throughout the world.

In his *Living Flame of Love* 1,15, John of the Cross gives witness to this way in which God is present within humanity: "The Father of lights [James 1:17] who is not closefisted but diffuses himself abundantly as the sun does its rays, without being a respecter of persons [Acts 10:34], wherever there is room – always showing himself gladly along the highways and byways – does not hesitate or consider it of little import to find his delights with the children of the earth at a common table in the world [Prov. 8:31]." Around these tables, mystics embrace and empower others to live meaningful lives amidst the problems and difficulties, joys and blessings, encountered in day-to-day living.

Mystical life is life lived in the Spirit of God within the one world that humanity and God share. The ethical and the mystical inextricably overlap in this world. Attunement to God's embodied Spirit (described as the mystical domain of human life) transforms the human heart and results in the transformation of human action (which refers to the ethical domain of human life). Mysticism has more to do with the passionate love affair between God and humanity that shows itself in social life than it has to do with private, extraordinary occurrences. It is this love affair that has resulted in the transformation and growth of individuals, faith communities, and society in many different ways over the course of the development of the Christian traditions.

Christian asceticism[06]

Origins of the word asceticism

The contemporary word *asceticism* finds its origins in the ancient Greek word *askesis*. *Askesis* referred to various practices of self-discipline: the disciplined exercise or training required by athletes and soldiers for physical and mental health; the acquisition of wisdom by philosophers; and the practice of religious observance by priestly officials in the temples. In short, *askesis*, translated as ascesis, refers to the methodical and intentional actions needed to meet the goals at hand. Rigorous ascetic practices were required by these various groups in the Greek culture to fulfill the tasks and obligations expected of them. Grueling physical exercise by the soldier preparing for combat, the detachment from the material world by the philosopher to achieve clear thinking, and the fasting and sexual self-control ritually required by priests in the Greek mystery cults were seen as necessary in the Greek world. Today asceticism is more closely identified with various religious practices or expressions.

The spiritual meaning of asceticism

The conventions of Buddhists, Muslims, and Christians all include a range of expressions of ascetic discipline that are described as ascetic exercises. Muslims, for instance, observe the rigorous annual fast of the month of Ramadan, where no solids or liquids are eaten between sunrise and sundown, even while normal routines of work and activity are pursued.

This pillar of Islam is complemented by another ascetic pillar, almsgiving, instituted by Islamic law as a contribution of part of one's possessions for the sake of the disadvantaged.[37] In Islam, asceticism is generally viewed in terms of modesty and temperance, contentment with what the Divine will offers, and the denial of luxuries. Under the categories of Right Speech and Right Action in *The Noble Eightfold Path*, Buddhists are enjoined to refrain not only from self-intoxication through alcohol and drug use, but from misuse of the senses and from gossip or frivolous speech.[38] Fully fledged Buddhist monks must regularly observe far stricter rules of asceticism that include eating only one meal per day. They must also refrain from attending shows and entertainments, from sleeping on luxurious beds, from having sexual intercourse, and from possessing money of any kind.

In the Christian traditions asceticism has often been understood, incorrectly, as renouncing the pleasures of life for their own sake, or practicing harsh physical punishments, such as using the *discipline*. The discipline was a small whip used for self-flagellation in medieval times, but was also used in some places up until modern times.[39] Movies have portrayed this practice in sometimes graphic detail. The medieval procession of frenzied flagellants beating themselves bloody in Ingmar Bergman's *The Seventh Seal* (1957) and the image of the French nun Thérèse de Lisieux (1873–1897) forcing her rival to strike her with a handful of twigs in the film *Thérèse* (1986) are typical examples, as interpreted by Hollywood, of this kind of bodily asceticism. More recently *The Da Vinci Code* (2006) portrays members of a Roman Catholic community called Opus Dei following these kind of practices. Flogging, the wearing of hair shirts, and tight belts fitted with metal spurs that would dig into the flesh (called the *cilice*) were also practiced as forms of Christian asceticism in medieval and modern times.

Down through the centuries, asceticism and ascetic practices have been understood in various ways. Within Christian spirituality not all expressions of asceticism can be viewed in a positive light. Origen, a Christian writer in Egypt during the third century, understood asceticism in Platonic terms, as an opposition between spirit and matter: the soul and the body. For Origen Christian asceticism was fully expressed in chastity and the celibate lifestyle. He went so far as to emasculate himself in compliance with Matthew 19:12 (the making of eunuchs for the kingdom of heaven), which he took in a literal sense. Regrettably, this dualistic approach to asceticism, which placed flesh and spirit in opposition, continues to have a major impact on Christian spirituality and practices of asceticism up to our own times. When asceticism leads to expression of extreme bodily mutilation or opposes spirit and flesh, we have reason to question the Christian nature of such practices.

To understand Christian asceticism it would be helpful to explore further asceticism outside the context of any faith system. The practices and rituals described as asceticism within various faiths and Christian spiritualities can and do make sense outside the context of a specific faith system as we saw above with the Greeks and their practice of *askesis*. Asceticism in Christian spirituality can make a lot more sense once its non-religious meaning is better understood – or once it is understood in the context of human reality in general. From this perspective asceticism is appreciated as a human and humanizing reality before it is practiced within the values of a particular spirituality. Let us examine how this is true.

The non-spiritual foundations of the practice of asceticism

Asceticism forms part of the natural movements of humanity in the search for authentic human existence. To achieve the particular goals people have for their lives, people are constantly faced with choices that will lead them along one pathway while leaving others behind. All pathways cannot be followed; people need to make choices if they are to achieve their most important life goals. For example, if a student wants to pass a course he or she is taking at college or university and eventually graduate, he or she needs to choose to fulfill the requirements of the course. This may mean giving up nights out with friends – not that the evenings out with friends are bad or destructive (or it is hoped this is not so!), but because there is another long-term goal on the horizon that guides the student in making helpful choices to achieve it. Sometimes long hours of reading and studying alone are required to get the degree or diploma. Academic life, it can be said, involves a kind of asceticism.

Asceticism thus helps people find a balance in life between competing desires. When any one desire becomes so absolute that everything else is ignored, life can become a tyranny. This would be true even in the example above. Excessive studying to the neglect of exercising, eating properly, and maintaining a healthy social life can be as destructive as not studying at all. The human being is a mix of desires and impulses that sometimes compete with one another.

People constantly find themselves sifting through their desires to make the most helpful choices for healthy living. This is the essence of asceticism: making mindful choices within the framework of a particular value system with the goal, for example, of living a balanced, happy, and fulfilled life.

If desires get out of control and propel some people toward destructive self-indulgent behaviors or addictions, they may choose not to act upon them if they want to achieve their other goals in life. Asceticism, understood as making willful and wise choices to avoid excess, is necessary for everyone to constantly grow and mature.

People never stop becoming who they desire to be; the fullness of human life is not realizable once and for all. All human actions are temporary stopovers between realized selfhood and selfhood envisioned as an ongoing project. Thus the whole of human life, over many years, requires an asceticism that shapes feelings and actions to help people realize the deepest aspirations of the human heart.

> The ascetic task is to enhance the integration of the self through life-giving choices that respond to all of the self and not only one part of it. This is the task of asceticism: to work out an acceptable balance. The goal of asceticism is to strive to realize the deepest aspirations (passions) of human nature by the selective choices people make in everyday life. Asceticism is thus understood as the willful practical choices that guide the transformative process that leads toward ultimate goals in life. This is true for all of humanity, not just those who adhere to some spirituality of one kind or another.

Thus understood, asceticism is primarily a positive movement toward fulfillment in life. Human passions are first understood by a reference to an innocent quest for happiness in life, not first as expressed in their negative mode (for example, greed, abusive power, and vanity). The passions are not disordered in themselves, but are the powerful impetus behind the possibility for making appropriate human relationships possible in all areas of life. It is only later that we understand the excesses of the passions as departures or deviations from their original goal of constructive human living.

Although human desire is susceptible to corruption and evil, the primordial state of desire is first innocent. However, desire, as it is incarnated in the active choices of everyday life, can fall prey to the trap of excessive indulgence in life. A program of asceticism is needed to assist people in the ongoing task of becoming more of who they want to be, rather than getting stuck along the way. What is at stake here is the transformation of human desire. Asceticism is needed to help break out of the narrow boundaries within which people have a tendency to root their desires. Asceticism is needed to help awaken people to what is important in life, to what is permanent, or at least enduring. Asceticism, fueled by passionate desire, helps people get going again when they have become stuck in bad habits or negative relationships.

Asceticism, paradoxically, in its first expression, does not seek to remove people from this world, but to insert people ever more intimately and authentically in it. But in so doing, asceticism teaches the value of limits in life. Without asceticism, people are easily seduced into living under the pretense that there are no limits in life: desire and fantasy become one. Such a seduction tricks people into living superficially without concrete points of reference by which they become embodied in a real world.

The Christian context and meaning of asceticism

The above section on asceticism describes it as a journey in which all people are called to participate. However, this definition of asceticism, when mapped onto the framework of Christian spirituality, takes on particular meanings and contours. Christian spirituality provides its own goals and values that assist Christians in directing their ascetic practice. Since Christian spirituality identifies the fullness of what the self seeks with a personal and loving God, Christian asceticism involves both the individual and the community in their relationship with God.

> Christian asceticism reflects the values of Jesus and his life as lived in the Spirit of God. Just as he was self-giving, compassionate, forgiving, and kind, the Christian wishes to be so as well; thus, he or she practices asceticism to achieve those goals. Christian asceticism, therefore, should seek to assist believers to make responsible and life-giving choices that respond positively to the various ambiguous situations in life as Jesus did.

For the sake of growth and something more, Christians choose to place boundaries on some of their ambiguous desires – for example, the desire for misused sensuality, unjust possession, manipulative power, or abusive relationships. The path of Christian asceticism consists of the awakening and the transforming of the personal and communal heart of humanity to God's personal grace experienced in everyday life. Christian asceticism is lived in the marketplace, in the daily encounter of one's brothers and sisters.

This approach challenges the common assumption that Christian asceticism, interpreted as corporal punishment or as a negative view of human sexuality (based on a caricature of Greek dualist philosophy that repudiated the body and exalted the spirit) has little or nothing to offer people today. In the popular mind, Christian asceticism is often seen as an aberration that has been relegated to the historical past since it seemed to curb the more creative and spontaneous movements of the human spirit and body. However, the above assessment of asceticism helps us recognize the wisdom of the earliest Christian monks who practiced a healthy asceticism.

Contrary to what people's prejudices might lead them to expect, in the earliest Western monastic traditions, asceticism was primarily a therapy. It was only later, toward the eleventh century, that it was almost exclusively viewed as a world-denying corporal punishment.[40] Unfortunately, the earlier ascetic focus on enhancement and restoration of spiritual and physical-spiritual health was all but lost later in the Christian traditions. To a large extent, this focus is still lost today. Christian asceticism ought to assist the believer to make responsible and life-giving choices that respond positively to daily ups and downs, all the while recognizing God's graceful presence in everyday activities.

John of the Cross, the Spanish mystic, poet, and spiritual author, outlines one example of an ascetical program that achieves great balance in helping live healthier, holier, and more loving lives amidst these daily ups and downs. It is to his ascetical program, as described in the threefold classical spiritual itinerary, and built on the recognition that God is present in one's everyday encounters with others, that we now turn.

The threefold classical spiritual itinerary: mysticism, asceticism, and human-spiritual growth[41]

The traditional three ways of the Christian life – the *purgative way*, the *illuminative way*, and the *unitive way* – are often referred to as the *classical spiritual itinerary*. Although they are described separately, with their own salient characteristics and method of prayer, together these ways form a *singular journey* that leads the Christian ever more deeply in the life and love of God in this world that God and humans share. They are often presented in a linear fashion, but the three ways are integrated aspects of spiritual and human development – attempts to describe the *cyclical movements of grace in human life*. Even those who are supposedly advanced in their spiritual pilgrimage know that something of each of the three ways continues to deepen and grow as they strive to mature in faith over a lifetime. Even the most secular of psychologists recognizes that people never arrive once and for all. People are continually involved in the ongoing task of conversion and human growth.

History of the threefold classical spiritual itinerary

The foundations for the three ways of the Christian life are visible in the writings of Christian antiquity. In Hebrews 5:11–14 and 6:9–12, along with many other New Testament texts, such as Ephesians 4:12–16, we see signs that development in the spiritual life is viewed as progressive; it can be practiced and learned. For example, the texts from Hebrews indicate in a general way that there are people who are *beginners* in their Christian journey and people who are *masters*. The writer of Hebrews describes those "living on milk" because they are still "babies"; he talks about those who are "mature" and those who are "teachers." The author speaks of "training"; thus, along with those who are "beginners" and "masters" there are those who are *further advanced* – who are neither beginners nor yet masters. Likewise, the text speaks of those who have learned and practiced the Christian life but have fallen away from it and need to practice some more!

In the third and fourth centuries, with the growing emphasis on personal perfection and bodily asceticism, a significant number of people moved to the deserts of the Middle East to achieve the goal of personal perfection through living the Christian life as monks and religious. They described their journey of faith in various ways. Origen (†254) wrote of "purification, learning, and love." Basil the Great (†379) adopted the existing description of "beginners," "proficients," and "perfects" after he became a monk and dedicated himself to the ascetic lifestyle. Later Bernard of Clairvaux (†1153) wrote of the threefold progression of "fear, hope, and love" in the life of the Christian, with reference to the biblical Song of Songs. Thomas Aquinas (†1274) spoke of the progression of "virtue and charity" and the "three degrees of charity," once again accepting the widespread belief that the Christian life was a developmental one.

It is in the writings of a contemporary of Aquinas that reference to the purgative, illuminative, and unitive ways are explicitly mentioned for the ordinary Christian and not just for those who had dedicated themselves to the ascetic lifestyle as a monk or religious. Bonaventure's (†1274) *De triplici via* (the three ways) was based on the writings of an unknown author initially identified as Dionysius the Areopagite, the convert of St. Paul in Athens referred to in Acts 17:34. However, it is now known that St. Paul's convert referred to in Acts could not be the author in question (who had lived later in the sixth century).

As a result Dionysius the Areopagite is frequently referred to today as Pseudo-Dionysius or Pseudo-Areopagite. He was most likely from Syria. What is important for this discussion is that the Dionysian terms and writings, initially thought to be of apostolic authority were, as a result, widely diffused in Latin in Europe after the sixth century. Dionysius had described what would become for future Christian generations the classical spiritual itinerary of purgation, illumination, and union. Although many Christian writers used this terminology to characterize and describe the Christian journey, like Bonaventure, mentioned above, it would only be later, in the sixteenth century, that John of the Cross (†1591) presented a thorough and systematic analysis of the three ways. This happened at the height of mysticism in Europe and, paradoxically, at the height of the Spanish Inquisition.

John of the Cross carefully analyzes the threefold way in his commentaries *The Dark Night of the Soul* (DN), *The Ascent of Mount Carmel* (A), *The Spiritual Canticle* (SC), and *The Living Flame of Love* (F). Since he is recognized as one of the Western mystics who has described, systematized, and analyzed most thoroughly the purgative, illuminative, and unitive ways, his work will be used in a summary way as the basis for the presentation below.

The purgative way

The *purgative way* is commonly associated with the state known also as the *Beginners* (see *A* Bk II, Ch. 17 ff.). The need to set out on the purgative way comes when an individual realizes that, as he or she has grown into maturity and adulthood, there is a further desire for growth and maturation. The individual understands that the desire for *something more* can only be achieved by moving beyond current debilitating boundaries and dispositions. This awareness is not meant to negate everything about one's life, but to help correct what *is* debilitating and draining. Thus, the purgative way describes the journey of somebody setting out to re-form primary attitudes that, to date, may well have guided the individual but, due to his or her own limitations, are now preventing the individual from further personal and spiritual maturation.

Entry into the purgative way is characterized by the recognition that "I need to do something about my life!" The individual has become aware of the need for change and wants to do something about it. In Christian terms, this initial phase might be described as entering into an acute awareness of the sinfulness of one's life – that is, of past failures toward others, self, God, and creation. These failures may have expressed themselves by, for example, greed, sloth, pride, false opinions, and bad habits. During the first week of the *Spiritual Exercises* of Ignatius of Loyola (†1556) retreatants are extolled to examine their lives in great detail to become deeply aware of their personal need for growth and conversion in light of past failures.

Entry into the purgative way is not merely the onset of the felt need to confess one's sins. Rather, it is a state of consciousness that propels people toward an integral reformation of the foundations of their lives. Many people will set out to perform works of charity, become more intentional and habitual about prayer, and seek to refocus inordinate passions that distract them from their primary commitments in life. In short, people who are launched along the purgative way seek to become more disciplined about many aspects of their lives so they can move from self-centeredness to other-centeredness. The goal is to live with a greater freedom in relationship to others, to the world, to God, and to oneself.

The purgative way questions business as usual. For example, people may decide to schedule a regular daily time for personal prayer and meditation. The beginner may use scripture passages, religious statues, or icons to help them focus on what is known as discursive prayer (the conscious and deliberate saying of prayers that helps people conceptualize and evaluate their lives). What the purgative way begins to correct is people's false sense of reality and their relationship to it. Current values and categories of knowledge are questioned and reshaped. Most significantly, the purgative way seeks to purify one's image of God and reorient one toward the truth of God in one's life and in the life of the world.

In negative terms the purgative way is a movement away from bad habits, sinful behavior, and an unhealthy attachment to material things. In positive terms, however, the purgative way is a movement toward more truthful relationships, more authentic self-giving to others, and a more conscious decision to perform acts of charity, prayer, and almsgiving.

The dialectic of asceticism characterizes the purgative way: Christians *intentionally* open themselves up to God's grace in their lives to move more positively in this world. As old habits are replaced with new ones, God's transforming grace becomes ever more apparent and takes deeper root. Thus, the goal of the purgative way is not to gain a disciplined mastery over one's life, but paradoxically to lose control of one's life and hand it over to God's loving grace. In this way the Christian can live more fully and lovingly in this world that God and humanity share.

The illuminative way

After a period of transition, the Christian enters into what spiritual authors have termed the *illuminative way*, also known as the state of the *Proficients*. The entry into the illuminative way is characterized by a major shift from discursive prayer and active self-discipline to a more contemplative form of prayer and self-possession. The paradox here is that far from becoming self-absorbed and self-preoccupied in this more contemplative stance, the Christian realizes more than ever that life is lived from a well of life deep within that expresses itself in an active love toward others, the world, and God. The embodiment of spontaneous, self-giving love is the hallmark of the illuminative way.

The Christian is illuminated by the loving grace of God in life in the quiet prayer of loving contemplation, in contrast to the busy discursive mental activity that characterized the prayer of the purgative way. In the illuminative way, peace-filled moments of silence illumine, ever more profoundly, the truth about life in relationship to the truth about God, others, and the world. John of the Cross lists three signs that indicate an individual is leaving behind his or her central preoccupation with the purgative way to move more fully into the modality of the illuminative way:

> The first is the realization that one cannot make discursive meditation or receive satisfaction from it as before . . .
>
> The second sign is an awareness of a disinclination to fix the imagination or sense faculties on other particular objects [such as statues or icons] . . .
>
> The third and surest sign is that a person likes to remain alone in loving awareness of God, without particular considerations, in interior peace and quiet and repose . . . (*A* Bk. II, Ch. 13, 2–4)

The illuminative way is not some blissful state of ecstatic preoccupation of nothingness. It is a contemplation that has a certain noetic quality – that is, it is a source of knowledge or revelation – that accompanies it: one is illumined or learns more profoundly about the truth of life in all its aspects. The falsehoods of the self are even more finely stripped away to reveal a truer and more authentic notion of self in relationship to the loving presence of God in the world.

In the illuminative way the Christian becomes more attuned to a realm of reality that he or she was unaware of before. One's gaze on the world has shifted, as has one's relationship to it. In the illuminative way, one's affections are continuously reshaped to be in right relationship to things and others according to the Gospel of Jesus Christ. John of the Cross describes it this way:

> When this house of the senses was stilled (that is, mortified), its passions quenched, and its appetites calmed and put to sleep through this happy night of the purgation of the sense, the soul went out in order to begin its journey along the road of the spirit, which is that of proficients and which by another terminology is referred to as the illuminative way or the way of infused contemplation. (*DN* Bk. I, Ch. 14, 1)

The state of the illuminative way, in contrast to that of the purgative way, may last many years to conform the individual more completely to the illuminated heart and mind of God. In fact, in its initial phase, the illuminative way may not be experienced as illuminating at all. Because the individual is discovering new ways to be in relationship to the world and to others the initial part of this illuminative journey is fraught with confusion and uncertainty, as is to be expected when charting a new course into the unknown.

It is in the initial onset of the illuminative way that the Christian may experience trances, raptures, or lapses of memory. As the light of God's love shines ever more brilliantly into the soul, the resulting disorientation can take these forms. These phenomena are often popularly associated with the highest levels of mysticism and personal holiness. However, John of the Cross counsels that these should not be given special attention, but should simply be acknowledged without seeking to prolong them or see them as signs of holiness.

Just as the Christian seeks to be detached from material possessions in the purgative way, here he or she actively seeks to be detached from extraordinary phenomena that may occur in his or her spirit (John calls them "visions of the soul" – *A* Bk. II, Ch. 23, 2) due to the conversion or transition that is taking place in the person's entire being. In other words, the Christian is counseled to keep going about his or her business, mindful that no one thing is the definitive expression of God's loving activity in one's life. The goal of the three ways must always be kept in mind: to understand reality and the world in terms of God's perspective, and thus to be in loving relationship to the world in the same way as God is.

The illuminative way can be described, then, as a slow and gradual process of the "accommodation of the senses to the spirit" (*DN* Bk. II,

Ch. 2, 1). All parts of the body are being brought into harmonious accord with God's loving plan for the world. In the illuminative way, the Christian has become radically aware that only God's loving grace can achieve the fullness of life that is desired. As the pilgrim continues to experience this purification there eventually comes what is commonly known as the *dark night of the soul*.

The dark night of the soul

The *dark night of the soul* refers to the most intense experience of the purification process cited to this point. Due to the Divine light that assails the individual, John indicates that a pilgrim "feels so unclean and wretched that it seems God is against him and he is against God" (*DN* Bk. II, Ch. 5, 5). So intense is this experience that the individual appears completely lost:

> Clearly beholding its impurity by means of this pure light, although in darkness, the soul understands distinctly that it is worthy neither of God nor of any creature. And what most grieves it is that it thinks it will never be worthy, and there are no more blessings for it. (*DN* Bk. II, Ch. 5, 5)

This experience indicates the culmination of the illuminative way. What is happening here is a constitutive and fundamental reorientation of the personality structure. In the dark night, the individual can no longer sustain, in any way, comfortable illusions about who he or she is before others or before God: one stands naked before God and before oneself in this phase of the journey. John calls this a dark night since the natural light of one's own capacity to know and make sense out of things no longer functions in any familiar way, but the light of God has not yet been revealed in its fullness. The dark night of the soul is not a passing psychological state that one will get over. It is a theological and spiritual category that describes the state of existence that opens up the radical awareness of one's absolute and utter dependence on God. For this reason it reveals the very nature of God.

What needs to be stressed here, once again, is that the God of loving and sweet presence that one experiences in the purgative way is one and the same as experienced here in the darkness of the illuminative way. As the Christian continues in his or her journey, the intensity of the loving presence of God in life grows. This awareness, of course, is of no consolation during this most terrible of experiences called the dark night.

What does stand out, however, is that in the public forum, those experiencing the dark night of the soul will scarcely be seen to be doing so

at all. What will be seen abundantly are generous acts of charity, spontaneous acts of forgiveness and reconciliation, and extreme moral integrity.
The person will be perceived as joy-filled and will exude intense happiness
as well as depth of character. There is an acute awareness of the profound
love of God that is embodied in the day-to-day life of pilgrims in this
culminating phase of the illuminative way, which precedes entry into the
last part of the threefold journey: the unitive way.

The unitive way

Following the dark night of the soul spiritual pilgrims enter the *unitive way*.
Those who enter this way are known also as the *Perfects*. Unlike the marked
shift in prayer life that characterizes the transition from the purgative way
to the illuminative way, no dramatic change takes place in the transition
from the illuminative way to the unitive way, although there may be a change
in the degree of intensity of contemplative prayer. In the illuminative way,
the Christian would have experienced certain *touches of union* – that is,
transitory experiences of the closeness of God. In the unitive way, there is
a quality of immediacy in the relationship to God. John of the Cross
describes this as being "one with God." With the entry into the unitive way,
a "substantial" union is established with God (*SC* St. 20 & 21, 12–13).
Whereas before the Christian at times felt the absence of God, the habitual
presence of God is now experienced deep within (*SC* St. 2, 5).

John of the Cross speaks of the unitive way as the "highest state attainable
in this life," or the state of the *spiritual marriage*:

> This spiritual marriage is incomparably greater than the spiritual
> betrothal, for it is a total transformation in the Beloved, in which each
> surrender the entire possession of self to the other with a certain
> consummation of the union of love. The soul thereby becomes divine,
> God through participation, insofar as is possible in this life. ... It is
> accordingly the highest state attainable in this life. (*SC* St. 22, 3)

The unitive way represents the completion of the transformation as one's
life conforms to God's. The individual has been drawn fully into participation in the Divine nature. All aspects of his or her life have been directed
toward the love of God in this world. Inordinate affections, desires, or
impulses all but cease to exist and thus cease to drive the individual toward
unwanted actions or harmful decisions. In psychological terms, the individual
has achieved an extremely high level of personal integration and maturity.
The individual "ordinarily inclines and moves toward God in the first

movements of its intellect, memory, will, and appetites, because of the great help and stability it has in God and its perfect conversion toward him (*SC* St. 27, 7). In the unitive way, the Christian enjoys an incredible "habitual sweetness and tranquillity that is never lost or lacking" (*SC* St. 24, 5).

John cautions, however, that an individual who has entered the unitive way is still capable of falling into sin, even though this is highly unlikely. The attraction to evil is not as strong as the intense attraction to the love of God and the absolute Good. Evil has no compelling hold over the pilgrim in this journey of life. As John says, "old lovers hardly ever fail God, for they now stand above all that would make them fail him" (*SC* St. 25, 11).

John of the Cross makes an interesting observation about the way an individual comes to know things of the created order in the unitive way: instead of knowing God through the symbolic expressions of God manifest in the created order, an individual "knows creatures through God" (*F* St. 4, 5). At this point the pilgrim comes to know the created world through the loving perspective of God.

In a very strong way, people in the unitive state experience both their humanity and their divinity through the order of creation. All of created reality is experienced as being taken up into God's sublime love. The fullness of redemption has won its way in the life of the individual; the power of God shines forth in Divine and human glory.

With the unitive way one reaches the highest level of development possible in this life but John acknowledges that "love can grow deeper in quality . . . and become more ardent" (*F* Prologue, 3). Here we are reminded of the cyclical nature of human-spiritual maturation – it is not strictly linear in nature even though the model used to describe it here by John of the Cross presents various stages that can be described with some distinction. However, none of these stages is absolute in itself. John cautions that even in the unitive state people are still capable of falling into sin, and thus may still experience some of the dynamics of the purgative way.

Mortal, bodily existence prevents a more complete union with God, and thus the intense desire for an even fuller union with God remains (*F* St. 1, 27–28). Even though it is profound, one's knowledge of God is still obscure because it is incomplete. God, on this side of eternity, is unfathomable. In the unitive way life will continue, with its disappointments and losses, joys and celebrations, until mortal death ushers the Christian into the eternal embrace of God. At that time, in the fullness of the state of glory, the Christian will be "face to face" with God.

Conclusion

This chapter describes some of the critical issues that come before the explorer of Christian spirituality with respect to human-spiritual development. Since psychology is the partner-discipline that is most able to assist in this reflection, a detailed analysis of the relationship between Christian spirituality and psychology has been presented. We discovered that, inasmuch as psychology can greatly contribute to studies in Christian spirituality, some caution is in order: we need to acknowledge the, at times, ambiguous and ambivalent relationship that exists between Christian spirituality and psychology, at least the more empirical psychological frameworks. Keeping this in mind will help keep the student of Christian spirituality attentive to the specific needs of Christian spirituality as he or she looks to a range of psychologies to aid in the understanding of human-spiritual maturation.

We looked at key concepts that are frequently associated with Christian human-spiritual development such as mysticism and asceticism. Mysticism, we discovered, involves a richly colored emotional life and consciousness that reveal the dynamic reality of the *mysterium* (God) embodied-in-the-world. The path of Christian mysticism consists of the awakening of the human being to God's indwelling Spirit and Christ's incarnate, redemptive love.

Our perusal of the concept of asceticism led us to appreciate its rich pragmatic flavor: it involves the positive choices that move individuals toward more in life. Asceticism is not a renunciation of what is good in life; it is a renunciation of what is harmful, or at least not helpful. It seeks to help people live complete and authentic human lives. Christians choose what is helpful using as a principal point of reference the life of Jesus and the way he went about dealing with the ambiguous and oftentimes messy situations of life.

Finally, we undertook a detailed analysis of one spiritual writer, John of the Cross, who deals with human-spiritual growth, the everyday nature of mysticism, and the dynamics of asceticism in his description of the threefold classical spiritual itinerary. We learned here that Christian spirituality has deep insights into the nature of human-spiritual growth. For this reason the writings of John of the Cross, along with a host of other Christian spiritual writers, continue to be mined for their contributions to this area of Christian spirituality: human-spiritual development.

RECOMMENDED READING

Bouyer, Louis (1980) "Mysticism: An Essay on the History of the Word," in *Understanding Mysticism*, ed. Richard Woods, Garden City, NY: Doubleday, 42–55.

McGinn, Bernard (1991) "Theoretical Foundations: The Modern Study of Mysticism," in *Foundations of Mysticism*, New York: Crossroad, 265–343.

Meissner, William W. (1987) "The Development of Spiritual Maturity," in *Life and Faith: Psychological Perspectives on Religious Experience*, Washington, D.C.: Georgetown University Press, 61–83.

Perrin, David B. (2005) "Mysticism," in *Blackwell Companion to Christian Spirituality*, ed. Arthur Holder, Oxford: Blackwell, 442–458.

Principe, Walter H. (1977) "Mysticism: Its Meaning and Varieties," in *Mystics and Scholars: The Calgary Conference on Mysticism 1976* [Collection Studies in Religion Supplements, 3], eds Harold Coward and Terence Penelhum, Waterloo: Wilfrid Laurier University Press, 1–15.

Soelle, Dorothee (2001) "Purification, Illumination, Union: The Three Ways of Classic Mysticism," in *The Silent Cry: Mysticism and Resistence*, Minneapolis: Fortress Press, 81–84.

References to research topics from this chapter

American Psychiatric Association (1994) *The Diagnostic and Statistical Manual of Mental Disorders*, 4th edition, Washington, D.C.: American Psychiatric Association.

Bache, Christopher (2000) *Dark Night, Early Dawn: Steps to a Deep Ecology of Mind*, Albany: S.U.N.Y. Press. (Upholds the need for personal experience of the inner spiritual journey in order to have authentic knowledge of it and journey with others.)

Conn, Joann Wolski (1989) *Spirituality and Personal Maturity*, New York: Paulist Press.

Dicken, E. W. Trueman (1963) *The Crucible of Love: A Study of the Mysticism of St. Teresa of Jesus and St. John of the Cross*, New York: Sheed & Ward.

Dreyer, Yolanda (2003) "Beyond Psychology: Spirituality in Henri Nouwen's Pastoral Care," *Hervormde Teologiese Studies* (*HTS*) 59:3, 715–733.

Elkins, D., L. Hedstrom, L. Hughes, J. Leaf, and C. Saunders (1988) "Toward a Humanistic-phenomenological Spirituality: Definition, Description, and Measurement," *Journal of Humanistic Psychology* 28, 5–18.

Emmons, Robert A. and Raymond F. Paloutzian (2003) "The Psychology of Religion," *Annual Review of Psychology* 54: 377–402.

Ferrer, J. (2002) *Revisioning Transpersonal Theory: A Participatory Vision of Human Spirituality*, Albany: S.U.N.Y. Press.

Flood, Gavin (2004) *The Ascetic Self: Subjectivity, Memory and Tradition*, Cambridge: Cambridge University Press.

Fowler, James W. (1981) *Stages of Faith: The Psychology of Human Development and the Quest for Meaning*, New York: HarperCollins Publishers.

—— (1984) *Becoming Adult, Becoming Christian: Adult Development and Christian Faith*, San Francisco, CA: Harper & Row.

Grof, Stanislov (1985) *Beyond the Brain: Birth, Death, and Transcendence in Psychotherapy*, Albany: S.U.N.Y. Press.

Harkness, Georgia (1973) *Mysticism: Its Meaning and Message*, New York: Abingdon Press.

Helminiak, Daniel A. (1987) *Spiritual Development: An Interdisciplinary Study*, Chicago: Loyola University Press, 41.

Herrick, James A. (2003) *The Making of the New Spirituality: The Eclipse of the Western Religious Tradition*, Downers Grove, IL: InterVarsity Press.

Kavanaugh, K. and O. Rodriguez (1991) *The Collected Works of St. John of the Cross*, Washington, D.C.: Institute of Carmelite Studies.

Keirsey, D. and M. Bates (1978) *Please Understand Me: An Essay on Temperament Styles*, Del Mar, CA: Prometheus Nemesis Books.

Kelcourse, Felicity B., ed. (2004) *Human Development and Faith: Life-Cycle Stages of Body, Mind, and Soul*, St. Louis, MI: Chalice Press.

Meissner, William W. (1987) *Life and Faith: Psychological Perspectives on Religious Experience*, Washington, D.C.: Georgetown University Press.

Metz, B. and J. Burchill (1987) *The Enneagram and Prayer*, Denville, NJ: Dimension Books, Inc.

Michael, C. P. and M. C. Norrisey (1984) *Prayer and Temperament: Different Prayer Forms for Different Personality Types*, Charlottesville, VA: The Open Door Inc.

Payne, Steven (1990) *John of the Cross and the Cognitive Value of Mysticism*, Dordrecht, The Netherlands: Kluwer Academic Publications.

Perrin, David B. (1996) "Mysticism and Art: The Importance of Affective Reception," *Église et Théologie* 27, 47–70.

—— (1997a) *For Love of the World: The Old and the New Self of John of the Cross*, Bethesda: International Scholars Press.

—— (1997b) "Asceticism: The Enigma of Corporal Joy in Paul Ricoeur and John of the Cross," *Pastoral Sciences* 16, 135–162.

Riso, D. R. (1987) *Personality Types: Using the Enneagram for Self-Discovery*, Boston, MA: Houghton Mifflin Company.

Ruffing, Janet (1990) "Psychology as a Resource for Christian Spirituality," *Horizons* 17:1, 47–59.

Russell, Kenneth (1989) "Asceticism: The Transition from Therapy to Punishment," *Église et Théologie* 20:2, 171–193.

Soelle, Dorothee (2001) *The Silent Cry: Mysticism and Resistence*, Minneapolis: Fortress Press.

Streib, Heinz (2003) "Faith Development Research at Twenty Years," in *Developing a Public Faith: New Directions in Practical Theology*, eds R. Osmer and F. Schweitzer, St. Louis, MI: Chalice Press, 15–42.

Wilber, Ken (1995) *Sex, Ecology, Spirituality: The Spirit of Evolution*, Boston: Shambhala Press.

—— (1999) "Spiritual and Developmental Lines: Are There Stages?" *Journal of Transpersonal Psychology* 31, 1–10.

—— (2000) *Integral Psychology: Consciousness, Spirit, Psychology, Therapy*, Boston: Shambhala Press.

NOTES

1 Jean Piaget (1896–1980), a Swiss psychologist, is best known for his early work on the mental development of children. Lawrence Kohlberg (1927–1987) did extensive work on moral reasoning. James Fowler (b. 1932) extends Piaget's and Kohlberg's findings in the area of faith development.

2 Edward Howells (2002) provides an analysis of their unique ways of describing the spiritual journey in *John of the Cross and Teresa of Avila: Mystical Knowing and Selfhood*, New York: Crossroad Publishing Company. See especially "Some Important Differences Between John of the Cross and Teresa of Avila," 129–137.

3 Examples of psychologists who have developed psychological insights from the Christian perspective include: James W. Fowler (1981) *Stages of Faith: The Psychology of Human Development and the Quest for Meaning*, New York: HarperCollins Publishers; William W. Meissner (1987) *Life and Faith: Psychological Perspectives on Religious Experience*, Washington, D.C.: Georgetown University Press; and W. W. Meissner and Chris R. Schlauch, eds (2003) *Psyche and Spirit: Dialectics of Transformation*, New York: University Press of America. In Meissner's *Life and Faith,* see especially "The Development of Spiritual Maturity," 61–83. Ken Wilber has outlined a detailed theory of spiritual development, but not specifically Christian. See the bibliography for references to his work.

4 See Karl Rahner (1967) "Reflections on the Problem of the Gradual Ascent to Perfection," in *Theological Investigations* 3, London: Darton, Longman and Todd.

5 Cited in James Gollnick (2005) *Religion and Spirituality in the Life Cycle*, New York: Peter Lang Publishing, 41. The reference is to Dalai Lama & H. Cutler (1998) *The Art of Happiness: A Handbook for Living*, New York: Riverhead Books.

6 For example, Erik Erikson (1902–1994), the influential German-born American psychoanalyst, identified eight successive stages of the human life cycle. See Erik Erikson (1985) "Life Cycle," in *Life Span Development: Bases for Preventive and Interventive Helping*, M. Bloom, ed., New York: Macmillan, 35–44. Each stage prepares the individual for that which follows.

7 The British philosopher John Locke (1632–1704) greatly influenced this perspective. Locke emphasized the importance of the experience of the senses in the gathering of knowledge. Intuition, or speculation, was not a sure path

to knowledge. Locke expressed these views in his influential publication of 1690: *Essay Concerning Human Understanding.*

8 The word "Buddha" is a general term that refers to the "enlightened one." It also refers to an actual historical person born in present-day Nepal in 566 B.C.E. – Gautama Siddharta (also known as Sakyamuni) – who, at the age of twenty-nine, opted for a solitary, ascetic life and thereby achieved the enlightenment of Buddha.

9 See the extensive bibliography in D. M. Wulff (1997) *Psychology of Religion: Classic and Contemporary,* New York: Wiley (2nd edition).

10 David Fontana (2003) refers to the psychology of spirituality in *Psychology, Religion, and Spirituality,* Malden, MA: Blackwell Publishing. See especially "Why the Current Neglect of the Psychology of Religion and Spirituality?", 3–5.

11 An instrument to measure these may be found in Elkins *et al.* (1988), cited in the research bibliography for this chapter.

12 The standard psychological manual used by clinical psychologists today is *The Diagnostic and Statistical Manual of Mental Disorders* (*DSM*). It is currently in its fourth edition: thus the title is abbreviated (*DSM-IV*). Only with the publication of *DSM-IV* in 1994 did the manual recognize religious and spiritual problems among the normal difficulties encountered during various periods or situations of life (for example, problems associated with "questioning of spiritual values" or "loss or questioning of faith"). *DSM-III,* published in 1980, makes no reference whatsoever to religious or spiritual problems (i.e. questions on spiritual issues were not part of the inquiry of the clinical psychologist).

13 See, for example, Roy Schafer (1981) *A New Language for Psychoanalysis,* New Haven, CT: Yale University Press; Kenneth Gergen (1985) "The Social Constructionist Movement in Modern Psychology," *American Psychologist* 40, 266–275; Amedeo Giorgi (1970) *Psychology as a Human Science: A Phenomenological Based Approach* New York: Harper & Row; Carol Gilligan (1982) *In a Different Voice: Psychological Theory and Women's Development,* Cambridge, MA: Harvard University Press; Pamela Cooper-White (2003) *Sharing Wisdom: Use of the Self in Pastoral Care and Counseling,* Minneapolis, MN: Augsburg Fortress Publishers.

14 For example, James A. Herrick supports elimination of any spirituality that has as its basis a belief in God. Instead he would like to replace spirituality with a strictly scientific world view that does not support a belief in the non-material aspects of life. See, James A. Herrick (2003) *The Making of the New Spirituality: The Eclipse of the Western Religious Tradition,* Downers Grove, IL: InterVarsity Press.

15 Daniel A. Helminiak (1998) *Religion and the Human Sciences: An Approach Via Spirituality,* New York, S.U.N.Y. Press, 166. Helminiak uses Eric Fromm, Victor Frankl, and Dan Browning to back him up in this perspective.

16 For an example of a secular approach to measuring spirituality see D. Elkins, L. Hedstrom, L. Hughes, J. Leaf, and C. Saunders (1988) "Toward a Humanistic-phenomenological spirituality: Definition, Description, and Measurement," *Journal of Humanistic Psychology,* 28, 5–18.

17 Division 36 of the American Psychological Association is working on these issues in a very intentional way. See their website: http://www.ppc.sas.upenn.edu. The work of Phyliss Zagano and C. Kevin Gillespie (2006) "Ignatian Spirituality and Positive Psychology," *The Way* 45/4 (October), 1–18 is an example of this work.

18 For an analysis of the hidden assumptions inherent in the human sciences see Brent D. Slife and Richard N. Williams (2004) *What's Behind the Research? Discovering Hidden Assumptions in the Behavioral Sciences*, Thousand Oaks, CA: Sage Publications.

19 These are summarized from John Shea (2005) "Spirituality, Psychology and Psychotherapy," in *The New Westminster Dictionary of Christian Spirituality*, Philip Sheldrake, ed., Louisville, KY: WJK Press, 52.

20 James Gollnick (2005) *Religion and Spirituality in the Life Cycle*, New York and Oxford: Peter Lang, 43. This summary on transpersonal psychology is taken from Gollnick (2005), 43–47.

21 See the work of Stanislov Grof (1985) *Beyond the Brain: Birth, Death, and Transcendence in Psychotherapy*, Albany: S.U.N.Y. Press and J. Ferrer (2002) *Revisioning Transpersonal Theory: A Participatory Vision of Human Spirituality*, Albany: S.U.N.Y. Press.

22 For a survey of how self-help resources have entered spiritual sensitivities under the guise of responsible psychology, see Paul C. Vitz (1977) *Psychology as Religion: The Cult of Self-Worship*, Grand Rapids, MI: William B. Eerdmans Publishing Company. Vitz argues that psychology, practiced as religion, has been ultimately detrimental to individuals and society in general.

23 This is a personality test, based largely on the work of Carl Jung, that helps individuals identify themselves with a fundamental personality type and its characteristics. The goal is to show both strengths and weakness so one can feel affirmed in the positive aspects and attend to the areas that need some change. See D. Keirsey and M. Bates (1978) *Please Understand Me: An Essay on Temperament Styles* and C. P. Michael and M. C. Norrisey (1984) *Prayer and Temperament: Different Prayer Forms for Different Personality Types*, listed in the bibliography for this chapter.

24 The origins of the Enneagram are not clear. Some writers suggest that it was first shaped by certain orders of the Sufis, a mystical sect of Islam prominent in the tenth and eleventh centuries; others believe it originated as long ago as 2500 B.C.E. in Babylon or elsewhere in the Middle East. See D. R. Riso (1987) *Personality Types: Using the Enneagram for Self-Discovery* and B. Metz and J. Burchill *The Enneagram and Prayer*, listed in the bibliography for this chapter.

25 Some of the material in this section was previously published as "Mysticism and Art: The Importance of Affective Reception," in *Église et Théologie*, 27/1 (1996), 47–70. Used with permission.

26 Cited in Dorothee Soelle (2001) *The Silent Cry: Mysticism and Resistance*, Minneapolis: Fortress Press, 11–12.

27 Bernard McGinn (1991) *Foundations of Mysticism*, New York: Crossroad, 322.

28 Cuthbert Butler (1922) *Western Mysticism*, London: Constable, 3–4.

29 For a survey of the various interpretations and use of the word mysticism see: Walter H. Principe (1977) "Mysticism: Its Meaning and Varieties," in *Mystics and Scholars: The Calgary Conference on Mysticism 1976*, Collection Studies in Religion Supplements, 3, H. Coward and T. Penelhum, eds, Waterloo: Wilfrid Laurier University Press, 1–15. On the origin of the word "mysticism" see, Louis Bouyer (1980) "Mysticism: An Essay on the History of the Word," in *Understanding Mysticism*, Richard Woods, ed., Garden City, NY: Doubleday, 42–55.

30 Rudolph Otto states that in the Christian Scholastic tradition, " 'Mystica' was originally an adjective qualifying the substantive 'theologia.' The essence of the mystical theologia in distinction from the usual theologia lay in the fact that it claimed to teach a deeper 'mystery,' and to impart secrets and reveal depths which were otherwise unknown." Rudolph Otto (1957) *Mysticism East and West: A Comparative Analysis of The Nature of Mysticism*, New York: Meridian Books, 141.

31 Karl Rahner states: "There is only *one single* mystery in the strict sense, that of God's self-bestowal by which he extends himself into the dimension of that which is most interior to existence (Spirit) and into the dimension of the history of man (Incarnation)." K. Rahner (1974) "Reflections on Methodology in Theology," *Theological Investigations* XI, London: Darton, Longman and Todd, 109.

32 This is at the heart of the teaching of many mystics: for example, Meister Eckhart (1260–1329). See in particular his "Sermon 52: *Beati pauperes spiritu, quoniam ipsorum est regnum caelorum (Mt. 5:3),*" in (1981) *Meister Eckhart: The Essential Sermons, Commentaries, Treatises, and Defense*, tr. and intro. Edmund Colledge and Bernard McGinn, New York: Paulist Press, 199–203. See also Rahner, "Reflections on Methodology," 106–109.

33 Rudolph Otto points out that the etymology of the word "mysticism" had nothing to do with "union" with God. See Otto, *Mysticism East and West*, 141. According to Otto: "Mysticism is not first of all an act of union, but predominantly the life lived in the 'knowledge' of this wholly 'other' God. God himself is mystical, for a relationship of union is only possible with an object which is itself mystical in the first instance." Ibid.

34 References to the *Living Flame of Love* of John of the Cross are to the following translation: Kieran Kavanaugh and Otilio Rodriguez (1991) *The Collected Works of St. John of the Cross*, with Introductions by Kieran Kavanaugh, revised edition, Washington, D.C.: Institute of Carmelite Studies. References use the following format: F=*The Living Flame of Love* (commentary, 2nd redaction), followed by the stanza number and paragraph number.

35 See Thomas Merton (1969) *Contemplative Prayer*, Garden City: Doubleday Image; (1972) *New Seeds of Contemplation*, New York: New Directions.

36 Some of the material in this section was previously published as "Asceticism: The Enigma of Corporal Joy in Paul Ricoeur and John of the Cross," in *Pastoral Sciences/Sciences Pastorales*, 16 (1997), 135–192. Used with permission.

37 See Peter J. Awn (1984) "Faith and Practice," in *Islam: The Religious and Political Life of a World Community*, Marjorie Kelly, ed., New York: Praeger Publishers, 9–10.
38 See John Snelling (1987) *The Buddhist Handbook: A Complete Guide to Buddhist Teaching, Practice, History, and Schools*, London: Century, 58–60 and Peter Harvey (1990) *An Introduction to Buddhism: Teachings, History, and Practices*, Cambridge: Cambridge University Press.
39 Some members of *Opus Dei*, a group in the Roman Catholic Church, continue to use the cilice, a small bracelet with pointy edges worn around the thigh, for bodily mortification.
40 See Kenneth Russell (1989) "Asceticism: The Transition from Therapy to Punishment," *Église et Théologie* 20:2, 171–193.
41 'Some of the material in this section was previously published as three separate dictionary articles: Purgative Way, Illuminative Way, Unitive Way in *The New SCM Dictionary of Christian Spirituality*, Philip Sheldrake, editor, SCM Press 2005 and *The New Westminster Dictionary of Christian Spirituality*, Philip Sheldrake, editor, Westminster John Knox Press, 2005. Used with permission.'

8

Questions of spiritual practice

"Christian practice . . . can be understood as a rich tapestry of historically mediated, identity-forming, patterned actions through which . . . [we undertake] faithful witness to and participation in God's own active presence in and for the sake of the world. These inherited actions should be seen in dynamic not static ways because, as they are handed on from one generation to the next, practices are continuously shaped and reshaped through the ongoing dialogue we orchestrate between present sociocultural circumstances and the historic Christian witness of faith. Christian practices are the patterned, cooperative, and informed ways that our lives as Christians are caught up into the things that God is doing in the world already."

Susanne Johnson, "Remembering the Poor"

Introduction

SPIRITUAL PRACTICE IS A VERY FLUID TERM that refers to a large variety of activities in relationship to Christian spirituality. It can mean anything from the prayers said before meals, to the rites and rituals celebrated in places of worship, to the tending of the needs of the poor in local soup kitchens or the homeless on streets. It may also refer to such mundane activities as preparing food – for some people, "growing, cooking and eating food" is a spiritual practice.[1] Art (such as painting, firing clay, music, and dancing) could be considered one as well.[2]

Spiritual practices express in action the values and beliefs of Christians; they help Christians grow in those values and beliefs *as they are practiced*. In other words, beliefs organize and shape people's actions while endowing them with, for example, emotional intensity, personal values, and bodily expressions. Spiritual practices join together what is believed to be true and the reality of people's lives – including past experiences, current realities, and future potential. Through spiritual practices, all these are brought into the current moment to be expressed, explored, and deepened.[3]

Thus, the word *practice* refers to two things: the *event* that is the practice, and the idea that we *practice these events*, beliefs, hopes, and so on, to get better at them – just as one would practice a skill (such as throwing a football) to improve one's ability to do it. But spiritual practice is more akin to developing an art than it is to repeating by rote other skill-building activities that have predictable outcomes. Spiritual practices are an art because they require the contribution of all levels of our person. There is no single way of expressing or doing spiritual practices; certain ones will appeal at specific times in people's lives, but not at other times. As we reflect on spiritual practice here, we will refer to both these uses of the term *practice*, that is, the activity itself and the artful practice to grow in it.

> *Spiritual practice* in Christian spirituality is all the activities Christians
> engage in to grow and mature in their relationship to God, to each other,
> and to the world under the impulse of the Holy Spirit. Without practice
> there is a tendency to end up in theory – believing without living out the
> beliefs in daily life as witnessed to by Jesus.

Many Christian spiritualities have specific spiritual practices associated
with them, each emerging from particular values or beliefs. It is important
to be aware of the nature of these spiritual practices and the role they play
in people's lives, especially as people borrow spiritual practices from non-
Christian sources (such as tai chi body movement, Buddhist incense-burning,
or Native American purification rites) and use them within Christian
contexts.

This chapter will highlight the nature of spiritual practices and then
introduce some examples of spiritual practices that are often part of
Christian spiritualities.[4] We will discover that Christian spiritual practices
have the following qualities:

- link contemporary Christians to the past *and* insert them more integrally
  in the present;
- are personal *and* communitarian; they link people intimately with
  themselves, others, the world, and God;
- involve total embodiment;
- exercise a range of selves;
- are not necessarily utilitarian, that is, one thing done to cause another
  to happen;
- are subversive, transformative, and reformative;
- teach new things by helping acquire wisdom.

The nature of spiritual practice

Spiritual practice as a link to the past

Spiritual practices are passed along in the forms of traditional rites, songs,
readings, particular types of social outreach, along with countless other ways
in which people have creatively constructed, expressed, explored, and
deepened Christian spiritualities. As such, spiritual practices are located in

a precarious place – they are a link to the historical past and the traditions out of which they arose, while at the same time being a link to the actual circumstances and context of *people's* lives.

In this way, the historical past is brought into active dialogue with the present. This dialogue can be life-giving yet challenging. Spiritual practices that were developed in the past reflect values, a world vision, images, and symbols meaningful to people living in a context that may be radically different from the current one. Some, although prescribed as mandatory by faith communities or spiritual groups, may no longer be relevant. Life has changed, but the spiritual practice may not have evolved to reflect new realities.

For example, the spiritual practice in the Roman Catholic Church of honoring the Sacred Heart of Jesus began in the late seventeenth century, following the witness of Margaret Mary Alacoque (1647–1690), who reported conversing with Jesus about establishing a devotion to his Sacred Heart. Eventually, by the late nineteenth century, the devotion was firmly in place. Families and church communities would unite in prayer before a picture of Jesus, his physical heart exposed. His face was often depicted with fine features (almost to the point of being effeminate), with one hand raised in blessing and the other touching or pointing to his heart. His hair was long and he was dressed in flowing robes resembling a Roman toga.

When we begin looking at this devotion in context – in its historical origins and its spirituality – it makes a lot of sense. The giving of one's heart, seen as a symbol of self-sacrificing love, points to giving oneself wholly. This is exactly what Jesus offers – his entire person in love. However, a young person today who is exposed to an image of the Sacred Heart of Jesus – as it was portrayed a hundred years ago – would most likely find it unappealing, or even gruesome. Even though the spirituality behind the practice is sound, it literally needs to be reframed for people today.[5]

Spiritual practices must be continually renewed and made relevant or meaningful to the contemporary individual and community. It is not a matter of importing practices blindly from the past, or of doing away with former spiritual practices when they no longer seem to fit. Instead, to appropriate the tradition faithfully, practices that have been proven to be helpful in the past need to be interpreted responsibly and shaped anew for current times. Spiritual practices have their own history of development, but they need to be fluid enough to reflect current existential concerns.

What we need to discern in spiritual practices are the insights into Christian spirituality that underlie their exterior expressions. Often the insight can be preserved, but the exterior manifestation of the practice may take on fresh ways of expression or be structured in a new way.

The personal and communitarian dimensions of spiritual practice

We have seen that spiritual practices are linked to traditions: to a history of the use of a particular practice that a community of persons has found important over time. For this reason, spiritual practices enjoy a reciprocal relationship with the communities that employ them. While "communities shape their practices" for their own needs, we can say that "practices also shape communities."[6]

For example, extended time in quiet prayer may be the practice that gives a community its deep-felt identity and be the very purpose for its continued existence. This practice thus shapes who the community is at a profound level. Monastic communities are of this kind – their life of prayer shapes their community on all levels. Or, if a faith community has accepted to run a home for people living with AIDS, this responsibility (which is a spiritual practice) will shape the community in many ways – from the way they organize their time to care for the residents to the way they gather funds for their work. The needs of the spiritual practice shape the community's activities and thus the community itself.

But spiritual practices go beyond the communitarian dimension: they are *embodied by individuals* within those same communities. Spiritual practices are cooperative undertakings that depend on the investment of each individual. In prayer, ritual movement, or response to social needs, it is the individual's current state of feelings, self-perception, social location, world view, and the like that shape the concrete nature and actual expression of spiritual practice. This is the case regardless of how old the tradition is, how highly structured the practice in question, or how the community as a whole participates in spiritual practices. Each individual is responsible before the tradition and the community to embody spiritual practices that are important to the life of the community as a whole.

With the lived expression of spiritual practices, beliefs do not remain abstract. Instead, their meaning stems from the circumstances, joys, disappointments, failures, and successes of an individual life.[7] This is the personal nature of spiritual practice. After all, spiritual practices are performed by a real flesh-and-blood person – with all his or her personal traits, past experiences, and hopes for the future thrown into the mix and brought into dynamic tension with each other.

The role of the body

It is one's personal body, with all its history and potential, and no other, that feels, that sees, that smells – these arms that stretch forward in worship, this voice that proclaims the psalms in song, these eyes that gaze upon the marginalized and forgotten of the world. The role of the body in any spiritual practice, including prayer and meditation, is irreplaceable. Spiritual practices are situated in the concrete texture of personal corporeal movement, sight, smell, hearing, and other physical abilities. They are also situated within, for example, one's powers of imagination, creativity, forgiveness, and potential for growth.

These aspects of spiritual practice do not deny its communitarian dimension, for Christian spiritual practices are always in communion with others – even if those others are not physically present. They exist as the result of the thoughtful and reflective wisdom of those who have gone before. In a certain sense, spiritual practices are always received from within a tradition. But spiritual practices are much more than the manuals that describe, proscribe, or explain them. There is nothing automatic about their outcomes. A practice is seen as spiritual only when it is taken up by a living person, and its potential becomes intertwined with that person's potential. It is a relational encounter: for this reason, over time, individuals are shaped by the community and the community is shaped by the individuals who form it. People's bodies, with all their inherent qualities at the physical, psychological, imaginative, creative, intellectual, and so on, levels, are required for this to happen.

Spiritual practice in everyday life

Spiritual practices are not only scheduled at special times or on special days, such as Sundays or other days of worship; they are also part of, and reflect, the things done in everyday life. Through such activities as gardening (an example of nurturing life), walking (an example of care of the body), or quiet sitting (an example of the mindful recollection of life), the attitude that the Spirit of God is alive in all aspects of human life is fostered.

In this way, spiritual practices reflect the radical embodiment of Christian spirituality – they blur the lines between what we might think of as spirit and matter, mind and body, the holy and the unholy. They connect to the materiality of the spirit. We've already mentioned that the everyday nature of spiritual practices engages all of who a person is – not just his or her soul. The everyday experiences of mind, spirit, sight, smell, touch, imagination, thought, and other aspects may all play a significant role in a seamless expression of the self already known and experienced, and the self one wishes to be.

Along with the potential for personal transformation, and the transformation of the community, there is also the potential for the transformation of the spiritual practice itself. No matter how highly structured the practice may be, it is shaped according to the immediate context and the current meaning and needs of people's lives. With new insights gained from exercising the spiritual practice today, new ways of doing the same thing that will renew the practice and make it relevant for today's world may be found. This openness to transformation keeps spiritual practices fresh and vibrant for the changing needs of individuals and the communities to which they belong.

The range of selves that *exercise* spiritual practices

Closely tied to the everyday nature of spiritual practices is their capacity to bring out a *range of selves*. As we saw in Chapter 4, human beings operate from different centers – different profiles of the self – depending on their circumstances. These selves or profiles are interconnected, but each takes on a particular level of importance in different settings in people's lives.

In the same way, one spiritual practice may exercise or appeal to one aspect of a person's being, while another may call forth a different aspect. For example, someone doing the pilgrimage of El Camino de Santiago (an 800-kilometer walk from St. Jean Pied de Port in northwestern France to Santiago de Compostela on the northwestern coast of Spain) will summon an entirely different set of skills than someone following a silent retreat in a monastery under the guidance of the *Spiritual Exercises of Ignatius of Loyola*. The *Camino*, as it is commonly called, began in earnest in the twelfth century. (We will look at this in more detail below, when we discuss pilgrimages.) The *Spiritual Exercises* were developed by the Spanish nobleman and founder of the Jesuit order Ignatius of Loyola (1491–1556) to help people be more aware of the meaning of their lives and the way the Holy Spirit is active in them. While the walking pilgrimage requires a radical commitment to physical endurance, the silent retreat requires a radical commitment to prayerful solitude and silence. It is interesting to note that each of these spiritual practices takes about thirty days to complete.

A careful comparison of these two spiritual practices reveals that they share many elements. One example is the practice of hospitality. On the road to Santiago, one meets many other pilgrims; on the retreat, one silently receives and welcomes others into one's life in a process that is powerful and real, even though most of the time is spent in silence. Nonetheless, the nature of each spiritual practice is unique and calls forth different profiles of the self. An individual may at one point in his or her life feel attracted to the grueling, physical engagement (which requires mental focus as well) of the pilgrimage, while at another time he or she may feel attracted to the quiet serenity of the silent retreat (which requires endurance of another sort).

The non-utilitarian nature of spiritual practice

Some spiritual practices, such as volunteering time at a shelter for homeless people, are aimed at meeting particular goals. Not all spiritual practices have this explicit utilitarian character, however. Not all are meant to accomplish something that can be clearly described, measured, and repeated with specific outcomes. And that is just fine. We need to acknowledge the gratuitous quality of many spiritual practices.

For example, when someone takes time to pause and peacefully watch the slow movement of the sun as it gracefully slips below the horizon, he or she is not setting out to accomplish a particular task. The moment speaks for itself – the moment, in itself, is the fullness of the practice. This moment may be one of peace-filled solitude, of thoughtful recollection on one's life; or there may emerge a feeling of immense gratitude to God for the life one has been graced to live. When silence is practiced in the presence of the sunset's beauty one never quite knows how the moment will unfold or fill up. It just is – it is a gift. In another example, when someone tastes the sweetness of slow, meditative reading of a favorite scriptural text or author, he or she simply savors the moment, taking as much time as wanted on a particular phrase, image, or thought that comes as a result of one's openness to go with the flow.

Spiritual practices, by their very nature, sometimes draw us away from orderliness and coherence. Committed spiritual practices lay a foundation of stability and community within which the person can become open to something beyond. Feelings, memories, and images at times will pour into one's consciousness, seemingly out of nowhere, leading the individual in a new and unexpected direction. For example, while helping an elderly person in a nursing home to eat, you may be overcome by memories of your own parent, who died before needing this kind of care from you. You recall the love you shared with them and regret their passing all over again; you express gratitude for who they were in your life and how they shaped who you are today. People don't plan these kinds of moments – they come as gift, for those who are open to receiving them.

Another example that brings to light the unpredictable nature of spiritual practices is the *Clearness Committee* invented by the Society of Friends, now known as the Quakers.[8] The Quakers were founded in the mid-seventeenth century in England. The Quaker Clearness Committee provides a setting for individuals to let go of their ordinary way of thinking, feeling, and doing so they can be receptive to new possibilities for their lives. In a posture of submission, they meet in prayerful worship with others to discern God's direction for them. Silence and attentive listening to their own feelings, as well as the comments or questions from others, characterize this time together. People never quite know what the outcome will be – the Quaker community listens in silence to hear God's authentic voice for the individual and the community as a whole.

What happens in spiritual practice, as we see in the example of the Quaker Clearness Committee, is that the potential of the immediate transforms the ideal and the abstract. The current moment is broken apart into a living reality that has a heart of its own; it develops its own meaning, its own unique place in people's lives. The moment, if you like, breathes on its own. What one thought to be the controlled moment of the ideal is thrown into the ambiguity and the messiness of life. Spiritual practices, therefore, dissolve the artificial boundaries people have constructed to keep reality away. Through these practices people are taken up into reality as an entire being that cannot close off one part of its life from any other. At times this experience may be overwhelming, especially if pent-up emotions and unresolved issues surface. These emotions may be painful, or they may be feelings of joy, gratitude, awe, and wonder before a God who suddenly takes on a whole new meaning in our lives.

This is the paradox of spiritual practices: while an individual may exercise one profile of the self in any spiritual practice, his or her entire being is affected. People cannot control the outcome. Spiritual practices take people far beyond one part of their being – especially their rational intellect, which encourages them "to do it properly"[9] – mixing all elements of their selves. Because of this helpful aspect of spiritual practice – helpful in the sense that one desires to allow God's graceful presence to emerge spontaneously from within the entirety of life – we must avoid the tendency to see spiritual practices as a spectator sport.

Spiritual practices are not a spectator sport

Spectators are present for the action, but they are not involved intimately in it. They participate from a distance. In Chapter 2, we made the distinction between space and place; being a spectator is a psychological space occupied more by rational thought than by heartfelt participation. Spectators of spiritual practices may go through the ritual movements (such as prayers) but without real personal investment.

For example, many Christian traditions expect members to gather weekly as a faith community. The question individuals need to ask themselves is whether they are embracing active participation in this spiritual practice as mature, free, and responsible adults, or going through the motions as passive spectators to fulfill a requirement. These two positions (passive spectator or active participant) are not necessarily separate from each other – there are degrees in-between the two extremes – but they do characterize two points of view. While fulfilling one's Sunday obligation may be deeply satisfying on one level, how much value is involved for the individual and the community if a person is not actively and personally engaged in it? Can passive participation in the scriptural readings, song, prayers, and rituals of the weekly gathering lead to the transformation that spiritual practice is expected to bring about?

It is difficult to answer these questions. But as we have seen, it is authentic encounter that shapes the place, the potential, for authentic transformation. Without a true meeting of the individual and what is going on – an encounter that may lead to tension and to ambiguity about how someone sees the truth of his or her life – the transformative potential of spiritual practice is diminished.

> Spiritual practices of Christians are not meant solely to stabilize their lives as they are, or to affirm the way they view the world, themselves, or God. Instead, these practices transform and reform who they are; they shape them in new ways and renew their lives in God.

We saw the transformative process in action in Chapter 6, in the understanding moment in interpreting texts. In that chapter we emphasized that authentic interpretation, as authentic spiritual practice, challenges the status quo and helps open us up to new ways of viewing ourselves, the world, others, and God. This is only possible if someone invests personally in the process and chooses to let go of previous ways of seeing themselves or doing things. The same is true for spiritual practices.

The cognitive nature of spiritual practices

> "Through lifelong engagement in practices we come into awareness of certain realities – we come *to see* and *to know* and even *to be* things – that apart from such participation would otherwise remain beyond our ken. There are certain goods, values, and virtues internal to particular practices that can be acquired only from the inside out, through sustained participation in practicing communities."[10]

What Susanne Johnson is saying in the above text is that spiritual practices have a certain cognitive element: we can learn from them. This does not merely mean learning to do something better, as in becoming more accomplished at a certain kind of prayer. Rather, it means becoming aware of other dimensions of life that have been overlooked. For example, through the practice of meditation someone may discover insights into the value and preciousness of life, or become mindful of the love God has for all creatures. Even if someone knew these things before, they have moved from mere head knowledge and have become an integral part of his or her very being. This heart knowledge now lives in one's body; from it one naturally acts and engages others in life as a result of it.

Our bodies participate equally in the advancement of this heart knowledge, because it is through our bodies that we interact with and know our world. During times of quiet reflection or silent meditation, people not only listen to what is happening in their thoughts and feelings, but also listen attentively to their bodies and to their experiences in order to gain insights. People's physical senses are as tied to belief and knowledge as are their thoughts, feelings, and imaginative wanderings.[11]

The kind of knowledge described above is not easily obtained. As Susanne Johnson says, it requires "lifelong engagement" and "sustained participation" with others. People cannot pick up a book and acquire this kind of knowledge: it comes from the active and intentional participation in the issues of life, subsequent reflection on those issues, and openness to allowing this kind of knowledge to become part of who one is. In this way, the Christian traditions are appropriated – in the entirety of the person – so that spiritual practice becomes part of everyday life and forms part of one's spontaneous responses to experiences in life. Christians do the right thing in accordance with the wisdom of the scriptures and the witness of the men and women who have gone before them – with the values, beliefs, and practices of the believing community in which they participate.

But it is not merely a question of blindly appropriating the wisdom from the traditions. Spiritual practices and their cultivated wisdom are dynamic, for as they are passed on from one generation to the next, they are adapted and reshaped for current contexts. The wisdom gained from them is renewed as well. It is new knowledge in the sense that it fits today's times, which are different from, let's say, those of a hundred years ago. It is new to the life being lived today, with all its associated meanings and consequences.

The historic witness of faith must be taken seriously. Only then can wisdom retain its authenticity; otherwise, it loses its flavor, its salt (to use a biblical expression), and is no longer wisdom at all. There are no automatic answers to the often complex and messy situations of life – only hard-won learnings (which is what is called *wisdom*) that spiritual practices help shape in the depths of people's being. From this deep seat of truth, learnings emerge and provide light and guidance for people's lives.

Spiritual practice in the classroom

What has been stressed above is the experiential nature of spiritual practices as they are interwoven with the practices of everyday life or the formal moments of highly structured rituals. But what about the way someone learns about spiritual practices in the classroom during a university or college course or weekend workshop? What influence does classroom learning have on everything we have discussed above? Can spirituality be taught, or is it something we just do? Should spiritual practice even be part of academic courses?

The first task here is moving from the academic knowledge of spiritual practice to living out one's spiritual practice, which influences self-understanding and communal relationships. The second task is reflecting critically upon the appropriateness of spiritual practices in the classroom. Hot on the heels of this second task is the associated task of determining how to measure the success of what is taught. These tasks are not easy, but they form part of the pedagogical considerations of the educator and student working in the academic study of Christian spirituality. For this reason they must be carefully considered when spiritual practices are introduced as part of an academic curriculum.[12]

Let us now briefly examine a number of practices that have been helpful in embodying the principles and nature of spiritual practice outlined above. The treatment below is not meant to be exhaustive, but will introduce the reader to a number of key spiritual practices that have been recognized as such by many faith communities down through the centuries. Not all of these have had equal importance throughout the history of Christian spirituality, but they all have played, and continue to play, a significant role in the development of Christian spiritual life.

Prayer

"Action and contemplation do not pertain to separate spheres: the sacred and the secular, church and world, spiritual life and the domain of the mundane and profane. The one God who is constantly 'adventing' is not only for us but for the whole world. Prayer is well thought of as awakening to the divine presence in every dimension of everyday living."[13]

The New Testament contains many references to prayer. Perhaps the best-known example is the Lord's Prayer, found in Matthew 6:10–13. Others include Paul's advice to "Pray without ceasing" (1 Thess. 5:17); "Rejoice in hope, endure in affliction, persevere in prayer" (Rom. 12:12); and "Be alert and always keep praying" (Eph. 6:18). Clearly, prayer was a key activity for the early Christian communities. It has continued to be part of Christian practice down through the centuries.

But what does it mean to pray? What does it mean to keep praying? Prayer, according to Clement of Alexandria (150–214), means "keeping company with God." This is consistent with the way Jesus viewed prayer. The central message behind Jesus's invitation to prayer was to nurture relationship with God and, as a result, with other people and with all of creation. Nurturing one's relationship with God means doing what is done to nurture a relationship with a close friend or a spouse: one's concerns, joys, successes, and failures are brought before them. Time is spent together. In doing so there is a discovery of who each is at a deep level. In short, one trusts the other with his or her life, knowing that the other will cherish, honor, and love that life – no matter what. Prayer is all about nurturing companionship, as Origen, a celebrated writer and teacher in Alexandria, Egypt, also taught.

Origen was one of the first people to write at length on Christian prayer and its meaning.[14] He maintained that the entire lives of those who closely follow the teachings and spirit of Jesus Christ can be considered *to be prayer*. For Origen, prayer isn't just something Christians do or accomplish (such as reciting prayers or psalms from scripture). Instead, it is something that is lived, a lifestyle – the spirit in which people live and do all things as they grow in their relationship with God, others, and creation. For Origen, living the Spirit of Jesus, the Holy Spirit, in life constitutes authentic Christian prayer. Living in the Spirit of Jesus fosters authentic relationships: love of God, and love of others.

Prayer, according to Origen, can be unceasing if one allows every moment of one's life to be touched by the Spirit of Jesus, the Holy Spirit. Such an understanding of prayer has had an enormous impact on the practice of Christian prayer throughout history and up to our own times. It places the practice of prayer at the heart of everyday life, and ties it to the mystery of relationship with God as it is lived through the relationships with other people. Every moment of life has the potential to become prayer-ful!

Authentic prayer leads people to become ever more engaged in the issues of the world – not removed from them. This is true even for those who have chosen lives that are cut off from explicit engagement in the world. For example, Thomas Merton (1915–1968), a Christian monk, lived many

> Prayer is not a one-sided effort – an individual doesn't suddenly decide to pray. Prayer is a cooperative effort. The Holy Spirit first invites the Christian to prayer and from this invitation comes a response. This makes prayer possible in the life of the Christian. Prayer is first a gift, a grace, that is received and responded to. This gift is unwrapped by expressing actively the animating presence of God in life through, for example, the recitation of psalms, quiet moments of recollection, communal worship, mindfulness about God, and good works.

years behind the monastic walls of Our Lady of Gethsemani in Kentucky in the United States. Despite his solitude he remained very involved in the world through his writings and conferences on such contemporary issues as peace movements, civil rights, and concern for the poor and homeless.[15]

We must not confuse Christian prayer with carefully constructed psychological methods that may lead people into intense experiences of the self, or cause people to uncover self-deceptions or falsehoods. Psychological techniques may be useful to enhance the awareness of who one is, and how one is in relationship to others, but until these revelations are held and considered within the reality of God's presence in life, they are not necessarily Christian prayer. In Chapter 7 we examined the relationship between Christian spirituality and psychology. It might be helpful for you to go back and review those sections that deal with this relationship and reflect upon them, keeping in mind the characteristics of Christian prayer summarized below. The list is not exhaustive; so much more could be said of Christian prayer, especially as it is reflected in the various Christian traditions. So rich is the practice of Christian prayer that no one tradition reflects fully all the elements of it as it has been practiced and lived through the centuries.

Bible reading

Reading the Bible (often referred to as *scripture* or *holy scripture*) is a spiritual practice that is more common today in Christian communities than ever before. But what does it mean to read the Bible? Are Christians meant to learn something from it? Extract knowledge? Define principles? Look for absolute truths about Christian life? Bible reading as spiritual practice involves allowing the word of God to enter one's heart, rather than distilling abstract truths from it. What does this mean?

CHARACTERISTICS OF CHRISTIAN PRAYER

Prayer does not happen exclusively within one's private thoughts and feelings, or at some specific time and place; it also occurs in relationship to other people, with God, and with all of creation from day to day. Prayer is not the opposite of action: service and presence to others are key aspects of Christian prayer.

God does not live "up there" somewhere. Prayer ought to seek God in *this* world, where God and humanity live together, not outside of the world. In this world God lives and in this world relationship with God is nurtured – which is Christian prayer.

Christian prayer is embodied – it involves all one's humanity as an embodied creature in this world: for example, sight, smell, movement, feelings, mind, and soul. God's grace does not limit the form prayer may take in life. Dancing, singing, shaping clay, reading psalms, reflecting on scripture, and other activities may all be valid Christian prayer forms.

Prayer is influenced by models of God. A particular model of God will result in a particular approach to prayer. Basic to all models of God is God's active presence in one's life and in the world, which allows authentic communication and relationship to be nurtured.

Prayer seeks to foster self-awareness so that there is a growing sensitivity to God's unfolding presence in life. One can become transparent and honest in the depth's of one's being – thoughts, attitudes, and feelings (even those someone doesn't like) are allowed to bubble to the surface in prayer. Everything may be brought to God in prayer, because God is part of all aspects of one's life. Prayer draws people closer together as individuals draw closer to God. Healthy prayer finds individuals in some form of community (communion) with others – which may take different forms at various times in life. The nature of God is relational; this needs to be reflected in Christian prayer.

Christian prayer, because it is focused on the life, death, and resurrection of Jesus, looks explicitly at the person of Jesus and his manifestation of God alive in the world through the power of the Holy Spirit.

When someone reads a biblical text, it isn't read in the abstract. It is read from within the context of a life and a community of believers that lives in the here and now. The Bible, as a *living text*, is a *living witness* to the life of Jesus for the world today. The Bible doesn't pretend to give absolute answers to all the woes or questions of current times. The Bible is understood to be the word of God – but we also understand that it was produced from within a community of believers, now resides in the life of the community of believers, and continues to breathe new life into the heart of the Christian community, into its most profound reasons for existence.

From this perspective, the spiritual practice of bible reading is not so much about simply reading a text, but living it out. In Chapter 6, in the discussion of the interpretation and appropriation of texts, we saw how this works. When Christians come together in prayer, when they feed the hungry, when they forgive one another – when they follow Jesus in living and treating people the way he did – Christians *perform* what is found in the word of God. The word of God becomes a living word, not only for those performing it, but for others as well.

Francis Young describes the performative character of bible reading this way:

> The biblical canon, then, is as it were the repertoire, inherited, given to be performed. Selections are performed day by day and week by week in the liturgy. . . . All preachers and congregations are the performers and the hearers on whose inspiration the communication of the Word of God depends. The Word is both "incarnate" in a time-bound text and yet eternal, transcending the limits of human language and culture. Amateurs and professionals have a go with varying degrees of skill, fostering an audience which will be able to recognize the truly masterly performance. But any good performance has an authenticity of its own.[16]

When a Christian or someone else reads a text from the Bible, he or she might ask the following questions: "What am I (or are we) being asked to perform? How is this text addressing me personally; how does it speak to the actual situation of my life? What text am I (or are we) being invited to write through my (or our) actions?" In this way bible reading, as spiritual practice, becomes sacramental – a visible sign of God's invisible presence in one's life and in the world around one. To understand the Bible is not so much to question its principles and beliefs as to allow it to instruct in the mystery of living Christian life every day as people struggle to follow Jesus in the varied and unpredictable situations of life.

The Bible does not provide ready answers to the difficulties or complex questions people face in today's world. Reading the Bible in the context of one's life is not an invitation to undertake a frantic search for a scriptural passage that responds (most likely according to one's current way of thinking) to the burning problem of the day. Rather, bible reading invites the reader into a receptive and reflective stance before the text that nourishes and transforms his or her life in Jesus. Ultimately, bible reading and study leads into authentic prayer.

Benedict of Nursia (c.480–c.547), an Italian monk who founded many monasteries and whose followers came to be known as the Benedictines, outlines a way of reading the Bible that reflects what is said above. In the norms he set out for community living, recorded in the *Rule of Benedict* (Chapter 52), he describes reading the Bible as *lectio divina* (translated literally as *divine reading*). *Lectio divina* was not a fervent reading of the Bible aimed at distilling some truth or clear message. Instead, it was geared to spending some leisure time with God through a peaceful meditation on a biblical passage. In a place of quiet repose Benedict's monks were invited to savor the word of God in slow, peaceful reading – either alone or in community. Benedict's instructions to his monks emphasized a quiet attention to God's presence through attention to God's word that comes alive in *lectio*. *Lectio*, at one time, was essentially reserved for monks and nuns in monasteries, but now all Christians are invited to partake of this kind of spiritual nourishment.

The contemporary practice of *lectio* owes a great debt to Martin Luther and Huldrych Zwingli (1484–1531). They and others made the Bible more accessible to ordinary people outside the walls of monastic life – and in their native tongues. Before this time, the Bible was largely available only in Latin. Because of the importance of bible reading, and its place in spiritual practice, Luther supported it being published in the common language of the population. His little book entitled *A Simple Way to Pray* (1535) emphasizes the importance of reading the Bible as a form of prayer, of meditating on scripture to allow the Holy Spirit to fill people's lives and hearts. The fruit of this presence is a reconciling and loving attitude toward oneself, others, the world, and God.

We shall conclude this brief exploration of bible reading as spiritual practice by listening to the words of the Baptist preacher Charles Haddon Spurgeon (1834–1892):

> The Spirit has taught us in meditation to ponder its message, to put aside, if we will, the responsibility of preparing the message we've got to give. Just trust God for that. But first, meditate on it, quietly ponder

it, let it sink deep into our souls. Have you not often been surprised and overcome with delight as Holy Scripture is opened up as if the gates of the Golden City have been set back for you to enter? A few minutes' silent openness of soul before the Lord has brought us more treasure of truth than hours of learned research.[17]

Spiritual direction

"We define Christian spiritual direction . . . as help given by one Christian to another which enables that person to pay attention to God's personal communication to him or her, to respond to this personally communicating God, to grow in intimacy with this God, and to live out the consequences of the relationship. The focus of this type of spiritual direction is on experience, not ideas. . . . Moreover, this experience is viewed, not as an isolated event, but as an expression of the ongoing personal relationship God has established with each one of us."[18]

The Christian practice of spiritual direction[19] dates back to the movement of Eastern desert monasticism in the third and fourth centuries. Later, in the Christian traditions of both the East and the West, the idea of having a guide to assist individuals with their personal and spiritual maturation is reflected in the writings of many well-known figures. For example, in the West we find teachings on spiritual guidance by Basil the Great, Augustine of Hippo, and Gregory the Great (540–604). In the East, Evagrius Ponticus (345–399) and John Cassian (360–435) are the best exemplars of the desert tradition of spiritual direction.

In the Eastern desert tradition, an individual who accompanied a disciple along the path of holiness and virtuous living was known as a *pneumatikos pater* (spiritual father – the women were known as *ammas* and the men as *abbas*). The Celtic (Irish) Church had the tradition of the *anmchara* (translated as spiritual guide, spiritual director, or, perhaps best, soul friend). By the fifteenth century, the practice of spiritual direction had spread to Russia, where great spiritual guides were known as *startsy* – meaning the old and wise ones. Nilus of Sora (1453–1508) and Nicodemus the Hagiorite (1748–1809) are notable figures. A clear and detailed explanation of the role of the spiritual director is found in the *Spiritual Exercises* of the Spanish nobleman Ignatius of Loyola. The *Spiritual Exercises* is a handbook that helps the spiritual director to guide individuals seeking to discern God's active presence in their lives. Teresa of Avila considered spiritual direction so important that she had harsh words for those who did not fulfill their role responsibly.[20]

Many more examples of outstanding figures who viewed spiritual direction as important for Christian growth could be cited. But even the cursory lists above show that spiritual direction has been an important part of Christian spiritual practice. This continues to be true in current times, for Christians as well as for people of other faiths, as the discipline of having a spiritual guide is common to a number of traditions. For example, in some aboriginal cultures there is the *witch doctor*; in South Africa the *chimbuki*; or the *shaman* in North American Native communities. The Hindu guides are known as *gurus* and the Buddhist guides as *bhikkus*. All these figures perform the role of spiritual guide in the context of their specific beliefs and practices.

Although the role of spiritual director and the nature of the spiritual-direction relationship is described in many ways today even within the Christian traditions, the basic goal of spiritual direction remains the same: to assist individuals to grow and mature in their relationship with God. The opening quote at the beginning of this section reflects this fundamental goal. It is worth noting that here the *ongoing* relationship that God establishes with each person is the primary concern of the spiritual-direction relationship. It is only over time that an individual can articulate in some way the movements of God in his or her life. One practitioner of spiritual direction puts it this way:

> First spiritual direction is a process. It is not a single or occasional consultation about some particular problem but an ongoing relationship characterized by a certain continuity and consistency. In practice, spiritual direction usually involves regular . . . meetings between the two persons.[21]

These regular meetings may be weekly, bi-weekly, or monthly. At times, they might be just a few times a year. The key, however, is that they are regular and planned. Spiritual direction is not crisis intervention, therapeutic pastoral counseling, or psychotherapy. All these approaches may be needed to resolve particular issues that arise at specific times, but spiritual direction is focused squarely on the movements of faith in one's life – faith reflected in all parts of life and living. The boundaries between therapeutic pastoral counseling, psychotherapy, and spiritual direction are not always clear – it takes great skill to recognize when the resources of the psychotherapist rather than those of the spiritual director are needed.

What are you seeking? The differences between helping relationships:
"If you are interested in learning about the beliefs, observances, and texts of a religion because you want to know more or seek to more fully identify with that faith community, you are seeking *religious education or formation*.

If you want to relieve your anxieties and learn how to understand and deal with their causes, you are seeking *psychotherapy*.

If you want insight into how the wisdom of religious tradition might help you understand and respond to your problems, you are seeking *pastoral counseling*.

If you wish to deepen your relationship with God so that you can recognize how God's spirit might be calling you and moving in your life, you are seeking *spiritual guidance* [direction]."[22]

The spiritual-direction relationship strives to construct the story of God's life that is developing in the life of the Christian so that he or she becomes God's loving presence in the world. We talked about this in Chapter 4 as being the activity of the narrative self. During the telling of his or her story the directee articulates the ongoing movements of God perceived in his or her life. The director assists the directee to sift through various events, feelings, insights, and so on, and helps coordinate all these into a meaningful whole. This process helps the person to see how God is meaningfully present and active in his or her life.

Some people keep a journal in which they describe events, record feelings and perceptions, or simply jot down random thoughts that will eventually be brought to the spiritual-direction relationship. Journal keeping can be a spiritual practice unto itself. Many people find that rereading what they have written in their journals gives them greater insight into their own lives, their life with others, and their life with God. Some record their dreams in their journals and reflect on these in their spiritual-direction relationship.

"One very important way to befriend our sorrow is to take it out of its isolation, and share it with someone who can receive it."[23]

In spiritual direction, the consciously organized events we refer to as prayer (discussed above) are not necessarily the privileged moments when

God most intensely self-reveals in people's lives – or when someone has the greatest insight. Sometimes, even in one's busiest moments, there occur flashes of the meaning of one's life and how God has been active in it. As mentioned above, dreams can be a great source of insight. Moments of God's inbreaking in someone's life may not be recognized until carefully discerned within the patterns of God's presence shown in any one life over an extended period of time. The spiritual director, as an objective voice, shines light on one's experience so that he or she may see things that the individual is too close to see. After listening to the directee's reflections, the spiritual director offers his or her perspective on what has been shared. The dialogue that follows deepens the reflection in a respectful and transparent way. All this prayerful reflection takes time, which is why continuity and regularity in the spiritual-direction relationship are so important.

Although each person's story is unique, in a way the same Christian story – the story of God's mysterious transforming presence in people's lives – is being told over and over again. The spiritual-direction relationship is a wonderful place to discover and tell this story so the Christian can live it ever more consciously in his or her daily life.

We have focused on discerning God's presence in one's life as the main goal of the spiritual-direction relationship. But there are other benefits and goals as well. For example, as one tells his or her story in spiritual direction one recalls and highlights certain aspects of it. This thoughtful recollection gives an opportunity not only to analyze one's storied past, but also to set a particular story or event into the larger framework of one's life – for example, one's values, commitments, long-term goals, and world view.

This storytelling process relativizes any one part of one's personal story, but also gives the opportunity for truth checks. The following question may be asked: "Am I living the life I thought I was living?" In answering this question, the individual may decide to do some things differently or think about the world in a new way. We begin to see that with the discovery of how God is present in someone's life comes an invitation for transformation and change. This leads to personal freedom, self-awareness, humility, and so on such that he or she can reflect God's loving presence even more strongly in his or her day-to-day living.

When the fruits of God's Spirit are recognized personally in someone's life (fruits such as peace, charity, availability for others, and humility), he or she may also come to know those things that may hinder relationship with God and others (such as anger, resentment, envy, jealousy, and pride). Spiritual direction helps uncover these hindrances so people can be truly free and whole.

Pilgrimage

"Pilgrimage is always a search for God and God's goodness. True pilgrimage has to do with a change of heart. The outward journey serves to frame an inner journey: a journey of repentance and rebirth; a journey which seeks a deeper faith, greater holiness, a journey in search of God."[24]

Pilgrimage is found in the spiritual practices of all major world religions. Muslims journey to Mecca; Hindus to Benares, India; Buddhists to Lhasa, Tibet; Jews to Jerusalem; and Christians to Canterbury, Rome, and Jerusalem. Of course, the above list of sites is not complete; all these religious traditions have other places of pilgrimage as well. In all these centers stand monuments, temples, mosques, churches, or synagogues that mark foundational events for the faith of these traditions. In going to these sites, pilgrims believe they share in the special grace that these events brought to their faith communities. Somehow, in going to these shrines, pilgrims become involved with the past – which is now celebrated in the present through praying, reflecting, and learning more about the events and the places themselves.

Not all traditions within Christianity have taken up the practice of pilgrimages to the same degree. Frequently Christian pilgrimages are identified with the Catholic traditions. Pilgrimages in general, however, have become an expression of spirituality for people of faith and no faith alike, as the pilgrimage of Santiago de Compostela, which is discussed below, indicates.

The holy sites in Jerusalem mark the traditional places of Jesus's life, death, and resurrection. These sites, such as the Church of the Holy Sepulchre (the place that marks the spot where Jesus was raised from the dead; close by is Golgotha, the site of the crucifixion), were the initial destinations for pilgrims from all over Europe. During the early centuries of Christianity, a pilgrimage, for those who had the time and financial means, became interwoven into the spiritual practice of Christians. Sometimes a pilgrimage to Jerusalem served as restitution for sins – travel was fraught with danger. The trials and tribulations of a pilgrimage were a kind of penance and purification.

When Muslims restricted access to the holy sites of Jerusalem in 1078, keeping most Christians out, other places of pilgrimage in France, Germany, and northern Europe gained importance. One of these (in the twelfth century) is Santiago de Compostela, where the tomb of James the Apostle is enshrined in a magnificent church. Today, pilgrims from all corners of Europe and elsewhere walk, bicycle, or find their way by some other means, to his tomb.[25] The cathedral church at Santiago records the number of pilgrims who reach its doors each year. In the year 2000, approximately 55,000 pilgrims made the journey – a number that appears to be increasing annually.[26]

There are many reasons why people, individually or in a group, make a pilgrimage. Here we use the word *pilgrimage* in a particular way; a pilgrimage is not simply a tourist excursion whose focus is on history, culture, and recreation. And yet, what begins as a tourist trip could very well turn into a pilgrimage! As a tourist, because of the different setting or unexpected situations, someone may have a new experience of themselves and the world, an experience that may reflect, for example, the sacred nature of life – which is one of the goals of the pilgrimage as spiritual practice. There is a certain element of unpredictability in any pilgrimage – planned or unplanned.

Some people go on a pilgrimage to mark a new stage of life, such as retirement. This journey could provide an opportunity for prayer and reflection at this crucial juncture – a time to reassess the significant moments in one's life and identify new priorities and interests. But there are many other reasons to go on a pilgrimage. Some people are seeking forgiveness for past wrongs, or praying for recovery from an illness; Lourdes, France (a Roman Catholic pilgrimage site honoring Mary, the Mother of Jesus) draws many pilgrims seeking healing. Some people go on a pilgrimage just to get away from it all. Perhaps life has become overwhelming; a change of scene may result in a clearer sense of self-identity and goals. Clearly, pilgrimage as spiritual practice continues to be an important part of the lives of many Christians today.

While going on a *journey* is one type of pilgrimage, there are other ways to understand it. Some people may go on a *retreat*, taking time away at a retreat center that provides room and board for a few days, a week, or even a month, to spend time in prayer – or just be in a setting conducive to reflection. Retreat houses are located close to major urban centers around the world, but some are in remote desert areas, such as the Lebh Shomea House of Prayer in Sarita, Texas, in the United States. Retreats allow an individual to be in a different space physically, but also interiorly. A change in setting can lead an individual to experience a change of self, to discover new things about oneself, or to evaluate one's perspective on life, spirituality, and actions that reflect all of these. Galilee Center, a small retreat center located on the shores of the Ottawa River near Arnprior, Ontario, Canada, is located less than an hour away from where this book was written. For me it has provided the occasion for many pilgrimages that resulted in new perspectives on life, new attitudes toward others, and a new sense of self before God. Not far from the Galilee Mission Center lies another center, this one known internationally: the Madonna House Apostolate.

Located in a serene wooded area on a quiet lake just outside Combermere, the Madonna House Apostolate offers a unique pilgrimage experience. Madonna House was founded by Catherine de Hueck Doherty (1900–1985), otherwise known as the Baroness De Hueck, in 1947. The Baroness had fled Russia with her family in the throes of the 1917 Revolution. She recounts this pilgrimage from oppression to freedom in *My Russian Yesterdays* (1990, 2nd ed.). Once in Canada, stripped of all the prestige, money, and power she had known in Russia, she nurtured a particular expression of Russian spiritual practice that reflects the idea of an *interior* pilgrimage.

The ingredients for this kind of pilgrimage are simple – quiet, solitude, a very sparse setting, and a reduced amount of food. This is the Russian Orthodox Church experience of *poustinia*. *Poustinia*, a Russian word for desert, refers to a small cabin or room, often in a remote place, set aside for silence and prayer. The pilgrims are known as *poustinikki*. The *poustinik* will enter *poustinia* for a single day (usually a minimum of twenty-four hours), several days, or even weeks – often with only a bible and a little food. This is the desert pilgrimage Catherine de Hueck Doherty speaks of below.

> Deserts, silence, solitudes, are not necessarily places but states of mind and heart. These deserts can be found in the midst of the city, and in the everyday of our lives. We need only to look for them and realize our tremendous need for them. They will be small solitudes, little deserts, tiny pools of silence, but the experience they will bring, if we are disposed to enter them, may be as exultant and as holy as all the deserts of the world.[27]

At Madonna House Apostolate, individuals can find solitude and quiet in one of the numerous *poustinias* located in remote parts of the woods. Ultimately, as Catherine de Hueck Doherty teaches, the *poustinia* is found within, where one is immersed in the silence of God, always listening to the word of God, "forever repeating it to others in word and deed."[28]

A third kind of pilgrimage (the first being that of a *physical journey*, and the second a *retreat*) is that of the *labyrinth*. Labyrinths are usually, but not always, circular geometric patterns that contain a singular pathway from the exterior ring into the center. These patterns are usually quite large, measuring many meters in diameter. The pilgrim begins the pilgrimage from the outer ring at a designated place of entry and slowly follows the path to the middle. One must focus – that is, meditate – solely on the path below in order to follow the correct route – the only route – to the center. Once in the center, one passes some time in quiet reflection and prayer. During this pilgrimage, music may be playing or there may be just the rustle of other pilgrims on this journey of self-discovery.

The spiritual practice of the labyrinth is little known today, but the great cathedral churches built in Europe in the twelfth and thirteenth centuries often contained labyrinths placed in stone in the design of the floor. The most famous is found in the floor of Chartres Cathedral in France. This labyrinth, which dates back to 1201, became a designated pilgrimage site when Jerusalem was occupied by the Muslims later in that century.

> "In the pilgrimage tradition, the center of the labyrinth is named The New Jerusalem and the path is referred to as the *Chemin à Jérusalem* (the Road to Jerusalem)."[29]

Some retreat centers have added labyrinths to their sites. If located outside, these may be made from patterned hedges, or paving stones embedded in the ground, or another imaginative path. The same is true for interior installations. The Episcopalian Grace Cathedral in San Francisco in the United States recently added a woven tapestry labyrinth on the floor at the back of the church.

In general, pilgrimages invite individuals to step outside of themselves, to look at the world in a different way. Pilgrims leave familiar places, ways of doings things, and comfortable attitudes to explore what else might be possible for their lives. This can be done in a number of ways, such as by trekking to a distant place, taking time away at a nearby retreat center, seeking out a *poustinia*, or walking a labyrinth. Pilgrimage is not limited to a physical journey; it is essentially a disposition of the heart that requires imagination, courage, and faith. Once the pilgrim sets out on the journey, he or she never quite knows how it will unfold – or how it will end. What is important is being open to the Spirit of Jesus, which the Christian pilgrim invites into his or her life along the way.

Conclusion

> Lived spirituality "is constituted by the practices by which people remember, share, enact, adapt, and create the stories out of which they live. And it is constituted through the practices by which people turn these stories into everyday action. Ordinary material existence – especially the human body – is the very stuff of these meaningful practices. Human bodies matter, because those practices – even interior ones, such as contemplation – involve people's bodies, as well as their minds and spirits."[30]

As we can see, spiritual practices are not about merely doing something, as meaningful as this may be. They also involve a deepening and appropriation of the traditions, or some element from them. For this reason, spiritual practices go far beyond the mere repetition of rituals or activities labeled as spiritual. Worship, prayerful reflection, penitence, pilgrimage, care of the sick and homeless, and countless other activities are the containers for the fundamental beliefs and values held by Christians. Through these spiritual practices, and many others, Christians grow in relationship with God, with each other, and with all of creation. Spiritual practices are not about mindless repetition, but a deepening of what is already happening: God's Spirit is allowed to shine forth ever more brilliantly in people's daily lives. God's presence literally becomes a habit, a spontaneous way of living and acting.[31]

We have reflected in this chapter on principles of spiritual practice and some specific examples: prayer, bible reading, spiritual direction, and pilgrimage. Many other practices could be explored as well, such as volunteerism. Many people today practice – that is, live out – their spirituality through volunteering their talents, time, and resources in church and community settings. In this way, Christian spirituality is truly embodied in day-to-day living and not just in those activities, rituals, or actions such as prayer or community worship that tend to be identified more easily with Christian spirituality.

RECOMMENDED READING

Chase, Steven (2005) "Prayer as a Way of Life," in *The Tree of Life: Models of Christian Prayer*, Grand Rapids, MI: Baker Academic, 19–53. (Provides an embodied approach to prayer. Excellent bibliography that represents a wide spectrum of the Christian traditions with respect to prayer and its various models or expressions.)

Cunningham, Lawrence S. and Keith J. Egan (1996) "Hearers and Doers of the Word," in *Christian Spirituality: Themes from the Tradition*, New York: Paulist Press, 29–46. (Good introduction to bible study from a Roman Catholic perspective.)

Harris, Paul T. (2001) *Frequently Asked Questions About Christian Meditation: The Path of Contemplative Prayer*, Ottawa, Canada: Novalis Press. (A very readable and practical guide for the beginner to the art of Christian meditation.)

Inge, John (2003) "Place and the Christian Tradition: Pilgrimage and Holy Places," in *A Christian Theology of Place*, Burlington, VT: Ashgate Publishing Company, 91–122.

Johnson, Susanne (2004) "Remembering the Poor: Transforming Christian Practice," in *Redemptive Transformation in Practical Theology*, eds D. R. Wright and J. D. Kuentzel, Cambridge: William B. Eerdmans Publishing Company, 1–27.

McClain, George D. (1998) "Spiritual Practice and Social Action," in *Claiming All Things for God: Prayer, Discernment, and Ritual for Social Change*, Nashville, TN: Abingdon Press, 13–22.

McGuire, Meredith (2005) "Why Bodies Matter: A Sociological Reflection on Spirituality and Materiality," *Spiritus* 3:1, 1–18.

Moore, Thomas (1995) *Care of the Soul: A Guide for Cultivating Depth and Sacredness in Everyday Life*, New York: HarperCollins.

Peterson, Eugene H. (2005) *Eat This Book: A Conversation in the Art of Spiritual Reading*, Grand Rapids, MI: Eerdmans Publishing. (Follows closely the tradition of *lectio divina* as discussed in the section on bible reading in this book.)

Rahner, Karl (1997) "Prayer in the Everyday," in *The Need and the Blessing of Prayer*, tr. Bruce W. Gillette, introduction by Harvey Egan, Collegeville, MN: Liturgical Press, 37–47.

Rolheiser, Ronald (2001) "Contemplation as Respecting the Holiness of God: The Protestant Contemplative Tradition," in *The Shattered Lantern: Rediscovering a Felt Presence of God*, revised edition, New York: Crossroad, 106–136.

Scaperlanda, María Ruiz and Michael Scaperlanda (2004) "Developing a Pilgrim Heart," in *The Journey: A Guide for the Modern Pilgrim*, Chicago: Loyola Press, 13–39. (Contains an excellent introduction to pilgrimage as spiritual practice. Lots of practical advice.)

Sobrino, Jon (1981) "Christian Prayer and New Testament Theology: A Basis for Social Justice and Spirituality," in *Western Spirituality: Historical Roots, Ecumenical Routes*, ed. Matthew Fox, Santa Fe, NM: Bear & Company, 76–114.

Wiseman, James (2004) "The Body in Spiritual Practice: Some Historical Points of Reference," in *Reclaiming the Body in Christian Spirituality*, ed. James Wiseman, Mahwah, NJ: Paulist Press, 1–20.

Wuthnow, Robert (2001) "Art as Spiritual Practice," in *Creative Spirituality: The Way of the Artist*, Berkeley: University of California Press, 107–138.

References to research topics from this chapter

Addison, Howard A. (2000) *Show Me Your Way: The Complete Guide to Exploring Interfaith Spiritual Direction*, Woodstock, VT: Skylight Paths Publishing.

Ball, Peter (1998) *Anglican Spiritual Direction*, Boston, MA: Cowley Publications.

Bourdieu, Pierre (2005) *Outline of a Theory of Practice*, tr. Richard Nice, Cambridge: Cambridge University Press.

De Certeau, Michel (1988) *The Practice of Everyday Life*, Berkeley: University of California Press.

De Certeau, Michel, Luce Giard, and Pierre Mayol (1998) *The Practice of Everyday Life, Volume 2, Living and Cooking*, Minneapolis: University of Minnesota Press.

Doheny, William J. (1950) *Selected Writings of St. Teresa of Avila: A Synthesis of Her Writings*, Milwaukee: Bruce Publishing Company.

Doherty, de Hueck Catherine (1975) *Poustinia: Christian Spirituality of the East for Western Man*, Notre Dame, IN: Ave Maria Press.

Houck, Anita (2002) "Spirituality and Pedagogy: Faith and Reason in the Age of Assessment," *Spiritus* 2:1, 50–63.

Immink, Gerrit F. (2005) "How Faith and Life Interconnect," in *Faith: A Practical Theological Reconstruction*, Cambridge: William B. Eerdmans Publishing Company, 43–69.

James-Abra, Karen (1991) "An Introduction to an Ancient Ministry: The Practice of Spiritual Direction," *The Conrad Grebel Review* 9:1, 16–22.

Jay, Eric G. (1954) *Origen's Treatise on Prayer: Translation and Notes with an Account of the Practice and Doctrine of Prayer from New Testament Times to Origen*, London: SPCK.

Leech, Kenneth (1980) *Soul Friend: The Practice of Christian Spirituality*, New York: Harper & Row.

Liebert, Elizabeth (2000) *Changing Life Patterns: Adult Development in Spiritual Direction*, St. Louis, MO: Chalice Press.

—— (2005) "Practice," in *The Blackwell Companion to Christian Spirituality*, ed. Arthur Holder, Oxford: Blackwell, 496–514.

McGuire, Meredith (1996) "Religion and Healing," *Social Compass* 43:1, 101–116.

McNally, Michael (1997) "The Uses of Ojibwa Hymn-Singing at White Earth: Toward a History of Practice," in *Lived Religion in America: Toward a History of Practice*, ed. David D. Hall, Princeton, NJ: Princeton University Press, 133–159. (Views the generative capacity of hymn-singing as spiritual practice.)

Orsi, Robert (1997) "Everyday Miracles: The Study of Lived Religion," in *Lived Religion in America: Toward a History of Practice*, ed. David D. Hall, Princeton, NJ: Princeton University Press, 3–21.

Paulsell, Stephanie (2003) *Honoring the Body: Meditations on a Christian Practice* [The Practices of Faith Series, Dorothy C. Bass, Series Editor], San Francisco, CA: Jossey-Bass.

Perrin, David B. (1998) "Spiritual Direction, Hermeneutics, and the Textual Constitution of Selfhood," *Eglise et Théologie* 29:1, 31–62.

Peterson, Eugene H. (2006) *A Conversation in the Art of Spiritual Reading*, Grand Rapids, MI: William B. Eerdmans. (See especially Section II *Lectio Divina*, pages 79–117, which reflects separately on *lectio* [spiritual reading], oratio [speech/oral prayer], *meditatio* [meditation], and *contemplatio* [contemplation].)

Post, Paul, Jos Pieper, and Marinus van Uden (1998) *The Modern Pilgrim: Multidisciplinary Explorations of Christian Pilgrimage*, Leuven, Belgium: Peeters.

Ruffing, Janet (2000) *Spiritual Direction: Beyond the Beginnings*, Mahwah, NJ: Paulist Press.

Schmidt, Leigh E. (1997) "Practices of Exchange: From Market Culture to Gift Economy in the Interpretation of American Religion," in *Lived Religion in America: Toward a History of Practice*, ed. David D. Hall, Princeton, NJ: Princeton University Press, 69–91. (Highlights the potential for gift-giving to be viewed as spiritual practice.)

Singletary, Jon E. (2005) "The Praxis of Social Work: A Model of How Faith Informs Practice Informs Faith," *Social Work & Christianity* 32:1, 56–72.

Turner, Victor and Edith Turner (1978) *Image and Pilgrimage in Christian Culture: Anthropological Perspectives*, New York: Columbia University Press.

Vest, Norvene, ed. (2003) *Tending the Holy: Spiritual Direction Across Traditions*, Harrisburg, PA: Morehouse Publishing. (Spiritual direction described in a variety of world religions: for example, Buddhism, Sufism, Hinduism, and Judaism, as well as Christianity.)

NOTES

1 See Meredith McGuire (2003) "Why Bodies Matter: Sociological Reflection on Spirituality and Materiality," *Spiritus* 3:1, 10.

2 See Robert Wuthnow (2001) "Art as Spiritual Practice," in *Creative Spirituality: The Way of the Artist*, Berkeley: University of California Press, 107–138 and Don Saliers (2005) "Sound Spirituality: On the Formative Expressive Power of Music for Christian Spirituality," in E. Dreyer and M. Burrows, eds, *Minding the Spirit*, London, UK: Johns Hopkins University Press, 334–340.

3 Thomas Moore, a monk for twelve years, is a best-selling author who has guided many people in the "practice of everyday life" through his 1992 publication *Care of the Soul: A Guide for Cultivating Depth and Sacredness in Everyday Life*, New York: HarperCollins. The phenomenal success of this book testifies to people's desire to integrate the sacred into the practices of everyday life.

4 I would like to recognize in a special way the article by Robert Orsi that inspired many of the ideas on spiritual practice in this introductory section. See Robert Orsi (1997) "Everyday Miracles: The Study of Lived Religion," in *Lived Religion in America: Toward a History of Practice*, David D. Hall, ed., Princeton NJ: Princeton University Press, 3–21.

5 For a spirituality of the Sacred Heart see: Bernhard Haring (1983) *The Sacred Heart of Jesus and the Redemption of the World*, Slough, England: St. Paul Publications.

6 Susanne Johnson (2004) "Remembering the Poor: Transforming Christian Practice," in *Redemptive Transformation in Practical Theology*, Dana R. Wright and John D. Kuentzel, eds, Cambridge, UK: William B. Eerdmans Publishing Company, 3.

7 In reflecting on the nature of "practice" in relationship to hymn-singing of the North American Ojibwa Indians, Michael McNally states: "Practices are immersed in life's shifting demands and oriented toward practical concerns of survival." See Michael McNally (1997) "The Uses of Ojibwa Hymn-Singing at White Earth: Toward a History of Practice," in *Lived Religion in America: Toward a History of Practice*, David D. Hall, ed., Princeton, NJ: Princeton University Press, 146.

8 This is described in Parker J. Palmer (2004) *A Hidden Wholeness: The Journey Toward an Undivided Life*, San Francisco, CA: Jossey-Bass. See especially pages 134–149.

9 As the sociologist Pierre Bourdieu affirms in his reflection on practice in general, "No more logic is mobilized than is required by the needs of practice." See Pierre Bourdieu (2005) *Outline of a Theory of Practice*, tr. R. Nice, Cambridge: Cambridge University Press, 110.

10 Johnson, "Remembering the Poor" 3.

11 See Meredith McGuire (1996) "Religion and Healing," *Social Compass* 43:1, 112.

12 On the issues associated with the introduction of spiritual practices into the classroom, and measuring the success of what we teach in the classroom in the area of spirituality, see, Anita Houck (2002) "Spirituality and Pedagogy: Faith and Reason in the Age of Assessment," *Spiritus* 2:1, 50–63; Elizabeth Liebert (2005) "The Role of Practice in the Study of Christian Spirituality," in *Minding the Spirit: The Study of Christian Spirituality*, E. A. Dreyer and M. S. Burrows, eds, Baltimore, MD: Johns Hopkins University Press, 79–99. See also Susan J. White (1999) "Can Spirituality Be Taught?" *Christian Spirituality Bulletin* 7:2, 13–17.

13 Michael Downey (1994) "In the Ache of Absence," *Liturgical Ministry* 3, 98.

14 See Eric G. Jay (1954) *Origen's Treatise on Prayer*, London: SPCK, 79–219.

15 See Michael W. Higgins (1998) *Heretic Blood: The Spiritual Geography of Thomas Merton*, Toronto: Stoddart.

16 Frances Young (1992) *Virtuoso Theology*, Cleveland: Pilgrim, 25 cited in *Christian Spirituality: Themes from the Tradition*, L. Cunningham and K. Egan, eds, New York: Paulist Press, 16.

17 Cited in Alister McGrath (2006) *Christian Spirituality: An Introduction*, 2nd edition, Oxford: Blackwell Publishing, 54.

18 William Barry and William Connolly (1982) *The Practice of Spiritual Direction*, New York: Seabury Press, 8.

19 Much of the historical presentation of the various titles and roles attributed to the spiritual-direction tradition is taken from "Spiritual Direction in the Christian Tradition," in *Soul Friend: An Invitation to Spiritual Direction*, Kenneth Leech, New York: HarperCollins Publishers, 34–89.

20 See, for example, William J. Doheny (1950) *Selected Writings of St. Teresa of Avila: A Synthesis of Her Writings*, Milwaukee: Bruce Publishing Company, 245–251.

21 Karen James-Abra (1991) "An Introduction to an Ancient Ministry: The Practice of Spiritual Direction," in *The Conrad Grebel Review* 9:1, 19.

22 Howard A. Addison (2000) *Show Me Your Way: The Complete Guide to Exploring Interfaith Spiritual Direction*, Woodstock, VT: Skylight Paths Publishing, 37.

23 Henri Nouwen (1994) *Here and Now: Living in the Spirit*, New York: Crossroad, 45.

24 Sister John Miriam Jones, S.C. (2001) "An Irish Journey into Celtic Spirituality," *St. Anthony Messenger*, March. Downloaded April 2006. http://www.americancatholic.org/messenger/mar2001/feature1.asp#F5.

25 There are several legends that account for the body of James the Apostle being entombed in northern Spain instead of Jerusalem. Some historical accounts indicate that James evangelized in Spain after the death of Jesus. But James then returned to Jerusalem. After he was beheaded by Herod, his body was taken back to Spain by his followers, assisted by Divine intervention, sometime around 44 C.E. The appearance of the body of James in Spain follows a pattern of the supernatural translation of material relics (objects belonging to holy men and women, or even remains from their bodies) from the area of Palestine to various destinations in Europe. See Victor Turner and Edith Turner (1978) *Image and Pilgrimage in Christian Culture: Anthropological Perspectives*, New York: Columbia University Press, 168–171.

26 You can find additional information on the Santiago pilgrimage at www.csj.org.uk.

27 Catherine de Hueck Doherty (1975) *Poustinia: Christian Spirituality of the East for Western Man*, Notre Dame, IN: Ave Maria Press, 21.

28 Doherty *Poustinia*, 213.

29 Lauren Artress (2006) "Sacred Pattern, Sacred Path: Labyrinths and the Art of Pilgrimage," *Faith and Form: The Interfaith Journal on Religion, Art and Architecture* 2006/1, 8.

30 McGuire, "Why Bodies Matter," 15.

31 Pierre Bourdieu presents a detailed analysis of the formation of habits – called *habitus*. See *Outline of a Theory of Practice*, esp. ch. 2: "Structures and the

Habitus," 72–95. According to Bourdieu, *habitus* are internalizations of objective structures – the external structure is appropriated as part of the intimate life of the individual, community, or group. It thus shapes personal dispositions, thoughts, perceptions, and so on, and all the actions consistent with them.

9 Questions of critical edges

Introduction

THIS CHAPTER PROVIDES brief overviews of current work being done in the area of spirituality on a number of topics that we may not at first associate directly with general or Christian spirituality. Because none of the topics is treated in an exhaustive way, a select bibliography is provided for each for those interested in reading further or pursuing research on a specific question related to the topic.

Science

Contemporary reflection on the interaction of Christian spirituality and science inevitably involves the debates between religion (understood as a belief system in relationship to the existence of a Divine being) and the natural sciences (e.g. physics, chemistry, and biology). The dynamic encounter between religion and science has been framed in this way for some time. For example, the academic journal *Zygon*, published for over forty years, subtitled *Journal of Religion and Science*, is a key source of information at the frontier of the debates. However, with Christian spirituality emerging as its own academic discipline, its contributions need to be included as a partner in these conversations. This work is still to be done. As a result, the presentation here will use mainly religion and its theologies in relationship to science to expose the analogous issues that surface as a result of the connection between science and Christian spirituality.

Christian theologies bring to the debate their own sophisticated views of the physical universe, the nature and purpose of life, and the future destiny of humankind. This is what we have called a cosmology – a way of describing and accounting for the origins and structures of the world. What is at stake in the confrontation between religion and science are two different cosmologies – two ways of knowing not only the physical world, but also the meaning of that world, where it came from, and where it is going. Both religion and science ask many of the same questions, but from different perspectives.

For example, both inquire about the origins of the world and of humanity; the web of relationships that exists in the world; and what lies ahead for the physical universe and all its inhabitants. Clearly, both science and theology need to be aware not only of the questions being asked, but also of who is asking the questions, how the study is being done, and how racist or sexist biases might affect scientific inquiry. Issues of identity, social location, political bias, and so on must be acknowledged in scientific investigations as much as they are in theological ones.[1] At the same time, we must remember that each brings a unique analysis to the questions of human life and the world.

> Science looks at the world through the senses: what can be observed, measured, or quantified in some way. The classical scientific method requires proof that can be objectively understood: truth is characterized by a factual understanding of the reality being examined. In contrast, religion has as its foundation the enormous world of the unseen, which cannot be observed at will, measured with an instrument, or quantified by human means. It is this difference in the way the universe is viewed that has caused tension in the past between religion and science, and continues to do so today. In a general way, we could say that one works within the realm of hard facts, while the other works within the realm of faith.

We have already explored in Chapter 3 the rift that occurred between science and religion in 1543, when the ideas of Nicolaus Copernicus disrupted the tidy view of the universe held until that time. Copernicus, we recall, brought forward a scientific view of the world (proclaiming that the sun lies at the center of our universe) that seriously challenged accepted medieval cosmology (which stated that the earth lies at the center of our universe), a cosmology that had been suggested by biblical faith.

Even given these two different ways of looking at the world (which have been somewhat simplified to make the point), the main task is to avoid seeing science's way of looking at the world (caricatured as passive observation) and religion's way of looking at the world (caricatured as blind faith) as being in opposition to each other. Seeing the divide between religion and science in opposition implies that faith has no reason and reason has no faith, which is simply not true.

There is one world, viewed from various perspectives. The aim is to bring these perspectives together, despite what may appear to be irreconcilable differences. Both religion and science have valuable contributions to make to humanity's self-understanding, the understanding of the universe, and in general how everything fits together. Problems occur when one side feels it has exclusive access to truth about all these issues and refuses to accept insights from the other side.

For example, when we consider a specific scientific cosmology – the theory of the Big Bang, which is suggested as having occurred 13 billion years ago

– we are led to believe that the universe had an identifiable beginning. This evidence, from the perspective of Christian theology, and in turn Christian spirituality, indirectly suggests the principle of the creation of the world by God *ex nihilo* (from nothing). Such a belief on the scientific level as well as on the theological level can lead to a spirituality of the connectedness of all living creatures. That is, based on a common cosmological origin that is plausible from the perspective of science and of theology, we can find ourselves in empathy with not only all living creatures, but also all creation. We can make other connections between science and religion as well.

Both religion and science probe what is beyond humanity's immediate grasp in the universe. Both stretch the boundaries of what is known of life at this time to help gain an ever more profound, yet always incomplete, understanding of the world. We can say, then, that both religion and science seek an understanding of the transcendent quality of the world. Scientific discoveries continually bring us to a sense of awe and amazement in their exposé of the natural world, which takes people beyond their wildest imaginings. While science can describe and explain what is in front of us as well as what is beyond our immediate grasp, it cannot probe what the world can become based on the most profound characteristics of human nature. Science does not have within its capacity the possibility of giving birth to the fundamental ideas about human life and the potential for the success of *meaningful* human life. And yet, it can shed light on such things.

For example, science does not originate the idea of human self-giving or self-sacrifice,[2] but it can help us understand this reality, especially through the use of the human sciences, such as psychology or sociology. Science does not originate the idea of morality, but it can help us understand how morality is embedded in human nature. Science does not originate the ideas of individual human worth and the dignity of all life, but once we accept these as fundamental to the human condition, we can better understand them from a scientific perspective.

The realm of self-sacrifice, morality, and dignity of all life lies within the scope of the human spirit. As we saw in the first chapter of this book, spirituality lies at the center of the religious quest, even though it animates many people who are not religious in any formal way. This is how spiritualities illuminate the world of science. And, more and more, science is paying attention to their important contributions. Science is beginning to acknowledge that it cannot determine its agenda independently of all the other spheres of human living, including the spiritual, which contribute important insights to the scientific world.[3]

The brief reflection above has emphasized the different ways science and religion have viewed the universe, but also underlines their mutual interdependence. What needs to be added is that the classical division between science and religion, based on their respective world views, is no longer as rigid as it once was. The strictly empirical view of the universe (the universe that can be accurately observed, measured, and quantified) is no longer held by all those in the scientific profession. Many scientists, along with researchers in most areas of thought, agree that all scientific observation is partial: that is, at any one time, scientists view only a part of the whole. Therefore, conclusions ("the facts") are, in turn, partial and relative. Furthermore, scientists increasingly acknowledge that they don't passively observe the universe and then record their findings – they first come up with a theory (a best guess) and try to prove this theory in their research. Because the evidence may not account for everything that is going on, the scientist needs to use his or her imagination to fill in the gaps. Theories can be modified or thrown out altogether as research advances and new discoveries are made.

Scientific method today, along with the usual tasks of critical thought, involves creative insight and imagination. As a result many scientists today live with a healthy skepticism; they question anything that makes a claim to absolute truth. Tolerance and openness to new findings is necessary because many scientists realize that we have no way of finally proving that the last detail is known about any aspect of reality. Scientists who accept this perspective in our postmodern age have discovered a healthy mystery to the origins and nature of the universe that is compatible with the perspective of persons of faith. These scientists acknowledge that there is something mysterious beyond the observable that cannot be clearly identified. They know that we cannot account for all of life simply through what we can measure, see, or concretely observe in some way.

This understanding of the scientific method makes it a much friendlier partner to the religions and to Christian spiritualities, which also depend on critical thought, creative insight, and imagination to explore the world from their own perspectives. Science is not necessarily atheistic (denies the existence of God). But particular knowledge grows out of particular contexts and from within specific traditions. Not all scientists see the world as a closed system – a large mechanical structure that relies on continual, predictable, and identifiable cycles of cause and effect. Nature does have an intelligibility about it that we can explore but, from a faith perspective, not independently of the forces that brought it into existence in the first place.

Divine and human agency (the capacity to act and make a difference) have a role to play in this wonderful universe we call home. The task is to locate a vantage point whereby both Christian spirituality (that is, all religious traditions) and science will mutually contribute toward helpful answers to the mystery of the universe, the nature and purpose of life, and the future destiny of humankind. Science may give us a sense of the order and harmony in the universe, but it has a greater difficulty responding to the questions of meaning, of purpose, and of our final destiny. Christian spiritualities, along with the other great spiritualities in the world – such as Buddhist, Jewish, and Muslim – can help us better respond to the deep questions of life and understand the wonderfully mysterious world in which we all live.

What Christian spiritualities have to offer to the debates are their sensitivity to the vast number of ways that the mystery of God can be embodied in Christian life here and now. Christian spiritualities, because they strive to take seriously human experience, have a capacity to weave contemporary scientific understandings of the universe into their beliefs, reflections, and actions without denying their fundamental claim to the teachings of Jesus and the place of the Divine in the world.

Work and leadership

Workplace spirituality, although relatively new to corporate personnel at all levels, is not new in the history of Christian spirituality. Benedict of Nursia outlined a careful reflection of how everyday work is as important a meeting place with God – in short, a place for spiritual practice – as is the church, private home, or monastery. In his short book *Rule of Benedict*, he describes the foundations of a balanced life of prayer and work.[4] The monks had to be economically sustainable, but Benedict saw in this balance more than the means to achieve economic ends. He reflected on the holiness of work and its place in human happiness. Benedict taught that balance, harmony, hospitality, and moderation were keys to successful working and living. Who wouldn't recognize these same virtues as being goals in today's contemporary workplace, which is often fraught with stress, anxiety-provoking relationships, and the push to overachievement?

The long-standing Christian tradition of balance and harmony in work reflected in Benedict's *Rule* is now being given new foundations as theology, social psychology, sociology, business ethics, leadership and organization studies, and so on seek to study seriously the way spirituality influences the workplace in life-giving ways. The result is a *spirituality at work* movement that involves the way leaders lead and the way workers work – with each other, in groups, or alone – inside and outside the workplace. This movement recognizes that leaders and workers alike have responsibility for creating a more humanizing and egalitarian workplace whose values may overflow into society and be a transforming influence there as well.

The spirituality at work movement does not focus on introducing spirituality into the workplace, but rather recognizes that spirituality is already present in the workers. Many of them already have spiritual beliefs or are solidly committed to one spiritual tradition or another. It is a question of finding appropriate expression of these beliefs in the workplace so that they may enhance it and make it a more meaningful place for all. Given the complex mix of competing values, such as productivity versus meaningful social interaction (moments when personal interaction can lead to valuing, affirming, and supporting the other), spirituality may be seen as interfering with the main goal: the bottom line of financial success. However, many people today realize that the expression of spirituality in the workplace enhances productivity and gives workers a personal sense of meaning to their work.

To draw out people's best qualities in the workplace, to enhance the workplace so it is a meaningful place to be, and to engage individuals so they contribute to the common good – outcomes that are all supported by healthy spirituality – artful leadership is required. The capacity to awaken creative and imaginative participation in the workplace means that leaders must pay careful attention to the spiritual dimension of human living – whether one is a believer in God or not. We all ask the same questions in life: Who am I? What makes me feel most alive? Who inspires me in life? What values lie at the core of my being? We ask these questions in all contexts of life, including the context of work.

Consulting firms and centers now hold workshops to deal with these issues; for example, in Toronto, Canada, the Centre for Spirituality at Work has been offering programs in the workplace since 1998 to help people deepen the connection between who they are and the work they do.[5]

More and more people are coming to realize that if they cannot find meaningful answers to personal questions and issues in the world of work – a world that occupies the bulk of their waking hours – then they begin to feel dis-eased. People lose heart, start wondering if their labor is worth the effort put into it, and may even begin looking for another place of employment. Attention to spiritual issues by management and leadership may stem the tide of people feeling unhappy and unproductive at work.

With the increase in international travel, business relationships, and work placements in multinational companies that shift staff from one continent to another, it is essential that workers be aware of the various spiritual traditions represented in any one workplace. As we have seen, people's spiritual perspective or world view shapes and informs their attitudes, values, and actions. As co-workers or clients potentially have a range of world views, each based on a different religious tradition, the need to be sensitive to spirituality in the workplace becomes even more important. Buddhists, Hindus, Sikhs, atheists, Jews, Muslims, Christians and others, may find themselves all working together.

Understanding their different world views, that is, how these influence a range of ways of thinking, acting, and being in relationship with each other, is critical to the success of a workplace and the personal comfort of the individuals involved. Being able to work effectively in spiritually diverse environments is what spirituality at work is all about. Greater sensitivity to spirituality at work can provide a mutually supportive environment. It can also be a means of enhancing self-expression and identity within the workplace – as well as lead to increased organizational performance.

However, even though organizational performance can be improved through sensitivity to the spiritual beliefs of workers (this is sometimes referred to as *spiritual capital*),[6] organizational performance must not be seen as an end in itself. If this is the case, then spirituality is used as a tool and the individual becomes an object to be exploited, used, and eventually discarded when no longer needed. Rather, spirituality at work has as its focus the value, dignity, and honor of the individuals and groups in the workplace. This, in turn, may contribute to the bottom line (financial success) – but the bottom line is not the goal of the spirituality at work movement (or at least ought not to be).

Research in spirituality is increasingly being linked to the workplace. Topics being explored include the following.[7]

1. How spirituality and its expression in the workplace contributes to happier and healthier employees. Through spirituality at work, people are experiencing personal meaning and satisfaction through their work.
2. The practice of spirituality in the workplace and how it contributes to organizational performance: that is, increased productivity.
3. Interdisciplinary research: spirituality and, for example, psychology, social theory, leadership skills, and behavioral ethics, and their application in concrete settings in the workplace.
4. Relationships between differing, and perhaps even divergent, perspectives on spirituality (faith-based and non-faith-based), as well as the harmonization of interfaith expressions of spirituality.

5. How workplace spirituality enhances meaningful interaction with others which, in turn, leads to personal transformation, growth, and a sense of contributing to the common good even beyond the workplace.

Health

In that this book has placed much emphasis on holistic spirituality, which takes seriously all elements of the human being – body, mind, soul, feelings, and so on – the need to actively link spirituality and health should therefore come as no surprise. Indeed, research in the area of spirituality and health at all levels is becoming ever more important, not only in medicine, but also in areas such as counseling, spiritual practices such as yoga, and care of the bereaved and dying. *Spirituality & Health Magazine: The Soul/Body Connection*[8] publishes popular articles dedicated to all facets of holistic health. The magazine clearly shows that the concern for holistic living – living that usually emphasizes spirituality from a secular perspective – is at the forefront of people's lives. But that preoccupation has also led to the mass marketing of spirituality and health literature, workshops, and so on. We must proceed with caution before spending time, energy, and dollars that may not lead one closer to the goal of enhancing one's spirituality, or Christian spirituality in particular, in relationship to health, and vice versa.

Paying attention to the importance of spirituality, from a faith-based or secular perspective, is not a sentimental nicety. A large body of serious academic literature has been written on the positive influences of the spirituality–health relationship. The evidence shows that people with a strong spiritual foundation fare better than people who lack a strong spiritual core, especially when dealing with serious health issues in hospital settings, chronic-care facilities, hospices (health-care facilities dedicated to those who are dying), and the like. There appears to be good reason to believe that a causal relationship exists between spirituality and good health. Spirituality, as understood within the scientific world view of medicine and health care, may be difficult to fully understand and measure, but medical literature clearly supports its beneficial role in the practice of medicine.

The increased attention given to spirituality and health, a broad-based movement in contemporary society, has also attracted its skeptics. Those caught up in a purely scientific view of the world find it difficult to believe that there could be some relationship between spirituality and health. Despite this skepticism, more and more people are coming to understand that attention to spirituality must be part of the care they receive from public health facilities involving regular medical care. This is ironic, but not surprising – as we saw in Chapter 1, more and more people do not formally associate themselves with any traditional spirituality, yet they remain deeply spiritual. They want to draw on those spiritual resources, especially in times of need, such as failing health, the loss of a loved one, or depression. As we have discussed spirituality in this book, we have come to see it as a fundamental characteristic of the human person. For this reason, spirituality will seek to be expressed with or without the formal faith structures that have traditionally contained it.

This is not to say that better spirituality translates into better physical and mental health. A spirituality-for-health exchange misrepresents the dynamic relationship between the two. The bulk of Christians do not believe that spirituality makes a claim to faith to get what is wanted – health or wealth. Rather, healthy Christian spiritualities foster a healthy balance in all areas of life. Earlier in this book (Chapter 7) we referred to this practice as asceticism – the helpful choices people make in life to ensure the happy outcomes desired at the deepest level of one's being. Christian spirituality imbues the Christian's life with a sense of gratitude, hope, meaning, and self-giving love – all of which contribute enormously to mental and physical health.

We ought not to be surprised that Christian spirituality is interested in health, holistic living, healing, and medicine. After all, stories of the healing ministry of Jesus abound in the Christian scriptures. Jesus saw a clear relationship between healing and faith, as did the generations that followed him. Augustine of Hippo refers to Jesus as the "great physician." And yet, with the dawn of rationalism, and the skepticism that accompanied it in the seventeenth century, this relationship was all but lost. Even though work is being done to regain and nurture it in contemporary studies in Christian spirituality, much remains to be done.

For example, the question needs to be asked over and over again, "What does it mean to be healthy?" There is no obvious answer to this question. By whose standards do we measure health? Given our society's preoccupation with consumerism and our susceptibility to the logic of exchange, we are led to believe that we will find happiness and meaning in life if we buy this product, join that group, undergo such-and-such a treatment. That kind of skewed logic has shifted the contemporary understanding of health. We reflected briefly on this issue in Chapter 1, in the section "Spirituality Marketed as a Product."

Even our desires and needs are driven by market demands. Deeply personal values and beliefs may subtly become objects to be exchanged in the marketplace of life for other commodities. The dignity of the human person is at stake here. People's relationship with each other is at stake here. People's relationship with God is at stake here. If the notion of health depends on having all the right things or being able to enjoy all the right experiences, or requires certain prayers, devotions, or other spiritual practices to effect it, one's personal understanding of health and wellness needs to be questioned. It is here that Christian spiritualities, along the lines of many of the issues discussed in this book, can be of tremendous assistance to a happy, holy, and healthy life. Health is not merely the absence of disease (mental or physical). It is the capacity and actualization of a meaningful, vigorous, and productive life.

Politics, government and globalization

Prophetic visions are rarely lived out from the "pinnacles of power," but are most often realized from "movements of conscience working from the bottom up."[9]

> "Politics will, to the end of history, be an area where conscience and power meet, where the ethical and coercive factors of human life will interpenetrate and work out their tentative and uneasy compromise."[10]

At the center of the relationship between Christian spirituality and politics (politics here is understood as broad-based involvement in the life of society, as well as in formal political institutions) is the Incarnation of Jesus. Christian spirituality does not merely emphasize that the word was made flesh on the level of belief, but requires Christians to act upon this truth in the realm of Christian praxis (practice). This action leads Christians, among many other things, to care and service of the poor, and compassion toward the downtrodden. But it takes the Christian further as well.

The Incarnation also calls Christians to actively engage in an ongoing process of transformation of the social and political structures of the world that make and keep people poor, and oppress countless numbers of people. The link between Christian spirituality and politics is founded on the belief that God's grace is operative in the material and historical processes that influence governments, social structures, and the entire political realm. Christian spirituality cuts through the artificially constructed boundaries based on race and national identity to envision a hope-filled future for all people. Transformation, and not merely the addressing of problems associated with the status quo, is the nexus of the link between Christian spirituality and politics.

Transformation happens at various levels. It is not merely a question of becoming involved in one political party or another (the prevalent view of the 1960s) or in one movement or another. Transformation, rooted in the concerns of actual people, occurs when people take up the concrete and the real of the everyday and do what is possible to make this world a better place for everybody. These actions will contribute, even if in small ways, toward transforming political structures that are oppressive. Involvement in non-partisan politics through not-for-profit groups, or non-governmental organizations (NGOs) may help respond more effectively to the crying needs of the poor, the disenfranchised, those living with HIV/AIDS, and so on.

Christian spirituality ought not to engage itself in politics to suggest that it has a better or superior vision to offer the world (although many Christians would hold the superiority of the Christian vision over other systems); it ought to do so as one of many dialogue partners. Christian spirituality has a perspective to offer on life's concrete issues, but this perspective will always be in relationship with a multiplicity of voices that are also contributing to goals serving the common good.

People's commitment to equality and justice may take many shapes and involve various strategies to achieve: from supporting the local food bank to taking part in a peaceful demonstration against the destruction of rain forests by multinational businesses. Local, national, and international initiatives need to be part of any comprehensive initiative to transform, for example, one's personal life, the lives of those in need, and the structures that hold people in bondage. Some people, however, may choose to become directly involved in the formal political process to work at resolving these issues.

Indeed, the future of our planet, and those who live within its delicate life-supporting systems – which is all of us – depend on such involvement. The salvation of the world is as much humanity's work as it is the work of the Holy Spirit. Christian spirituality, in its incarnational dimension, invites people to consider how they can contribute in concrete ways toward the betterment of society and the planet as a whole. The emphasis needs to be on spirit-filled living in all of its aspects (for example, the political, the ecological, and the cultural) – not on abstract dogma from either the religious or the political side of things.

The Christian biblical tradition is a good resource for reflection on these issues.[11] Many things could be brought to the discussion here; let us take a look at a few examples. First, the biblical tradition relativizes all claims to ownership of land and material goods, emphasizing that these resources are to be shared by all people. Equal distribution of goods is paramount. Second, the Bible helps us understand that economic and political systems that ignore countless numbers of people will engender unrest, conflict, and even war. Christian spirituality teaches that more violence is never the solution to aggravation on any level. Third, the Bible helps us be aware that any progress that does harm to the ecosystem of the earth – that exploits the earth in any way – will eventually cause destruction to people as well. Without proper care of the earth – for its own sake, let alone for the sake of those who depend on it for survival – human history is bound for extinction. The Christian traditions, reflected in a large range of Christian spiritualities, call humanity to be accountable to all these areas of life.

Of particular interest in today's discussions on spirituality and politics is globalization: the increasing worldwide integration of world markets, including that of goods, services, labor, capital, and finances. Globalization has led to the fusion of cultures around the world – largely the mass (crass?) export of Western, North American culture to all areas of the globe. Values, knowledge, national policies, and even music were once perceived as being under the local control and management of one national culture, economy, or political system; this is no longer the case. As a result of globalization, international corporations and foreign governments now influence cultural values, economic development, and political autonomy in striking ways that are not always positive.

In his book *Religion and Humane Global Governance*,[12] Richard Falk reflects on globalization – the political, social, economic, and cultural factors that have an impact on the development of globalization in the world. He includes in his study the influence of spirituality and religious values. Falk concludes that, to understand what is occurring in the world, it is necessary to carefully examine what is happening in religion and spiritual movements, especially those that either provoke conflicts or struggle to establish peace. Spirituality has returned to the mainstream in political life in a remarkable way, as we can see from world conflicts that, on the surface at least, are based in religious difference (and intolerance). Following the tragic events of September 11, 2001, especially the attack on the World Trade Center in New York, much work is being done on the influence of religion and spirituality in the public realm, particularly on politics.

A tremendous amount of research and reflection in Christian spirituality is needed to help better understand the world as a global reality in all its dimensions: political, cultural, social, religious, and so on. Spirituality is not meant to pick up the pieces of human living that politics has chosen to leave behind – the crumbs that formal political structures could not be bothered with. Rather, using its own points of reference, spirituality (and Christian spirituality as we have studied it in this book) has a valuable contribution to make to the main issues influencing life in society today.

As Bill Ryan, a Canadian Roman Catholic priest and former director of the Center of Concern in Washington, says:

> Faiths are not private revelations but rather by their nature are both public and social. We know that in the past, and even in the present, faiths matter or have influence in public life, both by their power to transform public structures and institutions as well as individuals. We must admit too, that, like ourselves, our faith institutions have, just as those of science and politics, abused, and, in some cases, still abuse power in public life. However, since neither science nor politics have been expelled from public life for their abuses, so neither should faiths be banished from public life.[13]

The task for Christian spirituality is to help understand how Christianity can use its influence to foster the common good – now and for the future – in a practical way. Globalization has been very successful in creating more wealth, but unsuccessful in redistributing wealth. The result is increased inequality between people around the world. The prophetic dimension of Christian spirituality (the capacity to speak truthfully the realities that are now being lived) can invite others to reflect upon critical issues that affect all people as the effects of globalization reach even deeper into everybody's lives. Below are a few ideas for this reflection.

In speaking of the prophetic commitment that needs to align Christian spirituality and politics, Jim Wallis, in *The Soul of Politics* (1994),[14] emphasizes that Christian spirituality needs to relate:

- biblical faith to social transformation;
- personal conversion to the cry of the poor;
- theological reflection to care for the environment;
- core religious values to new economic priorities;
- the call of community to racial and gender justice;
- morality to foreign policy;
- and transcend the categories of *liberal* and *conservative* that have captivated both religion and politics.

Cyberspace

> "Cyberspace is a globally networked, computer-sustained, computer-accessed, and computer-generated, multi-dimensional, artificial, or 'virtual' reality. In this world, onto which every computer screen is a window, actual, geographical distance is irrelevant. Objects seen or heard are neither physical nor, necessarily, presentations of physical objects, but are rather – in form, character, and action – made up of data, of pure information. This information is derived in part from the operation of the natural, physical world, but is derived primarily from the immense traffic of symbolic information, images, sounds, and people, that constitute human enterprise in science, art, business, and culture."[15]

The language, ideas, and virtual experiences of cyberspace infiltrate the life of anyone who uses this technology beyond the use of the technology itself.[16] Erik Davis, in *Techgnosis: Myth, Magic & Mysticism in the Age of Information* (1998),[17] argues that cyberspace feeds people's dreams, hopes, and aspirations. That is, it feeds their spiritual imaginations beyond whatever practical application initially drew them to use cyberspace – whether for information, business contacts, or booking a holiday in some distant destination – in the first place.[18] We could say that a lot of *soul* exists in cyberspace, for cyberspace influences the deeper dimensions of being human. Let us use chat rooms as an example to see how this is true.

Cyberspace chat rooms (virtual meeting places where individuals go to exchange ideas or just to chat socially) provide a meaningful place of encounter with others. People report having deep and intimate encounters through this medium. Chat rooms have a transcendental quality to them – people transcend the limitations of their bodies and their lives; they even transcend their mundane experience of time through them. In chat rooms people are capable of transcending their current reality (at the level of the self as well as the domestic, social, and work levels) to explore new perspectives on the world, their relationship with others, and new aspects of the self. People experience exuberant freedom in this setting.

As a result, there seems to be no limit to the self people desire to be. In cyberspace, people can be virtually anyone they want to be. Consensual realities can easily be constructed in chat rooms, leading to feelings of security, belonging, friendship, and intimacy in relationship to others. But we have to ask this question: "What kind of relationships are these?" Among other possible answers, one answer comes to mind quickly: generally speaking, they are relationships devoid of personal commitment and obligations to the individual(s) as well as to the wider social arena. In cyberspace people construct virtual lives – but these lives disappear when the screen goes blank. Once people are disconnected from this virtual world, they are left once again to face their personal reality of the here and now.

Constructing this virtual world is not necessarily a bad thing, however. On the positive side, for example, someone may feel connected and understood by other participants in the chat room. Communicating from a physical distance – communication that can be terminated, literally, at the flick of a switch – one feels safe. This feeling of security may lead the individual to share personal and intimate parts of his or her life that he or she dare not share elsewhere. In this way the person can try on various aspects of his or her self and experiment with saying things he or she is normally too shy to say. This practice can be affirming, and may help some people share more easily in their daily face-to-face encounters.

On the negative side the individual does not know who he or she is communicating with at the other end. It is almost impossible to confirm who the other is, to verify their age and gender, or know if they are truthfully responding to the topic at hand. In virtual space there are no moral obligations – no reciprocal responsibilities that can be appealed to. The individual could, therefore, easily be objectified, made into an object, to appease the curiosity and playful, or even destructive, intentions of the other communicants.

Caution is always advised in such situations. The authenticity of the other, as well as the authenticity of one's own self brought to the virtual chat, is hard to determine. Because there is no physical interaction, people can fool themselves into thinking they have developed authentic relationships. Or, individuals may take on an identity that is not even close to what is actualized in their daily person-to-person contacts. Cyberspace, therefore, can feed an illusory sense of the self and of the other. There are no real social demands in cyberspace – no real accountability to the other. The experience of a gradual growth in interpersonal relationships, with all their give and take, is usually foreign to cyberspace relationships.

In some ways, cyberspace allows people to experience their *glorified bodies* without the limitations of the mortal flesh.[19] In cyberspace people experience themselves elsewhere, in a digitalized, disembodied form, without the actual presence – or limitations – of their physical bodies. However, people still have the real experience of the physical sensations (embodiment) that come with interaction in virtual reality – the experiences of gratification with instant communication, a sense of intimacy with the other, or profound feelings of trust and being cared for. There is a spiritual dimension to these realities that needs careful attention.

Is this not also what is promised in Christian life at the end of time – "the pleasures of the physical body, but without any of its weaknesses or restrictions"?[20] Around these experiences we can begin constructing a kind of spirituality that has at its foundation a particular world view and perception of the self, both of which may have little grounding in the actual limitations of everyday life. Interaction in cyberspace allows a veneer of bliss to smooth over the problematic areas of people's lives. Life in cyberspace is very seductive indeed. This seduction helps it become the repository of immense spiritual yearning.

> Margaret Wertheim suggests that "dreams of transcending bodily limitations have been fueled by a fundamental philosophical shift of recent years, the growing view that man is defined not by the atoms of his body, but by an information code – the belief that our essence lies not in our matter, but in an immaterial pattern of data. The ease with which many cyber-fiction writers shuttle their characters in and out of cyberspace is premised on a belief that at core a human being is reducible to an array of data. While atoms can only construct the physical body, according to this cybernautic view, data can construct both body and mind. Indeed the above fantasies imply that in the end we will not need physical bodies at all, for we will be able to reconstruct ourselves totally in cyberspace. . . . Transcendence, immortality, and resurrection – these are dreams beginning to awaken in the cyber-space religious imagination."[21]

The study of this yearning, with its shifts in self-perception and world view, its experiences of disembodiment and embodiment, could be called cyber-spirituality. The way the spiritual self is constructed, enlivened, lived out – and even the way it dies – in cyberspace can be documented and studied. Many novels and movies already portray for us the world of cyberspace *as if* it were real life. Cyber-spirituality is becoming a powerful force in the contemporary cultural landscape. Its interest for Christian spirituality is not just a question of how cyberspace disseminates information and makes it available to unlimited numbers of people around the globe (effecting evangelization, for example).

Rather, it is a question of how the potential of the Internet and the technology associated with it are affecting fundamental questions of human life that radically shift philosophies, theologies, and spiritualities – in short, for example, people's self-understanding before each other, their relationship to the environment, and their relationship to God or some other ultimate value in life. The problem is that cyberspace constructs reality with few, if any, fixed points of reference. Historical consciousness, as we examined it in Chapter 5, is altered significantly with frequent immersion in cyberspace.

Above we have touched upon a few issues that influence spirituality in relationship to cyberspace and the Internet. Since 1995, the annual European Christian Internet Conference has dealt with many topics related to Christianity and cyberspace, such as the delivery of pastoral care, education, and ethics – all by the Internet.[22] Many other resources are available to explore this exciting topic.[23]

It is important to follow closely how cyberspace is affecting Christian spiritualities in terms of how people perceive the world, themselves, their relationships, and so on. Concepts studied elsewhere in this book – such as the self, transcendence, community, human mortality, prayer, understanding of one's responsibilities in daily life, of the afterlife, of the soul, and even of God – are all affected by the way cyberspace affects or even changes one's world view. Cyberspace is a very fertile area, and a largely unmapped one, for researchers in Christian spirituality today.

New Age

"When it first appeared, under the banner of the 'Aquarian Conspiracy', the New Age was anti-establishment and politically and socially radical. However, over recent years, as it has been incorporated into the mainstream and produced by commercial industries, it has lost its early radicalism and become extremely middle-class and a kind of mystical add-on to ordinary life. There is quite a difference between the original Aquarian Conspiracy of the 1960s and today's largely conservative and politically reactionary New Age movement."[24]

Aquarian? Radical? Mystical? Commercial? Conservative? What, exactly, is New Age? What is it that began as a "conspiracy" and ended up as an "add-on to ordinary life"? These are difficult questions to answer – even with all that has been written on New Age in the last twenty or more years. The term *New Age* calls to mind such a vast array of beliefs, practices, and rituals, along with clothing lines and products of all sorts, that to pin down a precise meaning is all but impossible. Because of the diversity involved, it would not be feasible to make even a cursory summary of the main streams of New Age thought, or the rituals and beliefs associated with it. However, several historical references will help us understand the concept of New Age and its relationship to Christian spiritualities today.

The origin of the term *new age* is linked to the body of ideas called *theosophy*. Theosophy is founded on the belief that all religions are an attempt to get to know the one God. Therefore, all religions and spiritualities contain some measure of truth. Theosophy developed primarily from the writings of the Russian-born American Helena Petrovna Blavatsky (1831–1891).[25] It refers to any number of philosophies that claim that knowledge of God is achieved by personal spiritual ecstasy – a kind of direct intuition of God, a special knowledge of God that leads to personal enlightenment. Theosophists claim that the source of this enlightenment is within the individual: truth is sought within the confines of one's own experience. Theosophists trace the origins of this idea to many ancient philosophers: for example, to the Greek philosopher Plato. Theosophical writings used the term *new age* to describe a kind of breakthrough in cosmic consciousness in which human beings would become aware of their god-like qualities. This awareness would bring about the dawn of a new age on the planet, an age of peace, freedom, and harmony.

An American woman, Alice Bailey (1880–1949), picked up on the ideas of Helena Petrovna Blavatsky and referred to this cosmic breakthrough as *Christ consciousness*, equating it to what Christianity describes as the kingdom of God.[26] She and her husband, Foster Bailey, founded a school in 1923 called The Arcane School of Christianity (*arcane* means secret or mysterious) to teach followers how to achieve the kind of enlightenment fostered in the theosophist teachings described above. However, what was taught had little to do with traditional Christianity – it was a mix of Hindu and Buddhist doctrines, as well as socialist politics.[27] In The Arcane School of Christianity, Jesus was held to be little more than a person of great wisdom who taught others about their own Divine destiny. He was certainly not recognized as the Son of God.

From the foundation of theosophy as a fairly coherent ideology that included preoccupation with occult practices, parapsychology, and reincarnation present in the writings of Blavatksy, followed by the esoteric ideals of The Arcane School of Christianity, we jump to the counter-cultural events of the 1960s. It was during this time that New Age, as an ideology based on specific philosophical, psychological, and spiritual principles, entered the mainstream of popular culture. The time was right for a mix of the esoteric and the popular – a mix that would result in the adaptation of New Age for new times and for a broad spectrum of Western society.

The 1960s ushered in a dramatic social upheaval in Western countries – displays of alternative culture evident in, for example, the radical rejection of traditional morality (sometimes called the sexual revolution) and demonstrations by students against US participation in the Vietnam War). In general, this is where the "anti-establishment and politically and socially radical" theme mentioned in the opening quote in this section fits in. It was the era of flower power, peace, and unbridled personal freedom and love – the Age of Aquarius brought to popular consciousness through the smash hit Broadway musical *Hair* (1968). Through the media of song, dance, and storytelling, *Hair* questioned the current standards of morality, sexuality, racism, drug use, and social acceptance. It was the time of the Beatles – the British rock group that shook the world with its music, lyrics, and long hair! It was also the time of the Woodstock Music and Art Fair – the 1969 gigantic love-in of upperstate New York. The event, which has come to be known simply as Woodstock, was the biggest rock-and-roll concert ever, with more than 450,000 people attending. Although it was, and is, an enduring symbol of hedonism and sexual excess, it remains in the minds of many the event that opened the door to allow them to view and experience the world in a new, freer way.

The 1960s were also a time of mind-expanding hallucinogenic drugs, Eastern-style meditation, and a rise in popularity of humanistic psychology. The followers of Alice Bailey worked to package these themes not as counter-cultural, but as acceptable New Age culture, because of the values they engaged – such as personal freedom, peace, love, and harmony for all. The fit was remarkable – a convergence of ideology and popular culture that spawned the beginning of a new way of looking at oneself in the face of changing political perspectives and social norms, and, equally, in the face of changing views of religion and spirituality. New Age spiritualities developed when New Age ideals were transformed and embodied in the counter-culture movements of the 1960s, which then led to enormous changes in the popular understandings of religion and spirituality in general.

Throughout the 1960s and 1970s, New Age promoters launched educational seminars, self-help programs, meditation groups, and other activities to tap the revolutionary spirit of the time. The adaptation of New Age culture – which could be described more as an undergrowth than a direct frontal attack on any one establishment – seeped into the popular cultural environment. For example, in 1980, American author Marilyn Ferguson published *The Aquarian Conspiracy*, which capitalized on the emergent New

Age culture and its penchant for transforming the existing moral and social order. The book was a runaway success, for in it a broad spectrum of the population recognized themselves (their values, beliefs, and goals). Lynn Andrews's *The Mask of Power: Discovering Your Sacred Self* (1992) is clearly a throwback to theosophy. It would be easy to cite hundreds, if not thousands, of other highly successful books from the 1980s through to our own day that reflect New Age values. The content of the self-help seminars and workplace improvement workshops that are so common today smack of the same search for personal power and enlightenment spoken of in the work of Blavatsky almost 100 years earlier.

In most discussions of the New Age phenomenon, however, the political, historical, cultural, and social background that led to New Age publications, movements, and spiritualities is given little attention. Most often, the focus is on its popularized practices, concepts, and beliefs linked, for example, to self-help psychologies or the importation of Eastern religious practices. But as we have seen, it is clear that New Age has links to the ideology of theosophy mentioned above.

What needs to be emphasized is that New Age is not one seamless, coherent movement, spirituality, or even set of beliefs. Even though linked to theosophy, current manifestations of New Age are woven into people's thinking and practices on many levels in ways that are not always internally consistent. For example, in New Age there is an emphasis on the interdependence of all creation, yet there is also an emphasis on the radical autonomy and independence of each person. Furthermore, since the 1980s on, it is difficult to document or quantify in any systematic way the precise nature or focus of New Age concepts and practices, since they are so widespread in Western culture and its faith-based communities. In short, no clear boundaries identify New Age today.

In the early 1990s, New Age shifted even more dramatically into the mainstream due to an upsurge in multiculturalism and religious globalism. It is now just as easy to purchase materials for Buddhist spiritual practices as it is for Christian or Muslim ones. The Internet has made the dissemination of New Age–style practices such as retreats, self-help groups, and Eastern-style meditation accessible to almost everyone. Without realizing it, people are plugged into New Age culture, concepts, and ideas around the globe – for example, in the way they are exposed to advertising or health movements of all kinds.

Even though it is difficult to describe precisely what New Age is, we can summarize the following general characteristics of New Age thinking and ideology.

With respect to Christian spirituality, the positive side of New Age

- resists forms of hierarchy – stresses the equality of all persons;
- resists any form of dualism – (e.g. male/female; spirit/body; earth/heaven);
- values personal experience and the insights of each individual;
- emphasizes the wholeness or connectedness of all things; no one or no thing is more important than the other;
- emphasizes the need to discover one's inner spiritual self and to take personal responsibility for one's spiritual life;
- values the body; stresses good nutrition and health on all levels (mind/body/spirit);
- has an invested interest in the care of the earth as a partner in human growth and advancement; concern for the environment is central;
- recognizes the presence of the Divine within each person.

With respect to Christian spirituality, the negative side of New Age

- clings to a radical focus on personal experience as absolutely authoritative (i.e. without relationship to tradition, doctrinal norms, language, or historical context); personal enlightenment based on personal experience is paramount and the only sure guide to authority;
- views the self as the basis and originator of all knowledge – which means that the individual need not accept the authority of anyone or anything outside of oneself; the truth is what fits the life of any one individual;
- believes that there is a timeless knowledge about the spiritual aspects of life that is held within (at the center of) each person – New Age spiritual practices seek to tap and release the hidden wisdom and power deep within each individual as if it is present in some container located in our bodies;
- sees the self (body and psyche) as sacred, replacing the notion that God is sacred; in New Age thinking the sacred lies within each individual to be discovered through a personal, interior journey; in this approach there is a denial of God's grace operative in life; New Age relies on self-help techniques and practices to reach spiritual maturity;
- is suspicious of rational thought, since "reason may be something one has to obey; it may create hierarchies by judging some things true, others false; and it may reveal some people as cleverer than others."[28]

It seems that anything goes in New Age, as long as it does not contradict the personalized and privatized self that we examined in Chapter 4. New Age spirituality appeals to those who are looking for easily digested chunks of spirituality – ones that they can gulp down now to find an immediate solution to the problems and quandaries of life. New Age does not admit there is a God who, in some mysterious way, enters one's life and calls forth the individual and the community. Christian spiritualities hold that it is the personal Divine self that is responsible for calling Christians forward and responding to needs in life. Ironically, many aspects of New Age spirituality reflect the modernist view of the world with its emphasis on the privatized self. The rejection of this same view by the mid-twentieth century signaled the definitive shift into the postmodern era. We examined this shift in Chapter 2.

From a Christian perspective, New Age spirituality is a kind of consumer spirituality. Individuals may purchase whatever kinds of spiritual paraphernalia they find helpful for their personal quest without having to be responsible to any kind of regulating community. In New Age spirituality, there is little commitment to the collective dimensions of Christian spirituality we have been stressing.

It is easy to see that not all aspects of New Age spirituality are easily reconciled with Christian spirituality. Because New Age thinking has permeated most aspects of Western culture, for example, through self-help groups, meditative practices, workplace improvement seminars, personal power enhancing exercises, and even the way people approach Christian spiritual and personal development, it is helpful to be critically aware of where and how New Age thinking is taking root and to critically name both the positive and negative influences it may have. Christian spirituality, with its emphases on belief in a personal God, the role of grace in people's lives, and the centrality of Jesus Christ as the Divine Son of God, will always have much (both positive and negative) to dialogue about with New Age thinking, practices, and beliefs.

Gender

> "Gendered spirituality involves an ongoing process of mind-body-spirit practice by which the individual's gender identity can be expressed, produced and transformed."[29]

Gender is not a fixed characteristic of the human person. It is composed of a dynamic and fluid mix of cultural roles (assigned or chosen), personal identity, corporeality, race, and biological sex. Gender, therefore, is a social construct that is not determined merely from one's biological sex as male or female – although these influence gender, perhaps in the most significant way. Gender refers to our subjective feelings of maleness or femaleness. As a corollary, what is determined to be masculine and feminine is equally fluid as societies change their assessment of these categories.[30] Therefore, like ethnic or religious identity, gender identity involves a sense of "who I am" – how I locate myself in the world with respect to my sexual identity, my affections for others, and the way I construct meaningful, committed relationships. On this basis we can talk about gendered spiritualities.

Christian spirituality needs to take seriously this perspective on gender and gendered spiritualities as it struggles in the face of ignorance and prejudice that many Christian groups hold toward people who are not recognized as within the norm of gender expression. Regrettably, gendered spiritualities have long been considered outside the mainstream of Christian spiritualities. For example, the gay, lesbian, bisexual, and transgendered communities often find themselves disenfranchised by mainline Christian churches because they do not fit within the norm of heterosexual love. Given the homophobia, prejudice, and ignorance of the complexity of gender construction and its expression in both society and the churches, this situation is not surprising. But Christian spiritualities, founded on the love of God as revealed in the life of Jesus, have little reason, if any, not to recognize the positive witness of Christian spirituality that comes from the gay, lesbian, bisexual, and transgendered communities.

Love between same-gendered persons (read "same-sex couples") reminds us that God calls people to love deeply, regardless of the norms of society and or the churches at this time. Acts of love-making between same-gendered couples, as between different-gendered couples (read "heterosexual couples"), can be sacramental in the strongest sense of the word – in the same way as it is used to describe the love-making of committed heterosexual couples. If scripture has anything to teach people today, it is that God shows God's love in the most unexpected of places. Love between persons who belong to the gay, lesbian, bisexual, and transgendered communities exists independently of current trends or prejudices. We can, therefore, speak of gay, lesbian, bisexual, and transgendered spiritualities just as clearly as we can speak of spiritualities based on other unique sources of human experience.

It was emphasized in Chapter 1 that experience as experience is foundational to the construction of spiritualities, Christian or otherwise. Different world views will shape Christian spiritualities in different ways. Therefore, we can speak of feminist spiritualities (spiritualities that are constructed from the experiences of women, with their own embodiment of Christian life); liberation spiritualities (spiritualities that are constructed on the experience of being oppressed and marginalized, like many of the poor in Latin America); or spiritualities of people of color (spiritualities that are constructed from the experience of being a minority in societies that are predominantly white); and so on. Spiritualities are constructed from unique world views – people's views of the world are constructed on the basis of their embodied positions (ideological, social, political, spiritual, and so on) in relationship to that world.

We thus recognize that, within the wide range of experiences possible in Christian living, the gay, lesbian, bisexual, and transgendered communities also offer a unique perspective and wisdom based on their experience of God's love in the face of some very difficult challenges. This experience of God has yet to be identified and honored in the queer or gay[31] communities. It has never been easy to be different – society and churches do not tolerate difference easily. Even though great strides have been made in different societies and churches today to be open to and accepting of persons of all genders, and of their expressions of committed love, there is much progress still to be made before people will easily recognize that all people are God's children.

Spirituality in the gay, lesbian, bisexual, and transgendered communities resembles Christian spirituality when it is committed, sacramental, relational, and transformative. Many Christian groups may be challenged or even outraged by this affirmation. And yet, God's grace has been breaking through into the world in radical ways since the beginning of time. Christians are called to be open to the radical ways God's grace is breaking through in the world today. There is a certain prophetic quality to the committed love shared between persons in the gay, lesbian, bisexual, and transgendered communities. Because people in these communities perceive reality, and God, as part of that reality, in ways that may be at odds with the predominant cultures – both within society and within the churches – that surround them, they can reveal to the broader community new ways of loving, of being loved, and of embodying God's Spirit in the world.

Love, which is at the foundation of Christian spirituality, comes in many forms. Love, whether between same-sex or heterosexual couples, can bring God and God's love to others. This love can heal, renew, bring laughter and joy, engender hope, and transform people's lives in profound ways – whether people are queer or straight. Divine flesh, as we reflected in Chapter 4, does not take up life selectively according to gender constructions. Life is a gift given as *imago Dei*, the image of God, to all people. If Christian spiritualities take this affirmation seriously, they will recognize the wondrous gift of God's grace active in the lives of people of all genders, and be receptive to the unique gift each person offers.

Feminism

"Feminism . . . is a comprehensive ideology which is rooted in women's experience of sexual oppression, engages in a critique of patriarchy as an essentially dysfunctional system, embraces an alternative vision for humanity and the earth, and actively seeks to bring this vision to realization."[32] Feminist spirituality starts with the affirmation that God, as the ground of all being, and the giver of all life, supports and promotes female personhood as much as male personhood. Man and woman are equivalent as *imago Dei*.[33]

Although there is no universal agreement on what exactly feminism is, there is a general understanding that feminism, as understood today, is motivated by *feminist consciousness*. Feminist consciousness is the explicit awareness of the systemic and structural character of women's oppression that has been sustained either intentionally or indirectly through patriarchy (the domination of men in all areas of life). The eradication of women's oppression as sustained by patriarchy is not only directed toward the grievances of women, but also seeks to transform all kinds of oppressive structures, such as the exploitation of children as slave-workers or the destruction of the natural environment. Thus, women's movements that pre-date the nineteenth century are not motivated by feminist consciousness and cannot, within this understanding, be considered feminist movements.

For example, the social and political activities by women that began in the late nineteenth century in Europe, spread to North America at the beginning of the twentieth century, and then migrated to developing countries by the end of the twentieth century, focused on furthering women's interests so they would be treated in the same way as their male counterparts. The focus was on equality, but still defined within male patriarchal structures. Equal pay and opportunity in the workplace, access to vote at all levels in government as well as full participation in political life, and the implementation of laws to protect women from such dangers as male violence, were some of the issues women sought to have resolved to improve *their* lives.

These social and political activities were largely a response to the blatant oppression of women that became apparent in the workplace and in society in general during the various industrial revolutions. These are better described as *women's movements* that dealt mostly with equality issues.

A second wave of women's activity began in the 1960s, when women started to realize that the important thing was not simply a matter of becoming equal to their male counterparts. Rather, they knew they needed to begin a systematic analysis of the structures that kept women, and other disenfranchised groups, oppressed in the first place.[34] Critical analysis aimed at transformation of the status quo became the earnest work of feminist scholarship during the 1960s. Books cited as signaling the shift from issues of equality to issues of transformation include Betty Friedan's (1963) *The Feminine Mystique* and Mary Daly's (1968) *The Church and the Second Sex*.[35] Indeed, this is the time when feminist studies was recognized as a new academic discipline in higher education.

Another category, called third-wave feminisms, considers feminist perspectives that vary as a result of racial and cultural differences. Such differences have been largely ignored to date, with much of the feminist writings from the 1960s on being written by well-educated white middle-class women. Because the struggles of women of color in Latin America, for example, are different from those of white Euro-American women, distinct feminist perspectives emerge when the reflection is offered by Hispanic women. Third-wave feminisim also includes ecofeminism: the analysis of the exploitation of nature in relationship to political, social, scientific, and ecclesial structures. Ecofeminist theory holds that the domination of women and the domination of nature are closely linked.

In third-wave feminisms some women reject the *feminist* label, indicating that it aligns them too closely with the concerns of white Western women of privilege. For example, some Latin American women exploring contemporary women's issues prefer the term *mujerista*, derived from the Spanish word *mujer* (woman). Some black women distinguish themselves by using the term *womanist*.[36] Alice Walker, the author of the successful Pulitzer Prize-winning novel *The Color Purple*, subsequently made into an award-winning movie, is perhaps the most famous of womanist authors.

With its critical understanding of the way patriarchy and misogyny (hatred toward women) have crippled the role and power of women in our societies and churches, feminism has played a crucial role in liberating women to explore their own spiritual consciousness as well as loosening oppressive structures in other areas of society. For many women, this process has involved sifting through traditions and practices that were once held to be normative and life-giving. In doing so, they have discovered that traditions are constructed from within a particular world view, and that the practices that grew out of these traditions were often self-serving. They did not allow the women freedom to be open to other ways of expressing and embodying their full humanity.

What women have come to discover is that even though the imprint of their world view, which is usually shaped by patriarchy, is embedded deep within their psyches, they can be free to develop a new web of relationships that will inform and shape their lives differently. Indeed, feminist thinking has concluded that it is the *women's* web of relationships that functions as the catalyst for constructing meaningful lives that are not rooted in doctrines, rules, or regulations that have been put in place by male-dominated institutions and power structures.

Feminist spiritualities, therefore, recognize the unique experience of women as the basis for helpful and hopeful spiritualities that not only engage in the struggle for the equality of the sexes, but also acknowledge that sexism is at the basis of all oppression, for example, of men, women, children, visible and invisible minorities, and care of the earth. At the core of feminisms, and feminist spiritualities, lies the desire to expose the debilitating hierarchical structures of the world that, by their very nature, transform people and the natural world into objects to be exploited for ideological or financial reasons. As Sandra Schneiders suggests, all oppression is based on dichotomous dualisms: classism, racism, clericalism, colonialism, heterosexism, ageism, and so on.[37] Feminism works to expose hierarchical and dualistic relationships and replace them with structures, knowledge, and beliefs that recognize the implicit equality of people, the importance of the natural world, and the desire to construct justice for all – in society or in the churches. Feminist spiritualities are built on these principles of equality and justice.

To help us develop specifically feminist spiritualities based on the above understanding of different feminisms, it is helpful to consider five questions that Rosemary Radford Ruether brings to our attention:

1. How can the elements of a spirituality be reinterpreted from a female perspective so that they help to make women subjects of their own history?
2. Can the elements of a spirituality function to enhance the liberationist transformation of history rather than the sacralization of male domination?
3. How can stories and symbols drawn from spiritual traditions be translated from their androcentric form (male-centeredness) into one defined by and for women?

4. Should people continue merely to translate from androcentric traditions or do we need to go beyond them and create new stories and new symbols not directly related to patriarchal narratives and rituals?
5. Should women unite across religious boundaries in some synthesis of the perspectives traditionally perceived as set against each other, for example, Buddhism in relationship to Christianity?[38]

> "Feminism is a worldwide movement that envisions nothing less than the radical transformation of human history. It maintains that such a transformation is necessary in order for over half of the human race to be able to participate fully in the human enterprise. But it also maintains that until women participate in that enterprise, the human family and the earth as its home remain in mortal danger. Women do not seek to participate as imitation males or on male terms in a male construction of reality. Rather they have undertaken a deconstruction of male reality and a reconstruction of reality in more human terms. If the feminist enterprise succeeds, the future of humanity will be qualitatively different. . . . the change will be in the direction of salvation for the race and for the planet."[39]

Feminisms are made up of four essential components. These components, listed below, recognize that feminism in general is not merely a critique of the status quo. Feminisms also offer their own vision to replace the negative aspects of patriarchy as well as an action plan to put its vision in place.

Components of feminisms:

1. A *consciousness* that patriarchal culture inhibits the full human development of all peoples – especially women, the economically resourceless, and people of color – and that it destructively exploits the natural world;

2. A *vision* of what life could be like so that more and more people are able to find meaning, work, a sense of dignity, and the possibility of self-determination;

3. A *set of activities* that challenge the present social structures of politics, education, family, religion, and the economy so that the vision becomes part of history; and

4. An *evolving culture* (produced by the consciousness, vision, and activities) that shifts the total pattern of human behavior toward sanctifying every individual and cleansing the earth.[40]

Men's movements

We traced above the development of feminist movements – a response to the growing consciousness that women have been harmed or held back by patriarchal structures, debilitating ways of thinking (excessive rationalism), destructive dualisms, and so on.

Men, too, have galvanized themselves into identifiable groups that have formulated coherent responses to specific issues in their lives. These issues include: the rights of men to parent their children after divorce; the subordination of men to other men; male violence in the home and workplace; the preconceived notion that men live in their heads while women live in their hearts; and society's often harmful view of acceptable masculine behavior.

In the 1980s and 1990s, men's studies, which includes the study of men's movements, developed into its own area of academic research. The academic journal *The Journal of Men's Studies*, launched in 1992, testifies to this emergent discipline. The wide range of articles in *The Journal of Men's Studies* reveals that just as feminism can be expressed in many forms, so can men's movements. We will consider one of these, the *mythopoetic men's movement*, below. Other movements include men's recovery programs (e.g. from addictions and uncontrollable violence), pro-feminist movements, and men's/father's rights movements.

While feminism has focused on the transformation and change of social and political structures that lie at the root of so many problems in the world, men's movements, for the most part, are driven by the recognition that men need to change things in their *own* lives. Men have been the recipients of so many benefits of the current social and political arrangements, it is more difficult for men to see the compelling need to change these. Instead, men's movements have focused on personal issues that cause grief in their lives – in relationship to other men, their own families, women, society, or the workplace – and the dis-ease men feel in Western culture today because of the roles society has constructed for them.

Robert Bly, an American poet, songwriter, and leader of men's retreats, is frequently cited as being the father of the mythopoetic men's movement. To reveal the shifts that need to take place in the Western understanding of masculinity Bly returns to the examination of myths, fairy tales, and other ancient stories. One such story is Iron John, taken from the Grimm brothers' collection of fairy tales.[41] Bly uses this fairy tale as the framework for his 1990 book *Iron John: A Book About Men*.[42] What interests Bly is how the healthy masculine energy of the main character, Iron John, can become available to the contemporary male through the interpretation and appropriation of his story. Other examples of texts used for mythopoetic work include Homer's *Odyssey* and Virgil's *Aeneid*.

Bly, who has led many gatherings of men across North America, has worked hard to refute the commonly held view that men's ways of thinking and feeling are limited to linear, rational logic that distances them from deep and caring relationships. During these retreats, which often take place in woodland settings (but also in school auditoriums and other indoor locations), the tales of healthy masculine energy are recounted and sometimes even re-enacted to help participants find the source of this healthy masculine energy deep within them. In recounting the stories of bravery and valor of characters from long ago, these ancient stories are appropriated in a personal way to sustain and build hope today.

The work done during men's retreats allows men to reconfigure their outlook in life and break down controlling patterns of thinking and acting – even if only temporarily. These occasional glimpses of alternative ways of being, doing, and thinking are pursued with the goal of examining more critically what needs to change permanently in one's life. Reading and analyzing how men have behaved in texts such as those cited above, including the expressions of grief and joy, hate and love, tears and smiles, results in a more complete understanding of the male psyche and how men can live more healthily and happily.

Bly wants to show that men are just as capable as women of strong emotional and caring relationships, with women or men (in the latter case, without any allusion to homosexual attraction). Our culture has taught men to be independent, fiercely competitive, and emotionally barren. Only when we become consciously aware of how our culture has trapped them in the bondage of patriarchal values will they be free to enjoy committed, self-giving, and emotionally mature relationships. During the gatherings conducted by Bly, great emphasis is placed on how to get in touch with one's feelings, improve one's self-image and self-esteem, and become an agent of change in one's own life.

The mythopoetic men's movement led by Robert Bly has as its goal the replacement of destructive models of masculinity (characterized by, for example, excessive rationalism, oppressive power, and individualism) with models of masculinity that value feelings, see power as empowerment with and for others, and emphasize interdependent autonomy. The mythopoetic men's movement has helped men become more self-aware and given them opportunities to talk in a safe environment to other men who are facing the same issues around unhealthy models of masculinity. We could call this movement *men's liberation*.

The awareness that men, like women, have a unique way of being in the world has led to the development of specifically male spiritualities. At the foundation of the development of male spiritualities is the recognition that maleness is constructed on specific male phenomena, not that male experiences reflect the universal human. In the past, patriarchy assumed that the experiences of men define what is normatively human. Men were considered to be universal, generic human beings. As a result, women's unique experiences, such as those related to child birth, have been dismissed, but also disregarded are what might be considered specifically men's experience as *men*. We all share in a common humanity, but it cannot be defined exclusively by either male or female experiences.

Because there has been an attempt to define the normative human in relationship to male experiences in Western culture and its Christian spiritualities, there has not been sufficient reflection on those unique male experiences related to, for example, male physiology, growth patterns, and modes of consciousness, in relationship to God and faith. Everything that is important to a man's life ought to be given serious consideration in developing male spiritualities. Central to this way of thinking is men's self-identity in relationship to women, other men (male bonding and friendships), their bodies and sexuality, their fantasies, their emotions, their workplaces, their family, and so on. Although several major works cited in the bibliography for this section deal with these issues, much work remains to be done on the development of male spiritualities that take seriously the (misconstrued) notions of male identity in Western culture and in the Christian churches today.

> The work to be done in developing healthy male spiritualities is to understand that men, like women, have unique experiences not specifically related to the generic nature of being human, but are reflections of unique ways, for example, of being in the world related to their bodies, their psychological dispositions, and their preferences around ways of being together. This starting point will acknowledge as important the contributions of both men and women to the common project of developing holistic spiritualities. These spiritualities will not view men's and women's experiences as mutually exclusive and will hold in esteem the differences of the two.

Conclusion

This chapter has provided some general overviews of topics that are being critically studied today in relationship to spirituality and Christian spirituality. The topics chosen for presentation are a sampling of the broad range of work that is being done.

Other topics that could be pursued include education, marriage, ecumenism and inter-religious dialogue, liturgy, post-colonialism, and multiculturalism. Many of these topics, along with those presented above, intersect with each other. The key point to focus on is the genuine search to integrate spirituality (for Christians, this means Christian spirituality) into all aspects of life. The current interest in spirituality – Christian, Buddhist, Muslim, humanistic, and so on – has spawned a great deal of research and reflection that promises to be fruitful as people come to understand better the search for meaning and fulfillment in life.

RECOMMENDED READING

Science

Capra, Fritjof (1992) *Belonging to the Universe: Explorations on the Frontiers of Science and Spirituality*, San Francisco: Harper SanFrancisco.

Harding, Sandra (1991) *Whose Science? Whose Knowledge?* New York: Cornell University Press.

Horgan, John (2003) *Rational Mysticism: Dispatches from the Border Between Science and Spirituality*, Boston: Houghton Mifflin.

Knight, David (2005) *Science and Spirituality: The Volatile Connection*, New York: Routledge.

Matt, Daniel C. (1996) *God & the Big Bang: Discovering Harmony Between Science & Spirituality*, Woodstock, VT: Jewish Lights Publishing.

O'Murchu, Diarmuid (2002) *Evolutionary Faith: Rediscovering God in Our Great Story*, Maryknoll, NY: Orbis Books.

Richardson, Mark W. and Wesley J. Wildman, eds (1996) *Religion and Science: History, Method, Dialogue*, New York: Routledge.

Russell, Robert John (2005) "Natural Sciences," in *The Blackwell Companion to Christian Spirituality*, ed. Arthur Holder, Oxford: Blackwell, 325–344.

Work and leadership

Benefiel, Margaret (2005) *Soul at Work: Spiritual Leadership in Organizations*, New York: Seabury.

Boyatzis, Richard and Annie McKee (2005) *Resonant Leadership: Renewing Yourself and Connecting with Others Through Mindfulness, Hope, and Compassion*, Boston: Harvard Business School Press.

Costa, John Dalla (2005) *Magnificence at Work: Living Faith in Business*, Ottawa: Novalis.

Derske, Wil (2003) *The Rule of Benedict for Beginners: Spirituality for Daily Life*, tr. (from Dutch) Martin Kessler, Collegeville, MN: Liturgical Press.

Giacalone, Robert A. and Carole L. Jurkiewiz, eds (2005) *Handbook of Workplace Spirituality and Organizational Performance*, Armonk, NY: M. E. Sharpe.

Krishnakumar, Sukumarakurup and Christopher P. Neck (2002) "The 'what,' 'why,' and 'how' of Spirituality in the Workplace," *Journal of Managerial Psychology* 17:3, 153–164.

Roche, Marianne E. (2002) *On-the-job Spirituality: Finding God in Work*, Cincinnati, OH: St. Anthony Messenger Press. (Excellent sections on such topics as conflict, stress, boredom, workaholism, work as sacrament, work as a reflection of our *imago Dei*.)

Tredget, Dermot (2002) "'The Rule of Benedict' and Its Relevance to the World of Work," *Journal of Managerial Psychology* 17:3, 219–229.

Whyte, David (2001) *Crossing the Unknown Sea: Work as a Pilgrimage of Identity*, New York: Riverhead Books.

Health

Bregman, Lucy (2003) *Death and Dying, Spirituality and Religions: A Study of the Death Awareness Movement*, New York: Peter Lang.

Evans, Abigail Rian (1999) *The Healing Church: Practical Programs for Health Ministries*, Cleveland, OH: United Church Press.

Gilbert, Richard B., ed. (2002) *Health Care & Spirituality: Listening, Assessing, Caring*, Amityville, NY: Baywood Publishing Company.

Koenig, Harold G. (1998) *Handbook of Religion and Mental Health*, Toronto: Academic Press. (Includes reflections from Muslim, Christian, Jewish, Buddhist, Unity, Mormon, Protestant, and Catholic perspectives.) See especially "A History of Religion, Science, and Medicine," 24–49.

Matthews, Dale A. and Connie Clark (1998) *The Faith Factor: Proof of the Healing Power of Prayer*, New York: Viking.

Peel, Robert (1987) *Spiritual Healing in a Scientific Age*, San Francisco: Harper & Row.

Shuman, Joel J. and Keith G. Meador (2003) *Heal Thyself: Spirituality, Medicine, and the Distortion of Christianity*, Toronto: Oxford University Press.

Sulmasy, Daniel P. (1997) *The Healer's Calling: A Spirituality for Physicians and Other Health Care Professionals*, New York: Paulist Press.

Sweet, Leonard I. (1994) *Health and Medicine in the Evangelical Tradition: "Not by Might nor Power"*, Valley Forge, PA: Trinity Press International.

Swinton, John (2001) *Spirituality and Mental Health Care: Rediscovering a "Forgotten" Dimension*, London: J. Kingsley Publishers.

Politics, government, and goblization

Carlson, John D. and Erik C. Owens, eds (2003) *The Sacred and the Sovereign: Religion and International Politics*, Washington, D.C.: Georgetown University Press.

Falk, Richard (2001) *Religion and Humane Global Governance*, New York: Palgrave.

Finn, Geraldine (1992) "The Politics of Spirituality: The Spirituality of Politics," in *Shadow of Spirit: Postmodernism and Religion*, eds Philippa Berry and Andrew Wernick, London: Routledge, 111–122.

Lau, Cheryl (1998) "Spirituality and Government Policies." Delivered at the *International Coalition for Religious Freedom Conference* on "Religious Freedom and the New Millennium," in Berlin, Germany, May 29–31, 1998. Full text available at: www.religiousfreedom.com/conference/Germany/lau. htm. Downloaded June 6, 2006.

Leech, Kenneth (1992) "Stepping out of Babylon: Politics and Christian Vision," in *The Eye of the Storm: Living Spirituality in the Real World*, New York: HarperCollins Publishers, 95–144.

Roof, Wade Clark (1991) *World Order and Religion*, New York: S.U.N.Y. Press.

Ryan, Bill (2004) "Can Religion Shape Politics? Or is Religion Being Shaped by Politics in an Age of Globalization?" *Pastoral Sciences* 23:1, 25–34.

Snell, Priscilla (1986) "Spirituality and Economics: Promoting Gospel Values in the Marketplace," *Spiritual Life* 32:3, 145–152.

Wallis, Jim (1994) *The Soul of Politics: A Practical and Prophetic Vision for Change*, New York: Orbis Books.

—— (2005) *God's Politics: Why the Right Gets It Wrong and the Left Doesn't Get It*, San Francisco: Harper SanFrancisco.

Cyberspace

Babin, Pierre and Angela Ann Zukowski (2002) *The Gospel in Cyberspace: Nurturing Faith in the Internet Age*, Chicago: Loyola Press.

Baker, Jason D. (1997) *Christian Cyberspace Companion: A Guide to the Internet and Christian Online Resources*, Grand Rapids, MI: Baker Books.

Benedikt, Michael, ed. (1991) *Cyberspace: First Steps*, Cambridge, MA: The MIT Press.

Brasher, Brenda E. (2001) *Give Me that Online Religion*, San Francisco: Jossey-Bass. See especially "A Taste of Forever: Cyberspace as Sacred Time," 46–66.

Campbell, Heidi (2005) *Exploring Religious Community Online: We Are One in the Network*, New York: Peter Lang. See especially "The Internet as a Spiritual Network: Spirituality and Religion Online," 53–74.

Davis, Erik (1998) *Techgnosis: Myth, Magic & Mysticism in the Age of Information*, New York: Harmony Books. See especially "The Spiritual Cyborg," 129–163.

Dawson, Lorne L. and Douglas E. Cowan, eds (2004) *Religion Online: Finding Faith on the Internet*, New York: Routledge.

Mabry, John (2004) "Cyberspace and the Dream of Teilhard de Chardin," Downloaded on June 6, 2006 from www.watershedonline.ca/whatsnew/ archive/whatsnew04spring.html. Access Previous Editions.

Mayer, Jean-François (2003) "Religion and the Internet: The Global Marketplace," in *Challenging Religion: Essays in Honour of Eileen Barker*, eds, James A. Beckford and James T. Richardson, New York: Routledge, 36–46.

Stahl, William A. (1999) *God and the Chip: Religion and the Culture of Technology*, Waterloo, ON: Wilfrid Laurier University Press. See especially "Technological Mysticism," 13–34.

Wertheim, Margaret (2000) *Pearly Gates of Cyberspace: A History of Space from Dante to the Internet*, New York: W. W. Norton & Company.

New Age

Kemp, Daren (2004) *New Age: A Guide*, Edinburgh: Edinburgh University Press.

Klippenstein, Janet M. (2005) "Imagine No Religion: On Defining 'New Age'," *Studies in Religion / Science Réligieuses*, 34:3–4, 391–403.

Lewis, James R., ed. (2004) *The Encyclopedic Sourcebook of New Age Religions*, New York: Prometheus Books.

Perry, Michael Charles (1992) *God Within: A Critical Guide to New Age*, London: SPCK.

Pike, Sarah, M. (2004) *New Age and Neopagan Religions in America*, New York: Columbia University Press.

Saliba, John A. (1993) "A Christian Response to the New Age," *The Way: Contemporary Christian Spirituality* 33:3, 222–32.

Woodhead, Linda (1993) "Post-Christian Spiritualities," *Religion* 23, 167–181.

Gender

Downing, Christine (1990) *Myths and Mysteries of Same-sex Love*, New York: Continuum.

Goss, Robert (1993) *Jesus Acted Up: A Gay and Lesbian Manifesto*, San Francisco: Harper SanFrancisco.

Hefling, Charles, ed. (1996) *Our Selves, Our Souls and Bodies: Sexuality and the Household of God*, Cambridge, MA: Cowley Publications.

Johnson, Edwin Clark (2000) *Gay Spirituality: The Role of Gay Identity in the Transformation of Human Consciousness*, Los Angeles: Alyson Books.

McGuire, Meredith B. (2003) "Gendered Spiritualities," in *Challenging Religion: Essays in Honour of Eileen Barker*, eds James Beckford and James Richardson: London: Routledge, 170–180.

McNeill, John J. (1996) *Taking a Chance on God: Liberating Theology for Gays, Lesbians, and Their Lovers, Families, and Friends*, Boston: Beacon Press.

Ruether, Rosemary Radford (2002) *Gender, Ethnicity, and Religion: Views from the Other Side*, Minneapolis: Fortress Press.

Vasey, Michael (1995) *Stranger and Friends: A New Exploration of Homosexuality and the Bible*, London: Hodder and Stoughton.

Wernik, Uri (2005) "Will the Real Homosexual in the Bible Please Stand Up?" *Theology and Sexuality* 11:3, 47–64.

Feminism

Birnbaum, Lucia C. (2005) *She is Everywhere!: An Anthology of Writing in Womanist/Feminist Spirituality*, New York: Universe, Inc. a division of Barnes & Noble.

Conn, Joann Wolski (1986) *Women's Spirituality: Resources for Christian Development*, New York: Paulist Press.

Donovan, Josephine (1985) *Feminist Theory: The Intellectual Traditions of American Feminism*, New York: Frederick Ungar Publishing Company.

Eaton, Heather (2005) *Introducing Ecofeminist Theologies*, New York: T. & T. Clark International.

Fiorenza, Elisabeth Schüssler (1983) *In Memory of Her: A Feminist Theological Reconstruction of Christian Origins*, New York: Crossroad.

Isasi-Diaz, Ada Maria (1996) *Mujerista Theology: A Theology for The Twenty-First Century*, New York: Orbis Books.

Offen, Karen (1988) "Defining Feminism – A Comparative Historical Approach," *Signs* 14 (August), 119–157.

Plaskow, Judith and Carol P. Christ, eds (1989) *Weaving the Visions: New Patterns in Feminist Spirituality*, San Francisco: Harper & Row.

Purvis, Sally (1989) "Christian Feminist Spirituality," in *Christian Spirituality: Post-Reformation and Modern*, eds Louis Dupré and Don E. Saliers [World Spirituality: An Encyclopedic History of the Religious Quest, Volume 18], New York: Crossroad, 500–519.

Ruether, Rosemary R. (1984) "Feminist Theology and Spirituality," in *Christian Feminism: Visions of a New Humanity*, ed. Judith L. Weidman, San Francisco: Harper & Row, 9–32.

Russell, Letty M. (1985) *Feminist Interpretation of the Bible*, Philadelphia: Westminster Press.

Schneiders, Sandra (1991) *Beyond Patching: Faith and Feminism in the Catholic Church*, New York: Paulist Press.

—— (2000) *With Oil in Their Lamps: Faith, Feminism, and the Future*, New York: Paulist Press.

Zappone, Katherine (1991) *The Hope for Wholeness: A Spirituality for Feminists*, Mystic, CT: Twenty-Third Publications.

Men's movements

Arnold, Patrick M. (1991) *Wildmen, Warriors, and Kings: Masculine Spirituality and the Bible*, New York: Crossroad Publishing Company.

August, E. R. (1994) *The New Men's Studies: A Selected and Annotated Inter-disciplinary Bibliography*, 2nd edition, Englewood, CO: Libraries Unlimited.

Bly, Robert (1990) *Iron John: A Book About Men*, New York: Addison-Wesley.

Brod, Harry, ed. (1990) *The Making of Masculinities: The New Men's Studies*, Boston: Unwin Hyman.

Campbell, Joseph (1990) *The Flight of the Wild Gander: Explorations in the Mythological Dimensions of Fairy Tales, Legends, and Symbols*, New York: HarperCollins.

Carmody, John (1989) *Toward a Male Spirituality*, Mystic, CT: Twenty-Third Publications.

Hagan, Kay Leigh, ed. (1992) *Women Respond to the Men's Movement: A Feminist Collection*, San Francisco: HarperCollins.

James, David C. (1996) *What Are They Saying About Masculine Spirituality?* New York: Paulist Press.

Journal of Men's Studies, The (1992) Harriman, TN: Men's Studies Press.

Kipnis. A. R. (1991) *Knights Without Armor: A Practical Guide for Men in Quest of Masculine Soul*, Los Angeles: Jeremy P. Tarcher.

Lee, J. (1991) *At My Father's Wedding: Reclaiming Our True Masculinity*, New York: Bantam Books.

Meade, Michael (1993) *Men and The Water of Life: Initiation and the Tempering of Men*, New York: HarperCollins.

Nelson, James B. (1998) *The Intimate Connection: Male Sexuality, Masculine Spirituality*, Philadelphia: Westminster Press.

Perrin, David B. (2000) "The Mythopoetic Interpretation of Texts: Hermeneutical Considerations," in *Mythopoetic Perspectives of Men's Healing Work: An Anthology for Therapists and Others*, ed. Edward R. Barton, Westport, CT: Bergin & Garvey, 59–74.

Rohr, Richard (2005) *From Wild Man to Wise Man: Reflections on Male Spirituality*, Cincinnati, OH: St. Anthony's Messenger Press.

Upton, Charles (1993) *Hammering Hot Iron: A Spiritual Critique of Bly's* Iron John, Madras, Wheaton, IL: Quest Books.

NOTES

1 See Sandra Harding (1991) *Whose Science? Whose Knowledge?*, New York: Cornell University Press. Harding reflects on how perspective affects scientific outcomes.

2 This summary is taken from Philip Hefner (2006) "Editorial: Religion and Science – Two-Way Traffic?" *Zygon* 41:1, 4–5.

3 Hefner "Editorial: Religion and Science", 5.

4 See Dermot Tredget (2002) "'The Rule of Benedict' and Its Relevance to the World of Work," *Journal of Managerial Psychology*, 17:2, 219–229. Downloaded May 31, 2006, from www.emeraldinsight.com/0268–3946.htm.

5 You can check out the Centre for Spirituality at Work on their website: www.spiritualityatwork.org.

6 "Spiritual capital" is defined as "The effects of spiritual and religious practices, beliefs, networks and institutions that have a measurable impact on individuals, communities, and societies." Downloaded May 31, 2006 from "What is Spiritual Capital" on the Spiritual Capital Research Program website: http://www.metanexus.net/spiritual%5Fcapital/. A series of articles is also available on this topic under Resources/Articles.

7 This is summarized from Robert A. Giacalone and Carole L. Jurkiewiz, eds (2005) *Handbook of Workplace Spirituality and Organizational Performance*, Armonk, NY: M. E. Sharpe. See the publisher's website: www.mesharpe.com/mall/resultsa.asp?Title=Handbook+of+Workplace+Spirituality+and+Organizational+Performance.

8 You can view articles for free by registering at their website: www.spiritualityhealth.com.

9 Jim Wallis (1994) *The Soul of Politics: A Practical and Prophetic Vision for Change*, New York: Orbis Books, 42.

10 Reinhold Neibuhr (1960) *Moral Man and Immoral Society: A Study in Ethics and Politics*, New York: Scribner, 4.

11 The contribution from biblical spirituality is based on the ideas presented by Jim Wallis in *The Soul of Politics*, 40.

12 Richard Falk (2001) *Religion and Humane Global Governance*, New York: Palgrave.

13 Bill Ryan (2004) "Can Religion Shape Politics? Or Is Religion Being Shaped by Politics in an Age of Globalization?" *Pastoral Sciences* 23:1, 30.

14 See especially Chapter 3, "Politics and Religion: Toward a Prophetic Spirituality," 31–47.

15 Michael Benedikt, ed. (1991) *Cyberspace: First Steps*, Cambridge, MA: The MIT Press. *Cyberspace: First Steps* is a collection of papers from the conference on cyberspace held in Austin, TX, May 4–5, 1990. Quotation cited in John Mabry (2004) "Cyberspace and the Dream of Teilhard de Chardin," Downloaded June 6, 2006, from www.watershedonline.ca/whatsnew/archive/whatsnew04spring.html. Access *Previous Editions*.

16 For short, informative articles on sociological studies and cyberspace, see www.cybersociology.com. This website brings together multidisciplinary articles dedicated to the critical discussion of the Internet, cyberspace, cyberculture, and life online.

17 Erik Davis (1998) *Techgnosis: Myth, Magic & Mysticism in the Age of Information*, New York: Harmony Books.

18 Erik Davis coined the term "techgnosis." Since modern technology and religion continue to evolve together, it refers to identifying how new technologies lend themselves to some form of spiritual transcendence. "Tech" is the abbreviated form of technology and "*gnosis*" is the Greek word for knowledge. Thus, "techgnosis" literally refers to "technical knowledge."

19 Margaret Wertheim (1999) "Is Cyberspace a Spiritual Space?" September 1, 1999. Downloaded June 6, 2006, from www.cybersociology.com, 3.

20 Ibid.

21 Wertheim, "Is Cyberspace a Spiritual Space?", 4. The last sentence of this quote is from page 5.

22 Past conference proceedings and current topics being studied may be viewed at http://www.ecic.info.

23 A good starting place is Jason D. Baker (1997) *Christian Cyberspace Companion: A Guide to the Internet and Christian Online Resources*, Grand Rapids, MI: Baker Books.

24 David Tacey (2001) *Jung and The New Age*, Hove, East Sussex: Brunner-Routledge, 2.

25 *The Secret Doctrine: The Synthesis of Science, Religion and Philosophy,* first published in 1888, is her foundational work. This text is available in its entirety from the Theosophical University Press Online Edition at www.theosociety.org/Pasadena/sd/sd-hp.htm.

26 Carl A. Raschke (1996) "New Age Spirituality," in *Spirituality and the Secular Quest*, Peter H. Van Ness, ed., New York: Crossroad, 210.

27 Ibid.

28 Linda Woodhead (1993) "Post-Christian Spiritualities," *Religion* 23, 175.

29 Meredith McGuire (2003) "Gendered Spiritualities," in *Challenging Religion: Essays in Honour of Eileen Barker*, J. Beckford and J. Richardson, eds, London: Routledge, 170.

30 See Sherry B. Ortner (1996) *Making Gender: The Politics and Erotics of Culture*, Boston, MA: Beacon Press.

31 Some people who are attracted to others of the same gender prefer the term "queer" to "gay." In the 1980s, queer was chosen by many to identify themselves differently from the growing gay culture which had become mainstream in many ways; for example, it had become dominated by consumerism and lost its counter-cultural edge. "More importantly, queer was chosen to be inclusive of all sexual minorities, i.e. gay men, lesbians, bisexuals, transsexuals, and transvestites. ... Queer identification is an embrace of deviance and countercultural values and a rejection of conventional normalcy." Edwin Clark Johnson (2000) *Gay Spirituality: The Role of Gay Identity in the Transformation of Human Consciousness*, Los Angeles: Alyson Books, 9.

32 Sandra Schneiders (1991) *Beyond Patching: Faith and Feminism in the Catholic Church*, New York: Paulist Press, 15. Even though Schneiders specifically addresses the issues of feminism in relationship to the Roman Catholic Church, this little book is an excellent introduction to the foundational terminology used to discuss feminism and women's movements in general. Much of the material in this section is summarized from the first chapter of *Beyond Patching*.

33 Paraphrased from Rosemary R. Ruether (1984) "Feminist Theology and Spirituality," in *Christian Feminism: Visions of a New Humanity*, Judith L. Weidman, ed., San Francisco: Harper & Row, 11.

34 Examples of second-wave and third-wave feminism are described by Anne M. Clifford (2001) *Introducing Feminist Theology*, New York: Orbis Books, 21–28.

35 Betty Friedan (1963) *The Feminine Mystique*, New York: Norton; Mary Daly (1968) *The Church and the Second Sex*, San Francisco: Harper & Row.

36 See, for example, Lisa Albrecht and Rose Brewer, eds (1990) *Bridges to Power: Women's Multicultural Alliances*, Philadephia: New Society Publishers.

37 Schneiders, *Beyond Patching*, 27.

38 See Rosemary Radford Ruether (1986) "Feminism and Religious Faith: Renewal or New Creation?", *Religion and Intellectual Life* 3 (Winter), 7–20. Cited in Schneiders, *Beyond Patching*, 119. The questions here are paraphrased to focus specifically on Christian spirituality.

39 Schneiders, *Beyond Patching*, 36.

40 These are taken from Katherine Zappone (1991) *The Hope for Wholeness: A Spirituality for Feminists*, Mystic, CT: Twenty-Third Publications, 9–10.

41 For an interesting summary on how the two German brothers Jacob and Wilhelm Grimm (1785–1863 and 1786–1859) collected the various tales used in the mythopoetic men's movement see Joseph Campbell (1990) *The Flight of the Wild Gander: Explorations in the Mythological Dimensions of Fairy Tales, Legends, and Symbols*, New York: HarperCollins, 9–15.

42 See Robert Bly (1990) *Iron John: A Book About Men*, New York: Addison-Wesley Publishing Company. Charles Upton (1993) *Hammering Hot Iron: A Spiritual Critique of Bly's* Iron John, Madras, Wheaton, IL: Quest Books, takes exception to Bly's use of these myths. Upton focuses on the distortions of archetypal psychology that have entered the mainstream of popular culture through people like Bly. Upton recognizes the importance of the work being done by people like Bly in relationship to building strong male identities, but warns against the incomplete intellectual framework that lies behind the use of these myths.

Index

eBooks

eBooks – at www.eBookstore.tandf.co.uk

A library at your fingertips!

eBooks are electronic versions of printed books. You can store them on your PC/laptop or browse them online.

They have advantages for anyone needing rapid access to a wide variety of published, copyright information.

eBooks can help your research by enabling you to bookmark chapters, annotate text and use instant searches to find specific words or phrases. Several eBook files would fit on even a small laptop or PDA.

NEW: Save money by eSubscribing: cheap, online access to any eBook for as long as you need it.

Annual subscription packages

We now offer special low-cost bulk subscriptions to packages of eBooks in certain subject areas. These are available to libraries or to individuals.

For more information please contact webmaster.ebooks@tandf.co.uk

We're continually developing the eBook concept, so keep up to date by visiting the website.

www.eBookstore.tandf.co.uk